The French Parlements and
the Crisis of the Old Regime

BAILEY STONE

The French Parlements and the Crisis of the Old Regime

The University of North Carolina Press

Chapel Hill and London

© 1986 The University of North Carolina Press

All rights reserved

Manufactured in the United States of America

Library of Congress Cataloging-in-Publication Data

Stone, Bailey, 1946–

The French parlements and the crisis of the old

regime.

Bibliography: p.

Includes index.

1. France. Parlement (Paris)—History. I. Title.

KJV3747.S76 1986   328.44'361   86-1257

ISBN 0-8078-1701-5

To the Memory of Jean Egret,

and to Mme Egret

Contents

viii
Contents

Acknowledgments

I would find it impossible to acknowledge all advice and active assistance from which I have benefited in preparing this study; I must nevertheless record certain outstanding debts of gratitude here.

I am indebted most of all to the two individuals to whom I have dedicated this work: the late Jean Egret, eminent historian of the eighteenth-century *parlements* and longtime professor of history at Poitiers, and his charming and erudite widow, who resides in Paris. M. Egret's guidance greatly facilitated the research that eventuated (five years after his untimely death) in the publication of my initial book, a study of the Paris Parlement under Louis XVI. In 1976 and subsequent years Mme Egret was so generous as to entrust to me documentary material her husband had been collecting in anticipation of preparing a work on the Parisian and provincial parlementary opposition to Louis XVI's policies. I drew upon that material more than once in writing my first monograph and have utilized it again in preparing this more comprehensive study of the high magistracy (as the notes, especially for the first chapter, attest). The reader will note that at times I have taken issue with M. Egret's interpretations of parlementary motivation in the prerevolutionary crisis of 1787–88. Yet I would regard such criticism as constituting in its own way a further testimonial to the importance of Jean Egret's work on the political history of the late *ancien régime*. I can only hope that the present volume, as well as its predecessor, justifies in some small measure the assistance, encouragement, and hospitality unfailingly accorded me by M. and Mme Egret.

I must also thank the comte and comtesse J. d'Eprémesnil of Paris for having allowed me to consult the private papers of Jean Jacques IV Duval d'Eprémesnil at the Archives nationales. I hope that my portrayal of this prominent member of the Paris Parlement under Louis XVI assures him a fuller justice than some commentators upon that fateful period have meted out to him.

Again, special thanks go to M. Paul-Edouard Robinne, Secrétaire of the Commission régionale d'Inventaire du Limousin at Limoges, for having authorized my consultation of his important thesis (prepared for the Ecole des Chartes at Paris) upon the Rouen Parlement of the 1774–89 period.

I am similarly indebted to countless archivists (and to their staffs) in

Paris and, indeed, all over France. I would, however, single out for special notice the chief archivists at the Archives nationales in Paris and the Archives de Midi-Pyrénées et de la Haute-Garonne at Toulouse. Without the assistance of such dedicated individuals, I would have found it difficult at best to conduct the research this study required.

I should also acknowledge my many long conversations in France with Albert N. Hamscher of Kansas State University, who was on sabbatical leave, as I was, during the 1980–81 academic year. His trenchant observations upon judicial and administrative affairs in the old regime prompted me to conceptualize issues in ways that have, I believe, borne fruit in this study.

Recognition is due in addition to my colleagues in the Department of History at the University of Houston, who have offered critical and therefore valuable reactions to some of the ideas elaborated in my book, and to the University itself for having awarded me the Faculty Development Leave Grant that made my pleasurable and profitable stay in France in 1980–81 possible. I am also indebted to the University of Houston for assistance in the publication of this study.

Finally, I would cite again, as in connection with my first book, the unflagging support of my mother. That, too, has meant much to me at difficult junctures over the past several years.

The French Parlements and
the Crisis of the Old Regime

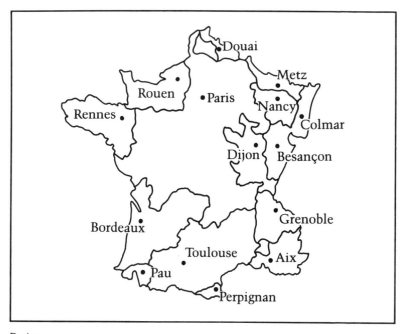

Paris
  (Île-de-France, Picardy, Brie,
  Champagne, Anjou and Maine,
  the Orléanais and the Touraine, Poitou,
  Auvergne, Saintonge, Dunkirk, and
  parts of Burgundy)
Toulouse (Languedoc, etc.)
Bordeaux (Guyenne, Gascogne, etc.)
Grenoble (Dauphiné)
Dijon (Burgundy)
Aix (Provence)
Rouen (Normandy)
Rennes (Brittany)
Pau (Navarre and Béarn)
Metz (Metz, Toul, and Verdun)
Douai (Flanders, Cambrésis, Hainaut)
Besançon (Franche-Comté)
Nancy (Lorraine and Bar)
Colmar (Alsace)
Perpignan (Roussillon)

The Parlements in History
and Historiography

In August 1786, France's Controller General of Finance Charles-Alexandre de Calonne, bedeviled by mounting government debt, gave Louis XVI a memorandum urging wide-ranging fiscal and administrative reforms. But how, the controller general wondered, could he and the king enact such measures, and thereby have a chance to retrieve government finances? If Louis did not choose to convoke the Estates General, the historic national assembly in desuetude since 1614, he could presumably have the *parlements* of Paris and fourteen provincial capitals "register" and thus legalize his edicts. The *parlements*, after all, had long played a quasi-legislative role in the kingdom's public affairs: they had never wanted to limit themselves to dispensing civil and criminal justice in their primal capacity as high law courts. But in this summer of 1786, Calonne knew better. A series of bruising encounters with the Paris Parlement over royal borrowing policies, and with certain provincial *parlements* over local controversies, had convinced him that this generation of judges would be as obstreperous as earlier generations had frequently been in opposing the crown's will. Hence, Calonne counseled Louis XVI to summon an Assembly of Notables to consider his legislation. The Notables' deliberations and approbation, so the controller general hoped, would facilitate the eventual registration of his program in solemn, carefully staged sessions (*lits de justice*) of the *parlements*. The government could then execute its reforms and put its financial house in order—all the while avoiding the risks attendant upon conjuring up that specter from past unsettled centuries, the Estates General.

Such were Calonne's calculations. All historians of the period know today that he failed even to secure the Notables' acceptance of his program; that his immediate successors failed even more resoundingly to quell the parlementary opposition to reform; and that this opposition, more than any other factor, brought Bourbon absolutism to its knees during 1787–88 and unleashed revolution within France. But historians have yet to explain satisfactorily why the regime's various opponents—and this means above all the *parlementaires*—acted the way they did during those dramatic years when the proud and venerable monarchy of France was stumbling toward disaster. This book describes the *parle-*

mentaires of that period and analyzes their motives in defying the beleaguered and reform-minded crown. The most effective way to preface such a study would be to recapitulate the confrontation between crown and *parlements* in 1787–88, summarize the historiography arising from that confrontation, and indicate the relationship between that historiography and the broader debate currently raging over the origins of the French Revolution.

Calonne's general intention in submitting his reforms to the Assembly of Notables early in 1787 was to rationalize the administration and finances of the Bourbon monarchy, thus establishing greater "equality of obligation" among taxpayers and augmenting government revenues.[1] More specifically, he wanted to replace the *vingtièmes*, taxes at 5 percent upon commoners' and lay nobles' lands, with a permanent "territorial subvention" of undetermined yield to fall in kind upon the lands of all three orders, including the clergy. Apportionment of the tax (at least in the *pays d'élection*, regions directly administered by agents of the central government) was to be entrusted to hierarchies of provincial and subordinate assemblies of landowners sitting and deliberating without regard for social rank. These assemblies were in fact to deal with a broad variety of administrative matters; in all their activities, however, they would be under the close supervision of the intendants, those most reliable of royal agents in provincial France. Calonne also wanted to extend the government's stamp tax; reduce the commoners' basic direct tax, the *taille*; exploit the royal domain more efficiently by leasing it out in fiefholds; enable the Church to emancipate itself from its huge debts; negotiate further loans for the royal treasury; and transform the Caisse d'Escompte (discount bank) into a national bank capable of shoring up the state's credit. The controller general intended moreover to stimulate agriculture and trade within the country, thereby increasing the yield from direct and indirect taxation. This would require eliminating internal tolls and duties, reducing the various salt taxes (*gabelles*), freeing the internal commerce in grain, and converting the peasantry's compulsory road labor (the notorious *corvée royale*) into cash payments additional to the *taille*.

Louis XVI and his ministers announced these reforms to the Assembly of Notables, which convened at Versailles on 22 February 1787. Among its 144 members were 33 magistrates from the kingdom's *parlements*; a number of these jurists soon joined many of the assembled prelates, great nobles of the sword, and deputies of the *pays d'état* and municipalities in finding fault with the government's proposals. In the end, Calonne failed to secure the Notables' approval of his program, incurred additional royal displeasure by appealing to the literate public for support, and on 8 April 1787 was dismissed along with Keeper of the Seals Armand-Thomas Hué de Miromesnil. The latter individual's post, the highest in French justice, did not long remain vacant.[2] On 13 April, Chrétien-François II de Lamoignon de Basville, fourth president of the Paris Parlement and a member of the Notables, received the seals from the king. On 1 May, the archbishop of Toulouse, Etienne-Charles Loménie de Brienne, also a Notable, became head of the Council of Finance and thereby assumed Calonne's erstwhile responsibilities.[3]

Lamoignon's dissatisfaction with French justice, and especially with its dispensation in the realm's most prestigious *parlement*, had long provided grist for the mills of Parisian gossip; accordingly, the educated public expected significant judicial reforms from his ministry in 1787–88. Brienne, for his part, had long enjoyed a reputation as a liberal ecclesiastical administrator, and had been one of the most articulate oppositionist Notables in the weeks leading up to his appointment as de facto minister of finance. For well over a year, from the spring of 1787 until late summer of 1788, Brienne and Lamoignon would labor to rescue the old regime's finances and rationalize its administration.

Ironically, Brienne, so outspoken in opposition to Calonne from the rostrum of the Notables, found himself as minister inheriting all of Calonne's headaches and adopting most of his program. Thus, Brienne carried over his predecessor's *subvention territorial*—although he modified its mode of assessment and judiciously limited its annual yield to 80 million livres—and also retained his extended stamp tax. Similarly, the new minister preserved Calonne's plans for hierarchies of provincial, departmental, and municipal assemblies in the *pays d'élection*, though he established the traditional social distinctions among the assemblymen and somewhat loosened their subordination to the intendants. Again, the archbishop-minister endorsed his predecessor's stance upon liberation of the grain trade, compounding for the *corvée royale*, and reduction of the *gabelle*, and he commissioned further inquiries into the kingdom's tolls and duties.

Brienne did, it is true, dilute or withdraw altogether certain other reforms that Calonne had submitted to the Notables. But the archbishop and his ministerial colleagues also applied some ideas of their own in the ensuing months. They initiated significant military reforms, reorganized the central administration of trade and finance, achieved savings in domestic expenditure wherever possible, and drafted legislation according a civil status to non-Catholics. Lamoignon, the disgruntled former *parlementaire*, set to work enthusiastically devising a simpler, less expensive, and more humane system of justice: he envisioned, among other things, thoroughgoing revision of the civil and criminal ordinances. In their own way, Brienne and Lamoignon and their confederates meant to succeed where Calonne had failed. But it was not to be. The new ministers could get nowhere with the Notables, who felt their assembly constitutionally inadequate to deal with matters traditionally reserved to the great law courts or, indeed, the Estates General. As the notion of recourse to the latter institution was still anathema in royal and ministerial eyes, there was nothing for it but to submit the new legislation to the Paris Parlement and its provincial counterparts. Yet, in announcing grandly at the Notables' final session on 25 May that the sovereign himself would now take in hand the regeneration of his government and realm, Brienne and Lamoignon must have already been anticipating parlementary opposition to their program.

And indeed, ominous parlementary rumblings had for some time been sounding from the provinces.[4] In the first place, many of the provincial *parlements* had engaged in acrimonious disputes with agents of the crown during the 1770s and early 1780s, and in at least four cases—involving the judges of Rouen (Normandy), Rennes (Brittany), Dijon (Burgundy), and Pau (Béarn and Navarre)—controversies of this type spilled over into the 1787–88 crisis. More disquieting, however, was the fact that one of Calonne's and Brienne's most cherished reforms, the monetary compounding for the *corvée royale,* had been drawing fire in recent months from both the Besançon Parlement in Franche-Comté and the Grenoble Parlement in Dauphiné. Calonne had introduced his reform of this labor obligation on a trial basis late in 1786; the magistrates at Besançon formally remonstrated against the initiative in February 1787 and their judicial cousins at Grenoble issued their own protests scarcely a month later. These reactions at Besançon and Grenoble adumbrated the more general rebellion later to come in provincial parlementary ranks.

But in June 1787 all eyes were upon the oldest and most prestigious *parlement,* the Paris Parlement or "Court of Peers" as it was styled when (as now) the Princes of the Blood and peers of the realm joined its permanent members to ponder great political questions. Trouble was not long in coming. To be sure, the first three acts the government submitted to the Princes, peers, and *parlementaires* won approval easily enough. On 22 June the Court of Peers ratified the edict establishing general guidelines for the new provincial, departmental, and municipal assemblies, although in an accompanying proviso it implored the king to assure the "stability" of these administrative bodies by submitting "particular regulations" governing their personnel and operations to the *parlements.* On 25 June, the Court of Peers registered the royal declaration freeing the grain trade. Three days later, the magistrates and peers, still in a cooperative mood, ratified the royal declaration converting the *corvée royale* into a surtax upon the *taille*. But then, on 2 July, the Parlement received the government's legislation extending the stamp tax, and the storm long augured in many quarters immediately broke. In the all-day session of 2 July, the Parlement rejected the stamp tax extension and insisted upon review of the crown's financial accounts.[5] Not surprisingly, Louis XVI refused this petition, but the jurists and peers returned to the charge with "reiterated" protests of 9 July and formal remonstrances of 16 July. The latter protests called for the summoning of the Estates General and were presented to Louis on 26 July; the following day, clandestinely printed copies were selling on the streets of the capital. On 30 July the government (without conceding defeat on this issue) sent the Parlement its edict levying the "territorial subvention" upon the lands of all three orders. Again the monarch and ministers were met with defiance as the Court of Peers, rejecting their legislation, called again for the Estates General. On 6 August a *lit de justice* at Versailles secured registration of both fiscal acts, but this only stoked the fires of parlementary defiance. On 7 August the tribunal declared the transcriptions of legislation made upon its registers the preceding day to be "null" and "void"; on 10 August the court attacked Calonne's stewardship of state finances and indicted the former minister; and on 13 August the magistrates formally condemned both the *lit de justice* of the sixth and the legislation registered at it. The government struck back immediately. On 14 August it quashed the jurists' actions and ordered execution of the new laws, and the following day its *lettres de cachet* banished the recusant judges to Troyes. The authorities also compelled two more specialized Parisian law courts, the Chambre des Comptes and Cour des Aides, to register the stamp and land taxes.

While these dramatic events were unfolding in the national capital, the magistrates in the provinces were also beginning to grapple with the ministry's reforms. The land and stamp tax edicts, it is true, never required provincial scrutiny because of the crisis they swiftly provoked in crown-and-peer relations; still, most of the provincial *parlements* had to reckon with the acts concerning the grain trade, the *corvée royale*, and the provincial assemblies during the summer of 1787. The measures deregulating the grain trade and reforming the *corvée* encountered little opposition, although the judges at Grenoble and Besançon continued to object to the latter act. The edict establishing the provincial assemblies, on the other hand, aroused more general judicial ire. Whereas three *parlements* (at Rennes, Dijon, and Pau) could ignore the edict because their jurisdictions coincided with *pays d'état* already boasting provincial Estates, the other courts, not so fortunate, exhibited varying degrees of hostility toward the proposed administrative innovation. The judges at Nancy, Douai, Metz, Aix, Toulouse, Rouen, Colmar, and Perpignan ratified the edict during July and August, but in most cases they emulated the Court of Peers by requesting implementing decrees upon the personnel and operations of the new assemblies. Moreover, several of the law courts forbade the new bodies to apportion any taxes lacking parlementary sanction and petitioned for restoration of their provinces' Estates. The Grenoble *parlementaires* grudgingly registered the edict on 11 August but would soon be at odds with the new Dauphinois assembly and with its sponsors at Versailles. The magistrates at Besançon and Bordeaux went further yet, flatly refusing to ratify the legislation at all. Besançon's judges demanded restoration of the Estates of Franche-Comté. The Bordeaux Parlement incurred the government's wrath by issuing a decree prohibiting the establishment of any provincial assembly within its jurisdiction! A royal decree of 17 August exiled the contumacious Bordelais to Libourne; they were not to be reinstated until late in 1788.

The banishment of the Bordelais to Libourne followed by only two days the exile of the Parisian *parlementaires* to Troyes. Such actions could not fail to elicit a chorus of protestation from the other law courts. In late August and early September nearly all of the courts issued decrees or wrote directly to Louis XVI on behalf of the Paris Parlement; protests over the fate of Bordeaux's justices came in the ensuing months. Additionally, the magistrates at Grenoble, Toulouse, Besançon, and Perpignan followed the Parisian example by censuring Calonne for his alleged misdeeds in office. Simultaneously, these jurists and their counterparts at Pau, Dijon, and Libourne solicited from the king that ultimate of ultimates, the convocation of the Estates General.

Meanwhile, Loménie de Brienne was named principal minister on 26 August. Having thus consolidated his position and desiring to end the stalemate at the center of power, he soon entered into negotiations with the exiled magistrates at Troyes. The result was the Parlement's acceptance on 19 September of a compromise: withdrawal of the land and stamp taxes and reimposition of the two *vingtièmes*. (The first *vingtième* would remain of indefinite duration; the second would be extended through 1791 and 1792.) The next day a royal declaration reinstated the judges in the capital, whose unruly elements celebrated soon thereafter by burning Calonne in effigy. But the compromise was precarious. The Parlement's endorsement of Brienne's terms had been far from unanimous and had been coupled with a decree reaffirming the necessity of the Estates General's consent to taxation.

The precariousness of the settlement of September 1787 became dramatically apparent two months later. On 19 November, the government at a hastily convened "royal session" of the Paris Parlement proclaimed parlementary registration of the first in a series of loans designed to restore royal finances over a five-year period. The judges, permitted to speak upon but not to vote upon the loan, regarded this *séance royale* as a disguised *lit de justice*, and the king's own cousin the duc d'Orléans denounced it as "illegal" to Louis's face. That the government also used the occasion to promise to convene the Estates General by the end of 1792 in no way mollified the *parlementaires*, who declared the whole proceeding void immediately after the king's exit. The next day, 20 November, the duc d'Orléans was exiled for his temerity and two of the more offensive *parlementaires*, Emmanuel Marie Michel Philippe Fréteau de Saint-Just and Abbé Honoré-Auguste Sabatier de Cabre, were imprisoned.

But the greatest casualty of the royal session of 19 November was Brienne's September compromise between crown and judiciary. In fact, relations between the two sides reached their nadir during the period from late November 1787 to early May 1788. The Parisian justices repeatedly decried the banishment of the duc d'Orléans, the incarceration of their colleagues, and the *séance royale* itself. The government maintained its own hard line throughout, quashing the judicial protest of 19 November and striking down every subsequent expostulation from Paris. As the quarrel dragged on, the parlementary polemics ineluctably broadened in constitutional scope. In January and March 1788, the magistrates condemned *lettres de cachet*; by late April they were censuring the ministers' taxes and "despotism"; and on 3 May, anticipating a ministerial *coup de force*, they passed their celebrated decree listing the "fundamental laws" of the French monarchy. The government, finding its revenues, reforms, and very legitimacy questioned, believed it had no choice but to break the parlementary opposition and break it for good.

What made the judicial resistance all the more worrisome to the authorities by the spring of 1788 was that it was undeniably nationwide. In the southwest, the Bordelais jurists, in exile at Libourne, remained as defiant as ever, refusing to ratify the ministers' edicts. They could take comfort from the fact that the first *parlement* of the realm had rejoined the opposition after its brief rapprochement with Versailles; they could draw additional solace from the protests that most of the other courts had made on their behalf. And those other courts were remonstrating on other issues as well. By tradition, government loans did not require the provincial judges' approval and so they did not have to confront Brienne's loan of November 1787. But they did have to consider the ministry's reimposition of the two *vingtièmes* and the extension of the second through 1792. With few exceptions, the provincial *parlements* either refused outright to endorse the extension of the second *vingtième* or hedged their ratification of the pertinent act in terms unacceptable to Brienne and Lamoignon. Judges in several provinces even encouraged local resistance to royal tax policies. In a few cases the authorities had to secure registration of their legislation in *lits de justice*. Moreover, the longer the imbroglio dragged on the more tempted the magistrates were to explore its constitutional ramifications. Like their judicial brethren at Paris, the provincial *parlementaires* turned from protesting the *séance royale* of 19 November to anathematizing arbitrary arrests and "ministerial despotism" and invoking the Estates General. And their debate with Versailles was becoming public: letters, decrees, and remonstrances intended solely for royal and ministerial eyes were giving way to published pronunciamentos as the judges sought to justify their intransigence by rallying local notables to their cause. For Brienne and Lamoignon it was high time to strike back, in provincial France as surely as at Paris.

On the night of 4–5 May 1788, government agents in the French capital attempted to arrest two of the Paris Parlement's most vocal oppositionists, Anne Louis de Goislard de Montsabert and Jean Jacques IV Duval d'Eprémesnil. The two justices fled from their residences to the Palais de Justice to invoke their company's protection. Eventually, during the dramatic twenty-nine hour session of the Court of Peers held on 5–6 May amidst an immense throng at the Palais de Justice, Goislard de Montsabert and Duval d'Eprémesnil gave themselves up to the Gardes françaises. They were incarcerated in the provinces, and on 8 May their associates were compelled in a *lit de justice* at Versailles to register Lamoignon's long-meditated judicial reforms. Henceforth, a Plenary Court composed of the senior Parisian *parlementaires*, the Princes and peers, and sundry other great personages was to assume the *parlements'* role of registering fiscal legislation and all acts affecting the kingdom as a whole. The Plenary Court could protest royal edicts up to a certain point, but in essence the *parlements'* political power would be broken. These high tribunals would also be reduced in their strictly judicial function, for they were now to share it with newly created Grands Bailliages at the intermediate level of justice and with presidial courts at the lowest level. This judicial reorganization would open new careers to the jurists, barristers, and proctors of the Third Estate and would facilitate justice for all litigants. Concomitantly, seigneurial courts and certain specialized tribunals would be weakened or eliminated altogether, and a new judicial ordinance would mitigate the rigors of criminal justice. During 8–10 May, royal agents forced all the other *parlements* in *lits de justice* to ratify Lamoignon's reforms as well as other royal edicts (such as that extending the second *vingtième* through 1792) where such edicts still lacked parlementary sanction. Finally, Brienne once again promised to convoke the Estates General by 1792. But the ministers' bold and desperate gamble did not succeed. They had hoped by promulgating judicial reforms (and by publishing the royal "budget" for 1788) to win the crucial support of ambitious jurists and barristers, grateful litigants, liberal men of letters, and bankers and financiers. Instead, they brought upon their heads a national parlementary revolt, local "popular" insurrections, and, by August 1788, the collapse of state credit.

Most of the *parlements* had issued decrees denouncing the government's long-rumored coup in advance, and from 8 May on they continued adamantly to oppose the ministry's regenerative policies. The magistrates at Douai in Flanders resigned en masse after their *lit de justice*. Normandy's *parlementaires* cut off communications with the keeper of the seals. Brittany's *parlementaires*, responding to local insurrectionism, convened publicly in defiance of royal orders, declared the reform edicts null and void, and anathematized all who would cooperate with the ministers. At Pau, in the Pyrenean south, mobs of city dwellers and mountain people reinstated the justices by force. Similar events transpired at Grenoble in Dauphiné. The king's troops were ordered to march on Rennes, Pau, and Grenoble. Bordeaux's judges, still in exile at Libourne, remained as intransigent as ever. All of the high courts without exception castigated the May Edicts and their authors. Of more significance from the government's point of view, the jurists' revolt found favor in many sectors of respectable society. Enough of the kingdom's legal personnel supported the parlementary cause to hamper operation of the new system of justice. The quinquennial Assembly of the Clergy called for the reinstatement of the *parlementaires* and refused crucial moneys to the authorities. In several provinces, traditional Estates or more popular assemblies declared their solidarity with the stricken law courts. Even the "enlightened" men of letters were severely divided on the great confrontation between the monarch and his magistrates; a majority may have sided with the latter.

On 5 July 1788, a royal decree invited all Frenchmen through the provincial Estates and assemblies to advise the government upon the composition and procedure of the Estates General. At this point, Brienne was apparently playing for time, hoping to hold off the convening of the Estates until the government's reforms could bear fruit; but he was undone by the collapse of the state's credit, a misfortune at least indirectly reflective of the unstable political situation. A new royal decree of 8 August promised the Estates General for 1 May 1789 and postponed establishment of the Plenary Court. On 25 August, Brienne resigned, giving way to former Finance Minister Jacques Necker, whose return to power seemed necessary to restore the state's credit. Necker, fearing civil war, felt that the *parlements* must be reinstated and the date of convocation of the Estates General moved up. And so Lamoignon, who had hoped to stay on and salvage at least some of his judicial innovations, followed Brienne into retirement on 14 September. A royal declaration of 23 September brought back the old judiciary and justice and announced the Estates General for the following January (though the original date of 1 May 1789 was later restored). The Parisian *parlementaires* on 24 September returned for the last time in triumph to the capital, which for days had been witnessing tumultuous merrymaking at the expense of the fallen ministers. The magistrates hurriedly took steps to curb the disorders, and on the next day (25 September) they registered the royal declaration of the twenty-third.

But in thus sealing their victory over Loménie de Brienne and their detested former colleague Lamoignon, the judges were sealing their own fate as well—and that of the entire high magistracy. For, in ratifying the legislation of 23 September, the *parlementaires* invoked the precedent of the last Estates General, which had been convened in 1614. This presumably would mean that the delegates of the clergy and nobility would outnumber the deputies of the lay commonalty by two to one in the upcoming assembly—and, more crucially, that voting on all issues would be by order rather than by head. By their reference to the 1614 Estates General, the judges conjured up for the Third Estate partisans the likelihood of a clerical and noble domination of the Estates General, and so forfeited at a stroke much of the popular support that had borne them through their recent tribulations. The provincial *parlementaires*, in registering the same legislation after their reinstatement in October, tried to preserve their own local prestige by skirting the issue of the upcoming convocation. But it was, alas, too late. The Paris Parlement's fateful pronouncement of 25 September had done much to transform a constitutional debate in which the magistrates could shine as intrepid foes of "despotism" into a sociopolitical conflict bound to pit most judges along with conservatives of miter and sword against liberal clerics and nobles and the Third Estate. A faction within the Paris Parlement, realizing this, endeavored as late as 5 December to restore their company's shattered popularity with a decree disavowing the earlier reference to the 1614 Estates General. But, again, it was too late. For that matter, the public's disenchantment with the erstwhile judicial heroes of the constitutional crisis can only have been growing at this time, as thirty-seven Parisian and provincial *parlementaires* attending the second Assembly of Notables joined that convocation's clerical and noble majority in perversely opposing reform of the Estates General. The harsh reality was that history had passed the magistrates by. And history would soon, very soon, summon both parlementary magistracy and absolute monarchy to a final reckoning.

This concludes our brief résumé of the political crisis that ushered in the Revolution of 1789. On the events of that crisis, historians concur; on the motivation of some prominent actors in the drama—most notably the Parisian and provincial *parlementaires*—they do not, and never have. Some scholars, mindful especially of the compelling financial needs of Louis XVI's government in the late 1780s, have been content to characterize the magisterial opposition as but an obstinate defense of old ways and privileges against the rationalizing policies of Calonne, Brienne, and Lamoignon.[6] Other analysts, more inclined to stress the constitutional dimensions of the late eighteenth-century crisis, have viewed the judges as actuated above all by a concern to do what they could to preserve a balance between the power of the crown and the influence of other institutions in French society.[7] Yet other historians, partial to one or another socioeconomic explanation of the advent of revolution in France, have pointed to the noble pedigree of nearly all these *parlementaires* and portrayed them as the instigators of the "aristocratic" revolt or revolution that supposedly preceded the "bourgeois" and popular insurrections of 1789.[8] Unsurprisingly, proponents of the first and third of these interpretations have scored the magistrates for their alleged hypocrisy in articulating popular interests and grievances, whereas adherents of the second perspective have been primarily impressed by the jurists' resolute stand against Bourbon "despotism" in 1787–88.[9]

However, in this welter of differing points of view about the *parlementaires*, argumentation has advanced far beyond the terra firma of established facts. Not one of the scholars writing in any of the traditions just mentioned has systematically studied what the magistrates, Parisian and provincial, had to say about themselves and their imperiled world in the late 1780s. It is true that French historian Jean Egret's *La Pré-Révolution française: 1787–1788*, published in 1962, offered a fuller analysis of parlementary attitudes during that critical period than had ever previously appeared.[10] Moreover, Egret's treatment of the subject was unprecedentedly sophisticated. He could underscore the expediency of judges who were nobles, privileged landowners, venal officeholders, and pretentious administrators, and at the same time discern in their pronouncements and activities an unfeigned solicitude for the material interests of French people of middling and humble station and for the "constitutional" rights of all. There are, nonetheless, two major problems with Egret's analysis of the judicial opposition in 1787–88. First, as helpful and significant as it is, it remains incomplete. Egret, conscientious political historian that he was, dealt with the totality of events in the late 1780s, not merely with those directly engaging parlementary interests and evoking parlementary responses. He was, of necessity, primarily concerned with describing the problems and elucidating the strategies of the king's policymakers in this period, and only secondarily concerned with exploring the magisterial "mentality." Second, Egret admitted that he had begun his study on the advice of Georges Lefebvre; it can hardly astonish us if at times Egret betrayed the influence of that illustrious scholar of modified Marxian persuasion by associating the *parlementaires* with a yet debatable "aristocratic revolution" of 1787–88.[11] Thus, Egret's study, important though it is, has not laid to rest the controversy over the high judiciary's role in the prerevolutionary crisis.

What we plainly require now is a thorough examination of Parisian and provincial parlementary attitudes toward public issues on the eve of the Revolution. "Public issues" would naturally include the celebrated ministerial reforms of 1787–88 but would also comprehend less familiar, purely local matters that the jurists of the high law courts had to consider during this period. If we want to understand fully and fairly why the judges opposed Louis XVI's government in 1787 and 1788, thus precipitating a national rebellion, we need to view through magisterial eyes the public questions, great *and* small, that from one day to the next caught up in their toils the interests of crown and commoners, of miter and sword, and of the judiciary itself.

In preparing this study we can turn to good purpose scholarship upon most of the major *parlements* of late eighteenth-century France. Of especial use to us will be three works that delve deeply into sociopolitical attitudes in individual law courts: Jean Egret's published dissertation of 1942 upon Grenoble's *parlementaires*,[12] English historian William Doyle's monograph upon the Bordeaux Parlement,[13] and my own study of the Paris Parlement.[14] Each of these works accentuates in its own way the complexity of judicial concerns in the twilight of the *ancien régime*; taken together, the three books would seem to portend a conspectus stressing the complexity of parlementary concerns throughout the length and breadth of France.

This project takes on additional significance in light of recent developments in the historiography on the causes of the French Revolution. Over the past thirty years, specialists on both sides of the Atlantic have become increasingly skeptical about attempts to explain the genesis of the Revolution in terms of "aristocratic" and "bourgeois" class revolts.[15] Because this revisionism has had to come to grips with the notion that the Parisian and provincial magistrates participated in (and perhaps even initiated) an "aristocratic revolt" against the monarchy, it has underlined the importance of thoroughly understanding parlementary attitudes and deeds for anyone essaying an alternative interpretation of the Revolution's origins.

This study will determine as accurately as possible the judges' role in the political crisis of 1787–88; beyond that, it will in its final pages address the challenge of satisfactorily accounting for the advent of the Revolution itself. Chapter 1 discusses the duties and personnel of the Paris Parlement and its provincial counterparts, with a primary stress among the latter institutions upon those tribunals whose members have already been extensively studied. Chapter 2 inquires how the all-important Parisian magistrates regarded the sovereign and his government and the various social classes on the eve of 1789. Chapters 3, 4, and 5 explore political, constitutional, and social perspectives in the provincial *parlements*, with a primary emphasis once against upon the most thoroughly studied of those courts but with frequent side trips as well to the other tribunals boasting parlementary status. The final chapter touches upon the revolutionary and postrevolutionary fates of some of our protagonists, summarizes their companies' role in the terminal crisis of the old regime, and advances some thoughts concerning the underlying "causes" of the Revolution that developed most immediately out of that crisis.

This study will argue that the Parisian and provincial *parlementaires* of the Prerevolution were not so much paladins of a "revolutionary aristocracy" as they were traditionalists striving to accommodate the diverse governmental and social interests composing the *ancien régime*, traditionalists striving thereby to safeguard their own enviable power and prestige. That they eventually came to grief in this endeavor was made inevitable by the failure of the late eighteenth-century French Bourbon state to marshal sufficient domestic resources—moral and financial—to compete successfully with the other European powers in the arena of international politics. To move away from a crude socioeconomic interpretation of parlementary behavior in 1787–88 will be, at least for the purposes of this argument, to move away as well from a crude socioeconomic rendering of the French Revolution's origins and to accentuate instead the ambitions and the dilemmas of the thousand-year-old French state in its international context.

The Parlementaires

Judges, Gentlemen, Bons Vivants

Of the myriad institutions obstructing reform in Louis XVI's France, none stood closer to the crown or derived greater power and prestige from monarchical traditions than did the *parlements* of Paris and the provinces. Undeniably foremost among these high courts of law was the Paris Parlement, the redoubtable Court of Peers, which customarily initiated magisterial debate with the king's government over public issues of national significance and did so in particular in the critical year 1787. Yet, if the Parisian *parlementaires* ignited the rebellion of 1787–88, their provincial counterparts rendered that rebellion truly national in scope. We should, consequently, have all the justices in mind when posing certain questions about parlementary activities and personnel in the last years of the *ancien régime*. The questions themselves are obvious enough. What functions did the *parlements* discharge in the eighteenth century, in what specific regions did they discharge them, and how were they organized internally to function? What were the social origins of Louis XVI's *parlementaires*? How affluent were these men, whence did they derive their wealth, and how was their enjoyment of it reflected in the social and cultural aspects of their lives? And, finally, who were the most influential personalities in these law courts in the late 1780s and how were they inclined by temperament and conviction to regard the great confrontation between the central government and oppositional interests?

We will answer these questions primarily with regard to the Paris Parlement and eight of the important provincial *parlements*, which have been subjects of prosopographical and procedural research. The eight *parlements* are the tribunals at Toulouse, Grenoble, Bordeaux, Dijon, Rouen, Aix, Rennes, and Besançon. When possible, we will also consider the *parlements* of Pau, Metz, Douai, and Nancy, as well as the "sovereign councils" of Colmar and Perpignan.[1] An inquiry into these fifteen courts of law will embrace nearly all the regions of prerevolutionary France.

The Institutions: Origins, Organization, Roles

An initial glance at the *parlements* reveals prestigious and influential institutions well positioned to obstruct the ministers' projects in 1787–88. A closer scrutiny of these tribunals discloses the apportionment of responsibilities and power among their constituent chambers.

In medieval France, the word *pallamentum* long denoted imposing convocations of various kinds held under the aegis of the Capetian monarchs.[2] By the end of the thirteenth century, however, a sedentary tribunal called the Parlement was emerging at Paris from the *curia regis* to hear the oral pleadings of cases that the sovereign, though supreme magistrate of his realm, had progressively less time to adjudicate in person. In a strict sense, the company of legal specialists that developed from these beginnings, and analogous institutions in what later became the outlying reaches of an expanding French realm, only "represented" the magistrate-kings, who, down to the very end of the old regime, reserved and occasionally exercised their right to adjudge litigation in their *parlements*. Nonetheless, in their more customary absence, the *parlements* settled litigation and rendered decrees (*arrêts*) in the royal name and thus bore witness to the historic expansion of France under her kings.

In the late eighteenth century the Paris Parlement reigned supreme in most judicial matters over the Île-de-France, Picardy, Brie, Champagne, Anjou and Maine, the Orléanais and the Touraine, Auvergne, Saintonge, and Poitou, as well as Dunkirk and parts of Burgundy. The oldest of the provincial *parlements*, that of Toulouse, held sway over a jurisdiction in southern France smaller only than that of the Parisian tribunal: it embraced Languedoc, Foix, about half of Gascogne, Rouergue, Quercy south of the Dordogne River, and several corners of Guyenne and the Limousin.[3] The *parlementaires* at Bordeaux dispensed justice in most of Guyenne, part of Gascogne, the Agenais, Labourt, the Limousin, Périgord, Bazadais, and parts of Saintonge.[4] Grenoble's *parlementaires* meted out justice in Dauphiné;[5] those of Dijon, Aix, Rouen, and Rennes discharged this function in Burgundy, Provence, Normandy, and Brittany, respectively.[6] The *parlementaires* at Pau administered justice in the erstwhile Pyrenean kingdoms of Navarre and Béarn;[7] those at Metz were responsible for the three bishoprics of Metz, Toul, and Verdun.[8] The *parlement* at Douai rendered justice in French Flanders, Cambrésis, and Hainaut.[9] Franche-Comté (the former "Free County" of medieval Burgundy) received its justice from the *parlement* at Besançon;[10] Lorraine and Bar, two ancient duchies in eastern France, made up the jurisdiction of Nancy's *parlement*.[11] Finally, two tribunals were *parlements* in all but name on the eve of the Revolution: the sovereign council at Colmar, whose jurisdiction was the eastern and German-speaking province of Alsace,[12] and the sovereign council of Perpignan, dispenser of Bourbon justice in Roussillon in the eastern Pyrenees.[13] Thus, fourteen provincial *parlements* shared with the primal *parlement* at Paris (and with a few more specialized law courts)[14] a multiplicity of judicial roles. Each tribunal was officially styled a "sovereign court"—that is, sovereign in the sense that it adjudged appeals from all presidial courts, *bailliages* or *sénéchaussées*, and lesser royal courts in its jurisdiction, and could only be overruled in such cases by the king's Council or by such high tribunal as the king himself should designate on appeal.[15] In addition, each tribunal functioned as a court of first instance for certain privileged litigants and in certain fields of litigation.

Highlighting the bewildering variety of civil and criminal suits that came on appeal to these fifteen sovereign courts were the so-called *cas royaux* which the *bailliages* and *sénéchaussées* judged in first instance at the intermediate level of the judicial hierarchy. These cases involved alleged crimes against the monarch's person or prerogatives or against the peace of his realm (for instance, *lèse-majesté*, forgery of the royal seal, or debasement of the royal currency). The *cas royaux* "came to include all instances of private war, of usury, of highway robbery, all matters pertaining to ennoblement or legitimization, to trade."[16] Moreover, by virtue of the theory of *prévention*, which stressed the subordination of seigneurial justice to royal justice, increasing numbers of disputes were taken out of seigneurial courts and tried by royal magistrates in the provost courts at the bottom of the judicial hierarchy; the *parlements* naturally had cognizance of such litigation on final appeal. Again, the *parlements'* appellate jurisdiction embraced the notorious *appels comme d'abus* from ecclesiastical courts that had allegedly exceeded their competence, transgressed in other fashion against the forms of French justice, or violated the liberties of the Gallican church. The *parlements* often capitalized upon such cases to champion royal justice against the pretensions of miter and sword. Ordinarily the jurists' decisions in all these matters were final, although (as indicated earlier) the king reserved and sometimes exercised the right to nullify their rulings (by decree of *cassation*) and "evoke" their litigation to his Council.

The *parlementaires* also adjudged a variety of momentous cases in first instance. For the Parisian magistrates in particular these included affairs involving the royal household, Princes of the Blood, dukes and peers, and great officers of the crown. For the judges in general, litigation in first instance could involve the stewardship of the royal domain and the monarch's right of *régale*, that is, his right to administer and draw revenues from vacant bishoprics. The Parisian and provincial justices also initiated proceedings in criminal lawsuits on behalf of or against lesser nobles, clerics, and judicial officers, and in civil disputes of those *privilégiés* whose royal letters of *committimus* entitled them to immediate parlementary justice. The *parlements'* competence might be circumscribed in certain specialized areas (mainly fiscal) by the jurisdiction assigned to other courts at Paris and several provincial capitals, and it might be limited by the will of the magistrate-king in his Council. Nevertheless, parlementary justice was the preeminent justice of the land in the ordinary course of affairs.

Furthermore, this judicial role carried with it an administrative function in a society whose justice and administration had always been closely intertwined.[17] It is true that each provincial tribunal had to share this latter function with the intendant, the military governor and/or lieutenant-general, the Estates if still active, the archbishop or bishop, and various municipal officers. And even the mighty Paris Parlement increasingly had to reckon in the eighteenth century with the *lieutenant-général de police* in the capital and with the intendants and their subordinates in the surrounding regions. Nonetheless, the judges all over France continued to have their fingers in a thousand and one administrative pies. In times of emergency, these justices could arrest or detain "seditious" individuals; ban public gatherings in city, village, or countryside; and impose curfews. Of greater moment on a day-to-day basis were the *parlementaires'* use of *arrêts de règlement*. By means of such regulatory decrees they helped to ensure the provisioning of foodstuffs and firewood to their communities, maintain the upkeep of urban thoroughfares and the sound condition of public and private buildings, and regulate hospitals, religious foundations, and prisons. Through their supervision of merchants, butchers, bakers, and a myriad of guilds and other associations the magistrates had much to say about wages, commodities, and working conditions in their cities and towns. They helped supervise universities, *collèges*, and academies, and charged the officers of lower courts with the same function. Further, the judges, in conjunction with the police, acted as censors of public morals and literature, investigating the conduct of public officials and sociable sons of nobility and sanctioning or burning books and pamphlets. Finally, the *parlementaires* could launch full-scale inquests into controversies within their jurisdictions. Let overseers of work upon the king's bridges and highways be accused of abusing their laborers, for instance, and the *parlement* within whose jurisdiction such malfeasance was reported would require from subordinate courts all particulars upon the matter. The *parlement* would then likely pass these findings on to the king's ministers or even remonstrate directly to the sovereign himself. The jurists in the peripheral reaches of France were rather more exercised about the kingdom's military security than their Parisian cousins had to be; hence, inquiries conducted by the Breton or Norman magistrates might

well concern naval affairs, whereas those launched by the Comtois or
Dauphinois might focus upon the fortifications on the eastern frontiers.
By means of such multifarious activities the sovereign courts did little
less than apply their own policies—policies that might or might not
dovetail with laws and regulations promulgated by the government. The
sovereign and his ministers, however, would usually endorse such administrative activities so long as the judges did not seem to be grasping
at the substance of a legislative initiative that belonged to the crown
alone.

Unfortunately for the cause of harmony between monarch and magistrates, the latter had in the eighteenth century a more potent excuse for
challenging the government on the legislative front. In the continuing
absence of the Estates General, the *parlements* had been conceded the
right to legalize many of the king's public policies. They did so by tran-
scribing legislation implementing such policies upon their official registers in formal plenary sessions. This ceremony of *enregistrement* was
essential for the legitimization of the monarch's edicts, for it—and it
alone—made them enforceable as law throughout the kingdom. *Enregistrement* simultaneously reaffirmed the legality of French kingship itself.[18] On the other hand, the *parlementaires* could protest against legislation they deemed "illegal" and/or harmful to the king and his subjects. It was in playing this quasi-legislative role that the judges loomed
so large in the political calculations of Louis XVI's ministers in the late
1780s.

A *parlement* finding fault with a specific piece of legislation had a
number of ways to signify its displeasure. Most innocuously, it could
send letters (or deputize its officers) to Versailles to explain its reservations concerning the measure in question. Somewhat more defiantly, it
could pass ad hoc resolutions (called *arrêtés*) that detailed secret court
deliberations upon the offending legislation. Moreover, it might publish
and circulate such *arrêtés*, thus violating the confidentiality of its own
proceedings as it announced to the world the reasons for its disagree-
ment with the ministry. More dramatically still, the tribunal could order that full-dress "remonstrances," or slightly less emphatic, less formal "representations," be made to the sovereign, explaining why it
found the legislation at issue to be "unconstitutional" or for some other
reason objectionable. In such circumstances, the court's chief officer,
the first president, would appoint a committee (composed for the most
part of senior judges) to draw up the formal protests, which a subsequent
"assembly of the chambers" would then consider and customarily approve by majority vote. The Paris Parlement usually had its first president and several other senior magistrates present its protests to the
monarch in person; a provincial tribunal would ordinarily content iself

with sending its remonstrances or representations to Versailles under cover of a justificatory letter to the sovereign. *Parlementaires* failing to receive satisfaction upon the question or questions they had raised could issue "reiterated" protests (and perhaps have them surreptitiously published), attempt through so-called *arrêts de défense* to paralyze local application of the contested government policy, refuse to dispense justice, or, as an ultimate act of protest, resign their offices en masse.

The king, for his part, would respond in kind to these varying degrees of magisterial defiance. He could always quash offending parlementary decrees, order an intendant or some other royal agent to reprimand a recalcitrant court in its own chambers, or lecture its disobedient members personally at Versailles. Ultimately, of course, the sovereign could threaten those judges who persisted in their refusal to ratify his legislation with a *lit de justice*, with banishment from their seat of professional operations, or, most drastically, with forfeiture of offices.

A *lit de justice* would be an especially impressive affair when staged in the Palais de Justice at Paris.[19] To this historic complex of legal chambers and courtyards, home of the Paris Parlement and several other more specialized sovereign courts, would come the magistrate-king, accompanied by his chancellor or keeper of the seals and by other great personages, to witness the compulsory transcription of his controversial acts upon the judges' registers. In these circumstances, the *parlementaires*, faithful to their own sense of drama and history and professional self-importance, might summon to their benches the Princes of the Blood, dukes, and peers, thus transforming their company into the Cour des Pairs. The king's *lit de justice*, highly formalized and imposingly staged in this glittering assemblage overflowing the central chamber (Grand' Chambre) at the Palais de Justice, would simultaneously recall the original judicial quality of French kingship and the medieval origins of the kingdom's first *parlement* in the *curia regis*.

A *lit de justice* at Pau or Perpignan in the Pyrenean far south or at Douai in the far north or even at a major provincial center like Bordeaux or Dijon would lack some of the fanfare attending such a session at Paris: the nation's capital, after all, was unique, and only the Paris Parlement could, as the Court of Peers, assemble upon its benches the most dazzling names of the French aristocracy. Still, Dijon might as well be Paris to the typical Burgundian: for him, a *lit de justice* held in the provincial capital by the intendant or military commandant would necessarily be an extraordinary event. And, for that matter, would "his" *parlement* fail upon such a solemn occasion to insist that it descended as directly from the medieval kings' *curia regis* and from the Frankish convocations of yet more distant days as did its overweening counterpart at Paris? Was not the *lit de justice* unfolding at Dijon a kind of *séance de la Cour des Pairs* once removed? Nor was this all. The Dijonnais *parlementaires*, heirs and custodians of local traditions predating "French" rule as well as servants of a royal master at Versailles, might try to have it both ways by invoking the glories of ducal and Imperial Burgundy. In the eyes of the intendant or commandant at Dijon, on the other hand, the only thing that would matter would be securing registration of the king's contested legislation as expeditiously as possible. After all, parlementary legitimization of royal edicts at Dijon, or elsewhere in provincial France, was important. It might be true that, unlike their Parisian cousins, the provincial magistrates did not have to ratify government loans, but they did have to pass judgment upon measures concerning taxation and other policies of vital public significance. In the final analysis, the Parisian justices could legalize the royal will in the national capital and much of central and northern France, but only the provincial judges could bring the entire realm into line with royal and ministerial wishes. Hence the government's insistence that its edicts be registered, voluntarily or, if necessary, forcibly, in provincial France as well as at Paris; hence its willingness to threaten especially obstreperous magistrates with exile and even forfeiture of their offices.

Actually, cooperation rather than confrontation prevailed between monarch and magistracy much of the time in the eighteenth century. Yet even in "ordinary" times the French ministers had to deal with the sovereign courts on a wide variety of judicial and political issues, and they could not have hoped to do so effectively had those tribunals been unable to maintain internal order. That such discipline prevailed within each *parlement* under Louis XVI—at least until the end of 1786, and in many cases even beyond—attested in part to the maintenance of a hierarchy of chambers and personnel and to a careful allocation of roles and responsibility in all of these law courts.[20]

None of the provincial *parlements* at this time could claim to approach the Paris Parlement's active membership of about 140 or its six functioning chambers, but in their internal organization and operations they all resembled the great court in the French capital. The *parlements* at Bordeaux, Rouen, and Toulouse boasted memberships of between 100 and 115; 90 judges or more served at Rennes and Dijon; between 60 and 80 jurists were active in the courts at Aix, Grenoble, and Besançon; and comparable or smaller numbers of magistrates administered justice in the lesser tribunals at Pau, Perpignan, Douai, Metz, Nancy, and Colmar. Within each *parlement*, business was conducted in a Grand' Chambre, a Tournelle, one to three Chambres des Enquêtes, and usually a Chambre des Requêtes (or in their functional equivalents, where the nomenclature first developed in the Paris Parlement had not taken hold). From time to time, other chambers appeared for temporary purposes in some of the sovereign courts; but the aforementioned chambers discharged their permanent functions.

The Grand' Chambre, staffed by the eldest *parlementaires* who had graduated into it from Enquêtes and Requêtes through seniority of service, wielded absolute power within each court. When in session with the much smaller chamber of criminal law known as the Tournelle, the Parisian Grand' Chambre in particular adjudicated criminal lawsuits of Princes of the Blood, dukes, peers, and other lords, as well as those of officers of the *parlement* itself and members of other tribunals upon petition. The Parisian Grand' Chambre also settled civil litigation engaging the interests of the Princes, peers, great officers of the crown, and such privileged "corporations" as the University of Paris and Hôtel-Dieu. The senior chamber in each of the fifteen *parlements* and sovereign councils settled disputes involving the vital interests of the crown. Again, each senior chamber judged on appeal the suits of privileged holders of royal letters of *committimus* who had applied in first instance to its Chambre des Requêtes, and indeed it had to corroborate *all* judgments rendered in the subordinate chambers. Each *parlement's* Grand' Chambre also received the *appels comme d'abus* in cases involving purported abuses by ecclesiastical tribunals. In addition, each Grand' Chambre would convene with its Tournelle (most of whose members were *grand' chambriers* in the first place) to decide whether government acts could be sanctioned without consultation of the inferior chambers or whether the substance of the legislation in question required convocation of a plenary session of the court. Needless to say, it was in accommodating plenary sessions devoted to discussion of controversial royal acts, and accommodating the *lits de justice* that could result from judicial rejection of those edicts, that the Grand' Chambre in each tribunal achieved its greatest prestige—and notoriety.

In the nature of things, the discipline that the representative senior chamber maintained within its company as a whole implied the existence of a formal or informal directorate, a coterie of veteran *grand' chambriers*, to administer that discipline. And in fact, several judges charged specifically with representing royal interests—that is, the first president, the *procureur-général*, and the two or three *avocats-généraux* —collaborated with a few subordinate presidents and untitled but influential *grand' chambriers* to preserve the order within the tribunal and the harmony between tribunal and crown requisite for the dispensation of justice and registration of legislation.

The first president had always been the chief officer in each *parlement*. His appointment, in theory a matter of royal discretion, had become by the late eighteenth century a mere formality due to his ownership of his office and the normal workings of promotion among the senior chamber's presidents.[21] The first president, as his title implies, presided over the deliberations of the Grand' Chambre and over the *parlement* as a whole when it convened in plenary session. In conjunction with the subordinate presidents of the senior chamber, he distributed among the court's membership special judicial assignments often carrying with them generous perquisites. He acted as intermediary between court and crown (especially in the Parisian case) by voicing his company's concerns and perhaps presenting its remonstrances to the king at Versailles and by relaying the monarch's responses back to his confreres. At *lits de justice* and other solemn assemblages he addressed the king on behalf of his associates. The first president and other presidents who sat upon the Grand Banc or "Great Bench" in the court's central chamber were officially styled *présidents à mortier* (for the *mortiers* or caps worn in judicial session) and "presidents of the court." They were indeed reigning executives, and of the whole company, not just the senior chamber.

Those three or four *parlementaires* known as the *gens du roi* or "king's men" were also, by their functions, indispensable members of the court's directorate. The king's men were the *procureur-général* and the two or three *avocats-généraux*: these royal attorneys, special pleaders for monarchical and public interests, composed the *parquet*, a term that also designated the place on the floor of the Grand' Chambre where these jurists stood when addressing their fellows. The *procureur-général*, as the king's chief "proctor" or solicitor, oversaw the pleading by the *avocats-généraux* of the royal side in any litigation involving the crown's interests; moreover, as *trésorier garde des chartes et papiers de la couronne* the Parisian *procureur-général* in particular (and, at a remove, all his counterparts elsewhere) championed the inalienability of the royal domain and all royal prerogatives. He also maintained order within the court (and within the teeming Palais de Justice) and exercised the same function throughout his company's jurisdiction in concert with local agents of the crown, city and town officials, and his own underlings ("substitutes") in the local *bailliages*, *sénéchaussées*, and provost courts. In addition, the *procureur-général* presented the king's edicts to (and sometimes upon royal command withdrew them from) his associates; sent his company's decrees to subordinate tribunals to be read, registered, and published; and supervised special investigations of administrative or judicial affairs mandated by his colleagues. In all these activities he was seconded by his associates of the *parquet*, especially the senior *avocat-général*. The latter also had the task of responding after the first president to the compulsory registration of royal edicts at *lits de justice* and might address the sovereign or his fellow jurists on other momentous occasions as well. Though the *Almanach royal* might

list the officers of each *parlement*'s *parquet* separately from the personnel of its senior chamber, and though Louis XVI and his ministers might
devoutly wish that these *gens du roi* would truly be the monarch's
"men" in all conflicts between crown and judiciary, their social ties,
daily routine, and mentality really made them *grand' chambriers* before
all else.

These traditional officers of the *parlement*—the *présidents à mortier*
and the king's men of the *parquet*—were joined in the late eighteenth
century, at least at Paris, by a semiofficial figure, the king's political
rapporteur.[22] In conferring this position upon one of the influential veterans of the Grand' Chambre, the sovereign was designating a political
agent to assist the court's leadership in explaining royal legislation and
arguing for its ratification in plenary session. As it turned out, the Parisian *rapporteurs* of the 1770s and 1780s (like their fellows of the Grand
Banc and *parquet* and the provincial counterparts of the latter) found
their loyalties increasingly divided between what successive ministers
expounded as fiscal *raison d'état* and what militant magistrates everywhere apotheosized as noble and necessary opposition to "ministerial
despotism." But, again, before the terminal crisis of the old regime this
was a manageable problem and not one that occupied many hours at the
Palais de Justice. In the humdrum routine of the judicial weeks and
months, the *rapporteur* and the other deans of the tribunal directed parlementary affairs in methodical fashion. At Paris and elsewhere, the
Grand' Chambre with or without the assistance of the Enquêtes and
Requêtes admitted new personnel into court, conferred special honors
upon those of its members who had distinguished themselves, and accorded *lettres de grâce* and *lettres de pardon* to disgraced individuals
petitioning for them. It frequently received delegations from inferior tribunals or from privileged associations imploring parlementary advocacy
or protection. But above all else, the justices of the Grand' Chambre
continued to distribute judicial assignments and royal favors among the
parlementary membership, thereby maintaining the intraparlementary
discipline and the rapport with the crown necessary for the administration of royal justice and legitimization of royal acts.

As noted before, the typical *parlementaire*, whether Parisian or Bordelais, Rouennais or Aixois, could achieve the envied status of the *grand'
chambrier* only through a long apprenticeship in one or more of the
inferior chambers and a slow advancement up the ladder of seniority.
One eighteenth-century observer (who was apparently speaking of the
situation in the Paris Parlement but whose commentary was applicable
likewise to the provincial law courts) aptly characterized the Enquêtes
and Requêtes as "the novitiate of the Grand' Chambre" and asserted
that promotion by seniority guaranteed for the most part that the senior

chamber "was composed of weightier dispositions, of more rational minds susceptible to the coolness and moderation that long reflection and experience produce." Somewhat equivocally, however, this observer conceded that although the Grand' Chambre had "the useful attributes of old age," it was not altogether above the suspicion of harboring "the vices of old age" as well.[23] The novices of the Enquêtes and Requêtes would have probably endorsed that last whiff of criticism, for they were constrained to take a back seat to their elders in prestige and power within the court, and certain zealots among their number at Paris were ever ready to assail the "vices" of the senior judges.[24] Not surprisingly, few of the grand' chambriers were willing to engage in professional self-criticism: as far as they were concerned, their juniors should be content to serve their apprenticeship in the lower chambers, as most parlementaires had since time out of mind, and defer to the company's veterans in all matters. The younger judges' turn would come later; in the meantime, what better schooling for the responsibilities of the Grand' Chambre than patient service in Enquêtes or Requêtes? So senior justices had lectured their junior colleagues over the generations; and they had doubtless reminded these neophytes as well that, as parlementaires, however junior, they participated in and profited from their company's unmatched prerogatives and prestige. They, along with their elders, meted out high justice; they, along with their elders, basked in the occasional glory (or notoriety) of lits de justice staged in the thronged and tumultuous Palais de Justice; they, along with their elders, might even wait upon the sovereign at splendid Versailles on especially grave occasions.

These last facts may have been irrefutable; no less, however, did each parlement's grand' chambriers continue to lord it over the apprentices of Enquêtes and Requêtes.[25] These inferior chambers had evolved originally in the primal Parisian Parlement to share its growing workload with the magistrates of the Grand' Chambre and to provide a more careful examination of the legalities involved in the suits destined for adjudication in the senior chamber. Specifically, the Requêtes approved or rejected the initial requests for parlementary consideration of cases, and the Enquêtes scrutinized the written evidence of parties to those disputes admitted into the court by the Requêtes and often conducted further inquests to ascertain other points in these cases. Long before the troublous last years of the ancien régime the Enquêtes and Requêtes in all the parlements had acquired the right to judge certain types of lawsuits in their own right; nonetheless, every junior parlementaire knew that his chamber's rulings required the approbation of the Grand' Chambre before they could actually become "law." The Requêtes, for example, might pronounce in first instance upon the civil litigation of those pri-

vilégiés holding letters of *committimus*, but all dissatisfied parties to such cases could appeal the junior chamber's decisions to the Grand' Chambre. And even though the Enquêtes might have appellate jurisdiction over *petit-criminel* transgressions punishable by fines, only the Grand' Chambre and Tournelle adjudged on appeal the more serious criminal suits that could invoke corporal punishment. Moreover, every president and ordinary counselor of Enquêtes and Requêtes was aware that the older men of Grand' Chambre and Tournelle, and they alone, would decide when the full court should convene to discuss controversial public issues and who should sit on committees to draft remonstrances if a majority of the membership should vote for such protests. Again, due to the fact that the chamber of Requêtes (at Paris and elsewhere) had never been as fully integrated into *parlement* as had been the Enquêtes, and thus had a somewhat anomalous status, its members, should they desire elevation into the Grand' Chambre some day, would ordinarily have to move over into one of the chambers of Enquêtes and endure the standard apprenticeship there.[26] Small wonder, in view of such realities, that service in the Enquêtes and Requêtes, the "novitiate of the Grand' Chambre," could at times engender frustration and impatience among the younger *parlementaires* and even provoke displays of what our anonymous eighteenth-century observer disapprovingly termed "the high-spiritedness which makes youth dangerous."[27] But although tensions between veteran *grand' chambriers* and newcomers of the inferior chambers had occasionally flared up at Paris (and most likely in provincial *parlements* as well) over the years, such intraparlementary friction would not customarily bode any great trouble for the law courts' directorates—except, of course, in the event of an unmanageable crisis external to these tribunals, such as impending government bankruptcy.

Such, then, was the standardization of functions and internal organization in fifteen law courts with disparate local origins, and it testified impressively to the aggrandizement and unification of France under her monarchs. Yet we should note that these same *parlements* bore witness as well to the incompletion of this grand and historic process. Each *parlement* in northern and central France jealously guarded the *coutume* or customary law of its jurisdiction; each sovereign tribunal in the south prided itself upon its stewardship of written Roman law. Perhaps more important, each *parlement* regarded itself as the supreme custodian and champion of the innumerable and antediluvian privileges and peculiarities of the provincials to whom it meted out royal justice. Besançon's *parlementaires*, for instance, defended an array of relics from the imperial past—including serfdom—that were largely unknown to the men of the other major courts.[28] Douai's magistrates celebrated the antiquity of Flemish customs in the far north; Colmar's jurists upheld Germanic and imperial tradition in Alsace; Pau's and Perpignan's justices stubbornly glorified the peculiar ways of Spanish-speaking mountaineers; and so on. Furthermore, the *parlements* displayed their own institutional and procedural idiosyncrasies. At Aix—and nowhere else—the *parlement's* first president served also as intendant of the province. (This produced some interesting case studies of divided loyalties.)[29] At Grenoble—and nowhere else—the court's chief officer could fill the shoes of the lieutenant-general or the commandant in their absence from Dauphiné.[30] At Rouen, the *présidents à mortier* served in *all* chambers of the tribunal, and judges transferring from the Requêtes to the Enquêtes automatically outranked the other members of the Enquêtes in seniority.[31] Such a state of affairs would have been inconceivable anywhere but in Normandy. Thus, in their internal procedures as in their variegated activities, the *parlements* unavoidably testified to a delicate balance between the writ of Versailles and the legacies of local history, to unique and colorful variations on the French national theme.

We shall see later on how these ambivalences were reflected in the politics of the *parlementaires* during 1787 and 1788. At this point, however, it behooves us to assemble some statistics regarding the social and professional recruitment of the judges dispensing Louis XVI's justice. Only by doing this can we determine whether, in reviewing this critical period, we can speak with as much assurance of a national pattern of parlementary recruitment as we can (with some qualifications) of a national pattern of parlementary organization and functions.

The Personnel: Social and Professional Recruitment

It would only be logical to speculate that magistrates wielding formidable influence in many spheres of eighteenth-century society were socially prominent and privileged men. And in fact enough genealogical research has been done in recent years to assure us in highly quantitative terms that this was so. We can ascertain easily enough that in the course of the eighteenth century, and more particularly during Louis XVI's reign, the *parlements* were recruiting most of their personnel from the nobility. The minority of *parlementaires* who were not full-fledged nobles knew at the very least that (depending upon where they were exercising their judicial *métier*) they, or their sons, or their grandsons, would acquire that envied status through uninterrupted service in parlementary ranks.[32]

At the same time, however—and this point may in some ways overshadow the first—we can hardly speak of a "caste reaction" manifesting itself among these judges in the decades leading up to the Revolution unless we are very careful to characterize that "reaction" in professional as well as social terms. If, in other words, it is possible to demonstrate that some of the sovereign courts (though not by any means all of them) were drawing new members somewhat more exclusively from the social elite during the years immediately preceding France's great upheaval than in times past, it is also noteworthy that in *all* of the *parlements* veritable dynasties of the robe were coming increasingly into being, providing for key judgeships men steeped in the traditions of proud judicial service. Robe and sword together were tending increasingly to monopolize parlementary offices—but they were doing so in a manner that especially underscored robe prestige and power. These conclusions, though most thoroughly documented for the law courts at Paris, Rennes, Aix, Toulouse, Grenoble, Besançon, Rouen, Bordeaux, and Dijon, seem (pending further research) to hold as well for the six lesser parlements and sovereign councils.

The labors of several French historians provide us with convincing data regarding the nobility of the Parisian *parlementaires*.[33] In 1715, 173 of 209 active judges (about 83 percent) were sons of nobles, 26 (about 12 percent) were sons of *privilégiés* in the process of acquiring nobility, and only 10 (about 5 percent) were apparently offspring of commoners. Over a half century later, in 1771, 119 of 155 active judges (about 77 percent) were of noble birth, 21 (about 13 percent) had fathers anticipating ennoblement, and the remaining 15 (about 10 percent) were commoners' sons. There were, then, a few more *roturiers* (commoners) in the Paris Parlement of Louis XV's senescence than were serving at the decease of his great-grandfather, but this hardly constituted a dramatic development. And what was true of the court's membership in general was even more emphatically true of its chief officers in particular. All 10 *présidents à mortier* in 1715 were nobles' sons; all 16 presidents in 1771 could claim noble fathers. All 4 king's men in the *parquet* of 1715 were nobles; the situation was unchanged in 1771. Finally, of 23 presidents of the Enquêtes and Requêtes active in 1715, all but 1 were of noble birth, and that one exception involved the son of a *privilégié* "in the course of ennoblement."[34] Of 26 presidents of the inferior chambers active in 1771, at least 24 were offspring of the noblesse. The long reign of Louis XV was manifestly paralleled by the reign of nobility in his greatest court of law.

Not much changed in this regard under Louis XV's grandson and successor. Of 71 lay counselors admitted into the Enquêtes and Requêtes during the 1774–89 period, and still holding office as of 1790, no fewer than 63 could boast noble blood; at least several of the remaining 8 magistrates could probably lay claim to a *noblesse commencée*, a nobility that would be fully achieved after the standard twenty years of tenure in the tribunal.[35] It also appears that each of the 5 *présidents à mortier*, 3 *gens du roi* of the *parquet*, and 3 presidents of Enquêtes and Requêtes received in the *parlement* after 1774 could vaunt a noble pedigree. There is no doubt that we must avail ourselves repeatedly of the adjective "noble" in characterizing the social provenance of our eighteenth-century Parisian *parlementaires*.

And how had the *parlementaires* (or their families) acquired their envied nobility? In a number of ways, which in relative proportions seem not to have altered radically during the seventy-five years before the Revolution. In general, we find few of the eighteenth-century magistrates displaying a nobility "of ancient extraction": most of them, perhaps eight out of every ten, could do no better than claim a noble status gained in the course of the seventeenth and eighteenth centuries. And, again, this was true for both reigns of the 1715–90 period. Of 590 families represented in the *parlement* from 1715 to 1771, only 33 (less than 6 percent) could trace a nobility back into the fifteenth century; another 106 families could document noble origins antecedent to 1600. These 139 magisterial families together made up not much more than 20% of the total. Of the 71 lay counselors entering the Enquêtes or Requêtes under Louis XVI, and still serving as of 1790, 44 were *hommes nouveaux* (judges of nonparlementary provenance), and of these 44, only 8 could pride themselves upon a sword noblesse dating back a century or more. A very few of the judges of distinguished parlementary lineage might be able to discover noble ancestors predating Bourbon times, but such jurists would very definitely be the exception, as most great families of the robe had achieved social prominence under Henri III's Bourbon successors. Thus, throughout the eighteenth century, most Parisian *parlementaires* would have had to concede a nobility of recent origin.

Among the mechanisms of ennoblement in their families, purchase of the prestigious post of *secrétaire du roi* and exercise of high office in the robe were by far the most common. Of 477 such families represented in Louix XV's Paris Parlement, 241 owed ennoblement to the former mechanism, and 132 to the latter. (Smaller numbers of magisterial families had obtained *lettres-patentes de noblesse* or had broken into the social elite by other means.) Of the 71 lay judges admitted into the court's inferior chambers during the 1774–89 period, and still in office in 1790, most (as with the majority of their elders) were sons and grandsons of prominent robe officers, *secrétaires du roi*, and holders of *lettres-patentes de noblesse*. Such were the modes of upward mobility in the families furnishing judges to the kingdom's primal *parlement* during the last seventy-five years of the *ancien régime*.

Yet the "professional recruitment" of the magistrates may have harbored as great a significance as did their social origins.[36] A pronounced dynastic tendency evidenced itself in the personnel of the eighteenth-century court, as the great robe families which had risen to prominence in the service of the earlier Bourbons (and, in a few cases, the later Valois) now gathered in a rich harvest of judgeships, passing them on as patrimony from generation to generation.

Hence the prominence of the d'Aligres, Lamoignons, Joly de Fleurys, Séguiers, Pinons, Lepeletiers, Ferrands, Bechard de Sarons, and Lefevre d'Ormessons in the justice, administration, and politics of the Paris Parlement. Associating themselves with a common *métier* and defending common privileges, joining sons and daughters and inheritances in matrimony, and mixing socially in townhouses and on country estates, these families came increasingly to monopolize the offices that really mattered and to furnish not a few judicial neophytes to the Enquêtes and Requêtes. The latter magistrates, moreover, exercised their vocation alongside other offspring of the robe, beneficiaries perhaps of somewhat less illustrious parentage and connections but equally formed in magisterial traditions and equally determined to avail themselves of all advantages of a parlementary career.

To follow the parlementary personnel from its reinstatement in 1774 after Chancellor Maupeou's disgrace to its political eclipse fifteen years later is to document the continuing thrust of this professional recruitment, in the Grand' Chambre and in the lower chambers. All five *présidents à mortier* received after 1774 bore the luminous names of the French judiciary: Gilbert de Voisins, Lefevre d'Ormesson, Pinon, Le Peletier de Saint-Fargeau, and Molé de Champlâtreux. Equally prestigious robe families continued to dominate the *parquet*. Guillaume François Louis Joly de Fleury had inherited the post of *procureur-général* from his father under Louis XV and maintained it in the post-Maupeou era until his death in 1787; his successor, the last *procureur-général* in the *parlement*'s long history, was his nephew Armand Guillaume Marie Joseph Joly de Fleury. The latter's father, President Jean Omer Joly de Fleury, was yet another prominent *parlementaire* from this famous family. The senior *avocat-général* throughout the 1774–89 period was Antoine Louis Séguier, bearer of an even more illustrious name. Séguier's junior colleagues, *avocats-généraux* Marie Jean Hérault de Sechelles and Charles Henri d'Ambray, were also of distinguished robe pedigree. In the court's inferior chambers, three new presidents were designated under Louis XVI, and their families—Dompierre d'Hornoi, Le Rebours, and Trousset d'Héricourt—boasted solid robe credentials. As for the new lay personnel of the Enquêtes and Requêtes, its recruitment testified similarly, if less strikingly, to the professional tradition in the *parlement*. Of the 71 lay judges entering the court's junior chambers from 1774 to 1789 and still holding office in 1790, 27 issued from families owing their social ascension to parlementary service, and at least 12 others came from families ennobled through comparable robe service—most notably in the Parisian Chambre des Comptes and Cour des Aides.

Of course, statistics can be read in different ways, and thus if roughly four out of every seven of these parlementary novices "arrived" socially as well as professionally due to their forebear's judicial careers, roughly three of every seven either traced their nobility to other sources, or, in a few cases, did not possess nobility at all. The presence of eight sons of the old military noblesse may reflect, however indirectly, the continuing attractiveness of a fusion of robe and sword in parlementary eyes. Yet the presence of twice as many sons and grandsons of *secrétaires du roi* and purchasers of *lettres-patentes de noblesse* speaks of ways in which new money and new blood could rejuvenate parlementary ranks without demeaning parlementary "honor." Finally, that eight of the court's newcomers had no more than a *noblesse commencée*, or perhaps not even that, suggests that no unprecedented "aristocratic reaction" was gripping this critical institution at the close of the old regime. In light of the foregoing discussion it would seem that it was the robe rather than the sword that was consolidating its influence in the prerevolutionary Paris Parlement.

Undoubtedly, though, there was in provincial France at least one *parlement* that stood out for its social exclusionism—that in Brittany. Yet this had ever been the case at Rennes. As far back as 1627, Desnos des Fossés had referred to the Breton magistrates as "les chevaliers de Malte de la Robe."[37] Only the Venetian Senate and a few other antique bodies could boast personnel of more illustrious lineage, claimed another old regime witness: the *personnes de naissance* serving in and controlling the Rennes Parlement made it "famous throughout Europe."[38] The modern authority upon the Breton *parlementaires* concurs. "What one appreciates in the magistrate of the Parlement of Brittany," observes Jean Meyer, "is less his office than the antiquity of his family's nobility. The Breton parlementaires are first of all nobles who, through familial custom or for some other reason altogether, occupy parlementary posts."[39] What Meyer terms "draconian institutional measures" restricted access to the benches of this *parlement* from 1672 on almost exclusively to sons of Breton nobility, and old nobility at that. Yet such measures only reaffirmed mechanisms of recruitment already long in place. Of 216 families supplying *parlementaires* to the sovereign court at Rennes in the eighteenth century, whose genealogies could be determined and confirmed, 6 were of nobility antedating 1300; another 14 could trace their nobility back into the fourteenth century; and another 112 vaunted nobility of the fifteenth century. Of the remaining 84 families, all but *one* had been ennobled prior to 1700. Indeed, adds Jean Meyer, the Breton nobility serving *in* the eighteenth-century *parlement* at Rennes was of more ancient extraction than the Breton nobility as a whole—a sure sign of the importance traditionally attached to membership in this tribunal by many of the most venerable families of the province.[40] It is no wonder, then, that at Rennes during the 1774–89 period, and only at Rennes, every single *homme nouveau* (that is, lay magistrate of nonparlementary background) admitted into the court was an undeniable *gentilhomme* of at least 100 years' noble extraction.[41] No room for commoners here in an institution whose members had to prove either ancient sword or illustrious robe origins! Nor, by the same token, could there be any room here for "aristocratic reaction," as "reaction" at Rennes could only amount to ongoing custom. Meyer's research, on the other hand, does underscore the prominence of robe (and, thus, of professional tradition) intimately allied with sword in this tribunal. For example, of 412 marriages by eighteenth-century Breton *parlementaires* studied by Meyer, 190 involved women from families of the sword, but approximately 135 involved women from families traditionally providing magistrates to the *parlement* or *Chambre des Comptes* of the province. (In the remaining cases, the wives' families were of very recent noblesse or of the *haute bourgeoisie*.) Thus, more than 75 percent of these spouses of Breton *parlementaires* claimed robe or sword lineage, and in a respectable proportion of these cases men of the robe had chosen "women of the robe."[42] But if marriage patterns point to a degree of "robe solidarity" within this most "noble" of *parlements*, so, too, do dynastic tendencies in parlementary service. In Brittany's *parlement* (and we shall see this to be equally true elsewhere) fathers and uncles tended increasingly to bequeath their offices to sons and nephews in the eighteenth century. Meyer found 7 families alone making 42 such transactions between 1700 and 1788, or about 11 percent of the 408 transactions of those years. Another 42 prominent families conducted 156 transactions, about 38 percent of the total. Some of these same families controlled posts in the Breton Chambre des Comptes as well. The de La Bourdonnaye and de Farcy families, the de Becdelièvre, Boylesve, and de Cornulier families—these, and others, proud of their centuries of nobility, were proud as well of their generations of professional activity in their province's greatest court of law.[43] A *parlement* regarded by many in the old regime as a bastion of noble exclusiveness would perhaps have been more accurately noted for its amalgamation of the interests of both sword *and* robe in Brittany.

A similar marriage of the interests of parlementary and sword noblesse characterized the situation at Aix-en-Provence, although here under Louis XVI the robe's genealogical role was greater and the sword was of less ancient extraction than at Rennes. It is surely true that 20 of the

21 lay counselors entering the *parlement* at Aix during the 1774–89 period were full-fledged nobles; the only judge who was not may at least have had a *noblesse commencée*.[44] But whereas 11 of these newcomers were *hommes nouveaux*, that is to say, sons of nonparlementary noblesse, only 1 of these 11 could trace his nobility back a century or more. The families of the other 10 novices had gained their nobility in the course of the eighteenth century by the usual means: judicial service in lower courts, or acquisition of *lettres-patentes de noblesse* or posts of *secrétaire du roi*. Furthermore, whereas at Rennes less than one-third (that is, 17 of 52) of the lay magistrates admitted to the Breton *parlement* under Louis XVI issued from the robe, at Aix nearly half (that is, 9 of 21) of the lay apprentices to judicial service reveal parlementary backgrounds.

Also meriting notice is the Aix Parlement's decree of 23 January 1769.[45] Although this *arrêt* resembled those of other *parlements* in the middle and later decades of the century in stipulating that candidates for office demonstrate either parlementary lineage or the standard four generations of nonparlementary noblesse, it also commented that candidates whose wives were daughters of *parlementaires* need only document three generations of noblesse. We can probably regard this latter provision as an additional, if minor, indication of the significance attached to "professional" as well as "social" pedigree at Aix. At the same time, it is true that the Provençal *noblesse de race* had not destined its sons for parlementary service in the sixteenth and seventeenth centuries and was not doing so in the eighteenth century either: as noted earlier, only one offspring of the "old" sword accepted parlementary responsibilities under Louis XVI. But the magistrates at Aix-en-Provence may have been too preoccupied with consolidating family dynasties within their tribunal to worry unduly about possible discrepancies between the genealogical requirements set forth in their decree of January 1769 and the recent nobility of their junior colleagues from sword families. Certainly dynastic tendencies abounded in the *parlement* at Aix.[46] The Rabasse family had held the post of *procureur-général* through seven successive generations. The Forbin family had provided two first presidents and four other presidents *à mortier* to the court; the Coriolis had furnished no fewer than seven presidents *à mortier*; the Grimaldi-Regusse, four presidents *à mortier*; and so on. If the nobility of the Aix *parlementaires* was of altogether more recent extraction than that of the Bretons, there was nonetheless in the Provençal *parlement* as in that of Brittany an ongoing aggrandizement of old robe influence under Louis XVI.

The situation at Toulouse was fundamentally the same, although here the Languedocien nobility's near monopoly of judicial office was more clearly overshadowed by an accelerating professional "caste" reaction after 1774.[47] Of the nobility of the Toulousains there could be no doubt. Of 27 lay counselors who entered the *parlement* during the 1775–90 period, 26 already enjoyed noble status or were in the process of acquiring it at the time of admission into the court, whereas the twenty-seventh, an exceptionally talented commoner named Pierre de Guiringaud, had to undergo a candidacy of eight years before finally securing a post in the lowly Requêtes in 1785. (A youthful Bertrand Barère, perhaps not as talented or as fortunate as Pierre de Guiringaud, was kept out of the *parlement* for lack of documentation of nobility and had to settle for an office in the presidial court at his native Tarbes.) Moreover, the tribunal at Toulouse could boast representatives of some very old aristocratic families: for example, the Lamote, Lecomte, Catellan de Caumont, Roux de Puyvert, and du Bourg families traced noble ancestry back into the Middle Ages and had given France ambassadors, bishops, chancellors, and other servants of high estate. Most of the Toulousain families, however, were of postmedieval extraction, having in many cases won their spurs of caste in the seventeenth-century competition for judicial and municipal office, *lettres-patentes de noblesse*, and the inevitable posts of *secrétaire du roi*. A few sixteenth-century families allied with the Languedocien *noblesse d'épée* and a few families ennobled only since 1720 also counted representatives in the highest court of the province. Overall, the pedigree of the Toulousain *parlementaires* could not rival that of the nobles who dominated the Estates of Languedoc—a fact that may help explain the endemic state of war between *parlement* and Estates throughout the eighteenth century.[48] Bickering over pedigree, prestige, and precedence, after all, could take on absurd importance in the *ancien régime*.

But some of the blue bloods of the Languedoc Estates who sneered at the less-than-immemorial nobility of the Toulousain *parlementaires* may have grudgingly admired the success of the latter in taking care of their own. The statistics here are arresting.[49] To begin with, every one of the 11 *présidents à mortier* serving in the court after Chancellor Maupeou's disgrace were sons of former presidents or counselors at Toulouse. Again, all 4 judges entering the *parquet* after 1774 were sons or nephews of *parlementaires*. But more significant are the backgrounds of the untitled lay personnel. Of the 27 newcomers to the tribunal under Louis XVI, only 1 seems to have lacked ties to the robe. Of the other 26 apprentices, 15 were sons of *parlementaires*, 3 were nephews of *parlementaires*, another was the grandnephew of a president, 4 were descendants of former members of the court, and the remaining 3 counselors could count officers of other law courts among their ancestors.

Furthermore—and this is especially interesting—statistics reveal the gradual waxing of robe dominance within the court during the latter half of the century. Whereas the sons of *parlementaires* entering the court after 1774 represented only 38 percent of the *entire* membership of the 1775–90 period, which of course included veterans of Louis XV's reign, those same parlementary sons composed fully 58 percent of the contingent *new to the court* after 1774. In other words, it may have been easier for nonparlementary offspring—sons of *militaires*, of Toulousain *capitouls*, of lower-court judges and *avocats*, of *receveurs des tailles*—to take up parlementary careers at Toulouse before 1771 than it was after 1774. Symptomatic of a *réaction judiciaire* at Toulouse were the dynastic and marital tendencies already noted elsewhere as well. The Catellan de Caumont family provided the *parlement* with nine counselors, three presidents, and an *avocat-général;* the de Rességuier were represented by nine consecutive generations in court service; the Cambon had supplied parlementaires for a century and a half; and the d'Assézat, de Segla, de Papus, de Boyer, de Rabaudy, and others in eighteenth-century service could point to sixteenth-century ancestors in the same institution.[50] It was not unusual for junior magistrates in the post-Maupeou period to join fathers and uncles in rendering the king's sovereign justice in Languedoc. Finally, that these judges were as eager to marry daughters and sisters of colleagues (or of the local noblesse) as they were loath to give their own daughters to *avocats* or lower-court judges or others of inferior station tells us something about their conquests in society on the eve of the Revolution. Like their counterparts at Rennes and Aix, they aspired to the very best that robe and sword could offer them.

At Grenoble, the situation was similar in many but not all respects.[51] The Dauphinois *parlementaires*, like their Breton, Provençal, and Languedocien cousins, had long prided themselves upon their noble origins, and their institution would remain a citadel of the social elite right down to the Revolution. At the same time, however, the tribunal at Grenoble experienced recruiting difficulties in the late 1770s and 1780s, difficulties apparently related to a reduced "colonization" of offices by established parlementary families and reflected in the increasingly disparate robe backgrounds of newcomers to the court. Yet the practical import of this latter development was not, it seems, very great.

On the first point, there was never any doubt about the local nobility's continuing monopolization of judgeships. Indeed, the magistrates had called for this explicitly in their *arrêté* of 5 March 1762, which required (as would the decree of 1769 at Aix) that all candidates for parlementary office possess either parlementary nobility or at least four generations of sword nobility. Judges must, in other words, continue to be "gentlemen" in one way or another. But statistics advanced by the *parlement's* major historian, Jean Egret, show that, at Grenoble as at Aix, discrepancies between genealogical requirements and social realities appeared in the waning years of the old regime. On the one hand, it is true that 25 of the 26 judges admitted to the company from 1756 to 1771 were either *nobles de robe* or *nobles de race*, and that at least 17 of the 19 lay counselors entering the tribunal under Louis XVI held similar credentials of judicial or military noblesse. Moreover, the jurists responsible for the *arrêté* of 5 March 1762 would never have had reason to question the ancient noble extraction of names in their midst such as de Chaponay, de Vaulx, de Murat, d'Yzé, de Beaumont, d'Agoult, de Corbeau, and de Revol. The problem (if it *was* a problem) lay with the *nobles de robe* rather than with the *nobles de race*. Of 20 ordinary counselors entering the *parlement* from 1756 to 1771, 15 issued from parlementary families; but of the 19 lay counselors joining parlementary ranks under Louis XVI, only 5 could be so categorized.[52] What of the other 14 novices in the years after 1774? Three issued from the "ancient" military noblesse, 2 at most may have been commoners, and the other 9—nearly half of the new lay counselors—would have to be described as *nobles de robe* whose families had won their noble spurs through means other than service in Grenoble's *parlement*. As in other *parlements*, this would mean that their grandfathers and fathers had served in lesser magisterial positions or had purchased *lettres-patentes de noblesse* or posts of *secrétaire du roi*.

The evolutionary tendency among the nonpresidential lay counselors at Grenoble, then, ran counter to that for the analogous personnel at Toulouse: away from, rather than toward, "colonization" of counselors' offices by established parlementary families. Yet the significance of this for parlementary policy and posturing in the closing decades of the old regime should not be exaggerated. The offices that really mattered, on the Grand Banc of the Grand' Chambre and in the *parquet*, remained the preserve of the Dauphinois "parlementary aristocracy" almost without exception. At Grenoble the names most closely associated with parlementary prestige and power under Louis XVI—de Bérulle, de Vaulx, de Montferrat, de La Croix de Sayve d'Ornacieux, de Barral, de Moydieu, de Reynaud—conjured up generations of parlementary service in Bourbon France. Despite the admittance of some nonparlementary *hommes nouveaux* into the tribunal's one chamber of Enquêtes, effective control of the institution lay as always with the established parlementary families.

Of all the provincial *parlements*, none has been more exhaustively studied, at least from a prosopographical viewpoint, than that at Besançon. Statistics of recruitment culled from Maurice Gresset's massive dissertation on the *monde judiciaire* of old regime Besançon suggest to us a parlementary membership especially similar to the analogous personnel at Toulouse.[53] In other words, we find here an institution staffed by nobles of relatively recent extraction, dominated increasingly by a network of entrenched robe families, and less and less accessible to moneyed and talented aspirants lacking noble and magisterial lineage. First there is the question of long-term evolution of noble recruitment to the tribunal.[54] During the period from 1694 to the Revolution, 34 of 35 presidents *à mortier* assuming office were nobles; 232 of 277 lay counselors (about 84 percent) were nobles; and 21 of 32 officers of the *parquet* likewise enjoyed noble status. Comparison of these figures with those for the incoming personnel of Louis XVI's reign reveals something of an evolution toward exclusion of commoners from magisterial ranks. All 3 presidents assuming office after 1774 were nobles; 31 of 35 incoming lay counselors were similarly favored; 3 of the 4 "commoners" were by expectations, pretensions, and life-style virtually nobles; and the king's men were without exception members of the social elite. Incontrovertibly, then, nobility at Besançon maintained its hold upon the *parlement*'s personnel and, at least in the cases of the *gens du roi*, even appears to have tightened its grip somewhat. This was true despite the fact that "nobility" in this court of law could claim nothing like the antiquity boasted by nobility in the Breton *parlement*. Only a smattering of the 180 magisterial families studied by Gresset for the 1676–1789 period had won their spurs of caste before 1500, and fully 100 families (55 percent of the total) were ennobled only in the course of the eighteenth century. The 13 families with noble origins antedating 1500 bore some of the proud names of Franche-Comté—Espiard, Benoit de Saint-Vandelin, Chaillot, d'Orival, Boudret—but by the late eighteenth century the court was obviously dominated by magistrates whose families' more recent nobility derived from judicial service or judicious purchases of one kind or another.

But, as Gresset's research convincingly demonstrates, the major story in Besançon's *parlement* from the late seventeenth to the late eighteenth century was the entrenchment of a particular type of nobility: robe nobility.[55] Most of the *parlementaires* serving Franche-Comté in this period issued from families steeped in the judicial tradition. Of the 180 magisterial families mentioned earlier, fully 112 (about 62 percent) could trace their association with justice back to judges or *avocats* or *procureurs* or humble *notaires* of fairly distant times: most of these apparent founding fathers of robe tradition had served professionally in the seventeenth or even sixteenth century. Of the remaining 68 families, only 16 could not boast of at least one judicial officer in their genealogies. Thus we find here, documented with unusual thoroughness, a parlementary membership deeply rooted in the local *monde judiciaire*. And, once ensconced in their province's highest tribunal, what did the heirs of this robe tradition, these descendants of humbler judicial folk, do? Predictably, they passed their posts on to sons and nephews and espoused sisters and daughters of other legal practitioners. On the former point, 14 of 37 *présidents à mortier* serving in this period had received their *mortiers* directly from their fathers, whereas another 14 could at least speak of fathers who had been counselors in one or another of the local sovereign courts. Of 277 lay counselors, 109 had been preceded in counselors' ranks by their fathers, and another 32 could point to fathers who had discharged similar responsibilities in other law courts. On the latter point, no fewer than 251 of 348 marriages of *parlementaires* studied for the same period at Besançon (about 72 percent) involved women from the local judicial milieu. (Another 50 wives were from families of the sword; thus, the milieus of robe and sword provided about 85 percent of these judges' spouses.)

Most intriguing, however, are the signs of an *evolutionary* development toward the end of the period. All 3 incoming presidents under Louis XVI, and all 3 officers of the *parquet*, were sons of the high magistracy. Of the 35 incoming lay counselors of the 1775–89 period, 17 were sons of *parlementaires*, and 17 of the remaining 18 could indicate other relatives or ancestors in sovereign court service or at the very least were closely associated with the judiciary through marriage. In fact, of 16 marriages of counselors studied for this terminal phase of the tribunal's existence, no fewer than 11 involved daughters specifically of *sovereign court* judges. It would be difficult to resist Gresset's conclusion that the upper levels of the magistracy in Franche-Comté were becoming more and more the preserve of a network of powerful robe families under Louis XVI. Yet, at the same time, access to judicial office at lower levels was apparently becoming *easier*. Expectations of upward mobility *within* the magisterial hierarchy, in other words, may very well have been rising—but increasingly coming up against the established "robinocracy" fortified by the ties of the *haute société robine* to the local military noblesse.

Paul-Edouard Robinne's research on the *parlementaires* meting out justice at Rouen under Louis XVI suggests that, in Normandy as in other provinces, robe reinforced by sword had the situation fairly well in hand.[56] Robinne's analysis embraces 173 jurists of the period from November 1774 to September 1790: 102 of these justices appeared in the post-Maupeou *parlement* of 1774 and the other 71 subsequently entered the court. As of 1774, about 74 percent of the members already possessed nobility and another 12 percent had a *noblesse commencée*; sixteen years later, the figures were 76 percent and 9 percent, respectively. Thus, about 6 of every 7 magistrates throughout the period issued from the social elite. There was, admittedly, a substantial minority of *roturiers* here that would not have been tolerated by the Bretons in their company. The Normans had passed their own exclusionist decree in April 1777, but discovered (as did their counterparts in several other provinces) that restriction of court membership to "gentlemen" and parlementary offspring was not always possible. Moreover, the nobles in Normandy's highest court did not, for the most part, issue from the oldest families of the province. Of the 155 families furnishing *parlementaires* at Rouen during the 1774–90 period, only 15 could trace their nobility back before 1500; 34 families could attest sixteenth-century noblesse; 46 families were of seventeenth-century extraction; and another 35 families displayed nobility acquired in the years since 1700. Here were social origins, to be sure, more impressive than those of the personnel at Besançon, and comparable to those of the membership of most other provincial *parlements*; yet they were still a far cry from those of the *chevaliers de Malte de la Robe* at Rennes.

The families of the *anoblis* (that is, of that heavy majority of judges whose noblesse was somewhat less than "ancient") had risen into the social elite by the usual means: *lettres-patentes de noblesse*, purchase of the office of *secrétaire du roi*, service in judicial and financial posts, and so on. The venerable families of the eighteenth-century *parlement* at Rouen—the d'Hugleville, the Couvert de Coulons, the Beaunay, the Des Roys, the Mézières, the Des Landes—must have cherished their "superiority" over these *anoblis* and positively scorned the consistent 13 to 15 percent of incoming judges not even able to certify an upstart nobility. Patently, the exclusionist decree of 1777 did not preserve an unsullied escutcheon at Rouen. On the other hand, the minority of commoners at Rouen, as elsewhere, occupied the inferior benches in the tribunal; representatives of nobility monopolized the key positions of parlementary power.

And what were the professional origins of this nobility? As elsewhere for the most part, so at Rouen, robe predominated over sword. Robinne's statistics do not permit us to attest the sort of long-term evolution of "robinocracy" at Rouen already noted for Besançon, but they do show the robe, with its inevitable family dynasties, to be very much in the ascendant. Of the 173 magistrates in the 1774–90 period for whom information is available, about 61 percent issued from the *haute société robine*: they were sons of *parlementaires* or of counselors in the local Cour des Comptes, Aides et Finance or were linked in other fashions with the high robe. Predictably, the robe enjoyed a near monopoly of posts in the *parquet* and on the Grand Banc, while supplying lesser proportions of nonpresidential counselors to the court's various chambers. The overall impression of robe ascendancy in the court is only confirmed by the fact that, of the 39 percent of the justices *not* issuing from the *haute société robine*, at least some were of humbler judicial origins. After all, barristers and lower-court judges could be as inclined as *militaires, seigneurs de fiefs,* or occasional men of trade and finance to place sons or nephews in the greatest court of the province. And then, of course, there were the great robe dynasties, success stories whose first chapters had been written by enterprising peasants and Parisian or Norman bourgeois of the fourteenth and fifteenth centuries. Acquisition of minor administrative or judicial posts had opened doors of professional opportunity; fulfillment had come with generations of parlementary service and "colonization" of important parlementary posts. In the eighteenth century, the Le Roux family could pride itself upon nine generations' presence in the court; the Du Val de Bonneval, Camus, Du Moucel, Le Cordier, Baillard, Le Bret, Montholon, Bigot, and Romé, among other families, were similarly represented over many generations in the *parlement* and other sovereign courts. When we note in addition the usual patterns of intermarriage within the robe, and "matrimonial policy" linking Norman robe with Norman sword, the consolidation of professional and social interests of many judicial families at Rouen becomes obvious.

Investigation of the *parlementaires* rendering justice far to the south at Bordeaux reveals a similar situation—reveals, that is, a fairly exclusive but not-so-ancient noblesse, a formidable presence of the robe, and an impressive solidarity of robe and sword interests. William Doyle's statistics leave no doubt as to the nobility of the preponderant majority of judges.[57] Of 162 magistrates serving during the 1774–90 period, only 13 were definitely commoners upon entering the court; significantly, all of these 13 held relatively inferior offices. Of the 127 families providing the 162 *parlementaires* of Louis XVI's reign, however, only 4 could positively claim nobility antedating 1500: Pichard, Piis, Degères, and Raymond de Sallegourde. Another 24 families could document noble origins extending back at least into the sixteenth century; these account for most of the prestigious presidential names of the late eighteenth century, such as Gourgue, Lavie, Le Berthon, and Gascq. Another 46 families could boast at least a seventeenth-century noblesse, and the 48 remaining noble families were of eighteenth-century extraction. Here was a nobility predominantly of Bourbon times, of extraction similar to that of the noble magistrates in most other provincial *parlements.* In a social sense, recruitment at Bordeaux, as elsewhere for the most part, was narrow without being altogether closed.

But recruitment at Bordeaux, as elsewhere, reflected a professional as well as a social concern. Of 153 judges of the 1774–90 period for whom information is available, no fewer than 71 were sons of *parlementaires;* moreover, 46 judges could point to paternal grandfathers in parlementary service, and 29 could make the same claim for great-grandfathers.

Perhaps 14 magistrates could boast more than four generations of parlementary service in their families: here, again, were presidential names such as Verthamon, Gourgue, Lavie, Gascq, and Le Berthon. During the 1774–90 period, 21 families were represented by two successive generations in the tribunal, with fathers passing offices on to eldest sons or perhaps purchasing posts for them and staying on in court themselves. But of equal interest are the statistics for those 82 judges *not* issuing from parlementary families. At least 45 of them had backgrounds in or bordering upon the local *monde judiciaire*: 11 were sons of Cour des Aides counselors, 9 were sons of "treasurers of France," 9 were sons of officers in lower courts, 11 others were sons of king's secretaries in chanceries of various sovereign courts, and the remaining 5 jurists were sons of *avocats*. Finally, abundant data reveal the usual intermarriage within the robe and the usual alliances linking robe with nonrobe noblesse. Of the 162 Bordelais *parlementaires* in this period, 33 married daughters of judges; a smaller number married daughters of the nonparlementary robe; and 45 others married daughters of the nonjudicial noblesse. Mothers of at least 50 of our 162 *parlementaires* were themselves of parlementary lineage. No fewer than 57 judges of the period had brothers-in-law among their professional brethren, and 15 judges counted from 1 to 3 sons-in-law in the company.

It would be only a slight exaggeration to assert that everyone was related to everyone else in Bordeaux's highest law court on the eve of the Revolution. And certain robe families counted for a great deal in the tribunal. The dynasties of the Verthamon, Darche, Marbotin, Filhot, and Castelnau families alone demonstrated the extent of "colonization" of offices and concentration of power by entrenched robe families in an important provincial *parlement*. Simultaneously, those forty-five weddings involving daughters of all but the most glittering sword families of the region indicate that here, as elsewhere, the parlementary robe had very nearly the best of both local worlds, social and professional. There was, to be sure, one idiosyncrasy in the social composition of this *parlement*: perhaps one-tenth of its members were "arriving" from mercantile families, and about one-fifth of the marriages involving parlementary husbands were uniting them with mercantile wives. But this was hardly surprising in a seaport internationally famed for its commercial prosperity, and in no way does it alter our impression of a continuing robe-*cum*-sword ascendancy in the *parlement* dispensing justice at Bordeaux.

Finally, among the eight "major" provincial *parlements*, there was that of Burgundy. At Dijon, as virtually everywhere else, an ascendancy of robe and sword characterized the years leading up to the Revolution.[58] Albert Colombet found that, of approximately 120 Burgundians administering parlementary justice in the twilight of the *ancien régime*, barely 10 entered their company as commoners, and at least 6 of those enterprising 10 had to content themselves with posts in the lowly Requêtes. Admittedly, 2 of the other apparent commoners were *avocats-généraux* Etienne Henri Colas and Louis Bernard Guyton de Morveau, but both had embarked upon parlementary careers long before Louis XVI's accession, and the latter at least was exceptionally gifted. Admittance to the court may have been rendered more difficult for commoners after 1774: one Crétin d'Oussières found himself rejected in 1783 because of credentials deemed insufficiently "dignified" by the justices. Yet here, as at Bordeaux and Besançon and elsewhere, noble exclusiveness in no way reflected a prevalence of ancient pedigrees. Inevitably, a few names of old Burgundian nobility illuminated the parlementary membership: Joly, Legouz, Espiard, Bouhier, Coeurderoy, Fyot, and Gagne, for example. But a noblesse of the Bourbon epoch, with roots in local commerce and agriculture, was more common. Indeed, magistrates such as Pierre-Anne Chesnard de Layé, Pierre-Antoine Robin d'Apremont, and François Maublanc de Martenet had leapt out of relative obscurity in two or three generations. The real *noblesse ancienne* of the province was to be found elsewhere; for the most part it would not deign to send its sons into judicial careers at Dijon.

And so the parlementary nobility at Dijon, as in most other cities of the great judiciary, was more remarkable for its tendency toward "robinocracy" than for its ancient extraction. Statistics attest the importance of robe backgrounds in Burgundy's highest law court. Of Colombet's 120 magistrates serving in the terminal period of the *ancien régime*, 55 were sons of *parlementaires* or of other sovereign court judges; another 5 were sons of *avocats*; and another 18 were sons of *officiers notables*—king's secretaries, royal notaries, *bailliage* lieutenants, *maîtres des eaux et forêts*, and so on—associated directly or indirectly with the administration of justice. Thus, nearly two-thirds of all the *parlementaires* were truly offspring of the robe. Furthermore, although his research did not permit comparison of the 1774–89 period with earlier phases of the tribunal's existence, Colombet clearly suspected an evolution toward "robinocratic" control of the Burgundian *parlement* under Louis XVI. He noted a distinct tendency for *parlementaires* to bequeath their offices to their sons, or—more significantly—to purchase judgeships for their offspring while remaining in court service themselves. Families illustrative of the latter practice included the Barbuot de Palaiseau, Carrelet de Loisy, Guenichot de Nogent, Joly de Bévy, Juillet de Saint-Pierre, Legouz de Saint-Seine, Macheco de Premeaux, Mairetet de Thorey, and Villedieu de Torcy. In some cases fathers might pass their offices on to their sons and then acquire presidential *mortiers*: President

Jean-Vivant Micault de Courbeton and his son Joseph were an example. In 1789 four presidents on the Grand Banc could boast sons in the counselors' ranks. Moreover, those judges willing to take wives from wealthy but nonnoble, nonparlementary families were apparently the exception: "matrimonial policy" at Dijon followed the national pattern in consolidating the interests of "robinocracy" at the sovereign court level.

And what of the lesser *parlements* dispensing justice on the kingdom's periphery during these years? Here we have less information at hand, but also fewer judges to investigate. What little we do know suggests some adherence to—but also some divergence from—patterns of socioprofessional provenance documented for the *parlementaires* serving in the more important provincial tribunals.[59] Of 15 *présidents à mortier* assuming their duties at Colmar, Douai, Metz, Nancy, Pau, and Perpignan under Louis XVI, at least 9 issued from parlementary families and at least 5 of the others displayed a nonparlementary noblesse. Of the 6 *procureurs-généraux* serving in these peripheral law courts on the eve of the Revolution, 4 were full-fledged members of their local "robinocracies," and a fifth, issuing from a sword family of recent extraction, owed his elevation to the *parquet* to his eminent success as parlementary counselor. On the other hand, only 3 of the 8 *avocats-généraux* entering the *parquets* of these *parlements* after 1774 issued from the magisterial nobility; 3 of the remaining 5 hailed from the nonparlementary noblesse, and the other 2—interestingly enough—were apparently commoners.

The most widespread evidence of parlementary newcomers lacking nobility concerns ordinary nonpresidential magistrates, as we would expect. Of 85 lay counselors embarking upon parlementary careers at Colmar, Douai, Metz, Nancy, Pau, and Perpignan under Louis XVI, 35 hailed from parlementary families, 21 came from nonparlementary noblesse, and the remaining 29 were seemingly commoners possessing at most a *noblesse commencée*. At one extreme, Nancy remained as unsullied by "common" blood as Rennes: all 10 incoming lay counselors at Nancy could display one sort of noblesse or another. At the other extreme, 4 out of 5 newcomers at Colmar lacked nobility upon entering the "sovereign council" of Alsace. At Metz, 8 out of 21 entrants were commoners; at Pau, 10 of 28; at Douai, 5 of 14; and at Perpignan, 2 of 7. If, then, in the lesser *parlements* recruitment to the key posts of power (the presidencies, the judgeships in the *parquet*) remained quite narrow, access to the less important positions of counselors was broader, at least at Colmar, Metz, Pau, and Douai.

Access was broader—but what about "commoners" who may have been already launched upon the way toward nobility? Such was the case with most "commoners" admitted to the major provincial *parlements*:

the Aixois, Toulousains, and Normans (to say nothing of the Bretons) seem to have been little inclined to lower social barriers very far in the waning decades of the *ancien régime.* In any case, relatively few of the *parlementaires* in Louis XVI's realm were to be found at Colmar or Metz. The vast majority of them were exercising their vocation in such cities as Paris, Toulouse, Bordeaux, and Rouen, and they were continuing to hail chiefly if not exclusively from the kingdom's second estate. Yet this was clearly not the whole story. Though the data marshaled on these pages do certify a persisting ascendancy of nobility in the *parlements* on the eve of revolution, they show as well that the judges were aggrandizing their influence as heirs of a professional tradition rather than as standard-bearers for a resurgent aristocracy. The high magistracy insisted nonetheless upon having very nearly the best of both worlds, professional and social. Their enjoyment of the latter will emerge more strikingly as we consider their sources of wealth and style of living in the city and in the country.

The Personnel: Wealth and Life-Style

Inquiry into the economic and social aspects of our magistrates' lives in the late eighteenth century yields several general conclusions. On the one hand, the jurists' affluence tended to vary from province to province (and, not surprisingly, within each institution), whereas the provincials as a whole were less wealthy (and less needful of wealth) than the Parisians. On the other hand, the *constitution* of magisterial wealth did not vary significantly from province to province or, for that matter, from the outlying reaches of the realm to the national capital, although admittedly the long-term valuational evolution of certain components of this wealth (such as the worth of the judges' offices) could be determined primarily by local factors. Finally, in the way they lived, and enjoyed living, the justices, be they Parisian or provincial, very much resembled their cousins of the sword—without, however, relinquishing certain distinctive traits of their *métier.*

The Parisian *parlementaire* had to support the dignity of his profession in the greatest city of continental Europe. Whether novice of Enquêtes or Requêtes, veteran counselor of Grand' Chambre, or officer of *parquet* or Grand Banc, he patently had to reckon with living expenses far exceeding those of most of his provincial counterparts. If, for instance, he were the first president, he would not only have to furnish lavish repasts and entertainment fairly frequently for his colleagues, but would upon occasion have to do so for foreign dignitaries and the king as well. It is only natural, then, that we should find more millionaires at

Paris than elsewhere, and more judges worth between half a million and a million livres. The former category included most of the court's great officers as well as a number of the influential counselors of the Grand' Chambre and even a few members of the inferior chambers. The latter category claimed a much larger number of jurists. The authority on the parlementary membership of Louis XV's reign assures us that having between 500,000 and 1 million livres made one "capable of maintaining an honorable rank . . . for a counselor if not for a president, it meant avoiding 'gilded mediocrity.' " Those judges with fortunes between 150,000 and 400,000 livres were unable, at least under Louis XV, "to lead a grand life at Paris," whereas the minority of magistrates with even less than that "knew considerable financial difficulties."[60] Most Parisian *parlementaires*, however, were not in truly straitened circumstances, and those who counted for the most in professional and political matters could usually call upon impressive reserves of wealth. Admittedly, the men of this crucial *parlement* were not for the most part as opulent as certain *grands bourgeois* of the capital or *nobles de la cour* at Versailles, but for that matter neither were the preponderant majority of nonrobe nobles and bourgeois in the realm; and in any case the *parlementaires* eclipsed all these other groups in prestige and power.

Glances at some of the tribunal's notables of this period tell us much about magisterial wealth at its most imposing.[61] First President Etienne François d'Aligre bought the marquisat de la Galaisière and its dependencies for 925,000 livres shortly after his company's reinstatement in 1775; he was known to be a millionaire several times over in the late 1780s. D'Aligre's eventual successor Louis François de Paule Lefevre d'Ormesson had as far back as 1765 purchased "the land, seigneurie and justice of Thiais" from Louis XV himself and was in later years lord of Noyseau, Thiais, Grignon, and other seigneuries. Another *président à mortier*, Pierre VII Gilbert de Voisins, bought the seigneurie of Orgeval from Louis XVI's brother the comte de Provence for 346,000 livres in 1779 and obtained other lands from a *négociant* for a mere 56,200 livres. As of the 1760s the presidential family Lepeletier de Rosambo held domains in at least ten parishes of Brittany: the family's patrimonial estates in that province alone were later evaluated at more than 1.6 million livres, with overall landed wealth put somewhere between 2 and 3 million livres. Still another president, Armand Guillaume François de Gourgues, owned "a great domain at Gonesse, northeast of Paris." Then of course there were the ubiquitous Joly de Fleurys. They had inherited enormous holdings from their forebear of mid-century fame, Procureur-Général Guillaume François Joly de Fleury. President Jean Omer Joly de Fleury was in the 1780s lord of la Mousse au Maine; his brother Guillaume François Louis Joly de Fleury, *procureur-général* until late 1787, was seigneur of Fleury itself; and the president's son Armand Guillaume Marie Joseph, the court's last *procureur-général*, was lord of the estates of Briosne. Long-standing counselor of the Grand' Chambre Adrien Louis Lefebvre d'Amécourt also qualified easily as a millionaire, holding vast lands near Lisieux in Normandy. Some judges' landed wealth derived from recent ancestral conquests in the worlds of finance, commerce, and colonies. The recent forebears of controversial counselor of the Enquêtes Jean Jacques IV Duval d'Eprémesnil had prospered in French India; their descendant of the 1780s could consequently draw upon handsome properties that included estates in the vicinity of Le Havre in Normandy. President Edouard François Mathieu Molé de Champlâtreux owed much of his fortune to his grandfather, who was none other than fabulous financier Samuel Bernard. These are the success stories of some of the Paris Parlement's luminaries on the eve of the crisis that would shatter all.

If now we turn to the provinces, we can say something about "average" wealth in the major *parlements* even if we cannot yet rank them with any precision in this regard. The Bretons, we can be fairly confident, were as a group the most affluent of the provincial judges—and, given their lustrous extraction, was this inappropriate?[62] Descendants even in the seventeenth century of many generations of the greatest Breton nobility, the judges and their families of Bourbon times acquired roughly 56 percent of the *grandes seigneuries* of Haute Bretagne (mostly from the Court noblesse) and dominated as well the northern coast from Saint-Brieuc to Morlaix, the environs of Nantes, and the Vannetais. Eighteenth-century millionaire families included the de Robien, de Langle, Le Prestre, de La Bourdonnaye, de Cornulier, Châteaugiron, Bopriac, de Gage, Huchet de La Bédoyère, and other great families. The great majority of magistrates in the 1770s and 1780s were worth a half million livres or more. To put it another way, the Bretons' modern historian has loosely categorized the "very richest families" (worth 2 to 3 million livres), the "average families" (200,000 to 1 million livres), and the "poor" minority (200,000 livres or less). The fantastic mercantile wealth of Saint-Malo and Nantes might outstrip most parlementary fortunes during the 1750–89 era, but magisterial affluence put the fortunes of most other local groups in the shade. Proud blood and proud wealth reinforced each other powerfully in Brittany's highest court of justice.

Somewhat less moneyed than the Breton *parlementaires* were the Frenchmen rendering justice at Toulouse, Besançon, Bordeaux, Dijon, and perhaps Aix-en-Provence. It is at these seats of parlementary influence, if anywhere, that we find degrees of wealth typifying the provincial judiciary of the first rank.

Especially useful are Jean Sentou's data treating magisterial fortunes at Toulouse.[63] Here, we can reach some highly quantitative conclusions. Of those judges serving at the outbreak of the Revolution, 5.88 percent were millionaires, 19.6 percent were worth from 398,000 to 1 million livres, 47.05 percent fell into the 158,000–398,000 livre category, another 25.49 percent belonged in the 63,000–158,000 livre category, and just under 2 percent were worth from 25,000 to 63,000 livres. Prominent millionaires at Toulouse included Procureur-Général Jean Gabriel Aimable Alexandre de Riquet de Bonrepos, President Bertrand Bernard de Boyer Drudas, and ordinary counselor Etienne Louis Marie de Guillermin, baron de Seysses. Notable among those in the next highest bracket were President Jean Jacques Marie Joseph Martin d'Ayguevives, counselor Charles Blanquet de Rouville (vicomte de Trébons), and counselor Jean François de Pérés. (First President Jean-Louis-Emmanuel-Augustin de Cambon may have been straddling the line between these two brackets of affluence.) The overall average fortune of all Toulousains in 1789—339,488 livres—conceals two more meaningful statistics: the average wealth of the *présidents à mortier*, which was 435,156 livres, and the average wealth of the nonpresidential counselors, which was by contrast only 289,861 livres. Roughly speaking, then, whereas the majority of *parlementaires* at Rennes on the eve of the Revolution fell into the 500,000–1 million livre category, most of their counterparts at Toulouse could claim something less than 400,000 livres in personal wealth.

The next most impressive documentation of magisterial wealth in this period is that of Maurice Gresset for the judges at Besançon.[64] Gresset's statistics strikingly resemble those of Sentou. Of thirty-four known parlementary fortunes in Franche-Comté during 1770–1800, two fell into the millionaire class, six ranged from 400,000 to 1 million, thirteen belonged to the 160,000–400,000 bracket, another twelve ranged from 60,000 to 160,000 livres, and one failed to amount to as much as 60,000 livres. Perhaps a few more magistrates in Franche-Comté than in Languedoc fell into the second lowest of these five brackets; otherwise, the figures for the Comtois and Languedocien institutions are comparable. One of those two millionaires at Besançon was Procureur-Général Claude-Théophile-Joseph Doroz; among those with fortunes superior to 400,000 livres were First President Jean-Claude Perreney de Grosbois and presidents from the Mareschal de Vezet, Mouret de Chatillon, d'Olivet, and Terrier de Santans families. Although the average fortune at Besançon was comparable to that at Toulouse (about 365,000 livres in the former case as opposed to 339,000 livres in the latter), the gap between the average presidential fortune and untitled counselor's fortune was markedly wider at the Comtois capital than at Languedoc's capital. Indeed, Gresset's research indicates that presidential wealth was averaging about 759,000 livres in this period, whereas the counselors' wealth approached a mean of 172,000 livres. On the other hand, the comparable disparity between the yearly expenses of a *président à mortier* and those of an ordinary counselor at Besançon, as estimated in individual cases by Gresset, may have done something to reduce the significance of wealth and income differentials within the higher ranks of the *monde judiciaire* of Franche-Comté. Again, Besançon, it need hardly be stated, put less of a financial demand upon the typical counselor than did more dynamic, fast-paced parlementary capitals such as Rennes and Bordeaux, let alone Paris. The jurist in eighteenth-century Besançon with a personal fortune of, say, 150,000 or 200,000 livres would have an income annually of perhaps 7,500 or 10,000, which, especially when considered in conjunction with the prestige and power flowing from his vocation, was not inconsequential.

Bordeaux has been mentioned in this context, and Bordeaux's *parlementaires*, though hardly capable of establishing an economic dominion in a city internationally famed for its opulent wine merchants, planters, and slavers, seem as a rule to have been comfortable enough.[65] Certainly there were more millionaires at Bordeaux than at Besançon or Toulouse: they included François-Armand Saige, an *avocat-général* (worth possibly 10 million), counselor Jacques Pelet d'Anglade (a millionaire possibly four times over), First President André-Jacques-Hyacinthe Le Berthon, President Nicolas-Pierre de Pichard, and President Paul-Marie-Arnaud de Lavie, among others. A considerable number of judges, including Procureur-Général Pierre-Jules Dudon, President Jean-Baptiste-Maurice Verthamon, and counselor Jean-Martin de Lasalle, were easily worth half a million. But most magistrates at Bordeaux, as at Toulouse and Besançon, held fortunes ranging from 100,000 to 400,000 livres. Disposing of annual incomes varying from 4,000 to 20,000 livres (and most frequently from 5,500 to 9,500 livres), they were comfortable enough, if not opulent. A minority of jurists were worth less than 100,000 livres—a situation that might be supportable for bachelors but that would ordinarily spell problems for judges with wives and children. For most *parlementaires* in late eighteenth-century Bordeaux, a personal fortune of 80,000 livres (meaning a yearly income in the neighborhood of 4,000 livres) would represent the lower limits of financial respectability. All in all, the justices of the Bordeaux Parlement were somewhat less moneyed than their Breton cousins, about as affluent as the Toulousains, and perhaps slightly better off than the magistrates of Franche-Comté. They could never hope to outshine the fabulous traders and slavers of their community, but even the high and mighty Parisian *parlementaires* had to share the limelight with financiers and courtiers and other Frenchmen of dazzling prosperity.

From what we know, the situation at Dijon just before the Revolution was more or less comparable with the situation at Toulouse, Besançon, and Bordeaux.[66] The Dijon Parlement vaunted its millionaires (Alexandre Mairetet de Minot, President Nicolas Jannon, Antoine Esmonin de Dampierre) as well as a sizable number of "demimillionaires" (President Bénigne Bouhier de Lantenay, President François Marie Bernard de Sassenay, First President Legouz de Saint-Seine, Bénigne Antoine Carrelet de Loisy). In Burgundy, though, as elsewhere, the majority of *parlementaires* were of more modest means. Many, perhaps most, could attest fortunes ranging from 100,000 to 500,000 livres, while others fell beneath that strategic demarcation zone of 80,000–100,000 livres. An average figure of 367,000 livres worked out for thirty Burgundians seems a bit optimistic and may indeed be more reflective of presidential ranks than of the untitled personnel of the court's constituent chambers. On the other hand, even the nonpresidential counselors (like their not-too-distant peasant ancestors) could be remarkably resourceful and opportunistic: witness Nicolas Jean Baptiste Baillyat de Broindon, Pierre Bénigne Guyard de Balon, and Jean-Antoine Raviot, whose wives brought with them doweries exceeding 100,000 livres! On the whole, the Dijonnais were perhaps slightly less affluent than their fellow *parlementaires* of Toulouse and Bordeaux and about as well off as their neighbors to the east in Franche-Comté. Like the latter, the Burgundians would not have much to fear from the quarter of merchants, *gens de finance*, or courtier millionaires.

We know less about the circumstances of the men dispensing the king's justice in the southeastern provinces of Dauphiné and Provence, but presumably they were not radically richer or poorer than their counterparts elsewhere. At Aix-en-Provence, a presidential *mortier* was still worth more than 100,000 livres as late as 1776, and counselors' offices in the 1770s and early 1780s were regularly changing hands for no less than 40,000 livres.[67] These were considerable investments and argue the presence of considerable wealth. Moreover, men such as First President (and Provençal Intendant) Charles-Jean-Baptiste des Gallois de la Tour, Procureur-Général Jean-François-André Leblanc de Castillon, and Avocats-Généraux François-Bazile-Casimir Maurel de Calissanne and Joseph-François-Paul Aymar de Montmeyan could not have discharged the duties and managed the expenses appertaining to their offices without substantial wealth. No doubt the presidents and king's men at Aix, as elsewhere, qualified as millionaires and demimillionaires, and counselors bequeathing or purchasing offices valued at 40,000 livres were themselves men of considerable substance.

At Grenoble, in the meantime, we find magistrates of widely varying degrees of affluence.[68] President François de Vaulx and his son President Pierre-Marie de Vaulx enjoyed a family fortune of at least 800,000 livres;

President Joseph-Marie de Barral de Montferrat's father, also a *parlementaire*, was "very rich, proprietor of a magnificent domain at La Tronche, on the banks of the Isère"; President Jean-Baptiste de Barral enjoyed an "immense fortune"; counselor Jean-François Anglès possessed a "considerable fortune"; and another counselor, Laurent de Garnier, reputedly held wealth of more than 600,000 livres. Obviously, the same must have been true for such personalities as First President Amable-Pierre-Thomas de Bérulle and his son and successor Amable-Pierre-Albert de Bérulle, Procureur-Général Jean-Baptiste de Reynaud, and Avocats-Généraux Jacques Fortunat Savoye de Rollin and Joseph-Louis de La Boissière. Serving in the same company, however, were judges (often of old aristocratic lineage) whose modest means confined them during long seasons to sojourns on their estates, where they would parsimoniously collect their revenues and whence they would bombard the government with requests for pensions and military posts for their sons. Was the "average" parlementary fortune at Grenoble slightly less impressive than the "average" fortune at certain other parlementary capitals? At present we cannot be sure, but, in any case, we are dealing here merely with relative degrees of affluence within the comfortable, privileged, and envied world of the high judiciary.

In shifting our focus northwestward to Rouen, we can document for the Norman *parlementaires* what we could only suggest for the Dauphinois: namely, a level of affluence somewhat inferior to that prevailing elsewhere.[69] Not that the *parlement* at Rouen lacked its affluent magistrates. President Nicolas Charles Armand de Bailleul was a millionaire nearly three times over; Presidents Esprit Marie Robert Le Roux d'Esneval and Thomas Louis César Lambert de Frondeville were millionaires at least twice over; Presidents Louis Paul Le Cordier de Bigars de La Londe and Bigot de Sassetot were worth between 1.5 and 2 million; and counselors Louis-Jacques Grossin de Bouville and Caillot de Coquéreaumont similarly qualified for this exclusive group. (First President Louis François Elie Camus de Pontcarré and several of his colleagues may have qualified as well owing to anticipated settlements, social and business connections, and far-flung sources of revenue.) Furthermore, perhaps a dozen judges were demimillionaires: into this bracket fell such notables as President Gilles Louis Hallé de Rouville and Guy Henri Marie Du Val de Bonneval, Procureur-Général Jean Pierre Prosper Godart de Belbeuf, and his son Avocat-Général Louis Pierre François Godart de Belbeuf. Approximately fifteen other parlementary families were represented in the 250,000–500,000 livre bracket.

If, however, 40 or 50 magistrates in all may have enjoyed personal fortunes of 250,000 livres or more, over twice as many judges—about 100 in all—possessed fortunes ranging from 100,000 to 250,000 livres. In other words, nearly two-thirds of the Norman jurists must have had no more than roughly 12,500 livres available to them as income from year to year. This was probably just about enough to ensure the typical counselor a comfortable if by no means luxurious existence at Rouen and in the countryside. Even further removed from luxury during this terminal period of the *ancien régime* in Normandy were 10 or 15 judges with no more than 50,000 to 100,000 livres in personal wealth. These unfortunates could find it difficult to maintain themselves in a style of life becoming a *parlementaire*; if largesse from the king's government was not forthcoming (and usually it was not), they might hope to mitigate their difficulties in some small measure by taking in extra judicial assignments at the Palais de Justice to bring in honoraria. Yet this minority of magistrates at Rouen hovering just above a sort of "poverty line" (judging "poverty" by parlementary standards) need not have felt intolerably humiliated, for in their daily professional lives they were continually rubbing elbows with colleagues of scarcely less modest means.

We might at this point recapitulate what we have learned from this survey of the levels of affluence in the principal *parlements* of Louis XVI's reign. It is clear that the degree of material well-being did vary from *parlement* to *parlement*, albeit within broad limits assuring to nearly all members of these institutions a comfortable as well as prestigious existence. The Parisians, as we would anticipate, led by far in this respect. Regarding the provincial law courts, the magistrates of Toulouse, Besançon, Bordeaux, Dijon, and (so it would seem) Aix and Grenoble fell somewhere between the relatively wealthy "chevaliers de Malte de la Robe" at Rennes and the relatively less moneyed men of the law at Rouen. Yet we may legitimately question the significance of such variations in general, and of the discrepancies between Parisian and provincial fortunes in particular. The provincial magistrates were probably as capable of defraying their expenses as were the Parisians; they lorded it over their small local worlds as confidently and effectively as the Parisians held sway over the greater *monde* of the national capital. Indeed, in communities not adorned with national finance or international trade (such as Dijon and Besançon), the richest judges probably shone with greater luster than the Parisian jurists could ever hope to do. We may similarly doubt the practical import of disparities of well-being *within* each tribunal. It may be true that, economically speaking, multimillionaires, millionaires, and near millionaires of Grand Banc and *parquet* could have little in common with untitled counselors for whom judicial perquisites were fiscally consequential. Still, the parlementary deans frequently had greater expenses to defray than did their juniors, and consequently were needful of more handsome incomes. Beyond that, all *parlementaires*, of whatever economic circumstances, had been formed by the same socioprofessional traditions and shared common institutional responsibilities. Would it therefore be unreasonable to predict that when push came to shove in the late 1780s they would manifest a formidable solidarity of outlook upon most public issues?

When we turn to the question of the *constitution* of magisterial wealth, we may again remark a divergence between Parisian and provincial realities—and yet again question its practical significance. Diversification in sources of income was much more the rule among the Parisian *parlementaires* than it was among their provincial counterparts.[70] There were those judges of the French capital for whom *rentes* (that is, annuities of various types) constituted the principal form of revenue; there were others for whom landed wealth or (somewhat less commonly) office and the perquisites associated with office were most important; and there were even a few Parisians whose fortunes consisted of roughly equal proportions of all these elements, along with urban real estate, furniture and furnishings, and perhaps liquid assets as well. For the typical justice of provincial France, however, land would matter more than all other forms of wealth. This can be easily documented wherever we have percentages to study. At Besançon, for example, one *président à mortier* studied by Maurice Gresset derived 45 percent of his income from his rural lands and properties, about 32 percent from real estate in the Comtois capital, about 18 percent from *rentes* of various kinds, and 5 percent from revenues associated with his office. More representative, Gresset suspects, was the ordinary counselor for whom the respective figures were 67, 14.4, 10.5, and 8–9 percent.[71] At Toulouse, the aggregate wealth of the *présidents à mortier* in 1789 derived as follows: 41.33 percent from rural properties, 28.96 percent from household furnishings, capital, and other "mobile" possessions, 20.61 percent from *rentes*, 8.29 percent from real estate at Toulouse, and less than 1 percent from stocks and similar investments. The analogous figures for counselors in 1789 were 53.15, 18.46, 15.90, 11.60, and less than 1 percent, respectively.[72] At Toulouse as at Besançon, then, the presidents evidenced somewhat greater interest in "liquid" forms of investment (*rentes*, furnishings, stocks) than did the nonpresidential judges; land, however, was obviously crucial for presidents as well as for counselors. At Rouen, the typical *parlementaire* apparently held from 60 to 80 percent of his wealth in rural lands, about 15 percent in *rentes*, from 7 to 15 percent in urban properties, from 3 to 10 percent in his office, and approximately 5 percent in furnishings in townhouse and countryhouse, liquid capital, and so forth. Again, the primacy of land is underscored: of 173 judges studied for the 1774–89 period, 140 or more (over 80 percent of the total) were essentially rural landowners.[73] Elsewhere the pattern, if not always as rigorously analyzed, holds true in its general outlines. At Rennes, Jean Meyer assures us, rural *biens fonciers* constituted by far and away the most important form of magisterial wealth; *rentes*, revenues from office (averaging from 5 to 10 percent of the total), and *éléments mobiliers* (cash, furniture, and so on) ranged far behind.[74] The Bretons, evidently, were as enamored of their country estates as were any other provincial *parlementaires*. Meyer's conclusions for Rennes are echoed by Albert Colombet for Dijon, by William Doyle for Bordeaux, and by Jean Egret for Grenoble.[75] Everywhere, then—at least in provincial France—the passion for land predominated.

And not only in provincial France, if the truth be told. The Parisian justice might be likelier than his provincial cousin to draw his income from a wide variety of sources, but for him as well as for the other, comfort and prestige ultimately lay in the acquisition, exploitation, and enjoyment of land. Whether hailing from Paris or Dijon or Douai, the representative *parlementaire* would hope initially to inherit a handsome patrimony or at least some arable and pasture. He would also continually look for opportunities to purchase from local proprietors of all classes and descriptions additional title to lands and meadows, forests and wastes, ponds and streams. He might want from time to time to consolidate scattered holdings by exchanging lands with fellow *parlementaires* or other neighbors. As a "feudal" lord he might even profit from the right of *retrait féodal* by absorbing the holdings of tenants lacking heirs, or might foreclose upon lands of peasants unable to pay quitrents or to discharge other "feudal" obligations. Then, again, he might seek concessions of crown lands or reclaim waste upon which he could very possibly enjoy several years' exemption from taxation. Upon occasion (and perhaps fairly frequently) he would also sell rural properties, whether for purposes of consolidation and further profit or from need of cash. In all these operations the *parlementaire* showed himself to be as passionately committed to the soil as any ancestral (or contemporary) peasant—and this despite his urban and magisterial orientation during nine or ten months of the year.

And how would he exploit his lands? If he were a *parlementaire* of Languedoc, wheat and to a lesser extent other cereals would be king.[76] If he rendered justice at Bordeaux, viniculture, fickle business though it was, would often take precedence over other enterprises.[77] Elsewhere, diversification in exploitation of the rural patrimony seems to have been the rule, although investment in arable and pasture ordinarily was more consequential than investment in such activities as glassblowing, brick making, iron forging, apiculture, and fishing and in such assets as tile works, oil works, and woodlands.[78] In the final analysis the revenue raised upon cereals and wine constituted most of the income of most provincial jurists (and quite a few of their Parisian counterparts as well).

The "typical" Parisian magistrate and his "typical" provincial counterpart were more likely to follow different drummers when it came to investment in those annuities or securities of the old regime known as *rentes*. We have already noted that there were some Parisians for whom *rentes* of various kinds constituted the principal source of income. Even when this was not the case, the judge of the French capital was still inclined to some outlay in this direction. He might place his capital in the so-called *rentes publiques*, public annuities drawn upon the Parisian Hôtel de Ville and covering such royal taxes as the *aides* and *gabelles*. He might also (or instead) invest in *rentes privées* drawn upon nongovernmental institutions and private individuals. Understandably, a certain number of the Parisian justices tended at all times to be extremely sensitive to fluctuations in the government's credit and would urge their company to declaim against any alleged government tampering with the securities at the Hôtel de Ville. By contrast, most of the provincial *parlementaires*, living as they did in their parochial worlds bound by parochial concerns, would have little or nothing to do with the vicissitudes of national finance. They were in fact less likely to inherit or to invest in *rentes* of any kind. What *rentes* they did hold would probably be upon local persons, in the form of loans to fellow magistrates or other practitioners of the law, or nonrobe bourgeois of various callings, or perhaps the peasants laboring upon their lands. Some of them might hold *rentes* upon local ecclesiastical communities or the local municipality—their modest version of the Parisian Hôtel de Ville—or even the provincial Estates where they still existed. Rare indeed was the provincial judge willing to trust any part of his fortune to the financiers of Paris and the policymakers of Versailles. *Rentes* were simply not of compelling importance to most of these magistrates.[79]

There was obviously one form of magisterial wealth that, both at Paris and in the provinces, defined the *parlementaire's* professional being: his office. Not that the Parisian, or the Aixois, or the Dijonnais anticipated that much revenue would flow from this source.[80] The annual *gages*, representing in theory a return of about 5 percent on the original capital value of the judge's office, were often reduced to virtually nothing in the eighteenth century by the bite of royal taxation—principally *capitation* and *vingtième*. Moreover, the jurists frequently complained about irregularities and long delays in the payment by the government of what remained of their *gages* after taxation. And, although the judges of all the *parlements* pocketed *épices* and other emoluments incidental to their exercise of judicial office, only the first presidents and a few of the most assiduous and favored *grand' chambriers* were likely to garner more than a few hundred livres annually in this fashion. But, after all, the typical jurist would draw most of his income from other quarters; he valued his office chiefly for the career and the public prominence it conferred upon him.

Of course, that career and public prominence were increasingly likely in the eighteenth century to constitute part of the magistrate's bequest to a son or a nephew. If this were not the case, and if in consequence the officeholder expected eventually to sell his *charge*, then all the more reason for him to be concerned about its market value. It would be pertinent therefore to inquire into the evolution of prices of parlementary offices during the eighteenth century. Data available for the Paris Parlement and our eight key provincial *parlements* suggest a general downward trend in prices before Maupeou's ministry but (at least in several cases) also hint at some stabilization and even recovery in the years after 1774.

At Paris, a presidency *à mortier* could command a price of 500,000 livres or more under Louis XV as well as under Louis XIV.[81] With non-presidential lay judgeships of the Grand' Chambre and Enquêtes, however, it was another story. Fixed at 90,000 livres in 1665, the value of these offices varied from 34,000 to 60,000 livres during 1725–56 and still had not recovered beyond 50,000 livres as of 1771. At Besançon, office prices (somewhat atypically) seem to have held up well throughout the eighteenth century. The value of a presidential *mortier* actually increased from 55,000 livres in 1712 to 80,000 livres in 1771; presidencies were still worth about 80,000 livres eleven years later. By the same token, offices of lay counselors of Grand' Chambre and Enquêtes fluctuated between 28,000 and 35,000 livres during the 1719–71 period and were still bringing in about 30,000 livres under Louis XVI. At Aix, the *mortier* declined in value from 120,000 livres in 1678 to 100,000 livres in 1701, but in at least one instance after Maupeou (that is, in 1776) it was still commanding a price of 101,200 livres. The price of lay counselors' offices turned downward from 64,000 livres in 1678 to 50,000 livres in 1708 to 33,600 livres in 1758, but stabilized in the 40,000–42,000 range during 1775–81. At Rennes, the *mortier* declined in value from a range of 160,000–180,000 livres to a range of 90,000–130,000 livres during the eighteenth century; on the other hand, the post of lay *conseiller originaire* (reserved in theory for the native Breton), after declining steeply from 100,000 livres in the 1660s to a range of 25,000–31,000 livres in the 1770s, seemingly leveled out between 30,000 and 32,000 livres during the following decade. (Offices of *conseillers non-originaires*, of less value, followed a parallel course.) At Dijon, lay counselors' offices valued at about 66,000 livres in the late seventeenth century were worth as little as 25,600 livres by 1771 and 24,000 livres six years later but had recovered to the vicinity of 36,000 livres by 1785–86. Presidents attempting to sell their offices in the 1770s and 1780s found it difficult to make profitable transactions; yet there were actually fewer vacancies in presidential as well as counselors' ranks at Dijon on the eve of the Revolution than ten years previously. At Rouen, *mortiers* going for 145,000 livres in the 1660s were fluctuating in value between 80,000 and 140,000 livres (and averaging 100,000 livres overall) in the 1750–89 period. Lay counselors' offices evaluated at 70,000 livres in the 1660s were worth closer to 40,000 livres in 1700, brought only 12,000–16,000 livres in 1775, and slipped further to 8,000–13,000 livres in 1777–79 before recovering to a range of 15,000–30,000 livres in 1785–87. At Toulouse, *mortiers* bringing around 120,000 livres through much of the eighteenth century were turning downward toward 100,000 livres as 1789 approached; counselors' offices, which had ranged widely in value between 30,000 and 60,000 livres early in the century, dipped somewhat in value before 1771 but recovered to the 38,000–45,000 range in the 1780s.

On the other hand, we have indications of long-term decline without stabilization or recovery at Bordeaux and Grenoble. In the former case, prices for presidencies, which averaged approximately 123,000 livres from 1739 to 1778, were on the whole slipping throughout this period. Prices for counselors' offices followed a vicissitudinous course throughout the century, peaking at about 39,000 livres in the 1730s, falling off during the 1740s and 1750s, recovering somewhat in the 1760s, but then falling off again toward 25,000 livres under Louis XVI. The situation was perhaps most serious in Dauphiné. Presidencies at Grenoble worth 100,000 livres early in the century were commanding only 60,000 livres in the 1760s and possibly even less after Maupeou; the figures for lay counselors turned downward from 50,000 livres in 1731 to 27,000 livres in 1761 to 19,000 livres in 1780 to 14,000 livres in 1784. That prices of offices at Grenoble apparently failed to rally in the closing years of the *ancien régime* may not have been altogether unrelated to recruitment difficulties experienced in Dauphiné's highest court of law.

In recapitulation, presidential and counselors' offices in eight of these nine major *parlements* had lost varying degrees of their value over the first seven decades of the eighteenth century but in all provincial cases save for Grenoble and Bordeaux were essaying a comeback under Louis XVI. It is difficult to explain these tendencies for any one tribunal, and patently impossible to account for office price fluctuations in all nine cases, but we can identify certain circumstances working to enhance or to diminish the value of such judgeships in the *ancien régime*.[82] On the negative side, restriction of recruitment to these "robinocratic" institutions would discourage middle-class bidding for office and thus exclude middle-class wealth. Moreover, the deteriorating political relationship between crown and magistracy no doubt could make investment in parlementary office seem risky. Again, the gradual decline in the *real* value of venal offices as prices generally rose over the eighteenth century might lessen the appeal of this kind of cash outlay. Furthermore, at a regional capital such as Bordeaux the availability of other types of ennobling offices would reduce in local eyes the attractiveness of posts in the *parlement.* And finally, the irregularity and tardiness in payment of *gages,* and general meagerness of revenues accruing from office, would hardly enhance the luster of this kind of investment. On the positive side, the prominence of justice and administration and the lack of opportunity for investment in dynamic overseas enterprise at cities such as Dijon, Besançon, and Toulouse may have helped in some measure to buoy market values for the Burgundian, Comtois, and Languedocien officeholders. When all else failed, there was the prestige and influence associated in the public eye with parlementary office, assuring it a minimum value year in and year out.

When it came to rounding out their annual incomes, nevertheless, most *parlementaires* would have resources more consequential than *gages* and *épices* in mind.[83] It was common for the judge of Franche-Comté, for instance, to speculate a bit in urban real estate and rent out townhouses or *appartements,* vineyards, gardens, and small fields and meadows in Besançon. Here and there we also find a magisterial family of Franche-Comté involved in the metallurgical industries or paper mills of the province. At Bordeaux, quite a few judges invested in the booming real estate market of this prospering coastal community. An occasional Bordelais might make an enormous fortune in the coffee, sugar, and slaves of the West Indies (no *dérogeance* from noble status threatened in wholesale and maritime commerce), although their heavy professional duties, and the undeniable risks of overseas trade, deterred most of Bordeaux' *parlementaires* from extending themselves too far in this direction. None of them seem to have invested in shipbuilding or sugar refining, as crucial as these activities were locally. Elsewhere (as, indeed, at Besançon and Bordeaux), few justices drew more than a small proportion of their income from urban properties, and fewer still profited appreciably from commerce and "industry." True, President de Brosses at Dijon held stocks in the Compagnie des Indes, and Procureur-Général de Riquet de Bonrepos at Toulouse invested heavily in the Canal des Deux Mers in Languedoc. But these men were exceptions to a rule that was further illustrated by the paucity of parlementary wealth in Brittany committed to overseas enterprise at Saint-Malo or Nantes, and by the lack of magisterial capital in Normandy sunk in the ironworks, glassworks, textiles, and maritime endeavors of that province. Of course the Parisian judge, as a member of the kingdom's most influential *parlement*, might receive a handsome royal pension, serve on a special royal committee looking into provincial *coutumes*, or counsel a Prince of the Blood.

After all is said and done, however, most magistrates, whether of Parisian or provincial derivation, impressed contemporaries as favored members of the landed elite who had little need to supplement their incomes in the ways detailed here.

Belonging to that elite, moreover, meant (among other things) enjoying elegant townhouses and charming châteaus and *maisons de campagne*—and this, in turn, reminds us that the Parisian and provincial judges lived urban lives and rural lives corresponding with the annual sessions and vacations of their companies.[84] Normally the working year extended from St. Martin's Day in mid-November to the end of the following August or early September; during the vacations of September and October a skeleton crew would stay on at each tribunal's Palais de Justice to render essential justice under the supervision of one or more *présidents à mortier*. Yet, not every magistrate religiously observed these seasons of the professional year. As the weather warmed and the daylight lingered in June, July, and August, the first president could never be sure of convoking all of his confreres upon all occasions: the justices, after all, were gentlemen farmers as well as specialists in French law, and desired in summer to be looking after their lands. By the same token, a few of these august jurists, occupied in subsequent months with the harvest (and with the delights of country life), might not make it back to their company in time to join their colleagues at the mid-November *messe rouge* inaugurating the new judicial year. Still, most of the typical law court's members would be conscientious enough in attendance at the Palais de Justice. They would, that is, spend nine or ten months annually in Paris or their provincial capital, dwelling the rest of the time in their beloved countryside.

However much the *parlementaire* as gentleman cultivator might pine for the rustic seat of his fortune and prestige in winter and spring, his judicial labors were compensated by the style of his urban existence. The representative judge might not possess the luxurious quarters of, say, the Parisian first president, whose *hôtel du bailliage de Paris*, located within the precincts of the Parisian Palais de Justice itself, was truly splendid, or (to cite a provincial case) Burgundian President Jean-Vivant Micault de Courbeton, whose huge townhouse on the rue Vauban in Dijon was magnificent in its outlines and furnishings. (During the Revolution, Micault de Courbeton's total *mobilier* was valued at 100,574 *livres*.) Nevertheless, the average magistrate would own a comfortable townhouse, whose *rez-de-chaussée* and first floor he and his family would occupy and whose upstairs *appartements* he would rent out to others; or else he would content himself with a rented townhouse suite. (Both in Paris and in the provinces, bachelors and clerics would be especially inclined to the latter arrangement; the clerical counselors in particular would be of modest means and modest needs.) In several parlementary communities judicial residences clustered in the most fashionable quarters; more commonly, perhaps, they were scattered over the urban landscape. Whichever tendency prevailed, these dwellings of the high magistracy, with their handsome façades, leafy drives, and anterior or enclosed courtyards; their symmetrical parks and gardens; and their sculptures, vases, and other external and internal embellishments, unfailingly impressed contemporaries and in many cases remain to impress us today.

The parlementary household would probably have a coach or at least a sedan-chair at its disposal for purposes of pleasure as well as of business. And pleasure the *parlementaire* would have on evenings and Sundays after working six long days a week at the Palais de Justice. Whether in the national capital or a provincial city, he would host suppers, salons, and concerts for professional associates and other acquaintances, and receive similar hospitality in return; he would attend the theater, or his Masonic lodge, or dabble in the mesmerism craze, or involve himself in the activities of a local *académie* or reading club; and he might possibly give alms (and some of his free time) to the local philanthropic society for orphans, indigents, and prisoners. Less conspicuous but ordinarily closer to his heart would be those events and activities that were strictly *en famille.* After all, the magistrate must not only congregate with wife and children daily and on special occasions but also see to financial and testamentary affairs, collaborate with his spouse in the management of the urban household, and—always this matter—ensure from afar proper stewardship of the precious rural patrimony.

Indeed, the jurist and his family, as we have already noted, would often long for the countryside in the very midst of the professional affairs and pleasurable pursuits of the town. Where better to spend the harvest time (and belike Yuletide and New Year's) than upon the family's rustic estates? Here were myriad links with the past as well as the great surety for the future; here was where the *parlementaire* and his closest kin could savor to the fullest the ultraprivileged existence of the robe noblesse.[85] And so, during the vacations of September and October, off the judge and his wife and children would go, happily exchanging their town existence for arcadia. Once ensconced in their venerable château, a residence most likely graced with modern gardens, parks, labyrinthine walkways, and grottoes, and perhaps even a medieval-looking moat and coat of arms, or more modestly established in an unpretentious *maison de campagne,* these fortunate folk of the robe would turn to the business and pleasures of the country.

For the *parlementaire* himself, of course, the business of his lands and those who labored upon them would claim the highest priority. No longer dependent, as he had been during the judicial term, upon a *fermier* or *secrétaire,* a *régisseur* or *intendant,* for proper management of his estates, he could now take the reins of affairs into his own hands. Thus, he would assiduously look after the ripening fields and vineyards. For hours he would pore over land registers and journals in order to keep abreast of clearing and drainage of lands, repairs and construction, workers' conditions, and collections of rents and dues. Aided no doubt by a *feudiste,* one of those lawyers versed in the Byzantine complexities of the local seigneurial custom, he would shrewdly exchange and consolidate lands, exact every rent and due that could be construed as legally his, and prepare, if need be, to litigate against his own peasants or against neighboring lords should he be challenged in any of his prerogatives or possessions. In all these activities the landholding jurist exposed concerns rooted in a genealogy of peasant and gentlemen farmers as much as in the contemporary soil itself.

And what kind of a master was he to his peasants? This would naturally hinge to some extent upon local law, so crucial in defining land leases, agricultural practices, and the rights and obligations of proprietors, tenants, and sharecroppers. The seigneurial regime reputedly weighed heavily upon the peasantry of certain provinces—Brittany and Franche-Comté were most often cited as examples—and not so heavily upon rural commoners in Dauphiné and Provence and other regions of Roman law. But careful research indicates that socioeconomic realities did not vary radically from region to region in late eighteenth-century France. *Parlementaires* everywhere were revising land registers and rent rolls and extracting from the local peasantry what they could legally claim in cash, produce, and labor. Moreover, they would insist upon the "honorific" as well as "useful" prerogatives of suzerainty: the honored pew and burial in the parish church, the gallows symbolizing the high justice ultimately rendered in their own company, precedence in festivals and processions, nomination of village officers, and so on. But these actions were in no way unprecedented; we have here no sudden "seigneurial reaction." Each succeeding generation of judges in the old regime had to some extent to reconstitute its domains, worry about landed bequests to sons and doweries for daughters and *légitimes* for widows and sisters, and maintain hierarchical patterns of deference and command.

In Brittany, that cradle of ancient noblesse, the millionaires among the *parlementaires,* we are told, would often lower rents and dues or extend credit in difficult times; it was the lesser judges of "median" income who were more likely to squeeze their unfortunate peasants. As for the justices of Franche-Comté, many of them did apparently wring whatever they could out of *mainmortables* as well as "free" peasants, although there are some documented cases of Comtois magistrates overtly or covertly aided by former tenants during the Revolution. Some Parisian and provincial *parlementaires* were, rightly or wrongly, detested as hoarders of and speculators in grain, and their châteaus might be among the first to be put to the torch in the summer of 1789. More often than not, however, the magistrates were spared; and it was to their credit that so many of them, in earlier untroubled times, revealed themselves to be *bienfaisants* within certain limits. They secured royal permission to sponsor fairs and markets for the local populace. They bequeathed substantial sums of money to the parish poor. They lent their support to local *collèges* and to the occasional primary school for peasant children. They assisted asylums and hospitals and institutions for the destitute. They reduced or canceled altogether the obligations of especially needy commoners and extended credit to them upon favorable terms. For the most part, then, these Parisian and provincial judges were not men devoid of humanitarianism: however sternly they might uphold the seigneurial regime with its inherently exploitative relationships upon the land, their private and professional actions often mitigated the worst rigors of that regime.

But of course the *parlementaires* could well afford a philanthropic penchant. In their rustic as in their urban setting they stood near the summit of society and savored living at its best in these twilight years of the *ancien régime*. The judges and their families staged plays in their own private theaters, sometimes taking roles themselves; or they attended theatrical performances in neighboring provincial towns. They were often "at home" to their neighbors of robe and sword noblesse, returning the hospitality of earlier suppers and receptions, concerts, and *soirées*. They were present at *fêtes champêtres* and all-night masked balls and passed idyllic hours at various games of chance, at riding and— that most aristocratic of pastimes—hunting. During an off season a magistrate might "take a cure" at one of the cold mountain spas of the south or east, travel to the north or west coasts, venture abroad to Italy or Switzerland or Spain, or make a pilgrimage to that alluring community of iniquity, Paris. Most of the *parlementaires*, however, had compelling home interests to attend to in September and October, and diversions aplenty that would beckon during leisure hours. We should hardly confess surprise if some of Louis XVI's *parlementaires* had a difficult time tearing themselves away from their rural existence to answer the call of professional duty in mid-November.

If the judges incontestably knew something of the eighteenth century's storied *douceur de vivre*, did they also contribute to its reknown as the *siècle des lumières*? A few of them did, though for the majority intellectual curiosity and cultural endeavor went only so far. To be sure, the average jurist would as likely as not inherit (and possibly even purchase) books treating a wide range of subjects: the inevitable jurisprudence, theology and devotion, romance and travel, science and political economy, and so on.[86] He was somewhat more inclined to secular literature, less predisposed to Jansenist and other religious writings, than his predecessors in the earlier decades of the century. The Enlightenment would contribute a few works to his shelves—though *Emile* and the *Nouvelle Héloïse* were more apt to appear there than the *Contrat Social*, and Voltaire would be tolerated as entertainment rather than appreciated as social criticism. (Montesquieu, naturally, was universally respected and, at Bordeaux, apostrophized by magistrates basking in his reflected glory.) Each *parlement* would vaunt its rhetoricians and academicians and historians of local fame, its collectors of *objets d'art* and patient compilers and editors of the local *coutumes*. In most of this, there is nothing extraordinary; indeed, leisured gentlemen of the sword and not-so-leisured barristers and lower-court judges were similarly addicted to such pursuits.

Some individual *parlementaires* merit mention for their cultural endeavors. At Paris, for instance, counselor Jean Jacques IV Duval d'Eprémesnil patronized notorious imposter Count Alessandro di Cagliostro and mesmerism while his youthful associate Charles Jean François Depont corresponded with Edmund Burke.[87] At Besançon, counselor François-Nicolas-Eugène Droz des Villars was known nationally for his scholarly authorship of his company's remonstrances; celebrated locally for his jurisprudence and his role as *secrétaire perpétuel* of his city's Académie des Sciences, Belles Lettres et Arts; and appreciated by his family for his virtuosity with the violin.[88] Several of his brethren had made the pilgrimage to nearby Ferney, though their acquaintance with the aging Voltaire had moderated not a whit their opposition to "enlightened" government policies. The judges at Bordeaux purportedly revered the memory of Montaigne and Montesquieu, but the most notable author among their number in Louis XVI's reign, President Charles-Marguerite-Jean-Baptiste-Mercier Dupaty, rendered himself persona non grata to his colleagues over political issues and spent the last four years of his life (1784–88) in Paris.[89] Among the Dijonnais, President Louis Philippe Joly de Bévy and Procureur-Général Bernard Pérard whiled away evenings in the country with their guitars; several associates were violinists in their leisure; and counselor Benjamin Edmé Nadault opened his country residence of Montbard to numerous distinguished artists and married the sister of the famous naturalist Buffon.[90] At Grenoble, Avocat-Général Joseph-Louis de La Boissière, philanthropist and man of letters, was reportedly encouraged by the celebrated philosophe Abbé Raynal to translate and publish the works of English novelist Laurence Sterne. One of his fellows, counselor Joseph Colaud de La Salcette, harangued a Masonic assemblage on the equality of all men and, in 1784, recorded his admiration for the existence of the simple shepherd during a journey over the Alps.[91] At Rennes, two presidents of the de Robien family kept a *cabinet de curiosités* widely admired among European cognoscenti; confiscated by the Breton revolutionaries in 1791, it was to form part of the nucleus of the modern Musée de Rennes.[92]

Among the Normans, two judges, Louis Formont de Clérondes and Pierre Le Cornier de Cideville, could reminisce about amicable correspondence with Voltaire (though, admittedly, the latter *parlementaire* had burned his letters during a controversy embroiling Ferney's sage and the French authorities.) President Alexandre Charles Marie Du Moucel and counselor Jacques Philippe Romain Le Bas de Lieville experimented with the strange phenomenon of electricity; counselors Jean François Asselin de Crèvecoeur and Philippe Auguste Morin d'Anvers, intrigued by the possibilities of aviation, assisted a friend in a balloon ascent in May of 1784.[93] The magistrates at Toulouse could pride themselves upon their patronization of the Académie des Jeux Floraux, whose foundation in 1323 made it one of Europe's oldest surviving cultural societies. They also superintended the local university, whose origins went back even further, to 1229. Languedocien counselor Louis Gaillard de Frouzins possessed at his château de Frouzins a collection of sixty-eight paintings by such masters as Le Nain, Murillo, Holbein, and Poussin, whereas First President Jean-Louis-Emmanuel-Augustin de Cambon was noted for his magnificent collection of Chinese porcelains and his Gobelin tapestries. Not to be outdone, another Toulousain of the de Montégut family exhibited prints by Rubens and de Teniers, 179 statues of Greek, Roman, Gallic, Egyptian, and Chinese provenance in clay, bronze, and marble, and precisely 2,862 Roman medals and coins.[94]

These literati, connoisseurs, and occasional amateur musicians of the late eighteenth-century *parlements* belonged to a generation and a professional elite that knew how to combine business and pleasure, how to exchange the sober mien of working hours for the elegant and cultivated demeanor of evenings, weekends, and holidays. This ability provoked comment, even in the lesser parlementary capitals. At Nancy, where the wives of First President Michel-Joseph de Coeurderoy and President Esprit-Claude Pierre de Sivry held popular salons on the eve of the Revolution, a contemporary saw in the first president a man "as distinguished *par ses lumières* as in his capacity as a man of the world; invariably grave and austere at the *palais* in the morning, no one was merrier company than was he in his friends' society in the evening." As for President de Sivry and his wife, they "contributed just as infinitely to the charm of society at Nancy."[95] And what obtained at Nancy was equally the case elsewhere—as, for example, at Besançon, where President Joseph-Luc-Jean-Baptiste-Hippolyte de Vezet exhibited, in his biographer's words, "the double physiognomy of the magistrate." The president "discreetly savors those modish books, those daring doctrines which he will excoriate . . . from his lofty judicial bench. . . . After a grave audience in which he has weighed, one after another, the interests of the poor and the rights of the crown, he gallantly entertains ladies at supper." This judge of Franche-Comté "belonged to that world, destroyed forever, in which one confounded political matters with judicial matters, liberty with privileges, the person of the sovereign with the image of the fatherland."[96] *Parlementaires* like him all over France, experiencing, in Voltaire's felicitous phrase, a "civil war in the soul," bore witness in numberless ways to the complexity and contradictions of a society in the throes of evolution and on the threshold of revolution.

The "double physiognomy" of the old regime magistrate undeniably manifested itself in part as the pursuit of the best that two worlds, the nobility and the robe, had to offer. Exemplary of the effort to secure and perpetuate the fruits of his professional life was the typical judge's immersion in calculations bearing upon the bequest of his *charge*, his judicial office. If, as was increasingly likely during the 1770s and 1780s, he viewed his eldest son as his natural successor in the parlementary *métier*, he would devote considerable time to his heir's upbringing. The proper lay or clerical tutor for the early years, the appropriate *collège* (perhaps staffed by former Jesuits or Oratorians), the year or two "abroad" on continental tour, the Parisian or provincial law faculty, the brief apprenticeship as proctor or barrister—all were matters of concern to the prospective judge's father. Frequently, too, "dispensations" were secured that would permit a son to enter the *parlement* as counselor (or, occasionally, as president or *avocat-général*) at less than the stipulated minimum age, with less than the minimum required legal experience, and despite the (legally proscribed) presence of close kinsmen in the company. Recent investigation suggests that such dispensations were as common in most of the major provincial *parlements* in the eighteenth century as they were at Paris.[97] Practically speaking, how could it have been otherwise, in view of what we know of dynastic and "colonizing" tendencies in these sovereign courts? In this connection, and so many others, we must acknowledge the potency of robe calculation and robe tradition even as we trace the Parisian and provincial magistrates' "noble" sources of wealth and describe their "noble" style of life.

But the "double physiognomy" of the *parlementaires* manifested itself most ominously to the crown in the form of the dichotomy between conscientious judicial service and fractious judicial politics. And this, of course, brings us to the subject of leading personalities in the sovereign courts of the late 1780s. The next section briefly identifies these individuals and their politics in the climactic confrontation between magistracy and crown.

Personalities in the Prerevolutionary Crisis

The current state of research upon the major *parlements* in the last years of the old regime does not permit as thorough a discussion of their internal politics as it does of their members' social provenance, wealth, and life-styles. What we do know, however, suggests that, on balance, the crown did not find many articulate magisterial advocates of its policies when that advocacy was most sorely needed. Perhaps, given parlementary attitudes toward basic public issues, it was inevitable that such an adherence to specific policies should have been lacking. To sketch some of the most talked-about "politicians" of these law courts is, in any case, to note how strongly the tide of oratory, energy, and initiative in parlementary chambers was running against the reforms of Calonne, Brienne, Lamoignon, and their confederates.

The government's problems were illustrated nowhere more strikingly than at Paris. Longtime First President Etienne François d'Aligre had in the mid-1780s fallen afoul of both Controller General Calonne and Keeper of the Seals Miromesnil over certain personal matters. Furthermore, like many of his brethren, he detested former Fourth President Lamoignon in 1787–88 for accepting a ministerial portfolio and essaying judicial reform. Not surprisingly, d'Aligre withheld support from the ministers' most crucial initiatives. D'Aligre resigned his post in October 1788; unfortunately for the government, his replacement, Louis François de Paule Lefevre d'Ormesson, though "an inflexibly honest and severe individual," was also "strongly attached to the old ways of doing things, and entirely devoted to parlementary pretensions."[98] Other notables on the Grand Banc included Louis-Michel Le Peletier de Saint-Fargeau and Jean Omer Joly de Fleury, but neither the eloquence of the former nor the unrelenting political ambition of the latter served the crown's imperiled cause in 1787–88. Imposing names of the robe adorned the *parquet* as well on the eve of revolution, but here, too, among the king's men, critical support was lacking for the king. Procureur-Général Guillaume François Louis Joly de Fleury could only bring a plodding conscientiousness to the service of Louis XVI, and the nephew who succeeded him upon his death in December 1787 attracted only the derision of observers in the French capital. Senior Avocat-Général Antoine Louis Séguier had long overshadowed his superior the *procureur-général* in contemporaries' eyes, but employed his celebrated forensic abilities in the cause of the opposition rather than in that of authority during the prerevolution. The two other *avocats-généraux*, Marie Jean Hérault de Sechelles and Charles Henri d'Ambray, briefly attracted notice as eloquent young champions of the judicial resistance before their company was swept away by the revolutionary torrent. As far as the court's general membership was concerned, few were the counselors, whether of Grand' Chambre, Enquêtes, or Requêtes, willing to take up the cudgels or even mediate on the embattled government's behalf in 1787–88. Longtime political *rapporteur* Adrien Louis Lefebvre d'Amécourt, the capable, energetic, and ambitious "eagle and oracle of the Grand' Chambre," tendered his good offices from time to time, as did *parlementaires* Abbé Gabriel Tandeau, Anselme François d'Outremont de Minière, Théodore Anne Bourré de Corberon, Edouard François Mathieu Molé de Champlâtreux, and Antoine François Claude Ferrand. But these would-be peacemakers, and their occasional allies of Grand Banc and *parquet*, were hopelessly outnumbered: contemporaries had a field day describing the antics of those magistrates who for whatever reason would brook no compromise with the ministers. Chief among the antigovernment rebels was counselor of the Enquêtes Jean Jacques IV Duval d'Eprémesnil. Reportedly an admirer of Montesquieu and the British Constitution, ardent adversary of "ministerial despotism," and paladin of France's traditional society of Estates, privileges, and "corporations," this tribune of the parlementary opposition could also patronize some of the most unorthodox cults in prerevolutionary Paris.[99] In raising the standard of revolt during 1787 and 1788 Duval d'Eprémesnil could count upon the adherence of *grand' chambriers* such as austere Jansenist and veteran jurist Pierre Augustin Robert de Saint-Vincent, feisty and oratorical Emmanuel Marie Michel Philippe Fréteau de Saint-Just, and clerical counselors Abbé Honoré-Auguste Sabatier de Cabre and Abbé Le Coigneux de Belabre. Of similarly turbulent disposition in the tribunal's inferior chambers were Charles-Louis Huguet de Sémonville, Anne Louis Goislard de Montsabert, and future revolutionary Adrien Jean François Duport de Prélaville. The defiant idealism of these incorrigibles appealed powerfully to a phalanx of youthful judicial apprentices flocking into the court during this period, and it could not be adequately countered by the maturity and prudence of older judges who were themselves of two minds about the ministers' plans for reform.[100]

A similar state of affairs prevailed at Aix-en-Provence. Charles-Jean-Baptiste des Gallois de la Tour served simultaneously as first president of the *parlement* and as intendant of Provence; hence he was torn between loyalty to his judicial comrades and fealty to his king. One observer characterized him as a "timid personage" and noted (unsurprisingly) that his intendancy rendered him "in general . . . disliked by the Magistracy, which regards him as a man sold over to the Court."[101] Nor did the government find much support for its policies among its other "natural" spokesmen, whether of the Grand Banc or of the *parquet*.[102] The *Journal* of President Alexandre-Jules-Antoine Fauris de Noyers de Saint-Vincent, still preserved today in the Bibliothèque Méjanes at Aix, shows how this *parlementaire*'s ingrained conservatism precluded acceptance of the ministers' initiatives.[103] Procureur-Général Jean-François-André Leblanc de Castillon, long celebrated among the Aixois for his oratorical and intellectual attainments, attracted national attention by inveighing against Calonne's proposed reforms at the Assembly of Notables in 1787 and by lashing out in his company at Third Estate aspirations in Provence. Avocats-Généraux Joseph-François-Paul Aymar de Montmeyan and Théodore-Joseph Simon de Beauval were "liberals" who opposed the government from the other end of the political spectrum. The most controversial liberal from the counselors' ranks was undoubtedly Antoine-Balthasard-Joseph André. This "gentleman" without a fief embraced the revolutionary demands of the Provençal Third Estate in 1788 and was later deputized by popular vote to the Estates General. André was seconded in his sympathies for the commoners' cause in 1788 by Arnaud de Vitrolles and several other counselors of "progressive" persuasion. Small wonder that "this divided Parlement, which was falling prey to a spirit of abandon," could offer little resistance to an increasingly revolutionary course of events in Provence.[104]

Prospects for judicial ratification of the government's program were even bleaker at Bordeaux, where infighting among the jurists and fractious opposition to royal projects had marred the expedition of public affairs since the Maupeou years.[105] First President André-Jacques-Hyacinthe Le Berthon ought to have been among the crown's most reliable partisans in 1787, but was rumored to be "anti-Calonne" and had long been at odds with Procureur-Général Pierre-Jules Dudon.[106] Rumor also had Dudon as "anti-Calonne" early in 1787, but this judge, "well versed in his duties and of great merit," emerged at year's end at the head of a small "ministerial faction" within the court.[107] Unfortunately for the ministers, however, Dudon's service during 1771–74 in Maupeou's Bordeaux Parlement had fatally prejudiced his reputation among his colleagues in the post-Maupeou Bordeaux Parlement after 1774; thus, his switch over to the royal side in December 1787 probably hurt rather than helped the ministers' cause at Bordeaux. In any case, the Bordelais were by then in exile and remained so until late in 1788. Although even in banishment the *procureur-général* retained some discreet allies, such as President Nicolas-Pierre de Pichard and President of Enquêtes Jean-Paul de Loret, who would have served the authorities for gain or from fear, most of the Bordelais adamantly rejected any thought of reconciliation with the ministers during 1787–88. They were of a mind with Presidents of Enquêtes Martial-François de Verthamon and Michel-Joseph de Gourgue and counselors Laurent de Loyac and Etienne-François-Charles de Jaucen de Poissac, who preached intransigent opposition rather than moderation at this critical juncture.[108] It was indicative of the hopelessness of the king's cause that the most distinguished of Bordelais justices under Louis XVI, President Dupaty, had retired in disgust to Paris in 1784 and died there four years later in the midst of the old regime's final agonies.

The story was essentially the same at Grenoble.[109] First President Amable-Pierre-Albert de Bérulle, an irresolute individual, could do little to further the royal cause. Two of his associates on the Grand Banc, Joseph-Marie de Barral de Montferrat and Pierre-Marie de Vaulx, occasionally endeavored to negotiate truces between Grenoble and Versailles in the months of the prerevolutionary crisis. But another president, Joseph-Arthus de La Croix de Sayve d'Ornacieux, lent his illustrious name to the opposition. President d'Ornacieux, whose impressive private library at Grenoble boasted many a magisterial text apotheosizing the eighteenth-century *parlement* as "the heir of the Merovingian Assemblies," displayed "virtues, a courage, a firmness and a devotion to the public weal which would have honored ancient Rome."[110] Contemporaries often paired him with another inveterate opponent of the government, a lay counselor named Louis-Jean-François de Corbet de Meyrieu. This judge, though seventy years old in 1787, still dominated his fellows through integrity and sheer force of personality: he was "an honest magistrate, truly clever and poised, enlightened and one of the most industrious of his Company." For Corbet de Meyrieu, the "law of *enregistrement*" was the supreme law, that which conferred upon all others "the seal of legitimacy"; the government could hardly confess surprise if, as reports had it, this dangerous *parlementaire* in the late 1780s was priding himself upon having received fourteen *lettres de cachet* during his judicial career.[111] But d'Ornacieux and Corbet de Meyrieu, the two most notorious oppositionists among the Dauphinois, were ably seconded by others. Counselors Laurent-César de Chaléon (a man "of spirit, intelligence, insight and especially greatheartedness") and Laurent de Garnier (a bachelor, rich, "exalted by temperament and by principle") had combated Maupeou's reforms and could be counted upon to inveigh against those of his successors. A younger counselor, Jean-François Anglès, admitted into the *parlement* in 1780 after a brilliant service at the bar, wrote many of the court's most powerful remonstrances from 1786 to 1789.[112] As for the king's men of the *parquet*, they, too, espoused the parlementary cause. Procureur-Général Jean-Baptiste de Reynaud had sympathized with and subserved his associates' contumacy on many public questions since the early 1780s; Avocats-Généraux Jacques Fortunat Savoye de Rollin and Joseph-Louis de La Boissière had long enjoyed local renown as ardent acolytes of the Enlightenment and as eloquent foes of "ministerial despotism."[113] At Grenoble, as at Paris, Aix, and Bordeaux, rare were the judges prepared to champion ministerial policies as the *ancien régime* headed toward its demise.

Although we know less about the outstanding personalities of Louis XVI's other *parlements*, all available evidence points either to political passivity or to open and unashamed antiministerial defiance in their ranks. At Toulouse, for example, First President Jean-Louis-Emmanuel-Augustin de Cambon assumed his position in the very midst of the political crisis, in December 1787; neither he nor his immediate predecessor, Joseph de Nicquet, did much (or realistically *could* do much) to succor the government in its hour of extreme financial need.[114] Likewise, the king's men revealed themselves to be the *parlement's* men when it really counted. Louis-Emmanuel-Elizabeth de Rességuier, senior *avocat-général* during 1787 and then *procureur-général* after February 1788, registered his opposition to royal wishes on more than one occasion. His successor as senior *avocat-général*, Jean-Antoine de Catellan de Caumont, drew national notice when his refusal to cooperate in the implementation of royal fiscal policies in Languedoc landed him in prison during March 1788. His junior colleague in the *parquet*, Jean-Jacques-Claire Lecomte de Latresne, protested bitterly against this incarceration and joined Procureur-Général Rességuier in denouncing the May Edicts of 1788 several weeks after their compulsory registration at Toulouse.[115] Other influential intransigents among the Toulousains included Joseph-Julien-Honoré de Rigaud, a counselor of the Enquêtes whose initial claim to local fame had been his recent vindication of a woman falsely accused of parricide, and Jean-François de Montégut, a counselor who wore the hats of academician, scientist, and *littérateur* as well as that of jurist.[116]

Although not all the reforms of the Calonne and Brienne ministries applied in 1787–88 in the highly privileged province of Brittany, those that did seemingly encountered a solid wall of parlementary resistance. One memorialist characterized First President Charles-Marie-François-Jean-Célestin du Merdy de Catuélan as a "weak, cautious, wavering magistrate" who, at the best, would "swim between two waters"; in other words, he hesitated before throwing himself wholeheartedly into the arms of his comrades' opposition.[117] The same commentator de-

scribed Procureur-Général Anne-Jacques-Raoul de Caradeuc—accurately
—as a "born enemy of M. de Calonne."[118] And, indeed, how much support could the controller general expect early in 1787 from this son of a
more famous *procureur-général*, Louis-René de La Chalotais, who in the
eyes of all good Bretons had been outrageously persecuted by Calonne in
a celebrated controversy of the 1760s?[119] Assuredly the *avocats-généraux* at Rennes, Hippolyte-Louis-Marie Loz de Beaucours and Saturnin-
Hercule du Bourgblanc, could not fail to follow de Caradeuc's lead and
thus maintain solidarity with their seniors' bitter memories. There were
at least two other oppositionists of note at Rennes: Jean-Vincent d'Euzénou de Kersalaün, a scarred veteran of many a clash between his company and the crown, and Amand Du Couëdic de Kergoualer, whose account of the "military" registration of the May Edicts at Rennes, clandestinely published "at the expense of the province of Brittany,"
breathed the good old parlementary hatred of ministerial malfeasance
and "despotism."[120]

At Rouen, too, we search in vain for judges willing to risk their associates' wrath in defense of the embattled ministries of 1787–88. Louis
François Elie Camus de Pontcarré, formerly of the Paris Parlement and
chief officer of the Rouen Parlement since 1782, resolved to "defend the
rights of Normandy vigorously" at the Assembly of Notables in 1787.
So, in any case, went one current report.[121] Procureur-Général Jean
Pierre Prosper Godart de Belbeuf was described by the same source as an
"elderly magistrate, highly esteemed, renowned for his impartiality"—
but was no less feared as a hard taskmaster by the peasants on his lands
and known generally for his adherence to the status quo in government
and society.[122] He was not likely to find his opinions challenged by his
son, Avocat-Général Louis Pierre François Godart de Belbeuf, or, for that
matter, by the other *avocat-général*, Louis Anne Grente de Grécourt.
Among these Norman jurists there were probably the usual "liberal"
and reactionary intransigents. Among the latter may have been Pierre-
Louis Le Charpentier de Chailloué, who was later to startle the Constituent Assembly by arguing that "there would no longer be a nobility
if it were condemned to pay [taxes] like the Third Estate, that he could
not conceive of nobility without privileges, that it was privileges that in
essence constituted its existence."[123] Defiance of the Constituent Assembly's revolutionaries cannot have been too different from earlier defiance of ministerial "revolutionaries" such as Calonne, Brienne, and
Lamoignon—though, unfortunately for all *parlementaires*, it was much
less successful in the long run.

That the king's imperiled cause could be served no better at Dijon and
Besançon than elsewhere was suggested by the influence wielded among
the Burgundian and Comtois judges by certain contentious and conser-

vative personalities outside the official leadership. At Dijon, First President Bénigne Legouz de Saint-Seine, Procureur-Général Bernard Pérard, and Avocats-Généraux Etienne Henri Colas and L.-J. Poissonnier de Prusley were overshadowed by President Louis Philippe Joly de Bévy. The *Gazette de Leyde* reported on 28 December 1787 that this fiery and inflexible tribune of the parlementary opposition "had the greatest influence in the deliberations of his Company."[124] Certainly the intendant of Burgundy would have concurred in this assessment of Joly de Bévy's sway over his associates: in writing to the ministers at Versailles about a month before, he had bemoaned "the difficulties the government will have in winning against a parlement led at will by a man so daring and so violent."[125] The intendant also singled out a counselor, Pierre-François Gauthier, for condemnation.[126] The object of Joly de Bévy's and Gauthier's ire in 1787 was what it had long been: the "Intermediary Commission" of the Estates of Burgundy, viewed by the *parlementaires* as too subservient to the government in matters of taxation. Burgundy was one of those provinces in which relations between Estates and *parlement* were as chronically troubled (and sometimes downright hostile) as relations between *parlement* and crown.

Similarly, at Besançon, First President Claude-Irénée-Marie-Nicolas Perreney de Grosbois, Procureur-Général Claude-Théophile-Joseph Doroz, and Avocats-Généraux Jean-François Bergeret, Hippolyte Bouhelier d'Audelange, and Charles-Bonaventure de Tallenay were somewhat eclipsed by two counselors, Claude-Joseph Bourgon and François-Nicolas-Eugène Droz des Villars, and by a president, Joseph-Luc-Jean-Baptiste-Hippolyte de Vezet. We have already made the acquaintance of President de Vezet, who in his professional days and social evenings so arrestingly exhibited "the double physiognomy" of the magistrate. We have also encountered Droz des Villars, that luminous and congenial academician, antiquarian, and jurisconsult who so delighted his family with the violin. He and Claude-Joseph Bourgon authored many of their company's political pronunciamentos in the late 1780s, explaining to king and ministers why they and their brethren could not accept critical royal reforms in their beloved Franche-Comté. We shall be returning quite frequently to Droz des Villars. He was, like his fellow Comtois President de Vezet, the classic magistrate exhibiting a "double physiognomy" in his professional and social lives, but in addition he was more prolific and versatile an author, and thus should prove more helpful to us ·as we explore parlementary attitudes on the eve of revolution in France.

The foregoing sketch of some of the more influential "politicians" in the major *parlements* of Louis XVI's reign leaves little doubt that in seeking legitimization of their reforms the monarch and his ministers had to reckon with politically neutralized or hostile presidents and *gens du roi*, intractable conservatives, and increasingly insubordinate liberals. Did they also have to reckon with an actual preponderance of unmanageable youths within these tribunals? Certainly there was a heavy influx of young inexperienced judges into the Paris Parlement during the last years of that court's existence, and the memoirs of Parisian counselors such as Ferrand, Guy Marie Sallier, and Etienne Denis Pasquier concur in portraying these judicial novices as ardent partisans of insurrection in the Cour des Pairs.[127] In provincial France the situation varied from *parlement* to *parlement*.[128] At Dijon, lay counselors under the age of thirty-five may have held an absolute majority in the "assemblies of the chambers" on the brink of the Revolution. At Rennes, those magistrates under thirty-five composed about half the membership. At Grenoble and Aix, the balance swung somewhat against the younger jurists. At several other places—for instance, Besançon, Douai, and Metz—the balance swung more decisively against those judges in their twenties and early thirties. At Toulouse, a relatively slow rate of replacement of *parlementaires* ensured an even heavier preponderance of those aged thirty-five or older at the end of the *ancien régime*. Analogous statistics for Bordeaux and Rouen could be cited on the basis of recent inquiries. But how much could such data really tell us? At Bordeaux, the average age of all judges in 1790 was about forty-seven and only twenty-two magistrates were under thirty-five; at Rouen, the influx of youth during the 1780s was decidedly greater.[129] Yet the Bordelais were if anything even more obstreperous in their politics than the Rouennais. The notorious antigovernment antics of the youthful Parisian judges notwithstanding, then, there was no correlation whatsoever between the ages of the magistrates and corporate parlementary behavior in the prerevolutionary crisis. At most, the biological assets of youth—energy, stamina, optimism—here and there reinforced a predisposition toward defiance of authority long nourished in magisterial stances upon public issues.

The most important conclusion to be drawn from this discussion of the organization, functions, and personnel of the late eighteenth-century *parlements* is that their members had to serve a multitude of masters. The judges dispensed the king's justice, helped administer the affairs of his realm, and legitimized his legislation. Thus, they were royal servants. The magistrates also excluded most nonnoble Frenchmen from their ranks and in their urban and rural lives were very emphatically of the social elite. Hence, they served "noble" interests as well. At the same time, the justices spent far more daylight hours in judicial chambers than upon aristocratic estates, and the familial dynasties they so painstakingly built over the generations were first and foremost dynasties of the robe. Indeed, as officers of the robe the *parlementaires* enjoyed not only the privileges of their noble cousins of the sword but also a raft of advantages that the latter could never hope to claim. In consequence, the men of the *parlements* promoted the interests of a specific profession—their own profession of justice. Yet in subserving the interests of justice, or at the very least averring that they did so, the judges had also to evidence some solicitude for the causes, real or imagined, of Frenchmen who were not of the king's government nor of the noblesse nor of the legal *métier*. As we look ahead, then, to an analysis of parlementary opinions upon public questions in the late 1780s, we can anticipate a portrayal of men who endeavored as always to reconcile a variety of advocacies—but who were fated to do so now against a backdrop of spreading paralysis in government and crumbling consensus in society.

The Court of Peers
Political and Social Attitudes

"The parlement," recalled one of the Parisian court's erstwhile members, Guy Marie Sallier, "was strongly committed to royalism, and at the same time retained a sense of its duties to the people. . . . regarding itself as the sole custodian of public liberty, it was unrelentingly suspicious of the ministry, which it was always ready to censure. . . . if it was incapable of lacking in fidelity to its king, it was not however safe from the influence of rising factions . . . seductively arrayed in an apparent solicitude for the public welfare."[1] Sallier's portrayal of ambivalence in the Paris Parlement of the prerevolutionary crisis finds an echo in the reminiscences of C.-L.-F. de Paule de Barentin, successor to Lamoignon as keeper of the seals in 1788. Barentin conceded that the great Parisian tribunal could still boast "a large enough number of virtuous magistrates, faithful to their God, to their king, to the interests of the people," but lamented that "their voice was stifled; they had the misfortune to see their ranks infiltrated by sectarian fanatics . . . who led the court's youth astray. These fanatical guides and their all too credulous disciples . . . opened the vast tomb which was soon to swallow up the majority of and the most meritorious in the membership."[2] Both of these judgments were rendered by men who knew through their experiences in 1787–88 whereof they spoke, and both attest to problematical parlementary attitudes and behavior at Paris.

We cannot help wondering whether, even in the absence of "rising factions," "sectarian fanatics," and overly impressionable apprentices of Enquêtes and Requêtes, the kingdom's oldest and most influential *parlement* could have avoided foundering upon the reefs of inconsistency and self-deception in the late 1780s. After all, in a time of political crisis how many masters could the judges serve, and serve well? Could they simultaneously be "faithful to . . . their king" and devoted "to the interests of the people" if "king" and "people" were falling out seriously, perhaps irreversibly, over public affairs? Both Sallier (the erstwhile *parlementaire*) and Barentin (the former minister) seem to have felt that most of the magistrates honestly endeavored to have it both ways—that is, to maintain allegiance to the governors and to the governed in their society. And, indeed, a careful analysis of parlementary pronouncements and actions indicates that Sallier and Barentin were fundamentally right to portray the jurists as advocates of a variety of interests in the prerevolutionary crisis, even though the two men did not in their commentaries adequately stress how irreconcilable those interests turned out to be. The Parisian *parlementaires*, in ordinary sessions as well as in glittering convocations of the Court of Peers, espoused the causes of monarchism, of clergy and noblesse, and of haughty and humble commoners. Yet, in their very attempt to accommodate all these interests, and thus preserve the comfortable world they had always known, the judges failed to champion any one cause—and most notably that of the embattled crown—unambiguously and consistently. Moreover, their increasingly rancorous debate with Louis XVI's insolvent government propelled some of them down strange paths of radicalism as the prerevolutionary crisis ripened toward revolution.

An Ambivalent Monarchism

There are abundant indications that the majority of Parisian *parlementaires* strove throughout the prerevolutionary crisis to remain loyal to Louis XVI even as they assailed the policies of his government. In so doing, they only pointed up the hopeless obsolescence of monarchist sentiments that failed to take adequate account of the administrative and fiscal requirements of an increasingly "modern" state. Yet these magisterial critics of Louis XVI's "administrative monarchy" were in one vital respect more "enlightened" than Louis's enlightened ministers themselves: they perceived and proclaimed the need for a new and more liberal constitutional pact between the rulers and the ruled in France.

In the cases of a few of the most influential judges, political ambition as well as ingrained professionalism counseled a continuing orientation toward the crown. The outstanding example of the ambitious "royalist" in 1787–88 was probably Adrien Louis Lefebvre d'Amécourt, who was on the verge of becoming fourth in seniority among the regular counselors of the Grand' Chambre.[3] He was one of the few *parlementaires* willing to second Abbé Gabriel Tandeau's vain attempt as king's *rapporteur* to secure a fair hearing for Loménie de Brienne's *subvention territoriale* at the court's plenary session of 30 July 1787.[4] Soon thereafter, according to reliable witness, Lefebvre d'Amécourt joined several presidents of the Grand' Chambre in the negotiations with the government that eventually terminated the Parisian Parlement's exile at Troyes and exchanged ministerial withdrawal of the controversial *subvention territoriale* and stamp tax for the reimposition of *vingtième* taxation. As part of the compromise, this indefatigable *parlementaire* eventually regained the post of king's *rapporteur* in his company.[5] Then, again, there were reports concerning an attempt by Lefebvre d'Amécourt, in alliance with his colleague and longtime confidant President Joly de Fleury, to use the aging former minister Jean-Baptiste Machault d'Arnouville to enter the government in April 1789.[6] The two judges' purported ambitions were still providing grist for the mills of Parisian gossip in the summer of 1789.[7]

But thoughts of political preferment, even in this most politically attuned of *parlements*, played second fiddle to professional instincts inculcated by long years of judicial service. The *parlementaires*, especially if not exclusively those of the Grand' Chambre, knew very well which side of their bread was buttered—knew very well, that is, how all of their interests argued for a continued identification with the monarchy. They demonstrated this time and time again in those last troubled years of the old regime.

An arresting case in point was the controversy in early 1787 over Calonne's proposal to parcel out the royal domain in fiefs to be exploited under a feudal regime.[8] The controller general hoped thereby to achieve a more efficient management of the crown lands, all the while leaving them under the "direct lordship" of the king. But "direct lordship" apparently was not enough for one of the veteran officers of the Paris Parlement, the aging and ailing Procureur-Général Guillaume François Louis Joly de Fleury. Speaking at the first Assembly of Notables, this *parlementaire* scored Calonne's plan for harboring disturbing principles "that could tend to weaken or pervert the maxim, immutable in France, that the king's domain is inalienable." As he had done upon many a previous occasion, Joly de Fleury asserted now that it was his duty as the king's lieutenant in the Parlement to draw a fine line between the royal and feudal regimes and to champion what belonged to the former. This meant, above all, declaring that the king's lands could under no circumstances be alienated, as they might conceivably be under Calonne's version of feudal contract. The *procureur-général* then spoke in a historical vein, discussing the ancient collection of legal titles of royal domain in France. The chief of the king's men in the Parlement proclaimed that such legal titles had existed "under the first and second races" of French kings; that these documents had been scattered and lost during the troubles and usurpations of feudal times; and that in more modern times the French monarchs "had taken greater care of these titles, and had had them placed above the treasury of the Sainte Chapelle of the Palace [of Justice] at Paris that St. Louis had built." Although this sacred treasure of royal titles, charters, and other documents had subsequently been transferred to another stronghold within the Palais de Justice, continued Joly de Fleury, it had remained and would always remain under the protection of the Paris Parlement and in particular the Parlement's *procureur-général*. Joly de Fleury and his successors would maintain that trust as they maintained their general surveillance over the "rights of the Crown." It would be difficult indeed to find in the archives of the *ancien régime* a more forceful evocation of the seasoned magistrate's identification with the cause of the crown.

Naturally, self-interest was also very much at work here. The *parlementaires* who most ardently championed the centrality of monarchy in France were precisely those most keenly aware of their company's utter dependence upon the continuation of that monarchy. And, in justice to the court's leaders, it must be noted that they had been perfectly willing upon at least one occasion earlier in Louis XVI's reign to acknowledge this dependence explicitly in a memorandum to the government. The issue prompting that acknowledgment had been the provisional establishment of several administrative assemblies of landowners by Director-General of Finances Jacques Necker.[9] It was only natural that in 1787 Calonne's pending legislation envisioning a more comprehensive network of provincial, district, and municipal assemblies in the kingdom's *pays d'élection* should have engaged the justices once again in a defense of certain monarchical (and, by implication, magisterial) interests.

Actually, a careful reading of Calonne's legislation (later carried over by Loménie de Brienne in an edict of June 1787) suggests nothing very revolutionary in the wind.[10] The government simply wanted to involve well-to-do landowners in local administrative activities that were still to be supervised by those right-hand agents of Bourbon absolutism, the intendants. But even the most cautious innovations made the judges uneasily aware that reform of royal administration in the provinces might affect the *parlements'* cherished political role of addressing the sovereign on controversial local matters.

It is not surprising, then, to find Procureur-Général Joly de Fleury voicing misgivings about the institution of provincial assemblies at the Assembly of Notables early in 1787.

> But can one in good conscience propose to the King that he renounce that exercise of the right of administering these provinces by his direct authority and give that function to a multitude of persons, who despite the best intentions, the most acute intelligence, the most active zeal, can never secure from their fellow provincials the most entire confidence, being in reality neither their mandatories nor their representatives, contrary to apparent insinuations?[11]

The speaker's brother, President Jean Omer Joly de Fleury, expressed himself on the same issue in April 1787 when he obtained from an acquaintance information concerning the administration of three small *pays* in southeastern France: Bresse, Bugey, and Gex.[12] From this information he developed an essay lauding the assemblies already established in those regions for, among other things, preserving intact the authority of the king's agents.[13] This was accomplished in part through utilization of the Third Estate contingent in these bodies to neutralize the clerical and noble contingents. Because the vote of the Third Estate was doubled in the governing councils of these assemblies, commented President Joly de Fleury, the "clergy and nobility could not dominate proceedings . . . the third Estate has two [votes] against their two, resulting in tie votes. The king's authority is undiminished because it retains the power to decide issues."[14] President Joly de Fleury and his brother were at this point especially disturbed, in all likelihood, by Calonne's intention that the new assemblies deliberate without regard for the social rank of their personnel. As cautious and conservative royalists they could easily see in this an innovation that, once become nationwide, might undermine the king's own authority and thus jeopardize the *parlements'* political influence as well.

Although Loménie de Brienne, after coming to power, restored the traditional social distinctions to his predecessor's controversial assemblies, the edict submitted for parlementary approval on 22 June 1787 encountered immediate opposition, motivated, so it would seem, by doubts similar to those already expressed by the Joly de Fleury brothers. Several of the judges at the plenary session of 22 June objected to the vagueness of the responsibilities assigned to the new assemblies. On the recommendation of the young counselor Antoine François Claude Ferrand, who retold the story years later, the court decided to ratify the edict with the proviso "that the King would be most humbly implored to complete his good work and insure its stability by sending to his courts the promised regulations to be verified in the ordinary manner."[15] This *arrêté*, which according to its author passed "by an immense majority," reflected magisterial concerns that contemporaries were quick to remark. The ever-attentive S.-P. Hardy reported that Grand' Chambrier Anselme François d'Outremont de Minière, though partisan of the government's policy on this as on so many other occasions, nevertheless reaffirmed the necessity of "maintaining the law of verification and registration in the Parlements" in all matters bearing upon "the welfare of the State and the relief of the People."[16] At about the same time, the *Gazette de Leyde* reported that those feisty *parlementaires* Duval d'Eprémesnil and Le Coigneux de Belabre had in the debate over the provincial assemblies assailed the intendants' plenitude of administrative roles in provincial affairs.[17] It is clear that the government's experimentation with novel deliberative bodies in provincial France upset many of the Parisian judges. In granting a new role in public affairs to prominent rural landowners, and possibly amplifying the intendants' role, such innovation could seem in parlementary eyes to place new barriers, or fortify old ones, between the magistrate-king and his most faithful judges. But if the behavior of intendants and assemblies of landed proprietors in the provinces occasioned misgivings at the Parisian Palais de Justice, how much more villainous in the view of the *parlementaires* were the "ministerial despots" at Versailles! And how desperately the magistrates wanted, even at this late hour, to distinguish between the old bugbear of ministerial despotism and the legitimate authority of their king! A most dramatic example in point was an incident at the tumultuous plenary session of 5 May 1788 which anticipated Lamoignon's judicial *coup de force*. One of the magistrates denounced to his fellows an anonymous publication that had the Parlement censuring "the enterprises of His Majesty upon the Magistracy" rather than "the enterprises of the Ministers upon the Magistracy" in a decree of 3 May. This incendiary squib was immediately referred to the *parquet*, and minutes later the court, upon the advice of Avocat-Général Séguier, condemned it to be "lacerated and burned" with standard ceremony at the foot of the Grand Staircase of the Palais de Justice. The judges condemned the work as "containing an insidious falsehood contrary to the respect due to the King, and designed to impute to the Court sentiments and expressions incompatible with its eternal and profound respect for the sacred person of the King." At the same session, Séguier denounced and demanded the suppression of another anonymous piece imputing disloyalty to the court; the suppression of this squib was accompanied by reiterated professions of allegiance to Louis XVI.[18]

Skeptical observers might view such actions as last-minute politicking designed to head off the heavy blows of the government, and as betraying in addition the jurists' hatred of their former colleague Lamoignon. The magistrates' action was assuredly both of these things, but it just as surely signified their desperate wish to stay in Louis's good graces and thus preserve their traditional relationship with the crown. Less than nine months earlier, in a fiery *arrêté* of 27 August 1787 from Troyes, the exiled *parlementaires* had testified to the same genuine if foredoomed hope by anathematizing unnamed "ministers who abuse the authority of the King" by abusing his subjects.[19] A hopelessly impractical distinction—but one to which the jurists nevertheless remained loyal to the end of their professional days.

As the preceding discussion suggests, royalism in the Parlement—old-fashioned, personal allegiance to the sovereign—was not confined to the more judicious veterans of the Grand' Chambre. Indeed, it actuated some of the most violent instigators of rebellion in the lower chambers, men who shared their seniors' determination to differentiate between ministerial malfeasance and the legitimate authority of Louis XVI. If there was any acknowledged spokesman of the junior *parlementaires* throughout the late 1770s and 1780s, any standard-bearer of revolt throughout the traumatic months of the "prerevolution" of 1787–88, it was surely Jean Jacques IV Duval d'Eprémesnil. Yet public and private sources alike make it absolutely clear that this *parlementaire*'s fundamental monarchism remained as unshaken by events as did that of the Joly de Fleurys and Lefebvre d'Amécourts and Séguiers and Outremont de Minières of the Grand' Chambre. In a widely publicized pamphlet on the upcoming Estates General circulating in the capital toward the end of 1788, Duval d'Eprémesnil, though candidly confessing his attachment to the "just prerogatives of the Nobility and Clergy," just as forthrightly branded "ministerial despotism" as the "common enemy of the King and of the three orders." The king and the traditional social order must remain; it was the perfidious innovations and capriciousness of the king's ministers that must go.[20]

But even more revealing, and convincing, is the unpublished correspondence from Duval d'Eprémesnil to his wife and other members of his family during his Provençal exile in 1788. Here, in an undated fragment of this fascinating correspondence, is the passionate tribune of the parlementary opposition, imploring his wife to intercede on his behalf at Versailles:

> If you do not come, *ma chère amie*, request frankly that I be restored to my wife, to my children, to my affairs. Expose your condition to the King, talk to his heart; implore His Majesty to consider that my distant exile is entirely unheard of in politics; and represent to him respectfully, but clearly, that his personal intention cannot possibly be to treat me severely, because the Kings reserve their severity for the guilty or for enemies: but the King has himself seen well that I was his servant, and his faithful servant. This, *ma chère amie*, is what will have to be said openly, respectfully: make the sacred laws of Justice, of Humanity, the rights of Nature all speak: let your petition breathe the sentiments that are in your heart, the sentiments of a wife, of a mother, of a loyal subject . . . such is the sole desirable objective, the only tone appropriate to your soul, to my character, to the reputation your courage has won for you, to my reputation, if I may dare to speak so, to the dignity of the Parlement, and especially to the Royal Majesty, which would be injured, no matter what they might say, by servile phrases, and by abject sentiments.[21]

In a letter to one of his children, written on 24 May 1788, Duval d'Eprémesnil continued in a somewhat naïve vein: "I persist in my belief that

it is all a misunderstanding. . . . convinced as I am that the King's intention has never been to have me pent up in a barred room, without being
able to leave it."[22] Clearly, the sovereign was being misinformed and
misled by his ministers. Would France, this judge wondered, be able
some day to revert to an ideal situation in which there would be no
despotic administrators interloping between monarch and people? A
hopelessly impractical vision, no doubt, stubbornly upheld in the face of
harsh realities in 1787–88. But the subsequent collapse of the *ancien
régime* only intensified Duval d'Eprémesnil's allegiance to Louis XVI
and to the monarchy. A fellow *parlementaire* whom we have already
encountered, Ferrand, later recalled Duval d'Eprémesnil's anguish at
"seeing the monarchy in flames" in 1789 and his vow to perish rather
than to have to see the crown utterly consumed.[23] As a matter of fact,
this controversial magistrate, regretting the violence of his opposition to
royal policies in earlier days, was in the Revolution to achieve a reputation as zealous paladin of the monarchy in the debates of the National
Assembly. Duval d'Eprémesnil eventually took his royalism with him to
the scaffold.[24]

   Another incorrigible opponent of the government in the Parlement's
Enquêtes was Huguet de Sémonville—yet he, too, shared the court's
basic orientation toward the crown. When, for instance, he addressed his
associates on 16 July 1787 in advocacy of reviving the Estates General,
he sought to allay the misgivings of many magistrates about such a
convocation by reminding them how many times in past centuries this
institution had supported French monarchs against the papacy, unruly
provincial "gentlemen," religious seditions, and other challenges to the
crown and to public quietude. The Estates General, he averred, would
enable the monarch to govern his realm more efficiently than ever before; surely it could not menace the monarchy itself.[25] An anonymous
tract attributed to this same jurist reinforced these sentiments by
roundly declaring that "France will remain a Monarchy, because that
form of government is perhaps the sole form compatible with its wealth,
its population, its extent, and the political system of Europe." This
was probably an echo of Montesquieu, and also an echo of Duval d'Eprémesnil and many another *parlementaire*, as Huguet de Sémonville went
on to cite as his guiding principles "the love of that liberty maintained
by the laws, the attachment to the forms of the Monarchy, the respect
for the royal person and for the royal prerogative, and the hatred of arbitrary power."[26] A similar orientation toward judiciously tempered monarchy appeared in a long speech on the religious situation in France
delivered in the Parlement on 9 February 1787 by another inveterate foe
of "ministerial despotism," Robert de Saint-Vincent.[27] There were a few
judges in the court—Adrien Duport, Hérault de Sechelles, Le Peletier de

Saint-Fargeau—who might cast off their allegiance to the *ancien régime* and enter wholeheartedly into revolutionary careers, but they seem to have been exceptions, at least among the articulate and influential judges. At the eleventh hour of the old regime, fidelity to a certain kind of monarchism continued to characterize *parlementaires* ranging from the cautious old men of the Grand' Chambre to some of the most notorious hotspurs of both senior and subordinate chambers.

However, it is obvious from what we have already seen that the Parisian magistrates' advocacy of monarchy in France was, indeed *had* to be, ambivalent in the extreme. For what could monarchy possibly mean in practice if not incessantly growing bureaucracy and taxation to serve the domestic and foreign policies of the French state? And how could the Parisian justices refrain from responding negatively to these growing pains of a dynamic Great Power? After all, if the judges were officers of the crown trained to champion the writ of royalty, they were also privileged landowners and spokesmen for all proprietors in their jurisdiction. Whether judicious veterans of the Grand' Chambre or firebrands of the lower chambers, the magistrates opposed heavier taxation. Or, if upon occasion they did not do so, they argued at the very least that new monetary tributes to the crown from the king's subjects required royal constitutional concessions to those same subjects. Thus, as the prerevolutionary crisis deepened, parlementary opposition to the government's fiscal policies inevitably became constitutional opposition as well—and put both the monarch and the magistrates themselves at risk.

To the chagrin of those seeking to restore the crown's finances in the late 1780s, the Parisian *parlementaires* stood foursquare behind the existing pecuniary privileges of clergy and nobles and others. And they announced this stance well before the convocation of the Court of Peers. Both Second President Lefevre d'Ormesson and Procureur-Général Joly de Fleury spoke out against Calonne's proposed *subvention territoriale* at the first Assembly of Notables early in 1787. Joly de Fleury, after alluding in his address to his colleague's rejection of the proposed imposition at an earlier session of the Notables, seconded his opposition:

> I will be satisfied simply with having the honor to observe that . . .
> the privileges of the clergy and the nobility have merited in all
> times the greatest consideration because of their antiquity and that
> one has always had a similar consideration in matters of taxation
> for all the other privileged bodies of which the State is composed.
>
> Thus, as the new plan . . . would tend to destroy all privileges
> and prerogatives whatsoever since it would tax a portion of the
> fruits of all the lands . . . of all persons regardless of estate and
> quality . . .

I think that the destruction of all these privileges and distinctions could have momentous consequences.[28]

That such an attitude, if taken up by other influential *privilégiés*, could spell permanent impoverishment for royal policies did not apparently dawn upon the *procureur-général*. After all, he would have insisted, monarchical policies had so far in French history been reconcilable with social hierarchy and privilege; why not, then, in the present and in the future? Unfortunately for Louis XVI and his ministers, the judges wanted to have it both ways: monarchy, yes, but monarchy reconciled with the trammels of hierarchy, privilege, property, and personal interest.

Calonne, we should recall, had not fixed the yield and duration of his controversial land tax. When Loménie de Brienne took this impost over from his predecessor in the spring of 1787, he established its permanence but hoped to mollify the *parlementaires* and others by fixing its yield at an annual 80 million livres.[29] Yet, in addition to being permanent, Brienne's *subvention* would, like Calonne's, fall as a lump sum upon *all* classes of proprietors within each administrative area, much as the *taille* fell as a lump sum upon all commoners. This meant that rich proprietors might very well have to pay more, absolutely *and* proportionately, than the less affluent paid so that fixed tax quotas could be met. The former might, in other words, be subjected to an "aristocratic" version of the dread and much denounced *contrainte solidaire* which, in the case of the *taille*, often saddled the most moneyed peasants with a disproportionate tax burden in the old regime.[30]

How humiliating for the "robinocrats" of the Palais de Justice and their fellow nobles of the countryside! Is it any wonder that the objections of Lefevre d'Ormesson and Joly de Fleury to Calonne's tax paled in comparison to the subsequent parlementary outcry against Loménie de Brienne's version of the *subvention territoriale*? The tempestuous sessions of the Cour des Pairs in the early summer of 1787 rang with excoriations of the proposed impost; but it was the redoubtable Duval d'Eprémesnil who most forcefully articulated his company's reaction. On 13 August 1787, a week after Brienne had compelled the magistrates to register his legislation at a *lit de justice*, Duval d'Eprémesnil persuaded his associates to issue an *arrêté* condemning the fiscal legislation and declaring its publication by the government "clandestine," "null," and "illegal."[31] Significantly, the decree also fulminated against the allegedly abusive principle of the *contrainte solidaire*: "It is no less contrary to the primitive constitutions of the Nation . . . to see the Clergy and the Nobility subjected to a solidary contribution for the *Subvention territoriale*. . . . it is only in our days that we have seen the concoction of a system to render the Nobility and Clergy *solidaires* for an imposition that each person owes on his own revenue after a deliberation and consent without which all demanded commitments constitute an attack upon property."[32]

In moving and securing passage of this decree, Duval d'Eprémesnil showed that he understood very well what the government was after with its tax legislation; he and most of his brethren rejected the ministers' design outright. The *contrainte solidaire* as imposed upon certain moneyed *taillables* incidental to the *corvée* was bad enough, they felt, but to make nobles and clerics yield up what peasants could not or would not pay, so that fixed local quotas of tax revenue might be met, would be downright insulting to the proprietors of the first two orders and perhaps economically disastrous as well for the wealthiest among them.

The Parlement's defiant decree of 13 August, we know, led almost immediately to its exile to Troyes. Although this banishment was later terminated by the compromise between ministry and magistracy that provided for withdrawal of the new impost and reimposition of the old *vingtième* taxation, the *parlementaires* remained dissatisfied. The *vingtièmes*, too, could be considered injurious to the interests of the privileged: had the judges not bombarded successive ministers over the preceding two generations with remonstrances attesting collusion between unscrupulous royal agents and peasants against seigneurs envied for their legitimate wealth?[33] In April of 1788, Goislard de Montsabert of the Enquêtes returned to this and similar themes in denouncing in plenary session the Brienne ministry's administration of the *vingtièmes*, and the company followed this up with a stinging decree on the subject.[34] The government intervened drastically soon thereafter with its coup against the judiciary, but could do nothing to shake age-old beliefs in and championship of privileges that were in fact rotting the *ancien régime*.

There was, however, more to parlementary oppositionism during the prerevolution than a sterile defense of privilege. Both directly and indirectly, the judges reacted to the inexorably growing demands of French *raison d'état*, to the inexorable bureaucratization of French governance. They did so in part by revealing their naïveté on the subject of state finances. No sooner did the government submit its legislation extending the stamp tax to the *parlementaires* in late June 1787 than the jurists, in "supplications" of 8 July 1787, voiced their incredulity over the need for such legislation "after five years of peace." The king, they said, would simply have to make his ministers' financial accounts available to his loyal servants at the Palais de Justice so that they might "verify the deficit" and convince themselves of the government's determination to streamline royal finances wherever and whenever possible.[35] Royal rejection of this request only elicited further "supplications" from the Palais de Justice; these were presented to Louis on 15 July. The magistrates now saw fit to remind the monarch that the government's financial accounts had just recently been submitted to the Notables. Could His Majesty refuse them to the Cour des Pairs, "obligated to give its suffrage where the Notables only proposed to give a simple opinion?" But in addition to betraying some jealousy of the Notables, the judges and their glittering aristocratic allies in the Cour des Pairs became bolder in their commentary upon the substantive financial issues: the royal deficit was "perhaps exaggerated," and the extended stamp tax was "an appalling impost, whose necessity is not demonstrated, whose duration is uncertain and whose amount (*quotité*) is unknown."[36] Once again Louis XVI was unimpressed, and once again he demanded prompt ratification of his legislation.

It was at this point that the jurists and aristocratic luminaries convened in the Palais de Justice decided upon formal remonstrances. On 24 July they chose the protests drafted for this purpose by Antoine François Claude Ferrand over those drafted by Duval d'Eprémesnil.[37] It may be, as Ferrand later maintained, that his language was less vehement and radical than that of his colleague; nonetheless, Ferrand's remonstrances, which the sovereign received on 26 July, certainly testified strikingly enough to the judicial conception of taxation as a *limited* and *temporary* resource for public policy. First, on the specific matter of the stamp tax legislation, Ferrand wrote:

> The declaration, vicious in almost all its dispositions, offers at all points the alluring ease of an extension, for which the pretexts are rarely lacking; experience furnishes on this score only too many examples; the two *sols*, the eight *sols pour livre*, the second *brevet* of the *taille* and so many other inventions dreamed up by the *esprit de finance* to overtax the people, are merely the extension of an impost that was simple in its origins; an extension that has in some cases . . . been implemented in virtue of a minister's letter, without your law-courts ever having obtained its revocation.[38]

But why should taxation ever be prolonged beyond its originally assigned period, unless for reasons of genuine national urgency? Here, a scarcely disguised swipe at the hated Calonne was perhaps inevitable:

> Your Majesty can recall under what point of view one presented to him, in 1784 and 1785, the situation of the State. It seemed then, or rather one wanted to make it seem, on the verge of liberation

from insolvency; and in this very moment, the State was more burdened than ever. Your Parlement, Sire, then endeavored in vain to expose the truth fully.[39]

Ministerial malfeasance and bureaucratic intrigue and corruption (but *not* the legitimate fiscal requirements of ongoing national policy) had prolonged the state's financial woes and produced the current crisis. Let the government, then, clean its own house before soliciting parlementary approbation of new taxes, and frightful extensions of old taxes:

All taxation must be proportionate to need and must terminate with it. . . . the people must not increase their contribution except in the case where [government] expenses are reduced as much as possible.[40]

Ferrand's remonstrances may have been couched in more diplomatic language than those of Duval d'Eprémesnil (which have not survived); they nevertheless made their point unequivocally.

Yet there was nothing in all this calculated to take the king and his ministers aback. The *parlementaires* were merely citing chapter and verse from earlier jeremiads against ministers who had sought to augment state revenue. Indeed, when, on 29 April of the following year, the court was spurred by Goislard de Montsabert's tirade against government assessment of *vingtième* taxation in the countryside to order an official inquiry into the matter, its *arrêté* explicitly linked the present with the past. "The progressive augmentation of the *vingtièmes* following upon the progressive augmentation of [proprietors'] revenues would be destructive of the citizens' property and destructive of their industry," declared the judges sententiously. Such taxation was "'contradicted by all the edicts and registrations of edicts since the establishment of the *dixième*, and overthrown utterly by the remonstrances of the Court, in 1778, upon the same matter."[41] And, in fact, the magistrates had assailed Necker in 1778 for essaying precisely what Calonne and Brienne were desperately essaying in 1787–88: namely, the securing of an adequate revenue base for French foreign and domestic policy, in the present and in the future.

It might be easy at this point to marvel at the Parisian judges for their ingenuousness in financial affairs, to dismiss them for their obstinate and selfish defense of privilege. Undoubtedly they were endowed with a normal measure of obstinacy and selfishness; but was their myopia in matters of urgent importance to the king's policymakers entirely their own fault? Or did the *parlementaires'* naïveté and shortsightedness derive ultimately from that dangerous constitutional flaw in the grand edifice of Bourbon absolutism, the growing isolation of the French kings from their more articulate and prospering subjects? We must believe that this was the case; these *parlementaires* in actuality leave us no choice in the matter, as their failure to appreciate the ministers' fiscal nightmare suggests so dramatically what civic support the monarchy forfeited through its splendid isolationism at Versailles.

Furthermore, the Parlement discovered very early in the prerevolutionary crisis that its worsening relations with the crown were compelling it willy-nilly to spell out the explosive constitutional implications of the government's difficulties. The Parlement, that is to say, found itself taking the lead in appealing for taxation with representation, civil liberties, and a highly novel conception of French kingship itself.

On the first issue, there had been occasional calls in the court for the Estates General all through the earlier years of Louis XVI's reign.[42] But what had only been, through 1786, a minority opinion rapidly became the official court position with the advent of the Lamoignon and Brienne initiatives. As early as 24–26 July 1787, Ferrand's remonstrances were heading in this direction:

> It was left to Your Majesty to revive those national assemblies that made the grandeur of Charlemagne's reign, that mended the misfortunes of King John, that cooperated with the Parlement in reestablishing Charles VII upon the throne. If ever the Nation could conceive that hope, it is doubtless in the celebrated epoch when the authorities have recognized that mystery leads only to distrust and weakness; that the more force [the government] commands, the more confidence it must command; and that to entrust part of the administration to the provincial assemblies is to enlighten and even to invigorate the government, and not to enfeeble it. It is in the era when Your Majesty, in calling the Notables around Him to aid Him with their counsel, has chosen those capable of telling Him the truth, as it was His will to hear the truth.

And what could provincial assemblies and Notables presage if not the Estates General?

> In bringing all zealous attention to the examination of the diverse objects submitted to their consideration, in announcing abuses which cried out for reform, in suggesting remedies that they judged appropriate, the Notables have prepared the way for the return to the Nation of that grand and noble censure, which it has so frequently exercised upon itself; the return of those incredible sacri-

fices which seem to cost it nothing, when they are requested by a sensitive monarch and necessitated by a genuine need.

After all, what could the king conceivably fear from the "grand and noble censure" of the Estates? The sovereign "can never be greater than when surrounded by his subjects, he has nothing to dread save for their excessive love, he has no precautions to take except to shield himself against offers that would be above their means; all must gain from that convocation."[43]

What Ferrand's proclamation did not quite state on 26 July, First President Etienne François d'Aligre insisted upon forthrightly at the *lit de justice* of 6 August:

> The constitutional principle of the French Monarchy is that taxes be consented to by those who must pay them; a beneficent king, Sire, cannot possibly have the heart to alter this principle which is associated with the primordial laws of your state, with those which assure authority and guarantee obedience.[44]

From this time forward, the Parisian magistrates, if not insisting unconditionally upon the Estates' resurrection (we shall soon see that not all of them relished this prospect), nevertheless did persist in something like the American colonials' principle of "no taxation without representation."[45] Given the inexorable financial implications of *raison d'état*, however, these two positions really came to one and the same thing. To some extent, the judges only anticipated in 1787 the following year's burgeoning national consensus on the need to revive the historic organ of consultation.

Then, again, there were the other rights of taxpayers—of all Frenchmen, for that matter, whether taxpayers or no. The parlementary advocacy of monarchy in France was, after all, predicated upon the distinction between the good, lawful sovereign (at this juncture, Louis XVI) and his evil and despotic ministers (Calonne, Brienne, and above all the turncoat Lamoignon). And so the judges in the heat of their confrontation with the crown over the stamp tax and the *subvention territoriale* opened a veritable frontal assault upon the ramparts of Bourbon absolutism. Here were the magistrates speaking from Troyes on 27 August 1787:

> the French Monarchy would be reduced to the condition of despotism if it were true that ministers abusing the king's authority could dispose of persons by *lettres de cachet*, of property by *lits de justice*, and of civil or criminal affairs by evoking cases from the

courts or quashing proceedings, and could suspend the course of justice by banishing individual judges and arbitrarily exiling entire tribunals.[46]

Yet these words were tame when measured against the increasingly radical rhetoric flowing from the pens of Duval d'Eprémesnil and other militant justices in the months that followed. Here, for example, in remonstrances against *lettres de cachet* voted on 11 March 1788, were the *parlementaires* discoursing very much in the manner of John Locke or Jean Jacques Rousseau:

Man is born free and his happiness depends upon justice. Liberty is an imprescriptible right. It consists in being able to live according to the laws; justice is a universal duty, and this [duty] is anterior to the laws themselves, which assume its existence and must direct it, but which can never sacrifice it to either kings or subjects.

Justice and liberty! there is, Sire, the principle and the object of all society, there is the unshakeable foundation of all power. . . .

The nature of man . . . leads him to join those of his own kind and live in society, subjected to general conventions, that is, to laws. But conventions that were to subjugate him without protecting him would no longer be laws, but rather irons. . . . all legitimate submission is voluntary in its principle. . . . the people's consent to the use of *lettres de cachet* would therefore be incompatible with the use of reason, but reason is man's natural condition as society is; thus the use of *lettres de cachet* is repugnant to man's nature, both as reasonable and as sociable.[47]

Is it any wonder that exactly one month later, in remonstrances voted by the judges to protest the *séance royale* of 19 November 1787, the king's plenitude of power should itself have been challenged?

The sole will of the king is not a complete law; the simple expression of that will is not a national form of law; in order for that will to command adherence, it must be published legally; for it to be published legally, it must be freely verified. . . .

God forbid that these principles should ever bear injury to Your Majesty's legislative power! The right to verify the laws is not the right to make them; but if the authority which makes the law could hinder its verification or arrogate that function to itself, then, verification being no more than a derisory precaution or a vain formality, the will of a man could replace the public will and the State would fall under the hand of despotism.[48]

The *parlementaires* and their partisans might argue that this was no more than Montesquieu's doctrine of tempered monarchy, no more than what the crown had tacitly conceded ever since the Regency. Viewed from Versailles, however, such assertions must have seemed little less than sheer madness, signifying as they did the Parlement's assumption of *carte blanche* (failing the Estates General) to obstruct implementation of desperately needed reforms.

By the end of April 1788, alarming rumors concerning the exasperated ministers' designs against the *parlements* provoked a desire at the Palais de Justice to anticipate any government coup with a comprehensive statement of parlementary constitutional beliefs. The upshot, of course, was Duval d'Epremesnil's famous *arrêté* of 3 May purporting to list the "fundamental laws" of the kingdom. This celebrated and incendiary decree proclaimed

... that France is a monarchy, governed by the King, according to the laws;

That among these laws, several which are fundamental embrace and consecrate:

The right of the ruling house to the Throne, from male to male, by order of primogeniture, to the exclusion of daughters and of their descendants;

The right of the Nation to accord subsidies freely through the organ of the Estates General convoked regularly and composed correctly;

The customs and the capitulations of the provinces;

The irrevocable tenure of the magistrates;

The right of the courts in each province to verify the King's laws and to order their registration only insofar as they conform with the constituting laws of the province as well as with the fundamental laws of the State;

The right of each citizen never to be brought in any matter before any judges other than his natural judges, who are those designated for him by the law;

And the right, without which all the others are useless, not to be arrested, in virtue of any order whatsoever, unless one is immediately remanded into the competent judges' hands.

The *parlementaires*, anticipating the heavy blows of the government, declared solemnly that they were now trustfully committing these "inviolable" laws "into the hands of the King, his august family, the Peers of the Realm, the Estates General and each of the Orders ... which together form the Nation."[49]

It would have been manifestly impossible for Louis XVI and his ministers, indoctrinated in the magnificent traditions of the French monarchy, to accept in the spring of 1788 a constitutional catechism guaranteeing absolute tenure to magistrates, the absolute right of all sovereign courts in Paris and the provinces to reject "illegal" legislation, the periodicity of Estates General freely according (or refusing?) tax revenue to the government, all provincial privileges and liberties, and all rights of habeas corpus to all subjects. Louis XVI (not to mention Henri IV or Louis XIV) could not have tolerated such a litany of constitutional liberalism as long as a fight for the absolute monarchy still seemed worth the candle; hence the crown's swift response in the form of Brienne's and Lamoignon's coup against the magistracy on 5 May. Unfortunately for Louis and his ministers, however, the attempt to drive a wedge between Duval d'Eprémesnil's faction in the Enquêtes and Requêtes and the presumably more cautious and responsible seniors of the Grand' Chambre foundered upon the rock of parlementary solidarity. One may still consult today at the Archives nationales the individual and collective letters signed by every one of the judges on 9 May 1788 as they refused service in the new Plenary Court and anathematized Lamoignon's comprehensive judicial reform.[50]

Embedded in this increasingly radical critique of the fiscal and constitutional aspects of French monarchy was at least one other notion that any sovereign of the *ancien régime* must necessarily have repudiated: namely, the idea that the monarch in France was unavoidably becoming little more than a distinguished servant of a dynamic and evolving master, the impersonal historic collectivity manifesting itself alternately as the "state" or as the "nation."

In a sense, this was anathema to the *parlementaires* as well as to the king and ministers they were so doggedly combating. In their very effort to distinguish between the good and lawful monarch and his sometimes despotic advisers and policymakers, the magistrates naturally wished to preserve Louis XIV's apocryphal definition of *personal* kingship: "l'état, c'est moi." Under the relentless pressures generated by the government's fiscal crisis in the late 1780s, however, the jurists gradually had to abandon the fiction that the state was reducible to the person of the king. We find them doing this as early as July of 1787 in the remonstrances against the stamp tax authored by that committed royalist, Antoine François Claude Ferrand, who stated that

... the Frenchman ... may believe his means to be as limitless as his love; but those very means should be carefully managed; those taxes which he pays to the King are a subvention which he owes only to the State ... the Sovereign is merely the dispenser of such funds . . . all that is not employed for public purposes belongs always to the taxpayers.[51]

In this astonishing statement the king seemingly ranks third and last in importance—after the taxpayers and "public purposes." He is, at most, the steward of public funds disbursed for public purposes. Although Ferrand and his colleagues may not have genuinely conceived the French monarch's role in such depreciative terms, their deteriorating relationship with the government was inexorably pushing them toward revolutionary pronouncements in their remonstrances and *arrêtés*.

How, after all, could they strike back at the ministers without invoking the interests of the state, the taxpayers, "public purposes"—and, ultimately, the nation? Accordingly, these collective interests gained ground steadily over monarch, ministers, and magistracy itself in parlementary propaganda as the prerevolutionary crisis deepened. Finally, in the "reiterated" protests of 30 April 1788 the judges sang a veritable paean to the "Nation":

> An excess of despotism being the only resource of the enemies of the Nation and of the truth, they have not feared to employ it. . . .
> The French Constitution seemed to be forgotten. They called the assembly of the Estates General an idle fancy. Richelieu and his cruelties, Louis XIV and his glory, the Regency and its disorders, the late king's ministers and their insensitivity, seemed to have effaced even the Nation from minds and hearts forever. . . . the ministry had neglected nothing . . . to make the French Nation fall. But the Parlement remained. . . . Advised suddenly of the condition of the finances, forced to comment upon two disastrous edicts, it . . . saw for the Nation only one resource: the Nation itself. . . . On 6 July, it called for the Estates General; on 19 September, it formally declared its own incompetence [to replace the Estates General]; on 19 November, Your Majesty Himself announced the Estates General; two days later, you promised them, you fixed their date, your word is sacred. Let men find on earth or search in history's annals for a single empire in which the King and the Nation have peacefully made such great strides in so little time: the King toward justice, the Nation toward liberty![52]

Furthermore, pursued the judges with a slight bow to their own profession, "it is precisely because it is not given to kings to be ceaselessly on guard against error or temptation, and to save the Nation from abandonment to the unfortunate effects of the abused royal will, that the Nation demands, in the matter of laws, verification in the courts." As for the cutting issue of taxation, the "prior concession" of the Estates General was in this area essential, "in order to be sure that the will of the King conforms to justice and his requests conform to the needs of the State."[53]

What a lecture to give to the king of France! Things had come to such a pass by 1788 that the "Nation" (whatever that was) could be portrayed as demanding registration of laws in the courts to ward off the consequences of royal error or weakness or naïveté, and portrayed as assuring itself (through the Estates General) of the justness of the king's will and of the public need for his taxes. Was the "Nation" then in practice to determine everything, and the recently absolute king nothing? It is not surprising that the Parlement's critics accused it then (and have accused it since) of abandoning the monarch with whom it ought to have been closing ranks at a juncture so perilous for both sides.

Although the foregoing analysis would not require that harsh a judgment upon the *parlementaires*, there is no denying a practical contradiction in magisterial attitudes toward the monarchy on the eve of the Revolution. The justices rendered homage to Louis XVI and to royal tradition with perfect sincerity, but as these rather old-fashioned monarchists increasingly wrestled with the reforms requisite for modernized state policy they could not avoid trumpeting ideas inimical to traditional as well as "bureaucratic" kingship. Part of the explanation for this paradox lies, of course, in the judges' conviction that they must also advocate a whole range of *social* interests.

Ambivalence toward the Social Elite

If the *parlementaires* were of two minds in considering their duties toward the crown, they were equally hesitant when it came to championing upper-class pretensions in 1787–88. This was as true for Duval d'Eprémesnil and other antigovernment incorrigibles as it was for the more prudent members of the tribunal—and not just on the notorious issue of the Estates General in September 1788. It was one matter to defend the established prerogatives of the elite; it was quite another to endorse ambitions in the first two orders that might upset the delicate balance of institutional forces preserving (among other things) magisterial influence in public affairs.

We would expect that the *parlementaires'* defense of clerical and noble privilege was informed as always by a profound attachment to the social hierarchy and inequality characteristic of the old regime, and this was certainly the case. Even as the kingdom was teetering on the brink of revolution late in 1788, Avocat-Général Séguier was still fulminating against subversive egalitarian principles at the Palais de Justice. A peer's denunciation of an anonymous squib offering political advice to the awakening Third Estate on 16 December provoked this outburst by the senior *avocat-général* the following day:

> We will consequently say that we envisage this publication as the first effort of an anarchy ready to break out, and if the guardian of the constitution does not hasten in his wisdom to ward off the effect of that seditious literature, it will become the seed of disorders which the system of equality pleases itself to introduce into the ranks and orders of society. . . .
> By what misfortune do we see these thoughtless assertions unceasingly reappearing? Is it possible to blind oneself to the point of asserting that the people by themselves constitute the whole Nation, that their interests alone must be consulted, that their consent alone suffices? Can one commit to oblivion the antique form of our general assemblies? The distinctions between the three orders, the right which they have to deliberate separately, and the equality of suffrage of each of the three orders? Destroy that respective independence, upset that equilibrium that is so wise, accord preference to the greatest number, and you will banish from society the spirit of concord that must penetrate all hearts.

This scurrilous work, pursued Séguier heatedly, menaced "the interests of the Clergy and the Nobility, all of whose prerogatives it erased."[54] Séguier's associates concurred in this indictment. Their *arrêté* committed the offending work to flames and condemned it as "seditious . . . attacking the rights of all the orders . . . contrary to the true interests of the third estate and of all the orders whose liberty and properties it compromises together."[55] Two days later the court reiterated these sentiments in reprimanding one Dr. Joseph Ignace Guillotin (of whom the world was soon to hear more) for stirring up elements within the Parisian Third Estate.[56] Two days after that, First President Lefevre d'Ormesson journeyed to Versailles to harangue the king on, among other things, the "dangerous effervescence" that was spreading throughout his kingdom thanks to "foolhardy spirits" peddling their "ideas of innovation" to all gullible enough to pay notice. The ruin of France would follow if Louis did not take arms against this threatening chaos.[57] The magistrates at times might be politicians enough to play for the popular favor, but in their hearts and (for the most part) in their remonstrances and *arrêtés* they were unabashed partisans and paladins of the social inequality so characteristic of the *ancien régime*.

In light of this philosophy (which of course served certain magisterial interests so well), what could be more natural than to find the *parlementaires* vociferously defending clerical and noble privileges throughout the prerevolutionary crisis? Thus, Procureur-Général Joly de Fleury inveighed against a proposal submitted to the Notables in early 1787 to abolish serfdom where it still existed in France. "The King has freed [the serfs] in his domain. The King has invited the seigneurs to follow his example. The King cannot force them to do so without doing injury to their property rights."[58] Thus, the *parlementaires* rejected out of hand Lamoignon's sharp curtailment of seigneurial justice a year later.[59] The *arrêté* offered by Duval d'Eprémesnil on 13 August 1787 put forth a spirited defense of clergy and nobility against the "unconstitutional" principle of the *contrainte solidaire* descried in Loménie de Brienne's legislation establishing the territorial subvention. The same decree, it is noteworthy, evoked the rural world of lords and peasants, a world the legislation at issue must rudely disturb:

> The highest Nobleman, like every seigneur upon his estates, must tremble to see himself responsible in common with all his vassals not only for the contribution of the poor or others whom vices common in the countryside prevent from cultivating their property; but also responsible for all the lands in common or waste or not amenable to cultivation that lie within the extent of the seigneurie.[60]

A week before, First President d'Aligre had said essentially the same in responding to the government's show of force at the *lit de justice* of 6 August. The *vingtième*, an *imposition de quotité*, had quite properly been set for everybody at the same "fixed and determined" rate, he had observed then; but the projected "territorial subvention," an *impôt de répartition*, would set off a mad scramble within each province, *élection*, and parish for undertaxation at the expense of the neighboring provinces, *élections*, and parishes. Within the same parish, fathers and sons (and, of course, lords and vassals) would soon be at daggers drawn in an unholy competition to avoid heavier taxation. The *impôt de répartition* would amount to a *contribution solidaire*, that constant bugbear of the *parlementaires*.[61] What d'Aligre had left unstated here (and what Duval d'Eprémesnil's *arrêté* verbalized the following week) was the suspicion that rich landowners of the sword—and of the robe as well—would be affected the most unfavorably by the new tax. And, insofar as social status coincided with wealth in the countryside, this would have been no more than true.

Parlementary advocacy of existing clerical and noble privilege, then, was not in doubt and never could be. This was to be expected. But was it also to be expected that in this crisis of the absolute monarchy the Parisian judges would countenance any radical concession of influence in public affairs to the upper classes? The evidence germane to this question is not and perhaps never can be entirely satisfactory, but it strongly suggests a negative response. The magistrates were not about to throw all other interests—royal, judicial, bourgeois, "popular"—overboard in order to embrace a new political state of affairs dominated by miter and sword.

True, we have seen the old *procureur-général* of the court muttering darkly against Calonne's enlightened proposal to abolish serfdom where it still existed in the kingdom, but this instinctive defense of a seigneurial right in no way contradicted Joly de Fleury's recognition that this and other vestigial institutions were continuing to retreat before the historic advance of royal (and, consequently, parlementary) authority. The judges might as conservators of legal tradition and as lords themselves assail Lamoignon's curtailment of seigneurial justice, but they had always been the first to proclaim the subordination of seigneurial justice to royal justice in the hierarchy of tribunals.[62] As for their adamant opposition to increased taxation of clergy and nobility, that was an old story at the Palais de Justice—but so, too, was the magisterial solicitude shown upon occasion for "common" taxpayers and about to reappear in the politics of 1787–88. The judges would articulate the interests of the social elite only so long as those interests were not perceived as pretensions to radical change in the corridors of administration and power.

Certainly the veterans of the court, weaned on the Gallican tradition, could have brooked no such pretensions in the First Estate. Only a few years had passed since the specter of reviving Jesuitism, and Necker's experimentation with provincial assemblies, had provoked parlementary protests against clerical influence and immunities in France.[63] Then, shortly after the Parlement's return from exile at Troyes in September 1787, First President d'Aligre sent Louis XVI an indignant memorandum entitled "Motive of hatred against the Parlements" in which he listed the parties allegedly guilty of slandering the judiciary to discredit it in royal eyes. Among these culpable interests were "the clergy whose pretensions are often beaten back, the Court of Rome whose enterprises have so frequently necessitated the remonstrances of the Magistrates," and "a powerful order that [attempts] incessantly to reappear and that believes the Parlements to be the authors of its destruction and an obstacle to its return"—a transparent allusion to the Society of Jesus. These factions, d'Aligre assured the king, "had an equal interest in debasing the Parlements" but could not possibly do so as long as the courts "had the support of the Sovereign and the people."[64] In an impassioned speech of 9 February 1787, Robert de Saint-Vincent, renowned Jansenist of the Grand' Chambre and confidant of Duval d'Eprémesnil, had already made an oblique attack upon the proscribed Jesuits, linking these traditional persecutors of Protestants with "those who destroyed Port-Royal."[65] The charges of the two men reflected a latent suspicion of clerical ambitions in their company that could very well have been fanned into open hostility by any striking revival of clerical influence in political and administrative affairs. When, on 17 December 1788, Avocat-Général Séguier complacently praised the First Estate for the "spirit of charity" which it derived from "the holy religion it teaches to us," he was but putting the clergy in its proper place. Who can say that Séguier, in going on to describe the most exalted order as "ready to honor itself by sacrificing its immunities," was not also betraying the noble landowner's satisfaction at seeing the First Estate's immense wealth liable, at long last, to taxation?[66]

More intriguing and significant was the *parlementaires'* wariness toward the secular nobility, a wariness they revealed well before promulgating their fateful decree of September 1788 concerning the Estates General. For example, in the very process of decrying Calonne's intention to levy additional taxation upon the nobility, the Parlement's *procureur-général* voiced his fear early in 1787 that such a policy could conceivably touch off increased political activity in the provinces. Was it not possible, asked Joly de Fleury at the Assembly of Notables, that the nobles would react by demanding that they be exempted as in earlier centuries from *all* compulsory taxation and that all "notables" would demand permission to assemble in the provinces to debate the issue? And could the sovereign afford to allow such assemblages?[67] Joly de Fleury's use of the term "notables" suggests that his misgivings on this particular issue may have extended to prominent provincial bourgeois; nonetheless, long and bitter historical experience indicated noblemen as the most likely instigators of rural "sedition."

For that matter, the specter of revived noble aspirations in the arena of provincial affairs had haunted parlementary minds just a few years previously in connection with Necker's provincial assemblies. The judges, we have seen, were jealous administrators who wanted to see no novel assemblages of landowners usurping their cherished roles of coadministering rural France with the intendants and articulating rural grievances in remonstrances to the king. Accordingly, Necker's administrative experiment had occasioned some unflattering comments upon ambitious rustic noblemen in parlementary papers, and in 1781 the court's leaders had gone so far as to complain to Louis XVI in a confidential memorandum about the inconvenient political pretensions of "each provincial gentleman."[68] Now, in 1787, provincial assemblies were once again the order of the day, challenging parlementary gentlemen anew.

The remarks of the Joly de Fleury brothers upon Calonne's new provincial bodies illuminate the social conservatism that held sway as always at the Palais de Justice. The *procureur-général* observed that "in general, all assemblies of residents excite much fermentation in minds, which renders them constantly tumultuous." Plainly he was worried about the potential in these institutions for subversion of the sacrosanct social order, for at another point in his commentary he spoke ominously of "a dangerous confusion of ranks . . . regarded as contrary to the constitution of the Monarchy."[69] But this very concern led him to view the first two orders as stabilizing elements in the social hierarchy and not as a resurgent political elite. The assemblies, the *procureur-général* remarked, might detract from the respect "due to persons of the order of the clergy and the order of the nobility," and this would be most unfortunate, because clerics and nobles "contributed eminently by their example toward containing the French people in the sentiments of love and submission they naturally show to their sovereigns."[70] Clerics and noblemen who led the way by loving and submitting to their sovereign conformed very neatly to the parlementary vision of an honorable but quiescent social elite that would never dream of fomenting political trouble in the state.

But President Joly de Fleury invoked this vision even more explicitly than did his brother. To see this, we need only reconsider a document analyzed for slightly different purposes earlier; namely, the president's laudatory memorandum of April 1787 upon the traditional assemblies of Bresse, Bugey, and Gex.[71] This essay, we recall, reflected its author's royalism precisely by positing a balance of all existing social forces as a prerequisite for the survival of monarchical authority in provincial France. If, on the one hand, the administrative bodies in these three small *pays* kept the commoners' delegates in their proper place, the Third Estate contingent on the other hand was useful for counteracting the influence of the clerical and noble contingents, and thus for preserving the king's authority. As noted in an earlier context, the vote of the Third Estate was doubled in the governing "councils" of these institutions. Consequently, the "clergy and nobility could not dominate proceedings, because the third Estate has two [votes] against their two, resulting in tie votes. The king's authority is undiminished because it retains the power to decide issues." The president summed up his remarks in a manner strikingly reminiscent of past parlementary statements on the issue of the provincial assemblies. "What is principally to be feared is that the clergy and nobility might have too much influence, or that one day they might have none at all."[72] For Jean Omer Joly de Fleury, as for his brother, preservation of the status quo in society required that the high and mighty, just as surely as humbler folk, know their proper place. Convictions akin to these probably help to explain the *parlementaires'* determination in July 1787 to solicit from Louis XVI those "promised regulations" that would ensure the "stability" of the provincial, district, and municipal assemblies whose establishment they had reluctantly endorsed.

At this point, however, an unavoidable question arises. If one of the Paris Parlement's most powerful elders could hasten in April 1787 to praise administrative assemblies in southeastern France for the equal influence they accorded to the first two orders and the third, how could this same magistrate and his colleagues call, less than eighteen months later, for an Estates General in which clerics and lay nobles could very well outvote the Third Estate by two to one? The reference here of course is to the notorious parlementary decree of 25 September 1788 recommending that the upcoming Estates General follow the precedent of 1614—a precedent that implied equal contingents representing the three orders and voting by order rather than by head.[73] This decree was hugely unpopular and almost overnight cost the Parlement the adulation it had won by its opposition to the Brienne and Lamoignon ministries. Did the judges upon this occasion (involving more than the fate of Bresse, Bugey, and Gex) betray their solidarity with a resurgent and reactionary aristocracy? The common impression that they did so seems untenable in light of available evidence.

In the first place, there was, at least initially, something less than a clarion call for the Estates General in the Parlement. True, the deadlock with the government over its finances gradually wore away magisterial resistance to such a risky constitutional expedient—but the resistance was very real and apparently died hard. There are many indications of this. The *procureur-général* had anticipated his associates' coolness toward the Estates General when, at the first Assembly of Notables in early 1787, he had expressed misgivings about the prospect of revived provincial Estates as well as about the establishment of Calonne's provincial assemblies.[74] Neither he nor his influential brother were likely to evince any great enthusiasm over the possibility of a general convocation of the Estates. Nor were their fellows of the Grand' Chambre, for the most part. When several members of the Cour des Pairs joined to their condemnation of "ministerial despotism" a demand for the Estates General in 1787, the young magistrate Etienne-Denis Pasquier noted the predominant reaction among the court's seniors: "The sober heads of the Grand' Chambre were troubled at the prospect. I could never forget what one of these old judges said to me then as he passed behind my bench and saw how enthused I was: 'Young man, a similar idea was often brought forward during your grandfather's time; this is what he always said to us then: "Messieurs, this is not a game for children; the first time that France sees the Estates General, she will also see a terrible revolution."' "[75] Not that doubts on the subject were limited strictly to the more seasoned jurists. When the Cour des Pairs eventually did decide, in late July 1787, to adopt the position that only the Estates General could legitimize the extended stamp tax and the *subvention territoriale*, the author of the resultant remonstrances of 24–26 July, the young counselor Ferrand, was penning sentiments that he actually found repugnant. He later recalled how he and another youthful *parlementaire*, Anselme François d'Outremont de Minière, strove vigorously but in vain to hold off a formal request for the Estates General, "so contrary to the Parlement's principles, so dangerous and so impolitic at all times." At least his remonstrances, "drawn up in a respectful form," had been preferred over the more radical draft offered by Duval d'Eprémesnil—perhaps one further sign of continuing apprehension in the court over the issue.[76]

As late as the dramatic *séance royale* of 19 November 1787, ambivalence on this question was manifesting itself in the court's senior chamber if not necessarily in the Enquêtes and Requêtes. Here was the king's *rapporteur* in the Grand' Chambre, Abbé Tandeau, addressing king, peers, and colleagues on the matter:

> Finally, can one regard the Estates General, themselves, as an effective remedy? Their convocation would probably bring great consolation to all hearts: Your Majesty would find salutary plans, wise advice, enlightened measures there. God forbid that I should seek to alienate Your Majesty from this grand means, the sole, perhaps, appropriate in the circumstances! But the moment of calamity is not always the most auspicious time for these great Assemblies. There are crises in Empires during which multitudes of advisers constitute an obstacle to the common welfare rather than a means for achieving it; and the diversity of opinions which a necessary diversity of interests must bring into that grand Assembly could only perhaps prolong the sickness instead of curing it.

In any case, continued Tandeau after having thus contradicted himself, the Estates General at best could only suggest new taxes or repudiation of the national debt, both of which expedients were unthinkable.

> Therefore it would perhaps be more prudent for Your Majesty to conceive in his wisdom a wise plan of financial retrenchment and liberation from debt; so that, once presented to that august Assembly, it would guide all deliberations, it would in a sense be consecrated by the Nation's unanimous desire, and it would leave to [the Nation's] zealous discretion only the choice of the means to confirm it and to accelerate its effects.[77]

Was the *rapporteur* arguing for or against the Estates General? Both, perhaps, in that, like many another moderate in the Cour des Pairs, he was being pulled in opposite directions by clashing and ultimately irreconcilable concerns.

As the months wore on, of course, the *parlementaires'* stance on constitutional matters became progressively more radical; the dangerous invocation of the historic national consultative assembly became more frequent and insistent. Yet, again, the reservations voiced at the Palais de Justice throughout 1787 make it logical to believe that the court's flirtation with such risky ideas reflected the unrelenting pressure of events (that is, the intensifying storm in relations with the crown) rather than wholehearted enthusiasm for Estates General dominated by the "aristocracy."

As it turned out, the issue was taken out of the Parlement's hands altogether in 1788 by the government's reluctant conclusion that the Estates General must convene the following year. The judges now were facing a fait accompli whether they liked it or not, and it was only natural for them to rally to their traditionalist principles by conjuring up and recommending the precedent of 1614 in their fateful decree of 25 September. Two participants in the session of 25 September later attempted to explain the motivation behind this decree, and, significantly, both underscored the purely conservative reflex of the court on that day. In an address at the opening session of the second Assembly of Notables on 6 November 1788, President Lefevre d'Ormesson had this to say:

> Already, by examining certain historical documents in the archives of Justice, your Parlement, Sire, has noted these two characteristics [that is, regularity and convenience] in the form utilized in 1614, and has resolved to call for it. It will merit all Your Majesty's attention, not only because of the legal formalities with which it is accompanied to preserve the rights of all and those of each person; but because its origin is ancient, and because . . . it seems to demonstrate the correct custom and habit of the Monarchy.[78]

"Regularity," "convenience," "correct custom and habit," and antiquity for the sake of antiquity—these had been the determining considerations behind the court's invocation of 1614, according to Lefevre d'Ormesson.

But it was perhaps even more telling that one of his junior colleagues of the turbulent Enquêtes, Guy Marie Sallier, should have recalled in later years a similar motivation behind the decree of 25 September:

> The preceding ministry had imprudently stated that there was no sure rule for the convocation, composition, and constitution of the Estates General. . . . The parlement judged that all would be lost, if no one could refer to certainties on this very important point . . .

and although it must certainly forfeit its popularity in pronouncing against democracy, it did not hesitate at this juncture to fulfill its duty by recalling the fundamental principles on the legal form of the Estates General; the last which had been convened, that of 1614, seemed . . . to be the appropriate model, having been perfectly regular.[79]

Again, we note that concept of "regularity." Lefevre d'Ormesson could have penned precisely the same words. The magistrates' constitutional radicalism may have been one of the factors contributing to the government's convocation of the Estates General in 1789, but when forced to regard this convocation as a certainty the Parlement's immediate response was to fall back upon what seemed to be the prescription of the past.

Yet the *arrêté* of 25 September 1788 was itself overturned a scant ten weeks later by a coalition of insurgents in the Grand' Chambre and Enquêtes. This action suggested to some contemporaries (and to some later historians as well) that Duval d'Eprémesnil and his confederates were taking up the cudgels in defense and furtherance of an "aristocratic" revolt or revolution as the political crisis deepened. But once again, the available evidence points to quite a different interpretation. To be sure, from the time of his entry into the Parlement in 1775 Duval d'Eprémesnil had (along with his judicious seniors of the Grand' Chambre) ardently championed existing privileges of the first two orders. But he had been equally quick (as in a controversy of 1784 pitting the mayor of Bordeaux against the marshals of France) to reject and even ridicule novel "aristocratic" pretensions that seemed to menace monarchical and judicial prerogatives.[80] Duval d'Eprémesnil maintained this orientation throughout 1787–88, although his royalist allegiance, so movingly attested by the correspondence cited earlier, was often obscured by his fanatical opposition to "ministerial despotism." As we know, he achieved notoriety in August 1787 with his decree condemning the crown's fiscal edicts and the *lit de justice* of 6 August that had compelled their registration. However, it is noteworthy that this decree, even while restating the Parlement's traditional opposition to heavier and demeaning taxation of clerical and noble lands, sketched the equally traditional parlementary picture of a *passive* lay nobility. Duval d'Eprémesnil's *arrêté* asserted

that the gentleman retired upon his domain, whom it is important for the State to cherish, finds himself virtually chased from his château or humble cottage, when he has to pay taxes upon the habitation that is only an object of continual expense and upkeep for him. . . . it is however that retreat that makes him love France, [it is] an asylum where, sheltered from ambition, he can practice virtue, in preserving for his posterity the inheritance that the preceding reigns did not at all begrudge his ancestors.[81]

Duval d'Eprémesnil here was the archetypal *parlementaire* of the French capital, idealizing the country gentleman as a quiescent soul desiring nothing more than to be left in peace to cultivate his lands and his rustic virtues. This judge, and the crushing majority in court who endorsed his statement, knew very well that to defend a rural elite living off its lands, privileges, and memories was in no way to jeopardize the influence wielded in judicial and political affairs by the sovereign courts.

Duval d'Eprémesnil established himself even more firmly in the government's bad books in the late winter and spring of 1788 with his outpouring of pronunciamentos against the ministers' "despotism." He was eventually imprisoned in Provence. But ten weeks after the Parlement's triumphant reinstatement in the fall, this irrepressible spokesman for the magisterial opposition signaled his own return to Paris by securing passage of the decree of 5 December 1788 over the scandalized protest of his more mature associates.[82] It was this *Arrêt sur la situation actuelle de la Nation* that overturned the decree of 25 September and that has signified to some the onset of "aristocratic revolution" within the kingdom's foremost *parlement*.

The decree of 5 December 1788 attempted in part to restore the tribunal's shattered popularity by disavowing the reference in the decree of 25 September to the 1614 Estates General.[83] It proclaimed the court's constitutional incompetence to determine the number of delegates representing the Third Estate, referred this matter to the king's wisdom, and implored Louis XVI to convene the Estates General as soon as possible. Furthermore, it accepted the equality of the three orders in matters pertaining to taxation. On the other hand, d'Eprémesnil's decree did not repudiate the principle of the "vote by order," and thus left open the possibility of domination of the assembly by the clergy and secular noblesse. The decree also pointed toward a close cooperation between the sovereign law courts and the regularly convening Estates General in the future. The royal ministers, answerable to the Estates General and *parlements* for their actions, were to be judged by the latter for any malfeasance in office alleged against them by the former. Finally, the *parlements* would ratify no impost, indeed, no law of any kind that lacked the sanction of the Estates General.

A most eminent historian has characterized this decree as "the supreme expression of that aristocratic revolution that Duval d'Eprémesnil, Huguet de Sémonville, Robert de Saint-Vincent, and the Abbé Le-coigneux had had in mind throughout the crisis."[84] Yet in the pamphlet he had published on 7 December to explain his position on the Estates General, Duval d'Eprémesnil revealed quite different intentions. He conceded candidly that he still supported "the just prerogatives of the Nobility and the Clergy," but he just as forthrightly endorsed "the lib-erty of all, the property of all, the rights of all." Yet the crucial argument in his tract was the argument for the traditional "vote by order" in the Estates General:

> Separate voting by the orders, each one so independent of the others that two of them cannot bind the third, that is the Constitution. . . .
> That having been stated . . . carefully preserve that vote by order, and preserve the orders' independence, and you will fortify them . . . against Ministerial enterprises, in giving affairs the time to ripen, individuals the time to become acquainted with each other, and Intrigues the time to betray themselves. . . .
> Oh! of course it is important that the Third Estate be fortified by number; but against whom? Against the Nobility and the Clergy? Not at all. . . . Against whom or what, then? It is essential to say it. Against Ministerial Despotism, common enemy of the King and of the three orders.

Thus, continued Duval d'Eprémesnil, let the clergy and nobility not take fright if the Third Estate should gain a more numerous representa-tion in the upcoming assembly than ever before: the "general interest," the "interest of public liberty," required it.[85]

A careful perusal of this tract makes clear that its author continued to be obsessed by "ministerial despotism"—he had, after all, recently been incarcerated by the government—and he was resolved to turn all avail-able means to the destruction of this bête noire. This meant, above all else, advocacy of a balance and collaboration among the three orders that would somehow preserve both the monarchy and "public liberty" while defeating the purposes of despotic ministers. Such institutional arrangements, by preserving each order's "independence" so that "two of them" could not "bind the third," would in effect preclude any drastic shift of power to the clergy and lay nobility or, of course, to any coali-tion involving the Third Estate. When we strip away the antiministerial polemics here, we seem to return to President Joly de Fleury's quest for a similar balance and collaboration among the social orders in his re-marks upon Bresse, Bugey, and Gex. Avocat-Général Séguier was soon to conjure up a like vision of a sacrosanct and stable social hierarchy embracing politically passive clerics, nobles, and commoners in his remarks to the plenary session of 17 December 1788, as well as in a pamphlet provocatively entitled *La Constitution renversée.*[86] For that matter, one of Duval d'Eprémesnil's alleged accomplices in "proaristocratic" politics, Huguet de Sémonville, had enunciated precisely the same ideas as early as 16 July 1787 in urging a summons to the Estates General.[87] If there was a single *parlementaire* who voted for the decree of 5 December 1788 in the belief that he was helping to initiate or to further an "aristocratic revolution," he has left no known commentary attesting to that intention.

There undoubtedly *were* certain strains of "revolution" harbored in the pronouncements of the Joly de Fleurys, Séguiers, Lefevre d'Ormessons, and Duval d'Eprémesnils, as well as in the rapturous enthusiasm of the youthful judges of the court's lower chambers who so readily embraced those pronouncements. We shall explore these strains of revolution presently. First, though, it would be worth our while to explore magisterial attitudes toward the commonalty that could be fully as complicated as magisterial conceptions of the crown and social elite on the eve of France's great sociopolitical upheaval.

Ambivalence toward the Third Estate

To examine parlementary attitudes toward the middle- and lower-class laity in 1787–88 is to plunge into a world whose infinite variety and complexities find no acknowledgment in the dry juridical term "Third Estate." Here we can locate the crushing majority of souls in the jurisdiction of the men of law ensconced in the Parisian Palais de Justice: businessmen and bourgeois *rentiers*, butchers and bakers and candlestick-makers, and many simpler folk besides, living largely uncelebrated lives in the capital and in the countryside. They, too, claimed the *parlementaires'* attention in this period, not only in the ordinary hours of judicial procedure and administrative surveillance but also in the extraordinary hours of magisterial preoccupation with controversial public affairs. And here again, ambivalence and inconsistency could manifest themselves as the Parisian jurists pronounced upon matters engaging their duty and their interest.

There were times during this troubled period when inconsistency at the Palais de Justice resulted from the intrusion into parlementary proceedings of demagogic considerations. The judges could not always resist the temptation to court the popular favor as their traditional relationship with the crown gradually broke down in 1787 and 1788. When, for instance, the court returned triumphantly from exile for the last time in September 1788, it immediately launched an inquiry into the public disorder then plaguing the capital. According to the young jurist Sallier, the inquiry sought to accuse the police, and not just the populace, of excessive behavior.[88] The tribunal issued two decrees on 23 September: the first ordered a further investigation into complaints of inordinate use of force by the police, and the second, although reverting to the customary parlementary ban against seditious gatherings in the streets, also enjoined the municipal police to exercise their duties with moderation. "The people understood that decree so well," commented Sallier, "that the tumultuous mobs and merrymaking continued as before, and the Parisian guard was regularly insulted during the evenings."[89] Less than three months later, Duval d'Eprémesnil's decree of 5 December, with which the majority of magistrates tried in vain to undo the damage wrought by the decree of 25 September, made it perfectly clear that some within the Parlement could woo public opinion. Still, the tribunal's willingness to "play politics" in such agitated times was limited. It is of interest in this regard that, whereas the decree of 25 September 1788 invoking the 1614 Estates General, a decree fated to be so hugely unpopular, was passed almost unanimously, the decree of 5 December 1788, designed in part to restore the court's popularity, could prevail only over the strenuous opposition of the more mature judges. The men of the Paris Parlement were attuned to the popular voice, but they were attuned as well to tradition and professional duty and their own elite class interests.

The company's elders in particular must have sensed the contradiction between endeavoring to appease street mobs and advocates of a "reformed" Estates General, on the one hand, and upholding the old social hierarchy, on the other. And uphold the latter they assuredly did. We are not likely to forget Procureur-Général Joly de Fleury's concern in 1787 that the new provincial assemblies might produce a "dangerous confusion of ranks ... regarded as contrary to the constitution of the Monarchy," or his conviction that clerics and nobles "contributed eminently ... toward containing the French people in the sentiments of love and submission they naturally show to their sovereigns." His presidential brother had emphasized that the Third Estate contingents in the administrative assemblies of Bresse, Bugey, and Gex were "composed only of deputies of the cities and principal market towns." After all, how could even those antique assemblages tucked away in obscure corners of the kingdom admit contingents representing an "order of peasants"? Unthinkable; and why? "It would be dangerous for France to create a fourth order; such an innovation would be contrary to the constitution of the monarchy."[90] Moreover, Avocat-Général Séguier and his confreres anathematized the subversive egalitarian principles disseminated by pamphleteers shamelessly wedded to the Third Estate's cause in December 1788. By the time Lefevre d'Ormesson addressed Louis XVI on 21 December 1788, parlementary oratory was becoming increasingly conscious of the specter of bourgeois assertiveness arm-in-arm with popular unrest.[91] The court's veterans, at least, remained faithful to the bitter end to the antediluvian schema of Estates in French society even if their company's sense of political expediency at times belied that allegiance.

In whatever forms, tradition and professionalism likely dictated parlementary behavior more consistently during the prerevolution than some of the tribunal's critics (and some of the judges themselves) allowed. But tradition and professionalism counseled championship of commoners' legitimate interests as surely as they counseled social conservatism. The Parisian magistrates demonstrated this convincingly in the summer of 1787 by rejecting Loménie de Brienne's stamp tax. This impost was to affect daily transactions in commerce as well as litigation in the courts; predictably, the Parlement was pressured by interests ranging from the booksellers and printers to the consular jurists (who dealt with lawsuits in business matters) to oppose the legislation.[92] Although the tribunal was forced to register the stamp tax along with the *subvention territoriale* at the *lit de justice* of 6 August, it struck back (as we know) at both legislative acts with Duval d'Eprémesnil's *arrêté* of 13 August. It is interesting that this decree stressed the abuse of *solidarité* in connection with individuals to be affected by the extended stamp tax even more than in connection with nobles and clerics to be affected by the new land tax. The stamp tax legislation would invoke fines against all those associated in any way with unstamped and hence untaxed documents. In his *arrêté* Duval d'Eprémesnil described the hardship likely to result from such a general provision:

> It is cruel to imagine that the lonely citizen living in the most profound solitude, the tranquil merchant working to increase the national commerce, by augmenting his personal trade, the wise practitioner consecrating his labors to the repose of families and to the service of his fellow citizens, all face the appalling prospect of finding themselves linked together in a common chain and subject, at the moment when they thought themselves least to be subject, to solidary fines, whose weight . . . would swallow up the totality of innocent as well as of guilty individuals.[93]

The decree also explained how the stamp tax would augment expenses in litigation through its levy upon documents used in justice. Palpably, then, the incendiary *arrêté* of 13 August 1787, considered in its entirety, transcended the cause of clerical and noble privilege: it exemplified the magistrates' advocacy of interests in all ranks of society.

Yet once again we are brought back to a cardinal paradox in parlementary attitudes. Defense of such a myriad of interests meant that no one institution or social class was likely to escape judicial censure altogether throughout this period. It was all very well, for instance, to applaud "the tranquil merchant working to increase the national commerce" when criticizing the government's stamp tax legislation; it was quite another thing to abide the fraudulent manipulations of "speculators" and "capitalists" involved in the trade with the Indies or in Parisian fire insurance operations, or unscrupulous activities of grain merchants that could jeopardize the supply of bread to the capital. In such circumstances, magisterial commendation could change very quickly to magisterial condemnation.

Parlementary interest in financial manipulations relative to the fire insurance business was awakened on 28 July 1787 by one Bourré de Corberon, speaking in plenary session "on behalf of the first chamber of Enquêtes." This counselor denounced certain unnamed managers of the Compagnie des Eaux de Paris who, taking advantage of royal legislation of the preceding year establishing fire insurance services within the Compagnie, were illicitly using proprietors' fire insurance premiums to speculate in the general stock of the company. Speculation, declared Bourré de Corberon, required unqualified condemnation by the court: it was "an extreme evil, that augurs a calamity for the Capital, and whose poison is already circulating throughout the Kingdom." The counselor spoke indignantly of "the criminal associations, the tortuous operations, the monstrous monopolies of the speculators," and of the "provocative stratagems of those greedy individuals whose conspiracies threaten society with imminent dissolution." Bourré de Corberon, warming to his subject, enlarged upon the nefarious cooperation between "speculators" and "capitalists" in the city:

> The most senseless sacrifices cost nothing to the speculators, provided that they can execute their operations. The capitalists who would blush to demand openly higher rates of interest than the law authorizes them to take, think that they can clandestinely share with [the speculators] the illicit profits of their transactions. Their cupidity increases by feeding upon the prodigality of those who borrow from them; it is thus that speculation comes in the end to absorb more monetary wealth than the most flourishing commerce can produce or send into circulation.

The offending parties would stop at nothing, including the diffusion of rumors attacking the reputations of individuals and the reliability of royal securities, to manipulate public attitudes toward various types of stocks and make a killing from investments in the Compagnie des Eaux. Bourré de Corberon demanded that the Parlement step in to "restore order" by proscribing "these shameful transactions in which some sell what they do not possess, what does not even exist; and others purchase what they cannot pay for."[94]

No immediate action was taken on the matter. The Cour des Pairs was at that time dueling with the ministers over their fiscal legislation. A week later, at the plenary session of 4 August, a magistrate of the Grand' Chambre launched into a tirade against unnamed "speculators" trafficking in stocks of the Compagnie des Indes as well as in shares of the Compagnie des Eaux de Paris.[95] This judge's indignation was apparently fueled in part by corporate pride, for he began by deploring the government's failure to submit for parlementary registration certain royal acts of 1785 reconstituting the Compagnie des Indes. For the most part, however, his address, like that of Bourré de Corberon the week before, was a philippic against the stockjobbing opportunities afforded all too many "capitalists" in the capital. He concluded, as had his predecessor, by exhorting his colleagues to intervene forcefully against activities as detrimental to general commerce as they were offensive to all principled Parisians. The court unanimously decreed that a special committee of jurists look into the scandal of "speculation" as it affected both the Compagnie des Eaux and the Compagnie des Indes and directed the committee to report back to the full assembly at a future date.

Almost immediately thereafter came the *lit de justice* of 6 August, followed by the Parlement's defiant response in the *arrêté* of the thirteenth and its subsequent banishment to Troyes. But the court was not yet done with the issue of stockjobbing and speculation in the capital. After the return from Troyes, renewed attacks against these activities in the Chambre des Vacations on 18 October led to further investigation by the substitutes in the *parquet*. Six days later, the Chambre des Vacations decreed that the inquest continue, pending the return of the tribunal's full membership in mid-November.[96] The court later sanctioned these actions, and although the ensuing silence upon this issue in the official minutes of proceedings suggests that more urgent affairs were occupying parlementary minds, continuing magisterial doubts about this flourishing sector of Parisian capitalism can be safely assumed.

Speculators in stocks and securities of every imaginable kind may have been multiplying in Paris just before the Revolution, but speculators in grain had been staple parlementary villains through much of the eighteenth century.[97] As judicial administrators obsessed by the need for social order, the *parlementaires* had always concerned themselves with the provisioning of grain to the capital, and had been inclined to blame shortages in this essential foodstuff upon hoarding and speculation by the grain merchants. Consequently, every ministerial campaign to remove the shackles of regulation from the grain trade had provoked protest at the Palais de Justice, for in the judges' eyes the economic freedom preached by the physiocrats and their partisans ineluctably encouraged just such hoarding and speculation, and thus meant deprivation for the needy and threatened social unrest in city and countryside. In the 1760s and 1770s the Grand' Chambre had heard myriad denunciations of alleged merchant monopolists and their defenders in high places.[98] Now, in 1787 and 1788, the old cycle of ministerial reform and magisterial censure repeated itself.

Procureur-Général Joly de Fleury signaled his company's concern on this as on so many other public issues at the first Assembly of Notables early in 1787. Calonne had submitted to the Notables his declaration reestablishing freedom in the grain commerce throughout the kingdom; the *procureur-général* was one of those who voiced serious doubts about the proposed reform.[99] The Parlement eventually ratified this legislation under Loménie de Brienne's ministry, on 25 June 1787, but Siméon-Prosper Hardy reported the following day that the vote for registration had been close. The judges, observed Hardy, were unimpressed by the "brilliant exposé and all the fair promises" included in the declaration. They recalled only too vividly how similar legislation sponsored by Turgot had fathered high prices and shortages of grain and bread which had eventually sparked widespread rioting in 1776. What was to prevent "rich and powerful persons" from using economic freedom, as they had used it before, to traffic in a vital foodstuff and so speculate upon the popular misery?[100] The court's ratification of the legislation, unenthusiastic as it apparently was, may have been facilitated by the act's provision authorizing the provinces, upon request of their assemblies or Estates, to suspend the export of grain in times of scarcity. However this may be, the following year was to see the court attentive once more to complaints from the marketplaces in the capital.

On 26 November 1788 the Parlement, reacting to the latest rise in the price of bread, ordered the officers of the *parquet* to ascertain its causes. On 13 December, Avocat-Général Séguier, speaking for the king's men, cited as contributing factors the meteorological disasters and poor harvests of the preceding two years but characteristically put the primary blame for the price increase upon the grain trade legislation and the cupidity of speculators and monopolists profiting from its provisions.

> It is not wheat that is lacking in France; the immoderate thirst for profit is making it disappear; insatiable avidity is monopolizing it; the opulent speculator still desires to enrich himself at the expense of the poor and the indigent. . . . It is time to recognize the danger of a confidence that is too blind, to reestablish a legal surveillance, to order an . . . inspection in moments of crisis, and to avert

through a wise and rigorous police the inconveniences and the abuses of an inhuman freedom that must every time victimize the people.[101]

A committee of judges was immediately appointed to recommend action on the matter. Five days later the court issued a decree reaffirming all existing regulations on the provisioning of grain to Paris. The decree restated the familiar prohibition of "any fraudulent maneuvers tending to impede the provisioning of the markets," and it enjoined the suppliers of grain to the markets to follow all existing regulations set by the police, "so that the first hour of business in the markets will be for the small consumers . . . the second for the bakers, the third for the merchants." The jurists ordered that their decree be sent "wherever need required" and that it be read out and published by all subordinate tribunals in the jurisdiction.[102]

The court also ordered its new first president Lefevre d'Ormesson to raise the matter when he next journeyed to Versailles. Accordingly, on 21 December Lefevre d'Ormesson asked Louis XVI to devote special attention to "the subsistence of the People, at a time when the severity of the season has reinforced the other causes of the high price of grain and the other misfortunes that make the People suffer." The judges could work no miracle in this vital area: "Your parlement, Sire, has done the most that it could do by issuing a decree that proscribes the schemes and intrigues employed to augment those high prices. The same decree establishes in the marketplaces the order of preference most favorable to poor persons unable to provide for themselves, but, Sire, there are insights of a superior order, resources more general and efficacious for the curing of such distressing ills."[103] In brief, the first president requested legislation to assure the poor their daily bread, but Louis, already under the shadow of the impending Estates General, put off Lefevre d'Ormesson and his colleagues with a noncommittal assurance of continued royal vigilance on the problem.

The magistrates, however, did not let the matter rest there. During February 1789 the syndics representing the Parisian bakers were called to the court to explain what they knew about the factors prolonging the economic crisis. In response, the syndics provided "some very curious information on wheat prices in France and in other countries and on the maneuvers employed to raise prices."[104] Unfortunately the court's minutes do not elaborate upon this "very curious information," but the *parlementaires* presumably were ready to believe anything concerning "maneuvers employed to raise prices," actuated as they were by unconquerable distrust of merchants trafficking in grain. The *parquet* continued its own investigation of the problem, and as late as 4 April 1789 the

Parlement approved reiterated protests on the bread issue to be delivered at Versailles. By now, however, the judges were preaching in the desert—with the Estates General almost upon them, the authorities had no further reason to heed expostulations from the Palais de Justice. The provisioning of the Parisians' daily bread was, like other matters, soon removed from the Parlement's cognizance altogether.

Patently, the magistrates' attitudes toward poor folk on the brink of revolution were as ambivalent as their attitudes toward prospering entrepreneurs. Given their allegiance to tradition, their enforcement of law and order, and their own personal interests, the *parlementaires* could not help but regard the *menu peuple* in a severely paternalistic fashion. But paternalism usually has its humanitarian aspects. It would be a bit too cynical to see in magisterial outrage over scarce and expensive foodstuffs merely an animus against grain merchants, spiced perhaps by a pinch of casual demagoguery. If, as we have seen, the jurists were humane enough to pride themselves upon their occasional acts of seigneurial philanthropy in the countryside, they were surely humane enough to pride themselves upon their cautious professional championship of the hungry in their jurisdiction. This is why parlementary oratory upon the popular misery wrought by the dearness and dearth of bread does not ring entirely false.

And, just as we can document parlementary efforts to succor the hungry, so we can record parlementary concern for those in Paris who were cold. The judges in the old regime were as active in surveillance over the trade in wood as they were over the trade in grain. Indeed, in the early 1780s the tribunal had repeatedly come to the defense of Parisians (of all classes, but especially of the lower ranks) allegedly overcharged for their firewood.[105] The officers of the *parquet* from time to time had endeavored to ascertain the reasons for price increases granted the *marchands de bois* by the authorities and had even launched inquiries into the methods used by these entrepreneurs to provision the capital. Predictably, the fiery Séguier had in plenary session accused the *marchands de bois* of conspiring to bleed the public, and the court had in formal remonstrances implored Louis XVI to roll back the price increases announced in his edicts and decrees; just as predictably, the parlementary protests had for the most part come to naught. But the justices demonstrated upon at least one occasion in the midst of the prerevolutionary crisis that the issue continued to interest them.

It was customary for the Parlement to receive reports from the *lieutenant de police* and the chief municipal officers in February detailing the state of provisions in the capital for the approaching Lenten season. The court would usually follow up these visits with a ritual plea to the archbishop of Paris to authorize the consumption of eggs during Lent.

Custom repeated itself in 1788 on 1 February, but this time with a difference. The *lieutenant de police* and his agents encountered some hard questions from the assembled magistrates about the purported dearth of foodstuffs destined for popular consumption during the upcoming religious season. After apprising the judges of the situation in the capital, the officers of both the police and the municipal administration asked for parlementary assistance in "providing for the subsistence of the poor."[106]

After thanking both groups of officials for their efforts and enjoining them to maintain their vigilance in the future, the court deliberated upon the problem in private session. In the course of the discussion, one of the *parlementaires* reminded the first president that the municipal officers had expressed fears that "in several years the wood necessary for the provisioning of Paris might be lacking." Further discussion only quickened the jurists' interest in this and related problems facing the Parisian consumers, and they consequently resolved to apprise themselves more thoroughly of the situation through the agency of their first president. Etienne François d'Aligre was to solicit from the administrators at the Hôtel de Ville additional details on the scarcity of wood that could threaten the capital in future years, and practical suggestions for averting the danger. The first president was also to ask the municipality's administrators for a "detailed report" upon "the shortage of coal that has occurred this year and upon the means for remedying it," as well as for precise information concerning the condition and maintenance of the canals upon whose waters the necessary wood, charcoal, and coal were transported to the capital. Finally, First President d'Aligre was instructed to inform the king and his ministers about what he had been able to learn from the administrators at the Hôtel de Ville and in general terms to attract royal and ministerial attention to the plight of the capital's consumers.

Subsequent minutes of parlementary proceedings fall silent upon these issues, but this is unsurprising when we recall that the court was at this very time moving into the final phase of its struggle with Lamoignon and Loménie de Brienne over French finances and the French "constitution." It is even uncertain whether the first president ever had the opportunity to air at Versailles the concerns voiced by his associates in their plenary session of 1 February. On the other hand, the government was bound to be cognizant of the judges' interest in the provisioning of fuel to the capital, just as it was ever aware of their strong reservations regarding an untrammeled trade in grain and other foodstuffs. That the king's legislation on the commerce in wood and alimentary commodities customarily endeavored to some extent to safeguard consumers' interests was not altogether unrelated to the germane magisterial investigations, decrees, and remonstrances of this era.[107] Within certain limits, then, the *parlementaires* were still sympathizing with the hungry and the cold on the eve of the Revolution. Were they similarly solicitous about the fiscally oppressed throughout their vast jurisdiction? The answer to this question would seem to be yes, again within certain limits. It is at least undeniable that parlementary polemics frankly supportive of the fiscal privileges of the first two orders in 1787–88 also paused at times to depict the grim situation of *roturiers* in the countryside overburdened by taxation and other hardships. In its first formal remonstrances of the prerevolutionary crisis, those presented to Louis XVI on 26 July 1787, the Cour des Pairs maintained that financial reforms

> are awaited every day by the unfortunate farmer, whose tears water the field which supports so many useless expenses before furnishing sustenance to the one who has planted it; they are awaited by the day-laborer, more unfortunate still, who has only his arms for his family's and his own sustenance, and who, deprived even of essentials, must somehow provide for the needs of the State out of his very poverty itself.
>
> Sire, these unfortunates, who are French, who are men, have in these capacities a doubly sacred right, even in the bosom of poverty; they cannot claim it themselves before Your Majesty, but may their fate and their rights always be in your mind's eye; may their laments always be heard; may your response always reach them and may they know that Your Majesty's benevolence and justice are the surest champions they can have around the Throne.[108]

Furthermore, these remonstrances (from Ferrand's pen) assailed those favorite popular villains, the agents of the Farmers-General, whose abusive collecting of indirect taxation was allegedly sucking the state dry. Here, on 26 July 1787, were echoes of popular complaints—if not specific suggestions for equalizing the burden of taxation.

True equality of fiscal obligations, from the greatest to the humblest of Frenchmen, may have been beyond most *parlementaires'* wildest imagining; yet, in a smaller way, they divulged their sympathy for "common" taxpayers. About a month before Ferrand's remonstrances conjured up the hardships of farmers and day laborers, the Parlement had to consider Brienne's legislation converting the *corvée royale* into a cash payment by commoners additional to their *taille*. The jurists registered this act on 28 June, but, as the *Gazette de Leyde* reported twelve days later, they attached a proviso "entreating ... the King never to allow the Contribution relative to the upkeep of the Roads to exceed one tenth of the Taille." Moreover, serious discussion ensued within the court as to whether *all* landed proprietors (including, that is, clerics and nobles) should not subsidize the commuted labor upon the kingdom's roads and bridges, rather than just the *taillables* themselves. The jurists eventually decided, by a reportedly narrow margin, to reject this notion. They did so, in the words of the *Gazette de Leyde*, "because it was observed, that the Individuals who were not *taillables* would no less end up paying the new Tax in the person of their Farmers, etc. Moreover, this is only a provisional arrangement; and the provincial Assemblies will decide, if it might be just and necessary, that all Taxpayers be taxed for this purpose."[109] The Dutch journal's account of the deliberations of 28 June tallied with those in several other contemporary sources.[110]

What was especially meaningful about the magistrates' reaction to the government's commutation of the *corvée royale* was that, like their statements upon the trades in grain and in fuel, it revived old subjects of contention between *parlement* and crown and dramatized the continuity of judicial concerns. Government attempts to devise more efficient and at the same time more humane means of highway maintenance than the traditional *corvée* of compulsory peasant labor had strained ministerial–magisterial relations under Turgot and Necker—to go back no further than ten or fifteen years. The Parlement's traditionalists had insisted that the responsibility for the upkeep of French highways and bridges devolved solely upon commoners. In defending this hoary principle, however, the justices had opposed substitution of professional road work for the peasants' own labor, arguing that the peasants were invariably overtaxed to defray the professionals' salaries and associated expenses. Moreover, the Parlement, however supportive of the old-fashioned *corvée*, had criticized abuses in its administration. In fact, in the late 1770s the court had conducted its own investigation of *corvée* policies within its jurisdiction: the result had been magisterial entreaties to Louis XVI to do something about labor abuses stemming from the traditional *corvée* and financial abuses resulting from the new-fangled alternative of professional road work.[111] More intriguingly still, the judges' opposition to heavier taxation of commoners as *corvéables* had been paralleled by their growing opposition to additional taxes of *any* kind levied upon commoners in the kingdom.[112] Thus, the proviso appended to the registration of 28 June 1787 represented a continuation of sincere, if limited, efforts by the Parlement on behalf of overtaxed *roturiers*.

Of course, self-interest played its role here as well, at least indirectly. The landed lords at the Palais de Justice knew very well that overburdened peasants would likely render less in cash and in kind to their seigneurs and might even require direct seigneurial assistance.[113]

Hence, their decision not to endorse the notion that the First and Second Estates were responsible along with the Third Estate for Brienne's compounded *corvée*. Nevertheless, the apparent support of a substantial minority within the tribunal for such a generous stance on this issue may have been one sign that gusts of reformism across the political landscape were beginning to penetrate the parlementary chambers at Paris. (Some of the provincial *parlementaires* were similarly moving toward a more generous position on this question on the eve of the Revolution, as we will see in chapter 5.)

A similar complex of motives lay behind the magistrates' occasional willingness to speak out on behalf of obscure commoners caught up in the toils of ministerial justice during this period. For an instructive example of this, we may consult the official parlementary minutes for 20 November 1787. This was the day after the stormy "royal session" that led to the exile of the duc d'Orléans and two fractious judges (mentioned in the Introduction) and the court was probably not in the best of moods. A magistrate arose in the plenary session of that day to discuss a petition just received from one Boyère and his wife, "goldsmiths and dealers in gold," alleging that "their child aged thirteen years and their journeyman in their shop, arrested without judgment and taken to the Hôtel de la Force on the eighth of the present month, for having thrown a firecracker on the Place Dauphine where they lived," were still "languishing and groaning in their prison without being able to secure their liberty from the police." The latter were "remanding them to the Baron de Breteuil."[114] What was to be done? There followed a general discussion of the matter. The court eventually instructed First President d'Aligre to "employ his good offices to secure the liberation of these individuals" and resolved to review the incident in the plenary session scheduled for 28 November. This is, however, the last we read of the affair in the court's minutes: the session of 28 November and those that followed were given over to the mounting magisterial outcry against the exiling of the king's cousin and the two judges. The first president may or may not have had the chance to "employ his good offices" on behalf of the two rambunctious youths apprehended in early November. That the justices considered this rather obscure matter at all is nevertheless of some interest. Obviously, the *séance royale* of 19 November had stoked antiministerial fires at the Palais de Justice, and protesting a minor police incident was one small way of striking back at the government. But at the same time, the magistrates' behavior on 20 November 1787 intriguingly resembled their behavior on earlier occasions in Louis XVI's reign when, with no particular antiministerial axe to grind, they had nonetheless spoken out on behalf of untitled Frenchmen in similarly distressing circumstances.[115]

Incidents like these will never appear in textbook accounts of the judicial opposition to Louis XVI's government, but they help to elucidate that opposition all the same. They lend at least some credibility to the *parlementaires'* contention that their indictments of reformist legislation, *lits de justice,* and *lettres de cachet* in 1787–88 served the interests of all Frenchmen and Frenchwomen, and not just those of the great in society. To understand the magistrates completely, however, we will have to acknowledge and account for certain radical tendencies in attitudes at the Parisian Palais de Justice.

Revolution for Magistracy or for the Commonweal?

We have seen how significant for the monarchy was the growing element of constitutional radicalism in the parlementary polemics of 1787–88. But this tendency also exposed a crucial subjectivity in the parlementary outlook at this time. The more the magistrates declaimed against ministerial despotism and trumpeted the rights of all Frenchmen, the more they seemed (or at least some of them seemed) to be elevating themselves and their institution and profession above the other individuals and institutions and professions of French society. Their public roles were so important and their zeal to play them so great that, by the time of the prerevolutionary crisis, the judges, already self-appointed advocates and censors of the monarchy and of all social interests, had almost become self-appointed oracles of a brave new world as well. This happened, ironically enough, in spite of the fact that most of the jurists would have preferred to cling to the old world they already knew, the old world that had been so very generous to them in so many different ways. Unfortunately, the relentless pressures generated by the government's financial crisis precluded that option. What remains to be noted is that parlementary commentary upon public issues actually envisioned two new worlds: one in which the judiciary would play an unprecedentedly influential role, and another in which the civic-mindedness of all Frenchmen would somehow achieve the common welfare.

Both visions, it is worth reiterating, derived from the parlement's increasingly radical stance upon constitutional questions. (This radicalism of course had roots in parlementary politics and polemics of past decades; still, as this chapter has shown, it matured fully only in the crucible of the prerevolutionary crisis.) It was as if the judges, having jettisoned the central and historic institution of absolute monarchy in their increasingly acrimonious debate with the ministers, had to cast about desperately for something to put in its place. One solution beckoned in the form of an unprecedented glorification of the magistracy's role in the state. Pertinent in this connection was the *parlementaires'* tendency to apotheosize their profession as a sort of "fourth estate" in France. Here, for instance, was Avocat-Général Séguier addressing his colleagues on 17 December 1788 in judgment of a popular tract to which we earlier alluded:

> That truly seditious work has only been so widely distributed in the present circumstances . . . to set the People in opposition to the Clergy, Nobility, and Magistracy, at the moment when the Clergy . . . is ready to honor itself by sacrificing its immunities; at the moment when the Nobility . . . seems to abandon its privileges and to retain only the honorific distinctions that constitute its essence; at the moment when the magistrates congratulate themselves for having been restored to their functions to exercise the worthiest ministry of the organs of the law, in inviting citizens of all ranks to occupy themselves with the misfortunes of the Fatherland.[116]

The clergy and the nobility recommended themselves to the *avocat-général* by their apparent relinquishment of their useful "immunities" and "privileges"; "citizens of all ranks" might ponder the country's woes; and the magistrates would continue as always to exercise crucial public functions.

At about this same time, Séguier's long-standing colleague Lefevre d'Ormesson was lauding the judicial profession even more extravagantly at the second Assembly of Notables:

> What would we be able to do for the Nation . . . if, around the Throne, and under the very shadow of the royal power, there had not been preserved that pure and free liberty of the Magistracy, which knows no other fear than that of being corrupted by flattery and complacency! . . .
>
> What happy security for Magistrates accustomed at all times to discerning the interests of the State through the least interests of the citizens . . . and to keeping constantly in view that long perspective through which one sees in advance . . . the public fortune extending with equal consistency through the most distant centuries![117]

The judiciary, declared the first president, "serves the Sovereign, defends the Fatherland, rules the citizens, and guards the sacred treasury of the Kingdom's Laws against all violation." If we took Lefevre d'Ormesson literally, we might be tempted to ask what responsibilities in the public realm would the robe *not* discharge? And, lest the message be lost at

Versailles, the first president reiterated it on behalf of his company when, on 21 December, he urged Louis XVI to expedite the convening of the Estates General.[118]

The burgeoning pride and pretensions of the *parlementaires* appeared even more strikingly in two crucial decrees of 1788 discussed earlier for other reasons. The *arrêté* of 3 May drafted by Duval d'Eprémesnil listed, as two of the "fundamental laws" of France, "the irrevocable tenure of the magistrates" and "the right of the courts in each province to verify the King's laws and to order their registration only insofar as they conform with the constituting laws of the province as well as with the fundamental laws of the State." The two "fundamental laws" immediately following in d'Eprémesnil's litany of 3 May 1788 guaranteed all citizens the right to be brought immediately after arrest before "competent judges" and to be tried by their "natural judges, who are those designated . . . by the law."[119] Here was an additional feather in the magisterial cap, as well as an essential right for all Frenchmen—though to Louis XVI and his ministers the *arrêté* of 3 May 1788 must have appeared to be parlementary pretension run wild.

But worse was yet to come. Duval d'Eprémesnil's later decree of 5 December 1788, in addition to wooing public opinion by disavowing the reference of 25 September to the 1614 Estates General, projected a future partnership between the regularly convened Estates General and the sovereign courts. Royal ministers accused of malfeasance in office "directly involving the entire Nation" would be judged in the courts, though this procedure must not "prejudice the rights of the Procureur-Général" of the Paris Parlement in such cases. Moreover, the sovereign courts would cooperate with the Estates General in legislating future taxation and, indeed, future ordinances of all kinds.[120] An increment in the judicial and political powers of the courts was obviously to accompany the new powers accorded the kingdom's future assemblies.

By this time the Parlement was past being able to provoke responses from Versailles, as the convocation of the Estates General was now occupying ministerial minds. But there was considerable indignation and concern within the tribunal itself as a result of the decree of 5 December. The counselor Ferrand later remembered it as "that *arrêté* which demonarchized France." The marquis de Bouillé learned from his neighbor in the country, First President Lefevre d'Ormesson, that the more moderate *parlementaires* had strenuously resisted its passage.[121] Yet most of the moderate judges who opposed the decree of 5 December had voted for the equally inflammatory *arrêté* of 3 May, and the more perceptive among them must have realized that their championing of parlementary prerogatives and criticism of government actions had long been pointing in this direction. The first president himself, in declaring grandly to the Notables that the magistracy served the sovereign, defended the fatherland, and ruled the citizens, had testified arrestingly to magisterial pride and ambition on the eve of revolution in France.

And individual political aspirations went hand-in-hand with corporate pretensions—a point driven home at the beginning of this chapter by the examples of Lefebvre d'Amécourt and President Joly de Fleury. There were other examples. Contemporaries were quick to note that at the plenary session of 27 February 1789 the Parlement had to pass an impromptu decree reminding those of its members anxious to be elected as delegates to the upcoming Estates General that they should not altogether neglect their professional duties at the Palais de Justice. The *Gazette de Leyde* in reporting this incident observed drily that in 1560 and 1576 the tribunal's decrees had not in this fashion authorized judges implicitly to "elect and be elected to" the Estates General of those years.[122] However, by the early months of 1789 the public had had its fill of magisterial politics: parlementary candidates for the Estates General were on the whole not upheld by their electorates.[123] Many Frenchmen would have agreed with the magistrates' insistence in their decree of 27 February "that the royal authority, the public liberty, and the tranquility of the kingdom" be maintained. But they emphatically refused to entrust that charge to the pretentious politicians of the Palais de Justice who were in part responsible for the parlous state of the realm. Corporate and individual ambitions in the Paris Parlement had in reality reached their logical dead end by 1789.

But another, more generous vision is to be found among the *parlementaires* in 1787–88. The heady expectation of national regeneration allied with the conviction that the judges should help achieve it by subordinating their narrow interests to the commonweal was a nebulous vision; indeed, it was more a mood of rapturous enthusiasm, of euphoric idealism, than a program for the future. Its main adherents were the youthful jurists of the Enquêtes and Requêtes, urged on by the unemployed barristers, lawyers' clerks, and law students of the court's *basoche*. One of these enfants terribles of the Parlement, Guy Marie Sallier, later recalled their mood and activities during 1787 and 1788:

> The young men of the *Enquêtes* came to the assemblies of the chambers as if they were going into combat, and everything assured them victory in a contest that was too unequal. Besides the advantage of number, they had greater unity than those whom they assailed. They even had some partisans in the Grand' Chambre. Their orators pleaded a cause generative of those eloquent mo-

ments that always produce a great effect upon large assemblies. They seemed to be defending the rights and interests of the nation. Their courage could not fail to win over ardent youths who passionately embraced generous sentiments and did not bother to open their eyes to dangers.[124]

Or, as Sallier's associate Pasquier said of himself and his fellows, "as soon as our interest was clearly put in the balance, we thought that the most glorious thing we could possibly do would be to sacrifice that interest to what we regarded as the public welfare."[125] Both men also recalled the contempt in which they and their comrades had held their seniors of the Grand' Chambre: they had ridiculed them as old cronies still slavishly obedient to tradition and to the whims of arbitrary government.

The politics of 1787–88 gave these precocious juniors of the Parlement repeated opportunities to resist authority, whether they perceived it in the government or in the informal directorate of the Grand' Chambre. They were, willingly, putty in the hands of judges such as Duval d'Eprémesnil, Robert de Saint-Vincent, Huguet de Sémonville, and Adrien Duport, who collaborated within and without the Parlement to raise opposition to the government.[126] Assuredly, it was they who voted most enthusiastically for the inflammatory constitutional pronunciamentos of 1787 and 1788; it was they who saw Duval d'Eprémesnil's decree of 5 December 1788 as a chance, perhaps the last chance, for the Parlement to redeem itself in public opinion. They failed throughout to notice (or at least failed to point out) that Duval d'Eprémesnil, Robert de Saint-Vincent, and some of the other veteran firebrands of the court had not yet jettisoned the old parlementary pretensions. They were aware only that the throngs noisily besieging and milling through the Palais de Justice were cajoling them, challenging them, cheering them on to reject the "despotism" of the government and to advocate the "rights" and the "liberty" of all Frenchmen—and, in the great majority of cases, they were more than happy to do this.

But it bears repeating that the court's enfants terribles were not really that different from their older or less ardent colleagues, who, despite considerable misgivings, were being forced down the same perilous path by the inexorable logic of the kingdom's situation. Thus, dukes and peers, seasoned grand' chambriers, and judicial apprentices of Enquêtes and Requêtes alike were in 1787–88 giving notice of a venerable institution wrenched increasingly out of its traditional role of mediating the variegated interests of the *ancien régime*. The monarchy, which had created France and held it together over a millennium, was now collapsing, and in the resultant political vacuum the *parlementaires*, like other

Frenchmen, could only brandish their own ambitions or optimistically preach regeneration and the public weal.

The more thoroughly we analyze and ponder parlementary attitudes at Paris on the verge of revolution, the more forcefully we are impressed by the great and growing discrepancy between the old regime that the magistrates still envisioned and wished desperately to retain and the new regime that was in hard fact starting to break out of the chrysalis of the old. In their private animadversions and in their public protestations the Parisian justices conjured up a world in which governance was still largely reducible to monarch and selfless servants, taxation was but a temporary inconvenience, clerics and nobles and lay commoners knew their proper places, and *parlementaires* like themselves mediated and harmonized all public and private interests. These judges visualized and apotheosized such a world because it was their way of endeavoring to preserve a state of affairs of which they were notable beneficiaries—in their professional and in their private lives.

Unfortunately for them, however, the emerging reality was otherwise in this France of the late eighteenth century. The monarch simply could not do without his policymakers and administrative agents, his financiers and taxes, and his frequent high-handedness toward his noble and common subjects. He himself was rapidly becoming but a dignified cog in a machine of state that, like other machines of state in Europe and often because of interaction with them, was willy-nilly pursuing more grandiose foreign policies and interventionist domestic policies. Concomitantly, nobles and literate commoners were proving less willing than ever before to accept their foreordained places. Better educated and better off than ever before, cognizant as never in the past of great events in France and in the world at large, and dreaming in some cases of playing in public affairs a role more active than that of taxpaying subjects, these enterprising individuals of whatever social rank were in their own fashion as likely as were reformist ministers and overweening bureaucrats to disarrange the Parisian *parlementaires'* static and precariously balanced world.

The justices bore witness to the geopolitical and social dynamics of this situation in 1787–88 when they railed against the *lits de justice, lettres de cachet,* and inexorably increasing taxes of the government and criticized what they regarded as the destabilizing aspirations of noblesse and literate commonalty. The ultimate irony, however, is that these conservators of timeless deference and stability were, like so many others, dragged into the whirlpool of unprecedented politicization that was the prerevolutionary crisis in France. The more widely yawned the chasm between the old world they wanted so to preserve and the nascent new world of bureaucratized governance, social equality, and mass politics, the more desperately and provocatively did these Parisian magistrates flaunt their corporate pretensions or their concern for the public weal. Yet in so doing they only accelerated the tempo of the whole crisis. When they anathematized "ministerial despotism" they politicized previously quiescent commoners as well as members of the social elite; and when they invoked the Estates General of 1614 in their decree of September 1788 they helped to crystallize latent and potentially explosive tensions between traditionalist clerics and nobles, on the one hand, and "liberal" clerics and nobles and bourgeois, on the other. Thus the proud *parlementaires* of Paris, caught up as much as any other Frenchmen in the implications of international power politics and domestic social change, contributed in spite of themselves to the demise of the *ancien régime*.

THREE

Provincial Judges, Politics,
and the "Constitution"

The Parisian *parlementaires* paid little notice to the stirrings of magisterial revolt in provincial France during 1787 and the first three months of 1788. By April 1788, however, they were trumpeting provincial as well as Parisian pretensions of the high robe in their philippics against the government. They ridiculed Lamoignon's use of the phrase "dangerous concert" to characterize "the unpremeditated agreement of all the courts which, penetrated by the same sentiments or struck by the same blows, have had to show an equal foresight or the same courage."[1] They accused the keeper of the seals of poisoning the king's mind against their plea on behalf of the cashiered Bordelais judges at Libourne; they endorsed those jurists' obstinate refusal to sanction the establishment of provincial assemblies within their jurisdiction prior to receiving specific operational regulations for these bodies; and they extolled the "heroic patience with which the magistrates confined at Libourne endure their disgrace."[2] By 30 April 1788 the Parisian judges were declaring that "the King's will, in order to be just, must . . . vary according to the provinces," and were exalting Normandy, Brittany, Languedoc, and all other "nations" within the nation.[3] Finally, on 3 May 1788, Duval d'Eprémesnil's most defiant *arrêté* cited as "fundamental laws" of the realm "the customs and capitulations of the provinces" and the provincial courts' duty to register royal laws "only insofar as they conform with the constituting laws of the province."[4] Forthrightly if belatedly, then, the embattled *parlementaires* in the French capital acknowledged the provincials' resistance to "ministerial despotism" and proclaimed their solidarity with their provincial cousins in the face of the ministerial wrath.

Solidarity was all the more easily achieved in that constitutional and social perspectives at Besançon and Douai and Toulouse differed little in most respects from those at Paris on the eve of revolution. The provincial *parlementaires'* attitude toward the monarchy, to consider only constitutional perspectives for now, was as ambivalent as their Parisian counterparts' attitude. On the one hand was the professional identification with the royal domain, the lingering Gallican defense of crown against Rome, the earnest and even agonized attempt to distinguish "good king" from "evil ministers"; on the other hand was the assault upon the "administrative monarchy," an assault directed in certain jurisdictions against the intendants and everywhere against ministerial malversation and the fiscal policies of Versailles. And, as at the center, so in the peripheral regions of France, the magisterial response to the deepening constitutional crisis raised specters of radical causes—only here, to a much greater extent, one of those specters throughout was the old-fashioned but unquenchable spirit of provincial patriotism.

The Magistrates and Their Monarch

From Pau in the Pyrenees to Metz in Lorraine, from Brittany to Provence, the very justices whose opposition to government policies helped doom the king's cause in 1787–88 were continuing nonetheless to associate themselves with their version of monarchy in France. They did so most fundamentally by rendering royal justice and acting in local spheres of royal administration (at least until the coup of May 1788), but in their responses to a variety of topical questions and controversies they provided additional evidence of their orientation toward the crown. Yet this orientation betokened no exclusive concern for Louis XVI's prerogatives, much less an acceptance of all that his ministers and other agents might do in his name. In upholding rights of royal domain, Gallican principles, and the traditional distinction between the trustworthy sovereign and his less reliable ministers, for example, the judges never abandoned the private interests of the realm, and did not even hesitate to circumscribe the king's own "constitutional" authority.

Parlementary commentary upon crown lands, which were scattered throughout France, reveals the sincerity and at the same time the expediency of the magistrates' commitment to their royal master's prerogatives. At Besançon, erudite and influential jurist François-Nicolas-Eugène Droz des Villars expatiated upon this subject in an essay of 1789. "Of all the revenues of the King," he declared, "the most legitimate is probably that of the domain."[5] Yet the king's subjects, too, had defensible rights, in Franche-Comté as elsewhere, and Droz des Villars and his professional brethren and all their illustrious predecessors had ever championed those rights and striven to reconcile them with crown prerogatives. Thus, in times past the *parlement* had resolutely defended crown properties in the "County" against the depredations of usurping proprietors—and had just as resolutely prevented royal administrators of various stripes from extending the sovereigns' lands and forests at the expense of law-abiding landholders of the region.[6] Still, Droz des Villars in 1789 had tangible reasons for believing that benefits would continue to accrue to himself and his associates from stressing their primal identification with the crown's interests. After all, the domain's revenues should constitute one small alternative to heavier taxation of the judges and their fellow proprietors in Franche-Comté—and the domain should be administered by, among others, the judges themselves.

Such must have been the thinking, not only of Droz des Villars, but of all the men meting out parlementary justice at Besançon. It would be difficult to account otherwise for their remonstrances of 30 August 1787. These protests were directed against the increasing tendency of the central government in the post-Maupeou years to consign the general administration of royal lands and forests in Franche-Comté to certain Parisian agents and the Paris Chambre des Comptes.[7] The Comtois *parlementaires* clearly resented having to relinquish any part of a traditional role in local administration to individuals (and a court of law) in the national capital. Very predictably, their remonstrances celebrated the Besançon Parlement's historic role in championship of all rights and revenues appertaining to the king's lands and forests in the "County of Burgundy." The judges also detailed their company's past efforts to ensure that those serfs and other individuals permitted to draw their livelihood from these properties had in fact been able to do so. With equal candor, they characterized the *parlement*'s role as a legitimate prerogative conceded to the Comtois magistrates explicitly from Louis XIV's time on. Only those legal experts resident in the province and thoroughly versed in local practices, they maintained, could successfully discharge such a complex function. The *parlementaires* at Besançon may have gotten nowhere on this matter—the government's will in this as in other disputed areas of public policy was "militarily" enforced the following May—but they had, at the very least, restated their appreciation for one of their company's significant traditions.

Moreover, at least four of the other provincial *parlements*—those at Pau, Rennes, Rouen, and Metz—invoked the rights of royal domain during the prerevolutionary crisis. The justices at Pau had for some time been complaining that a Franco-Spanish convention of 1785 readjusting the border between the two countries had ceded too much territory to the Spaniards.[8] Parlementary protests of December 1786 and August 1787 had candidly embraced the cause of aggrieved farmers and shepherds in the French Pyrenees but had also cited "inalienable rights" of crown domain allegedly sacrificed to Spain by the convention of 1785. The government had derided these protests in a lengthy memorandum, but the *parlementaires* of Navarre and Béarn returned to the attack in remonstrances of 14 December 1787. Once again the judges, though primarily interested in championing the claims of hardy mountaineering folk, broached the issue of crown properties in their jurisdiction. They recalled how, in 1590, Navarre's most famous son, the newly proclaimed King Henri IV of France, had attempted via letters patent to "separate from the domain of the Crown the great fiefs constituting his domain of Navarre." The Paris Parlement had courageously refused to register this legislation the following year, citing its duty to defend the integrity of royal lands and rights. Only in 1607, observed Pau's *parlementaires*, had Henri IV recognized his mistake: his edict of July of that year had revoked the letters patent of 1590 and thus "declared the reunion of his domains to the domain of the Crown." The Parisian magistrates' resistance to his will sixteen years before had been "as useful to the State as a timid deference to inadvisable orders would have been deadly." Now, insisted the judges at Pau, theirs was the obligation to discharge a similar duty in declaring that the recent revision of the Franco-Spanish border "attacked equally the inalienable rights of his [that is, Louis XVI's] domain, and the properties of his subjects."[9] Even though Pau's *parlementaires* here were likely more concerned about local proprietors' claims than about those of the crown, they no less ironically resembled the Parisian judges in past imbroglios with the government over Gallican principles in that, *plus royalistes que le roi*, they were insisting that the king had ceded too many of his own rights to a foreign power.

Brittany's *parlementaires* were also reaffirming the integrity of the royal domain at about this time, though for somewhat different reasons. On 18 September 1787 the substitute of the *procureur-général* at Rennes, one Joseph-Marie Brossays-Duperray, arose in the Chambre des Vacations to condemn a scurrilous pamphlet lampooning the Parisian *parlementaires*. In the course of his remarks he noted indignantly that "this audacious writer dares to assert that the King can alienate entire Provinces without rendering account of this to anyone," and he observed that this "antimonarchical assertion" contradicted "the fundamental law of the inalienability of the Crown's domain." This and other "fundamental laws" appertaining to the prerogatives of the crown could be adequately upheld in the absence of the Estates General only by those staunch bucklers of royal authority, the men of the *parlements*. So thought Brossays-Duperray, who went on to intone that "decrees of the Parlement ... must command respect, since love of justice has dictated them, and since they are generous and legitimate acts of the royal authority from which they emanate." The Breton justices, in solemnly censuring the squib in question for its "false, seditious assertions injuring and calumniating the Parlement of Paris," palpably had to have both royal and magisterial interests in mind.[10]

Normandy's *parlementaires* also found advantage in lecturing the king upon his rights of domain. At issue in this province were several royal decrees of 1785 and 1786 leasing out to local "developers" various crown lands and waste lands. The latter were claimed by lords and peasant communities as their own.[11] The government's announced intention was to encourage a more efficient exploitation of fertile lands in Normandy without permanently alienating crown territories or wronging individual proprietors. The *parlement* at Rouen, however, protested this policy in remonstrances of 8 August 1787. It did so in part by contesting the ministry's assertion that the land development recently authorized in Normandy was sanctioned as well by provisions of past royal ordinances, notably one of 1566. The Normans cited the first article of the ordinance of 1566 which stated in part: "the Domain of our Crown can be alienated only in two cases; the one for the appanage of the younger males of the royal House . . . the other for alienations in cash necessitated by War, in virtue of letters-patent issued for this purpose and published in our Parlements, and with perpetual right of redemption conceded to the Crown." The king's policymakers, argued the jurists, could not possibly use "the provisions of that law" to justify "illegal operations of his Council. . . . concessions made by simple decrees and without letters-patent."[12] Considered objectively, the controversy over the government's land concessions in Normandy exposed the familiar complexity of magisterial motives. When a Parisian memorialist, ordinarily no partisan of parlementary causes, described the Rouen Parlement's remonstrances as "necessary for . . . the King's own rights, for the quietude of the subjects and for justification of the Parlement's principles," he was only indicating an old triad of judicial concerns—concerns, that is, for long-sanctioned monarchical prerogatives, for individual proprietary rights, and for the cherished judicial review of royal acts.[13]

Finally, at Metz occurred perhaps the supreme irony: invocation of rights of royal domain to validate rights of taxpayers. The *parlementaires* in this community of Lorraine were as adamantly opposed to higher taxation as were the members of any other sovereign tribunal in 1787–88, and they demonstrated this by protesting repeatedly against the compromise legislation extending the *vingtièmes* late in 1787.[14] At one point in their "Declarations and reiterated Protestations" of 20 June 1788 the judges at Metz averred

> that such legislation can never be adopted in a Monarchy where
> the regal authority does not even have the power to alienate the
> Domain of the Crown, and where consequently that authority cannot have intended to assume the right to force the Citizens to pay
> taxes that they would never have freely accepted, and whose crushing burden would perhaps necessitate their alienating their properties, in order to be able to confront those taxes.[15]

It would seem, then, that the principle of "inalienability" could be invoked as justifiably in defense of the taxpayer as in championship of the king and his own. Parlementary advocacy of crown prerogatives in these troubled times was unquestionably sincere: this was attested most convincingly by the opposition of Procureur-Général Joly de Fleury and other judges at the first Assembly of Notables to Calonne's proposals regarding the management of the king's lands. But this advocacy could undeniably serve nonroyalist purposes as well.

Similarly expediential if equally sincere in this period were parlementary professions of fealty to the crown in connection with the Gallican question. Not much disputation, it is true, arose from this grand old issue in the twilight of the *ancien régime* (though the Revolution was soon to revive it in a new guise). Yet judges here and there were as ready as ever to return to an issue upon which some law courts in earlier times had waxed more royalist than the sovereigns themselves.[16] We have seen how, at Paris, influential jurists such as First President d'Aligre and Robert de Saint-Vincent inveighed against Jesuitical and other clerical pretensions in France. At Besançon Droz des Villars inevitably touched upon the question in his massive treatise of 1789 devoted to the "public law" of Franche-Comté:

> One should consult in the Parlement's registers the discourse of M. Jobelot upon the usage of the Gallican liberties, acclaimed long before the sway of France was acknowledged here, and notably the strictures against executing bulls not accompanied by proper state letters; similar precautions were taken against all abuses of excommunications; the wise settlement of 1680 restrains the ecclesiastical jurisdiction within its just limits.[17]

Such reflections betokened a rock-ribbed commitment to the supremacy of temporal justice (meaning, ultimately, parlementary justice) in France as well as to the principle of judicial review of Church-related legislation. And that commitment in turn presupposed a conscious allegiance to the supreme Magistrate and Legislator of the realm. The interdependence between judicial pretensions and judicial monarchism on this issue appeared nowhere more remarkably than in a polemic that the fiery Breton judge Amand Du Couëdic de Kergoualer turned out in 1788:

> There was a time when the Head of the Church, forgetting "that the Kingdom of God is not of this world," tried to subject all the Nations and all the Princes of Christianity to his temporal justice. . . . almost everywhere one could see the Pope conferring Crowns, excommunicating, deposing Kings, and placing Kingdoms in interdict. Only France had the courage to free herself from the yoke of this holy enemy. . . .
> The French believe without qualification that the King is the sole Chief of the monarchy of which they are members. . . . It is so

true that no Foreign Power can share the legislative Power here, that the Pope's Bulls, even those concerning Ecclesiastical Matters, are not received here unless accompanied by Letters-Patent registered in the Courts.[18]

The whole history of relations between crown and magistracy in the old regime suggests that, on this subject, Du Couëdic de Kergoualer was speaking for the vast majority of the high courts' jurists. And why should it have been otherwise? In ecclesiastical matters, at least, monarchist patriotism and the bent for public affairs could compatibly motivate parlementary behavior—and in 1788 there was no Louis XIV to call the judges to account for ultra-Gallican inclinations.

More problematical, because of greater practical import to the crown, was the parlementary endeavor in 1787–88 to maintain that superannuated distinction between the "good king" and his erring or evil servants. Here, too, was magisterial royalism in the final crisis of the old regime— sincere royalism, for all that it was hopelessly impractical in view of the increasingly bureaucratic and impersonal nature of monarchical governance.

When the more perspicacious jurists reflected upon the evolution of governance in France they could not help but voice nostalgia for the past and frustration about the present. Complained Besançon's Droz des Villars, "it seems that for a long time now, those in power, believing themselves to be invested with unlimited power, have no longer considered themselves bound to fulfill the obligations contracted by their predecessors. . . . if the promises of Kings, in matters upon which they can fully engage themselves, were more respected by their successors and their Ministers, one would not see the Government's inconsistencies expose the State to perpetual shocks." "As if," he added wistfully, "the King was not the unique center of administration."[19] But was he, or could he be? The Paris Parlement's most incorrigible hotspur, Duval d'Eprémesnil, sincerely hoped so, as we have seen. And the same pathetic hope (or was it merely drowning men's desperation?) actuated judges all over France in the prerevolution.

At Rennes, for example, the Breton *parlementaires* toward the end of 1787 wrote directly to Louis XVI on the alarming matter of the *séance royale* of 19 November. They implored him to reinstate the duc d'Orléans and the two judges arrested as a result of that dramatic convocation of the Paris Parlement. Their appeal to the king was not without its allusions to the "despotism" of recent ministries:

Your personal character, Sire, your love for your subjects, your desire to render them happy, the precautions Your Majesty took at his accession to ensure that the jails would no longer be open to any individuals not legally judged for crimes committed; all seemed to promise France that, under your reign, there would be no return to those unfortunate times, when the ability to form an opinion, the courage to express it, the attachment to one's duties, to the laws of one's honor and one's conscience, were misrepresented grotesquely as punishable offences.

The king's heart had "doubtless been rent" by his ministers' rigorous treatment of the duc d'Orléans, and only "with reluctance" had he acquiesced in the detention of the two intrepid judges of the Paris Parlement.[20] So, in any case, the Bretons purported to believe. They might not necessarily have been naïve to hold such a belief, for they must have known about Louis XVI's frequent expressions of benevolence toward his subjects. Furthermore, could *any* king fail in the pinch to be more sympathetic than the advisers surrounding the throne? So the Breton *parlementaires* must have felt in endorsing a letter whose practical chances of success were nil from the start.

The following spring and summer brought a flurry of appeals to the monarch from magistrates responding to the May Edicts and to the semimilitary means employed in some provinces to secure their registration. At Nancy, for instance, the justices issued a stinging indictment of the ministers' policies on 11 June 1788 but described themselves as "inspired by complete confidence in the justice of the Lord King, assured that the calamities of his people need only be made known to him in order to be mitigated by his grace." If the sinister forces besieging the throne made it impossible for the judges themselves to acquaint the sovereign with the ills afflicting his subjects, then all hope must lie with the mediation of those whose exalted rank assured them a royal hearing in spite of the ministers' baleful presence at Versailles. Accordingly, the *parlementaires* at Nancy voted to send their protests to the king's brothers, the Princes of the Blood, and even to the peers of France.[21]

Similar action was taken two weeks later at Rouen, although the Norman *parlementaires* lashed out even more savagely at the ministers responsible for the May Edicts.[22] In the concluding statement of their decree of 25 June ridiculing those reforms, the justices announced their intention to write "immediately if possible to the Lord King to denounce as traitors to him and to the State the Ministers guilty of having so misled His Majesty, and specifically le Sieur de Lamoignon Keeper of the Seals of France." The Rouen Parlement ordered its first president "from this moment on to cease corresponding directly" with Lamoignon about the tribunal's affairs. Moreover, the Normans, like their counterparts at Nancy, resolved to send their inflammatory decree to the king's brothers, the Princes of the Blood, and to the peers, and in covering letters invited these august personages to assist them in obtaining royal justice against the culpable policymakers at Versailles.[23] The court's entire membership signed this decree; it is no wonder that it was quashed by an *arrêt du Conseil* of 9 July.[24] Yet the judges at Rouen, like those elsewhere, would have insisted that they were only endeavoring to circumvent the monarch's malevolent advisers and sycophantic courtiers so that he might hear from their own lips (or, at least, read from their own pens) crucial truths as they saw them.

One other provincial *parlement* appealing directly to Louis XVI in the prerevolutionary crisis merits our attention. The justices at Pau, who had already written to the king on 31 August 1787 to protest the Paris Parlement's banishment to Troyes and to counsel a speedy convocation of the Estates General, had even more compelling reasons for wishing to communicate with him the following year.[25] The *parlements* had all been ordered on vacation after having involuntarily ratified the May Edicts. This, however, had not prevented the judges from remonstrating against the royal acts in one way or another, and at Pau, as we know, the magistrates were actually reinstated by a popular uprising on 19 June.[26] The government, willing to regard this *parlement*'s audacious resumption of duties as an action taken under duress, attempted by negotiation to induce it to relinquish its functions once again, but the tribunal, buoyed (or, perhaps, cowed) by the local rebellion, refused to do so.

In a lengthy missive approved on 17 July and sent off to the king himself two days later, the high justices of Navarre and Béarn sought to justify their defiance of the ministers by invoking the sovereign's presumed concern for the preservation of law and order in these mountainous and unruly regions of the south. They conceded that the entire realm, and not merely their own Pyrenean jurisdiction, faced a disordered future: to put the *parlements* on forced vacation, after all, could not but cripple the entire judicial system and thus bring about a situation favoring mischief makers and the guilty rather than law-abiding subjects and justly aggrieved litigants. Still, the effects of a cessation of parlementary justice would be especially serious in Navarre and Béarn as the inhabitants of those *pays*, accustomed as they were to the adjudication of so many of their civil and criminal suits in the Pau Parlement, would have little or no faith in the pronouncements of inferior tribunals. The king, maintained the jurists, must sooner or later recognize that his *parlement* at Pau, in refusing to defer to the ministers, was really obeying the truest promptings of his paternal heart.[27] Naturally the government rejected this argument and it was soon to summon the entire company to Versailles for a dressing-down by Louis himself. Nevertheless, this incident in the summer of 1788, arising in the first place from what one observer at Pau admitted was the "frightful misery" resulting locally from the government's judicial coup, illustrates once again the provincial judges' genuine if impractical fealty to a personal monarchy.[28]

Of course, drafting letters to the sovereign "informing" him of the parlous state of the realm or of purely local tribulations was only one way of trying to preserve an idealized relationship with the monarch and an idealized vision of the personal monarchy. The sovereign courts in 1787–88 also sent off myriad and more impersonal *arrêtés* and remonstrances to Versailles, while individual officers of the various *parquets* used their companies' plenary sessions to deliver attestations of principle, most notably in response to the compulsory registration of the May Edicts in 1788.[29] All of these magisterial manifestos and addresses attempted to make that antediluvian distinction between the monarch, well-intentioned if misled, and the ministers and their minions who were deliberately misleading him. Such a theme, however unoriginal, at once served parlementary purposes and betrayed the sincere if quixotic royalism of judges caught up with everyone else in a national crisis of unprecedented complexity.

Yet equally significant, and requiring greater elaboration, is the fact that the magistrates, in the very process of reaffirming solidarity with the king's "best intentions," steadfastly hedged his "rightful" powers with a variety of constitutional reservations. In the majority of cases these reservations appeared as cursory items in parlementary protests addressing a number of not necessarily related issues of the period. But in several noteworthy instances the provincial jurists, dueling with the authorities at Versailles, rebutted in great detail ministerial claims made on behalf of Louis XVI's powers.

Among the less rigorous treatments of this central constitutional question were the pronouncements of the judges at Grenoble, Toulouse, Dijon, and Perpignan.

In a decree of 24 January 1788 protesting the "royal session" of the preceding November and belaboring the government on numerous other points, Grenoble's *parlementaires* explicitly denied that the royal prerogative could take precedence over the subject's right to security from state oppression. "The legitimate authority of the Monarch," they asserted, "is distinguishable from the absolute Power of the Despot only because it is fixed by the Laws, which guarantee to each citizen the safety of his person, the first and most sacred of Properties."[30] The Grenoblois here were laying the groundwork for an indictment of *lettres de cachet*—which, indeed, follows almost immediately in this *arrêté*. The indictment itself, like the statement just quoted, is especially interesting from a constitutional point of view because of its delimitation, not of some minister's or faceless bureaucrat's influence, but of the king's own power.

In the pages of parlementary protest at Toulouse we find another brief but meaningful comment upon the sovereign's authority in France. This time the point of reference was the individual subject's right to property. Here were the Toulousains discoursing upon this topic in remonstrances of 12 January 1788 aimed more generally against the *vingtièmes*:

> Your Sovereignty, Sire, is full and complete. Well! Who has defended it more zealously than your Parlements! In a sense one can even say that it is absolute in that it is independent of all human authority. But it does not follow that your Government can be arbitrary; and one of the most conspicuous characteristics of that hateful government [that is, arbitrary government] is that the Prince disposes at his whim of his subjects' properties.[31]

What we have here is another intriguing example of how the provincial jurists, confronting one of the hotly debated issues of the day, could abandon the traditional distinction between the "king" and his "government" and explicate what the "Prince" himself could *not* rightfully do. If the king's principal agents in Languedoc, the comte de Périgord and Intendant Charles-Bernard de Ballainvilliers, had the opportunity to peruse these remonstrances, they must have snorted at the judges' specious invocation of "absolute" royal sovereignty "independent of all human authority." Dealing as they had to with the Toulousains' intractable opposition to higher taxation, they would have swiftly grasped the practical import of the *parlementaires'* remarks upon royal fiscal prerogatives.[32]

The intendant in Burgundy, Antoine-Léon-Anne Amelot de Chaillou, must have been similarly struck by inconsistencies emanating from the Palais de Justice at Dijon. In protests of 4 June 1788 against the May Edicts, the Burgundian *parlementaires* acclaimed "a government whose sovereign will always be cherished and respected as the father and protector of his subjects," but proceeded immediately thereafter to make of that sovereign's practical authority a questionable commodity indeed:

> The more just and charitable are His Majesty's views, the more reprehensible is the abuse made of them by those wielding his power; . . . to corrupt the sovereign's power to the point of altering its nature is a crime of *lèse-majesté* against him. . . .
>
> . . . that individual who wishes to destroy the national constitution by annihilating the intermediary bodies which direct the exercise of this power according to justice and the laws, alters the na-

ture of the sovereign power; . . . that individual who essays this change only to crush the people with taxes and stifle their defenders' objections, corrupts the sovereign's power; . . . finally that individual who announces his authority only by acts of violence, and who dares to lend the attributes of law to projects destructive of all laws, all engagements and all properties, corrupts the sovereign's power.

The magistrates would themselves be culpable should they "remain the passive witnesses of that subversion" and not endeavor to communicate "the truth" to the sovereign.[33] But what, then, did "sovereign power" amount to? In *this* rendering, not much, we suspect. The Burgundian judges' hostility toward Intendant Amelot de Chaillou and their furious squabbling with the Intermediary Committee of the Burgundian Estates over taxes and related matters scarcely represented a generous conception of governmental fiscal requirements and authority.[34]

Magisterial commentary upon the royal legislative prerogative was bound to appear especially ludicrous to the king and his partisans, and no more so than when it combined elements of monarchism and popular sovereignty. The judges at Perpignan in the eastern Pyrenees made bold to assure Louis XVI in a decree of 3 September 1787 that the "law" that required "the concourse of the nation for the establishment of taxation" did not in any way "injure the legislative power residing in the person of the Lord King." This "sacred right" which the king was "charged to protect" and which derived "from the policy and the constitution of the state," possessed "as unshakeable foundations as those of the throne." Pursued the jurists: "when, by free consent, the nation has diverted a portion of its property . . . toward the urgent necessities of the State, the legislative power, exercising its authority, converts a free gift into a tax, and establishes through a law emanating from the throne the obligation to pay this tax."[35] Doctrine such as this would be appreciated two or three years later by revolutionaries imperatively concerned with reconciling monarchical and popular claims to sovereignty; in 1787, however, it could hardly appear to the political authorities as anything but an offensive and nonsensical jumble of constitutional notions. Authority, they would insist, must be vested in the king, *sans dépendance et sans partage*; all talk of the "concourse" and "free consent" of the "nation" and of a tax as a converted "free gift" was, in a word, anathema.

As is well known, Keeper of the Seals Lamoignon forcefully lectured the Paris Parlement on the "immutable principles" of absolute monarchy in France at the *séance royale* of 19 November 1787.[36] Significantly, at least two of the provincial *parlements*, those of Rennes and Rouen, took Lamoignon to task for his "ultraroyalist" assertions in detailed critiques drawn up in the months that followed. In so doing, the Breton and Norman justices lent a new measure of temerity to the provincial assault upon the king's own authority.

The Bretons' rejoinder to the keeper of the seals came in remonstrances of 16 February 1788 ventilating their displeasure on a host of public issues.[37] The rejoinder took the form of a point-by-point review of the constitutional tenets advanced by Lamoignon on 19 November as "invariable principles of the French Monarchy." For example, Lamoignon, speaking in the royal presence that day, had stated: "to you alone, Sire, belongs the sovereign power in all your realm." The Bretons concurred in this assertion but reminded the king: "that power is tempered by the laws, and that is what distinguishes it from absolute power." Lamoignon had stated: "Your Majesty is accountable only to God for the exercise of the supreme power." And yet, observed the *parlementaires* in response, the king must recognize, as his august predecessors had recognized, that he was "happily incapable of undertaking anything against the Laws of the Monarchy." Lamoignon had stated: "the bond which unites you with the Nation is by its nature indissoluble." The judges, probably envisioning a "personal monarchy" with accessible monarch and without ministerial vexations, enthusiastically agreed: "Yes, Sire . . . such is the excellence of Monarchical Government, that it finds its stability in the intimate relations that exist . . . between the Monarch and the Nation." Lamoignon had stated: "The Nation, Sire, profits if the prerogatives of its Chief suffer no alteration." Riposted the magistrates: "The Chief profits if the Members of the Nation lose none of the essential rights that belong to them." Lamoignon had stated: "The King is the Sovereign Head of the Nation, and constitutes an entity with it." To this replied the judges: "He promises justice and protection to his people, under the religion of his oath." And then there was Lamoignon's most controversial pronouncement: "The legislative power resides solely in the person of the Sovereign, *sans dépendance et sans partage.*" To this the Bretons responded with the conviction of *parlementaires* everywhere: "Such however is the wisdom of the French Government, that before the Law has received its definitive form, and can be executed, it must be verified in the Parlement, . . . the true Consistory of the King. . . . that verification makes it possible to compare the new Law with the ancient Laws, . . . and to ensure that it affects neither the public order nor the Citizens' rights adversely."[38] Herein lay a practical warranty for observance of all the preceding (and rather theoretical) limitations upon the monarch's power: an ongoing judicial review of specific government policies. However, lest their critics charge them with threatening thereby to obstruct the king's reforms and thus paralyze public affairs, Rennes' *parlementaires* advanced one final point. "When the Nation's ills are extreme, and the constitution is in danger," the "Nation," insisted the judges, had the right to request from its sovereign the convocation of the Estates General. This is how they dealt with allegations that the jurists would frustrate public purposes, and with Lamoignon's claim that the king alone could pronounce upon the need for the historic organ of national consultation.[39]

It was entirely consistent with parlementary doctrine that the Bretons, at another point in their remonstrances, should have gone to great lengths to associate themselves with the king in the judicial and administrative affairs of the realm. The jurists' weighty responsibilities established "necessary and immediate relations" between sovereign and magistracy and conferred upon the latter "the right to communicate directly" with the former. "The dignity of the Parlement" was "an essential part of the King's dignity."[40] No wonder the Bretons endorsed Lamoignon's postulation of an "indissoluble bond" between king and nation: they regarded themselves as associates of the one and as tribunes of the other. But precisely because they did, they had to render unto the king's subjects what was theirs as well as serve the king's interests. This explains their point-by-point rejoinder to Lamoignon's litany of the absolute monarch's prerogatives. What to their many detractors seemed the height of inconsistency and hypocrisy was for the judges no more than advocacy of *all* interests in the realm (including, of course, their own).

The ministerial invocation of royal prerogatives at the *séance royale* drew even heavier fire from the intractable *parlementaires* of Normandy. In their decree of 25 June 1788 they not only assailed the ministers of Louis XVI but also challenged absolutism itself as displayed at the session of 19 November 1787. To begin with, the magistrates at Rouen averred that ministers who were "friends of truth . . . would have observed that until recently, our Kings' attendance in their courts of Parlement had not at all been regarded as an act of sovereign authority, obliged to deploy all its greatness, but rather as the simple and legitimate exercise of an incontestable right, whose exercise the nation has regretted to see become so rare." The royal presence at parlementary sessions had customarily signified the "mutual confidence" existing between monarch and magistrates and the determination of the former to "work for the common welfare, to enlighten himself through the insights of others so as to add to the solemnity of registrations of edicts, and thus merit the public's confidence all the more." Consequently, asserted the Normans—and here was the nub of the matter—"the purpose of . . . Sovereigns in coming to deliberate in the Parlement themselves on the verification and registration of these laws was not to disregard a plurality of votes that both the goodness and the wisdom of these same laws would assure them in advance." The Normans thus felt justified in daring to gainsay Louis XVI's right at the *séance royale* (or, by extension, at a session of any tribunal) to overrule the assembled magistrates. "Other ministers, friends of truth . . . would have observed finally that it was not possible to say that the plurality must not be formed *because it must not prevail in Parlement in the King's presence*, without professing a novel doctrine."[41] In deliberately underscoring and rejecting ministerial language in this last sentence, the judges of Rouen were, at least in this connection, jettisoning traditional absolutism itself.

Moreover, as if this were not enough, the Normans went on to assault absolutism as manifested in the recent institution of the Cour Plénière (Plenary Court). They ridiculed "the creation of an unprecedented Court of purely royal foundation" that would ratify laws "without regard for the plurality of votes, a plurality that could not be formed, much less prevail in the King's presence." The French nation, they declared, would recognize the legitimacy of "an indestructible and national Tribunal formed or solicited by itself" but would never brook "an assembly receiving its powers, its institution from the King alone."[42] The Normans were sufficiently circumspect to voice their conviction throughout their incendiary *arrêt* that Louis XVI had been outrageously counseled by his ministers, that the "despotism" of Lamoignon and his minions contravened the king's noble intentions, that there was yet time to apprise the monarch of all the evil being wrought in his name. The decree of 25 June 1788 nonetheless harbored some of the boldest of parlementary qualifications of royal absolutism in the prerevolutionary crisis. The decree, which as we noted earlier labeled Lamoignon a traitor and cut off all direct parlementary communication with him, struck one contemporary as being "the grand finale of the parlementary fireworks." There was, he thought, "no comparable decree in history."[43] The government, not far from rendering a similar judgment, formally quashed the offending decree on 9 July. It was not entirely amiss in censuring the Normans' *arrêt* as "seditious" and "injurious to royal authority."

We can see, then, that the provincial magistrates' attitudes toward their monarch on the eve of the Revolution were complex. The *parlementaires* undeniably dispensed justice and administered laws and regulations in the king's name, continued to uphold some of his most ancient prerogatives, and endeavored frequently to appeal to him over the heads of his advisers. They did these things to serve royal interests and other interests besides—including their own. At the same time, they did not hesitate to circumscribe the king's constitutional authority and did so upon some occasions in boldly specific detail. But from the viewpoint of the government, concerned as it had to be with its day-to-day operations and requirements, how the provincial justices reacted to ministers, intendants, and taxes was usually more crucial (at least in an immediate sense) than how they theorized upon royal sovereignty.

The Magistrates and the "Administrative Monarchy"

The provincial *parlements* may have viewed themselves as institutions still faithful to royalty in 1787–88, but they hesitated not at all to oppose the royal government's policies. To be sure, there were local variations upon this theme of judicial resistance. At one extreme, the court at Aix-en-Provence was more or less amenable to the ministers' wishes, at least before May 1788: its first president, after all, doubled as intendant, and its opposition to the extension of the *vingtièmes* late in 1787 abated with the government's concession to Provence of her long-dormant Estates.[44] Then, again, judges of minor courts (for instance, at Perpignan, Colmar, and Douai) could not be reasonably expected to initiate a magisterial revolt against Versailles. At the other extreme, the *parlementaires* at Bordeaux, Besançon, Grenoble, and Rouen had been tenaciously resisting the ministers on a plethora of issues throughout Louis XVI's reign and could be expected to cause major headaches for reformers in 1787.[45] Even in a lesser jurisdiction, the fires of magisterial defiance could burn brightly: witness the *parlement* at Pau, long given to articulating the perceived concerns of the hardy and mercurial folk of Navarre and Béarn, and fated to continue in this role in 1787–88.[46] Yet behind this façade of variations reflecting local circumstance loomed the edifice of a parlementary "mentality" that did not radically differ from one province to another. As a general rule, the justices assailed Louis XVI's most important ministers with varying degrees of ferocity, evinced suspicion of or candid hostility toward his intendants, and criticized the relentless growth of bureaucracy and taxation. In so doing, the jurists revealed an unedifying blend of spite, pettiness, and fiscal irresponsibility, but exposed as well a concern over political and constitutional issues shared by many of their most thoughtful compatriots.

Personal animus undeniably helped inspire the high magistracy's arraignment of the ministers in the prerevolutionary crisis. It was not altogether coincidental that of the three outstanding policymakers in this period—Calonne, Lamoignon, and Loménie de Brienne—the first two almost invariably bore the brunt of the law courts' criticism. Both Calonne and Lamoignon were former *parlementaires* and thus could be regarded as turncoats, as deserters from the parlementary cause.[47] Indeed, both men, in embracing the government's cause, had incurred magisterial wrath in controversies prior to 1787: Calonne in Brittany and Lamoignon at Paris.[48] Consequently, the politics of 1787–88 gave the provincial judges an excellent opportunity to vent old hatreds and (so they hoped) settle old scores. Yet in castigating Louis XVI's controller general and keeper of the seals the magistrates also raised some valid questions concerning those individuals' conduct in office and the proper uses of ministerial power in general.

Of course, Calonne was especially easy prey for the *parlements* in the months following his dismissal from government service. Not that individual tribunals had hesitated to combat him on local issues during his ministry; in fact, several of them were still engaged in such imbroglios at the start of 1787. But it was only in August and September of that year that the jurists in provincial France, reacting to the dramatic events at Paris and Bordeaux and beginning to elaborate their own critiques of the central government, focused their attack upon Calonne's *national* policies. Once having bestirred themselves, however, there was scarcely any accusation they were not prepared to hurl at the man so recently entrusted with the most crucial portfolio at Versailles.

Calculated to be most telling of all in the eyes of the literate public were the invidious comparisons a number of the courts drew between Calonne and that earlier finance minister and reputed worker of miracles, Jacques Necker. Grenoble's *parlementaires*, utilizing Necker's own figures, the fiscal revelations at the Notables, and their own biased computations, led the way in their *arrêté* of 21 August. As the king's "ordinary revenues" in January 1781 exceeded his "ordinary expenses" by 10,200,000 livres, how was it possible, queried the Grenoblois incredulously, that the government now could "still estimate the annual deficit at around one hundred and forty millions?" How horrifying that "in the interval of three or four years," during which time the authorities "ought to have profited from the advantages of peace to lighten the burden borne by the people," a "malevolent genius" had "compounded their misery by adding to the existing debts an overwhelming burden of more than two hundred millions!" How horrifying that "a vicious administration" had "in so short a time brought upon the state a more profound plague than could have been visited upon it by the longest and most accursed war!" In light of such realities, or what were accepted as such by the indignant judges at Grenoble, it was only logical for them to declare that "the glory of the . . . King, the interest of the nation and the security of the State" demanded that "someone thoroughly investigate the conduct of the author of such great confusion." These avatars of justice even allowed themselves the observation that Calonne seemed "convicted in advance" of "having exhausted the Royal Treasury" with "unheard-of depredations," of "having deceived the . . . King about the true condition of his finances, and of having betrayed public confidence with false assurances." It was essential, they pursued grimly, that this nefarious individual be punished, and punished severely, so that "a salutary terror might be struck into the hearts of those who could be tempted in the future to imitate his example."[49]

Parlementaires all over the kingdom lashed out in a similar vein at the disgraced Calonne, sometimes laying staggering fiscal sins to his account. In remonstrances of 1 September 1787 the justices at Besançon alleged that "at the very time when he appeared to be so sympathetic toward the People," Calonne had "announced a bankruptcy that supposed on his part a dissipation of three billions during three years of peace," and as a means of dealing with "this catastrophe" had "proposed new taxes, whose yield would be equivalent to that of six *vingtièmes*."[50] In an *arrêté* issued eleven days later the Burgundian magistrates disgustedly averred that "unbridled and revolting depredations in the administration of finances" had "swallowed up in a short interval sums which the most disastrous wars could not have consumed."[51] At Rennes, the jurists in protests of December 1787 declared that the mishandling of royal finances constituted a "crime of *lèse-nation*"—by which the Bretons presumably meant a misdeed fully as grave as the more traditional crime of *lèse-majesté*.[52] Even in normally quiescent Roussillon, Calonne could be invidiously contrasted to the wonderful Necker and accused of colossal malfeasance in office. In a decree they struck off on 3 September 1787, the judges at Perpignan echoed their counterparts of Franche-Comté by charging that the former controller general had managed somehow to "dissipate" more than "three billions in less than four years of peace." Perpignan's "sovereign councilors" flung accusatory fiscal computations about with an abandon characterizing parlementaires almost everywhere. They concluded their *arrêté* in the same spirit, urging an unsparing inquiry into Calonne's ministry and exemplary chastisement of the fallen minister himself—although, as they obliquely conceded, his recent flight from the country looked very much like an attempt to save him from anything more severe than punishment in absentia.[53]

In arguing thus that royal finances had suffered grievously under Calonne's stewardship, the provincial magistrates were patently exposing their animus against him, taking their cue to do so from the Parisian judges' denunciations of July and August.[54] Beyond this, however, they were testifying to the enormous hold upon public opinion of Necker's celebrated *Compte rendu* of 1781. Calonne himself recognized this very clearly at the time: indeed, he and Necker were engaged in a furious war of pamphlets over the hotly debated (and even today inadequately understood) question of the French state's finances.[55] Calonne and some of his contemporaries were quite right to accuse the *parlements* of extreme recklessness in their commentary upon this subject. Nevertheless, that the sovereign courts could indulge in such demagoguery in the first place also reflected public suspicion that the government's finances, as shrouded as always in mystery, were actually in a chaotic state. For that matter, magisterial polemics against Calonne usually contained kernels of much-needed criticism of administrative practices under the Bourbons. Let us return for a moment to the Burgundian *parlementaires'* *arrêté* of 12 September 1787:

> It is not at all by the establishment of new taxes, that exceed the strength of the People, that the Monarch must seek to establish order in his finances . . . he must derive his financial sustenance from a wise and honorable thrift, from the choice of administrators of unblemished reputation, and must allow the courts of justice to proceed against those whose waste and peculation have occasioned the crisis and distress of the State.[56]

Moreover, there is no denying that Calonne's policy of borrowing continually from 1783 to 1786 to keep royal finances afloat contributed substantially to the government's straits in 1787. The Paris Parlement had sharply criticized that policy at the time and had offered something of a blueprint for making the fiscal administration itself less costly and more efficient.[57] These representations naturally had been rejected by Louis XVI, but they look more impressive today in light of a new scholarly emphasis upon Necker's efforts to salvage the *ancien régime* through systemic administrative reform.[58] The indictments of Calonne's administration that rang out in the Cour des Pairs in the summer of 1787 sounded much like what had come before in the Paris Parlement. The censorious commentary of the provincial judiciary reinforced those indictments and thus raised a national hue and cry over the substantive and significant issue of malfeasance and inefficiency in the central government.

But the high magistracy reserved its most venomous language for the keeper of the seals in 1788. Admittedly, Lamoignon was not as universally attacked as Calonne had been the preceding fall: most of the sovereign courts spent their fury upon the May Edicts themselves, detailing and anathematizing the myriad ways in which they supposedly violated the age-old prerogatives of the judiciary and the provinces.[59] Nevertheless, *parlementaires* here and there did refer, scathingly, to the keeper of the seals or "the ministers." The judges at Rouen, we recall, signaled their intention on 25 June 1788 to denounce to the king "as traitors to him and to the State the Ministers responsible for having so misled His Majesty, and specifically le Sieur de Lamoignon." This individual, the Normans charged, had "against his own soul and conscience . . . not blushed to render himself" in oppressed Frenchmen's eyes "the apologist" of the hateful ordinances of May and of the equally hateful means employed to ram them through the tribunals of the realm.[60] The Normans even dared allude to "the mendacious speeches of the Keeper of the Seals."[61] The high justices at Rennes, though not mentioning Lamoignon by name in an outspoken decree of 31 May 1788, patently had him in mind in denouncing "to the King and nation as guilty of *lèse-majesté* and of *lèse-patrie* those who in the perversity of their hearts have dared to conceive, propose and execute projects leading to the total subversion of the civil order." The "enterprises" of such depraved individuals, averred the Bretons, were so "sacrilegious" as to "direct against the nation itself the very military forces it maintains for its own defense."[62] The *parlementaires* at Grenoble took the keeper of the seals to task in a decree promulgated on 9 May 1788, one day in advance of the government's judicial coup in Dauphiné. The jurists, referring the sovereign to "the constitution," entreated him "to be on guard against the insinuations of the author of that disastrous revolution, who, after having been the victim of a generous steadfastness at an earlier time when the destruction of the Magistracy was already envisioned, forgetting today his former principles, would like in his turn to annihilate it."[63] To listen to the Grenoblois, or *parlementaires* elsewhere, Lamoignon's apostasy was almost too hideous to contemplate.

But, once again, as sorry as was this spectacle of magisterial vindictiveness against one who would have saved the *ancien régime*, and with it some measure of parlementary influence, and as bent as the judges were upon preserving in toto a grievously flawed system of justice, they could not help but raise a constitutional issue recognized by even their severest critics as valid. Could a government steeped in a centuries-old tradition of absolutism now be trusted to do what it was claiming to set out to do? Or, to put it another way, would its success against the rebellious *parlements* be a triumph for the cause of reform in state and society or for the high-handed way in which reform was implemented? How could one be sure? Obviously, one could not be sure, responded the insubordinate magistrates—but, then, so did many others in France at this critical juncture. First, let us hear the *parlementaires* at Grenoble speak in their major decree of 20 May 1788 for their counterparts throughout the realm on that most passionately debated of the government's innovations, the Plenary Court. The judges declared

> ... that the members that must compose it, although chosen from among the most distinguished personages of the state, would be absolutely dependent upon the Government; some, because chosen by the Ministers in the Sovereign's name; others, because they oc-

cupy positions in his household or his council; and all, because of the favors they would expect. . . .

that they could be replaced if absent by councilors of State and *maîtres des requêtes*, whose will would always be that of the Ministers from whom they hold their public influence, their consideration, and their existence;

that they could oppose only a vain resistance to the views of the Ministers, since no provision of the law assures them the right to vote, and since every time authority showed its heavy hand, their zeal would be fettered and their functions destroyed;

that they would not be consulted on the necessity and consistency of loans, a fatal and ruinous resource, whose use the Ministers would like to determine by their own whim and caprice . . . and whose rapid increase, coming to surpass the resources of the State, would soon force it to default upon agreements struck up to the present day with creditors who have advanced loans upon the public credit.[64]

This was more or less the message from exasperated *parlements* all over the kingdom, though they dilated as well upon probable ministerial manipulation of the Plenary Court to dispose arbitrarily of subjects' properties and lives. Even the Aixois, hesitant the preceding year about joining the judicial opposition to the crown, expatiated now upon the evils likely to attend the operations of the new tribunal as well as the implementation of the government's other acts.[65]

Contemporaries might question magisterial motives in all this, but they could not deny that the judges had raised legitimate issues. No one was more fiercely critical of the *parlements* and their justice than Félix Faulcon, a member of the presidial court at Poitiers; yet he, too, profoundly distrusted the policymakers at Versailles. In a letter to a friend the preceding October he had derided Calonne's and Brienne's stamp tax as "the masterpiece of a diabolical or (what is the same thing) financial mind" and had alluded to "the ministers' vindictiveness."[66] Now, on the threshold of the summer of 1788, his mistrust was aroused again by the government's establishment of the Plenary Court. "It is . . . certainly obvious," Faulcon conceded in a missive of 20 June, "that we needed some kind of assembly or tribunal uniquely charged with registering laws for the entire kingdom." On the other hand, he commented, "the Plenary Court does not satisfy me altogether in that regard . . . its present composition would . . . expose it too much to the influence of the ministers." Indeed, "a Plenary Court bought over to the will of the Court would be extremely dangerous."[67] Faulcon was sufficiently alienated by the *parlementaires* and by the traditional judicial and administrative system they championed to give the Plenary Court and its authors the benefit of the doubt, at least for the time being. Nevertheless, the preponderance of "enlightened" opinion was with the stricken law courts on this and associated issues in the fateful summer of 1788. Condorcet, Mirabeau, and Lafayette were only the most renowned of those "Patriots" who, however sensitized to the magistrates' shortcomings, endorsed their opposition to the ministers' show of force.[68]

Apostles of enlightenment may have been somewhat less inclined to approve the harsh judgments pronounced by several of the provincial *parlements* in 1787–88 upon those sturdy and industrious agents of royal authority, the intendants.[69] Certainly it would have been only natural to have discerned an ad hominem element in such a bitter critique by judges long locked in combat with these administrators over a wide range of local as well as national issues. Yet here, again, personalities clearly were not all: charges leveled against intendants and their subordinates mirrored a multitude of local interests and widespread suspicions that the government was, after all, "despotic."

Probably the most thoroughgoing indictment of the intendants in the months before revolution issued from the jurists at Besançon. This was hardly surprising—the Comtois had been especially tenacious in opposing local application of royal reforms throughout Louis XVI's reign and would have to be forced in May 1788 to ratify legislation that for years had lacked parlementary sanction.[70] The question of the intendants' role was broached at Besançon as early as February 1787 in connection with the *corvée royale*. President de Vezet, Droz des Villars, and their colleagues had from the start disliked Calonne's decree of 6 November 1786 provisionally replacing this obligatory labor with an additional tax upon the *taillables*.[71] In remonstrating against this innovation on 5 February, Besançon's *parlementaires* almost immediately focused upon what they perceived to be the intendants' role in the affair:

> It is upon the advice of the *commissaires* of Your Council delegated to the provinces [that is, the intendants] that you have decided to establish the tax; but it is not upon them that the People will have to rely for the presentation to you of their plaints.
>
> In the form prescribed by the decree, not only are the Commissaires Départis charged with the assessment of the tax, they completely administer and manage it, without being held to a regular accountability; the more their power, their authority in that sphere grows, the more the People will fear being overtaxed.

The judges very candidly insisted that they, and their counterparts throughout France, should at least share with the intendants supervision of the employment of public moneys upon the kingdom's roads and bridges. They were, it is true, diplomatic enough to concede that in each intendancy this administrator, who could not "by himself know the condition, the needs of the People," was "so often exposed to deception in the explanations given him by others." Yet this, they argued, made it all the more reasonable to apprehend that "the unlimited power confided in this connection to the Commissaire Départi" would in the end become an "inexhaustible source of abuses of all kinds." No one, the magistrates assured the king, could better apprise him of "what in this sphere suits the Provinces, of what their particular conditions, their needs, their interests demand," than could those provinces' sovereign courts.[72]

Predictably, the Comtois received no satisfaction on this matter from Versailles. What they did receive, four months later, was a letter from Lamoignon reaffirming the benefits to be derived by all concerned from the commutation of the *corvée royale* and denying the *parlements* the right to do more than advise the monarch upon the administration of his realm.[73] The judges soon wrote back to the keeper of the seals to reject his exposition of the government's policy.[74] Moreover, events provided them with an opportunity to renew and broaden their assault upon the intendants. Before the end of July, they were refusing to ratify the establishment of a provincial assembly in Franche-Comté.[75] Their stated concern (common in the high judiciary) was that such an institution could be little more than a novel instrument of "despotism." And who should wield that instrument for the further subjugation of provincial Frenchmen if not the intendants? Hence, these unsparing comments in remonstrances of 1 September upon the intendants' administration:

> Your Majesty, fixing his eyes first upon the administration of the Kingdom, has recognized that in several provinces it is entrusted to a *commissaire*, who, whether absent or present, is authorized to adjudge important disputes in final instance, save for an appeal to the Council, which distance, expense, and delays render impossible; that this man is subject to no inspection; that his arbitrary activities, arbitrarily directed and executed, are regulated by no principle other than the most blind Despotism. His Mission, almost always won for him by years of service having nothing to do with administration, seems often to have supposed neither talent nor excellence nor knowledge on his part. His absolute power, like that of his underlings, is completely exempt from all accountability in financial matters and may with impunity effect the most shocking

vexations. It will one day be deemed incredible that such an astonishing administration could have maintained itself in an enlightened nation for more than a century.[76]

Harsh language, this—and hardly mitigated by the magistrates' occasional allusions in these protests (as in their earlier representations over the *corvée*) to benevolent intendants deceived "by others" or corrupted by their inherently abusive powers. And Besançon's *parlementaires* went even further, differentiating between the king's legitimate authority (we have encountered this already) and the intrinsically illegitimate force marshaled by the king's council! "The council ... to which Your Majesty calls only his Ministers," they dared to argue, "has never had nor claimed to have" any authority. Thus, the administrators dispatched to the provinces from that council were illegitimate; thus, all *arrêts du Conseil* affronted the "laws" of France. But the judges, we suspect, exposed the heart of their complaint in alleging that "all general officers, commanding or employed in the province, [including] the Bishops who counsel and guide it, the members of your Parlement, the municipal officers in the cities, all together do not wield an authority as absolute, as universal, as dreaded, as a single subordinate of the intendant." The gravamen of the judges' protest was that the central government, no matter how meritorious its agents, was encroaching upon the domain of *parlementaires* and other local "officers."

That such fault should have been found and such censorious language employed by Besançon's high justices in their commentary of 1787 upon the agents of the central government must have struck those partisans of the crown familiar with these remonstrances as wildly irresponsible—and as discouragingly redolent of the old magisterial oppositionism. Yet constitutional scruples were probably also involved here. When First President Perreney de Grosbois wrote to the ministers on 18 August to announce his company's decision to remonstrate formally against the provincial assemblies, he explained that "the great majority" of his colleagues "persisted in thinking that they must continue steadfastly to entreat the King in his goodness to grant the convocation of the Estates." They had in fact "gone so far as to say that since the Estates were part of the constitution of the Province, they had not the power to adopt another form of administration." The first president's arguments for the institution of a provincial assembly in Franche-Comté had been unavailing.[77]

Besançon's judges could at least remind the authorities that their court's jurisdiction coincided with a historic province for which Estates had actually functioned prior to 1674. Their professional cousins at Bordeaux could dredge up no analogous precedent. Nevertheless, whereas most of the provincial *parlements* were content to follow the Parisians' example of provisionally ratifying the legislation establishing the provincial assemblies, pending their subsequent review of regulations defining the powers and organization of these bodies,[78] the court at Bordeaux in July and early August refused utterly to sanction this legislation before seeing the supplementary regulations.[79] When the government went ahead anyway with implementation of its reform at Limoges, the Bordelais had the effrontery to respond with a decree of prohibition. Their subsequent banishment to Libourne only hardened their resistance to the royal and ministerial will on this and other public questions, as signified in decrees and remonstrances of the ensuing months. These parlementary apologias, akin to those emanating from Franche-Comté, assailed the intendants and other "despotic" figures.

The exiles at Libourne, for example, stated in a decree of 7 September that they recognized "how preferable the provincial assemblies, if well regulated, would be to the frequently arbitrary administration of a *commissaire départi.*" But they emphatically did not wish to see in their jurisdiction "several small provincial assemblies, scattered, incoherent, each one foreign to the others, which, under a domineering Minister, would have no will other than that of a few *commissaires* chosen by the administration, and which could favor the sway of oppression, far from safeguarding the people from it."[80] Then, in their widely circulated remonstrances of 31 October, the Bordelais selectively adduced testimony of the Notables to dramatize their misgivings about the prospective relationship between the intendants and the provincial assemblies.

> One of the most interesting points in the regime of the provincial assemblies [said the Bordelais] is that regarding the *commissaires départis*: the Bureaux of the Notables felt strongly that it was absolutely essential to the public interest that their authority be . . . circumscribed in a fixed and unchanging manner.
>
> Consequently some of them "desired that these assemblies be authorized to assess and allot all public taxes and other obligations, even that of militia duty, district by district and parish by parish, and as a result to act without needing any authorization other than that of the Council."
>
> The others expressed the wish "that the power of the Intendants be so interpreted that the provincial assemblies have a genuinely active role, which would not depend upon the Intendants."

Unfortunately, the judges observed, "events have borne out what the Notables in their prudence foresaw. The *commissaires départis* have assumed an authority over the provincial assemblies which has disheartened the presidents and the rank-and-file of several of these assemblies."[81] At least the Bordelais had the satisfaction of knowing that they were not alone among *parlementaires* in protesting such developments: they approvingly cited similar representations made by the Grenoblois in relation to events in Dauphiné.

The near unanimity of the Bordelais upon this question, signaled early on by First President Le Berthon in correspondence with the ministers, failed to give way in 1787 despite enormous pressure exerted upon the company by Versailles.[82] (By the following March, the court was wavering somewhat but was not yet overcome in its opposition.) Elsewhere, the sovereign courts were occupied with other issues, or in any case were a bit more circumspect in reflecting upon the regime of the intendants. There were nonetheless unmistakable signs that the sentiments articulated by Besançon's *parlementaires* and by their counterparts of Bordeaux in 1787 were widely held in the high judiciary.

The defiant Bordelais had referred in their remonstrances of 31 October to magisterial opposition at Grenoble, and with good reason. Although the Grenoblois were somewhat less disposed initially to challenge the government over its provincial assemblies (they registered the pertinent legislation on 11 August), their attitude hardened in the fall. By 7 October the intendant in Dauphiné, Gaspard-Louis Caze de la Bove, was reporting to Versailles "the currently well known vow of the majority in the company to resist with the greatest determination the establishment of the new administrative regime."[83] In fact, the Grenoble Parlement, taking a page out of the book of the Bordelais, issued an interdictory decree against the provincial assembly recently convened in the Dauphinois capital. As exposed in protests of 15 December, magisterial misgivings here were pretty much what they were elsewhere.[84] The Grenoblois objected that their provincial assembly's "absolute dependence upon the Commissaire départi could lead it to become the instrument of arbitrary power . . . at the least sign of . . . opposition to the Ministers' projects, its constitution . . . could be altered, to the detriment of the People, by a simple decree wheedled from the Lord King and his Council." That the magistrates, in the same breath, extolled the tribunals' role of registration as "the first and most inviolable of all laws," as "the safeguard of the Monarchy's constitution, of the Sovereign's authority, and of the Subjects' rights," demonstrates once again that, for the jurists, distrust of the administrative monarchy and advocacy of parlementary politics were two sides of the same coin. Caze de la Bove later informed the government that twenty-eight of thirty-six judges had voted for the protests of 15 December, and even the ministry's decision to hale the particularly recalcitrant President d'Ornacieux and counselor Corbet de Meyrieu to Versailles for a severe reproof in the dead of winter did little but confirm the Grenoblois in their intransigence.[85]

It is noteworthy that even a grudging parlementary decision in 1787 to cooperate with the government on this issue did not necessarily betoken trust in the intendants and their subordinates. The Toulousains, for instance, ratified the ministers' legislation without undue cavil, but in remonstrances of 12 January 1788 on the *vingtièmes* they could not forgo characterizing the provincial assemblies as "administrations created in each Province to supervise a myriad of interesting matters abandoned formerly to the will of a single man."[86] Again, toward the end of that pivotal year, the *parlementaires* at Rouen, taking heart perhaps from the collapse of the Brienne and Lamoignon ministries, let *their* true feelings about the intendants be known. In a letter to Louis XVI of 28 November requesting the restoration of the old Norman Estates, they savagely attacked these officials.

> It would doubtless be . . . interesting to know to what cause we must attribute the suspension of a right so precious to Normandy. It appears that we can find one of the principal causes in the establishment of the Commissaires départis under the title of *intendant*. . . . These antinational Magistrates affected all kinds of power, since legally they had none at all. They placed themselves between the Prince and the Subjects; but they showed themselves more often to be the harsh executors of the Ministry's orders, than to be the zealous paladins of the People entrusted to their care.[87]

An unjust portrayal, certainly, of men who seem for the most part to have labored honorably in the royal and public interest. We might add that such arraignments by no means emanated solely from the major *parlements*. In writing to the king on 12 July 1787, the sovereign judges of Colmar actually thanked him for conferring a provincial assembly upon Alsace—but only because, as they alleged, the administration of their intendant, Antoine Chaumont de la Galaisière, had been so "arbitrary" and oppressive.[88]

Yet obviously when the Alsatian judges and their counterparts in the other sovereign courts lashed out at the intendants, they were rejecting substantive royal policies as much as the purportedly "despotic" or deceitful means employed to implement those policies. Why, after all, were the provincial *parlements* so exercised about novel administrative bodies and their sponsors in the government? In part, we may reply, because of what the establishment of the assemblies by the authorities implied about bureaucracy and taxation. Here were the jurists at Grenoble, addressing the former issue on 6 October 1787:

This new form of Administration utilizes more than 11,000 people;
... it is composed of Municipal Assemblies, of arrondissement assemblies, of department assemblies, of the Provincial Assembly,
and of several intermediary commissions ... the complexity of
these various degrees, the relations among these different sorts of
Assemblies, ... and their mutual correspondence, would only
hinder their activities, and delay the expedition of affairs.

Moreover, even in "according perquisites, on the most modest basis,
solely to persons exercising regular and daily functions, and to those
obliged to travel, the expense would still rise to more than 400,000 livres." Yet, failing such compensation, "the zeal stimulated by patriotic
impulse and by the love of novelty would imperceptibly subside, and the
Assemblies would be deserted."[89] These were not unfounded concerns;
even the intendant, Caze de la Bove, came close to conceding as much
in a letter to the ministers of 7 October.[90] In addition, the Grenoblois
and their fellow magistrates in nearby Franche-Comté had just recently
been lamenting the government's provisional conversion of the *corvée*
into a tax on *taillables* for similar reasons—complaining, that is, that
administrative "reform" seemed always to swell expenses and the ranks
of petty officialdom.[91] (The Parisian judges had been making the same
point for years.) Many *parlementaires*, then, wondered where bureaucracy and its attendant delays and costs would ever end. But the word
"costs" brings us to that other issue, equally debatable and equally
timeless: taxation. The Besançon Parlement spoke to this issue in suggesting to Louis XVI what lurked behind the ministers' new assemblies:

> The principal operation which he who proposed that innovation to
> you had in mind, was a new assessment of taxes, under the pretext
> of equalizing them; this was the master purpose of his project; it
> was for this reason that he reserved to himself the choice of the
> members, and intended that those chosen should be irremovable
> for three years; he hoped likewise that this [project], by generating
> litigation in the Council between the Provinces, pitting some
> against others, would facilitate the overtaxation of all of them, one
> after the other.[92]

Was there, then, *anything* that the ministers and their myrmidons
would not do in their loathsome effort to pack the coffers at Versailles
with provincial wealth?

Lest this seem but cynical rhetoric designed to obfuscate the issue of
undertaxation of *parlementaires* and other *privilégiés*, we may recall
how Félix Faulcon, that severe critic of the sovereign courts, ridiculed
the ministers' stamp tax as "the masterpiece of a diabolical or (what is

the same thing) financial mind." We should also recall that the Bourbons and their advisers had never taken their most enlightened compatriots into their confidence where affairs of state were concerned, and yet had expected them to accept as essential every new tax or increase in existing taxation. How often had such imposts been styled initially as "temporary" and designated for specific purposes—and how often had they eventuated in permanent or frequently renewed tributes swelling the government's general revenues! Meanwhile, the governed, as utterly mystified by the fiscal requirements of French foreign and domestic policies as were (ironically) the sovereigns themselves, had no compelling reason to believe that they ought to submit indefinitely to taxation that was seemingly ever on the increase. Like taxpayers of any other era and realm, they would have preferred to pay nothing at all. Such attitudes, prior to 1789, were most faithfully represented in the kingdom's sovereign courts, whose polemics understandably advanced arguments diametrically opposed to those of the administrative monarchy.

The clash between the interests of the taxpayers (of whatever social rank) and those of the state was reflected in magisterial propaganda throughout the prerevolutionary crisis. The Dauphinois, for example, asserted on 21 August 1787 that

> the same laws that assure to the . . . King his Crown, guarantee to all his subjects possession of their property; . . . that property would only be a vain and illusory title . . . if its revenue could be absorbed by taxes; . . . the level of taxation must be regulated on the basis of a just combination of the requirements of the State and those of the citizens and . . . the genuine needs of the people must not be sacrificed to the imaginary needs of the State.[93]

Just nine days later, Besançon's *parlementaires* spelled out the implications of this stance for the monarch's finances by insisting

> that the immensity of the State's revenues makes it impossible to believe in the necessity of new subsidies, and ought to safeguard finances from the enterprises and schemes of the *esprit fiscal*; that these revenues would be more than sufficient to acquit all debts and obligations and to uphold the splendor of the Throne and the glory of France in magnificent fashion, if the public moneys were left in faithful and frugal hands and were not squandered in outrageous prodigalities.[94]

And so we have come full circle, back to the universal outcry against the ministers and their corrupt and spendthrift ways. Almost without exception, the provincial *parlements* associated the stated need for additional tax revenue with extravagance and peculation and borrowing policies at Versailles, and in the months to come some of them were even to chide the Paris Parlement for having acceded too readily to government demands for registration of new loans.[95]

That a veritable chasm yawned between magisterial and ministerial perspectives on the cutting issue of taxation was most strikingly attested by several law courts' picayune critiques of the *vingtièmes*. We recall that, under the terms of the compromise worked out in September 1787 between the government and the Parisian *parlementaires* in exile at Troyes, the *subvention territoriale* and stamp tax were withdrawn and *vingtième* taxation restored. The first *vingtième* remained of indefinite duration, the second was extended through 1791 and 1792, and the provinces or *généralités* were to bargain with the ministers through their Estates or provincial assemblies over the exact *abonnements*, or lump-sum payments, they would owe yearly to Versailles.[96]

That powerful social interests in the countryside would be adversely affected by this compromise is patent, and we shall soon have occasion to consider how the judges' remarks upon the crown's taxes illuminated their attitudes toward the various classes of society. For the moment, however, it is their static conception of state finances, and the implications of that conception for the state itself, that must claim our attention. Magisterial thoughts upon taxation varied little from one court to the next in 1787–88. Hence, since no parlement expounded those views more forthrightly—indeed, more painstakingly—than did that of Rouen, we may concentrate primarily upon what the Normans had to say, specifically in their *arrêté* of 20 December 1787, against the *vingtièmes*.

If Loménie de Brienne and his allies manifestly expected such taxation to be permanent and to yield more revenue as property values rose, the Normans just as plainly had radically different ideas. It was "an error" to believe that the *vingtièmes* must "increase gradually with the taxpayers' revenues," they declared. "This impost, like all others, could only have been established . . . to meet a momentary need." To maintain otherwise, they argued, "would be to profess that false and imprudent maxim, that the state's debts, instead of being amortized through order and savings, must grow in proportion with the taxpayers' properties." As nonsensical as such reasoning might seem to the crown's adherents, worse was yet to come. Much like the Parisian justices in past quarrels with Necker, the Normans subjected earlier tax edicts to hair-splitting interpretations in order to overthrow current ministerial doctrine on finance. For instance, had it not been self-evident since the *vingtièmes* first saw the light of day that their yield was not to increase as property values rose? The jurists averred

> that this truth was so clearly appreciated from the start, that the
> Edict of May 1749, creating the first *vingtième*, stipulated that

only those proprietors who had not been included in the tax-rolls established earlier for the collection of the *dixième* would be obligated to declare the value of their holdings; that by the declaration of 7 July 1756, the second *vingtième* was established in the same form, and upon the same principles as the first, even though the landed properties had probably already increased perceptibly in value since 1749.[97]

Of course the government had from time to time strayed from this sane principle, but never for very long. In 1777 and 1778 "harsh acts of absolute power" against landowners had unfortunately multiplied—an allusion to Necker—but respectful representations from the sovereign courts had restored the king's policymakers to their senses. They had once again embraced the essential maxim "that every impost is unalterable in its amount as well as in its duration." As proof of this, Rouen's *parlementaires* cited specific language from the act of January 1782 creating the third *vingtième*: "the three *vingtièmes* will be levied in a manner conforming to the rolls of the present year, without any taxpayer having to pay a higher rate of taxation." They construed this, and language from various other edicts on the *vingtièmes*, to mean that "all those who are taxed at rates higher than those anterior to 1749, would be authorized to seek redress in the ordinary manner," adding further that "those who pay a tax of precisely one tenth of their present revenue are in this situation exactly, because they should pay only one tenth of the revenue they had in 1749." Such an exegesis of past fiscal legislation made it logical for the Normans to assert that Louis XVI should now "have reduced the new tax rates to the level of the older ones, rather than raising the older rates to the level of the newer ones."

Normandy's jurists by the same token could envision no circumstances under which the legislation on the *vingtièmes* could be anything but injurious to local interests. To entrust determination of the province's *abonnement* to a provincial assembly would in magisterial eyes be tantamount to throwing the region's proprietors upon the mercy of the intendant, regarded invariably as the despotic power behind such an assembly. But the alternative, verification of land values by tax assessors and collectors, was equally unpalatable, conjuring up as it did memories of verifications undertaken during Necker's first ministry by "vexatious" and "arbitrary" fiscal agents in the countryside. Furthermore, as the judges continually reminded Louis XVI in their *arrêté*, there was the broader question of the duration and purposes of such taxation. Would the day ever come, they wondered, when imposts initially characterized as "temporary" actually expired when they were scheduled to expire, and were not turned to purposes other than those originally designated? Would the day ever come when wise administrators realized that debts must be paid off by cost-cutting measures at Versailles and by more efficient management of the king's sacred domain, and not by ruinous loans and even more ruinous taxes? Finally (and in the most crucial if quixotic of the judges' queries), would the sun ever rise over a France whose public policies, and expenditures for policy, were properly reined in by the taxpaying capacity of a long-suffering people?

If these questions were posed in particularly painful detail by the Normans, they were not evaded by *parlementaires* elsewhere. The Toulousains, in their *arrêté* of 27 August 1787, harped upon the government's obligation to put its fiscal house in order before seeking new tributes from the citizenry, and in full-dress remonstrances of 12 January 1788 chronicled the sad history of the *vingtièmes* much as the Normans had.[98] In remonstrances of 4 April 1788 the Dijonnais labored mightily to differentiate between "ordinary" and "extraordinary" expenses, only the latter of which could be justifiably defrayed by new (and, by definition, "temporary") taxes. Government expenditure, insisted the jurists naïvely, must be limited by available revenue; revenue must never become the servant, or slave, of capricious and ill-defined expenditure.[99] The Bordelais, unbowed in exile, quoted the Notables as having affirmed "that a time finally comes when taxation must cease, because the capacity to pay taxes has a limit." The government's deplorable deficit "could only derive from the errors and prodigalities of the administration."[100] Brittany's high justices voiced their astonishment that even "after five years of peace" (so unavoidable a phrase in parlementary polemics) the ministers could still be talking in terms of "crushing imposts." Did the authorities fail to realize that expenditure must be determined by revenue, and not revenue by expenditure?[101] The judges at Besançon and Grenoble, we know, were complaining about government expenditure even before they were confronted with the reimposition of the *vingtièmes* in October 1787. In Provence, Aixois President Fauris de Saint-Vincent might record his company's decision on 22 December 1787 to ratify reimposition of the *vingtièmes*, but this was done only when "we were sure of the convocation of the Estates of the province"— and even this timely concession by the authorities at Versailles would not prevent the Provençal *parlementaires* from going over to the opposition the following spring.[102]

Everywhere, then—and the protests of the lesser *parlements* could also be cited—magisterial attitudes toward the "administrative monarchy" were hostile in 1787–88. In vain did the controller general grandly announce his plan for rescuing royal finances and credit by the end of 1792. In vain did the keeper of the seals try to persuade Nancy's justices that his colleague's plan correctly estimated "the revenue and expenses for the five years from 1788 to 1792" and was "absolutely necessary to guarantee the treasury funds at this time for the service of those five years."[103] The provincial judges would have none of this. As noted earlier, their very failure to comprehend the fiscal and administrative requirements of an increasingly "modern" Power, a failure so widely shared by their countrymen, suggests what broadly based support the monarchy may have forfeited by adhering so resolutely to its absolutist traditions in the late eighteenth century. As it was, the citizenry's interest in public affairs could only manifest itself in sentiments truly radical in a constitutional sense. Inevitably, those sentiments, like so much else, found a voice in the judicial opposition of this period.

The Magistrates and the Radicalized "Constitution"

Although far from being citadels of youthful idealism and revolt in the style of the Cour des Pairs, the sovereign courts of provincial France were just as surely radicalized by onrushing events in the prerevolutionary crisis. In their pronouncements, perhaps even more than in those of the realm's primal *parlement*, we can see the Bourbons' proud scheme of things starting to unravel. More specifically, we can see here the resurgence of an ancient provincial patriotism, a more novel surge of national popular patriotism, and (unsurprisingly) the waxing political ambitions of the high robe. With hindsight we can also discern here in embryo several of those forces whose explosive interaction would rend the political and social fabric of France in the years that lay ahead.

It would be possible, but redundant, to show how each provincial tribunal vaunted local privileges and a local conception of history in dueling with the ministers in 1787–88. We would do well to focus primarily upon the example of the magistrates at Aix-en-Provence. The story of rising Provençal "patriotism" (and its apparent clash with French "patriotism") in an institution hitherto singled out for its amenability to royal and ministerial wishes in 1787 should suggest how powerful centrifugal forces of provincialism were throughout the high judiciary.

Procureur-Général Leblanc de Castillon gave warning of his company's identification with Provençal "nationalism" as early as March of 1787 in discussing the proposed *subvention territoriale* at the Assembly of Notables. This celebrated officer of the Aix Parlement declared to no less a Notable than the king's own brother, the comte d'Artois, that he could not "as a Provençal deliberate upon this subject, Provence having been neither conquered by nor joined to France." Provence, Leblanc de Castillon insisted, had "given herself freely" to the French "in confirmation of the Testament of King René, whose first article guarantees all privileges of the *Pays*, and notably that of never being subjected to any territorial impost." Not even the king of France, proclaimed this intrepid jurist, could "authorize" the imposition of Calonne's tax upon Provence.[104] The sensation created at the Assembly of Notables by this "protestation in favor of Provence" was duly noted by more than one memorialist of the time.[105]

About nine months later, it is true, the judges at Aix sanctioned the extension of the traditional *vingtièmes* through 1792, but it is significant that they did so in a manner underscoring their local patriotism. President Fauris de Saint-Vincent observed in his journal that his company had appended to its registration an *arrêté* affirming that its action was "without prejudice to the free acceptance" of the taxation by the Provençal Estates whose convocation was promised for 31 December. Moreover, the president and his associates assumed that the Estates would "offer" to the government in a lump sum only so much revenue as the province could fairly afford, and would have to consent to any future imposts or extensions of existing taxation before the *parlementaires* could even consider the question of registration. Even at that, Fauris de Saint-Vincent reported, several of his fellows had bridled at the thought of parlementary registration preceding action by the revived Estates upon the currently pending extension of the *vingtièmes*. The president, although supporting the court's decision to ratify this legislation, actually endorsed the dissenters' substantive points, including their assertion that the hallowed Provençal Estates were "national estates."[106] By this, he (and all like-minded brethren) seem to have meant that Provence was still what it had allegedly always been: a "nation" of ancient and independent extraction as well as a territory within France.

With the promulgation of the hated May Edicts less than five months later, the Aixois unavoidably came to trumpet this superannuated local patriotism. At the painful *lit de justice* of 8 May 1788, the senior *avocat-général*, Maurel de Calissanne, protested that the institution of a Plenary Court for the entire kingdom signaled "the annihilation of our constitutions, the neglect of all the pacts of our union and the subversion of all fundamental laws." The basic laws of Provence, he pursued, "were fixed . . . by the oath of Charles III [of Provence], sworn before our Estates-General assembled in 1482, acknowledged in his testament which in destining us to France requested that Louis XI [of France] preserve our rights and even give us more considerable rights. They were renewed by agreement of the Sovereigns and the nation convened in 1483." Maurel de Calissanne claimed that Louis XI's successor on the French throne, Charles VIII, had sworn "to join us to the Crown alone, without incorporating us into France." (An intriguing distinction, that, between the "Crown" and "France".) Charles VIII, furthermore, had pledged that he would "protect us and preserve us and never harm nor jeopardize nor diminish our laws, rights, liberties, customs and statutes . . . accorded us by our Kings and our Counts." But the sacred duties of the kings were now devolving upon the magistrates' shoulders. "We are the primary custodians of these laws, their conservators and defenders, and we must not allow . . . anyone to injure the rights of our *patrie*. Not to immolate ourselves if need be for the *patrie* would be a crime of State."[107]

Much like his counterparts in the other *lits de justice* staged concomitantly by the ministers, Maurel de Calissanne was exhibiting the dual loyalties of the provincial justices of those transitional years. On the one hand was the undoubted allegiance to the French monarchical tradition—fortified by an appreciation of the unique prestige and influence associated with service to Louis XVI. On the other hand was the equally sturdy fealty to "our constitutions," "the pacts of our union," "our Estates General," "our laws, rights, liberties, customs, and statutes," "our Kings and our Counts," and even "our *patrie*." It was at once so natural and so politic now, in countering the central government, to fall back upon and exalt the Provençal past, and with it a host of local privileges and practices bound to command widespread support.

Implied in all this rodomontade was a vision of the historical formation and present constitution of France irreconcilable with the historical and constitutional perspective at Versailles. The Aixois explicated this vision in formal protests of 7 June 1788. The ministers' notion of "regenerating the constitution already existing under Philip the Fair" was "false," they said, "since most of the Provinces have only been joined to the Kingdom since that period." Provincial Frenchmen owed the conservation of their rights "not to the concession of a French Monarch but rather to a genuine contract between the nation's representatives and their sovereigns." The Plenary Court, contemptuously referred to by the Aixois as a "foreign tribunal," could never replace "the *conseil éminent* of the Counts of Provence, the Conseil Delphinal, the *échiquier* of Normandy," nor any of the other provincial *parlements*. Provence, the jurists emphasized, "being *a major state equal to France and not subordinated to nor incorporated into France*, must have a continuously existing court of registration to verify . . . all laws whatsoever emanating from the authority of the Count of Provence." For that matter, "in Provence any law in which the King does not take the title of Count of Provence cannot even be presented for registration."[108] That the Provençal magistrates in their pronunciamento so pointedly invoked the pre-French origins of regions and regional institutions long considered very French indeed by the monarchs and ministers at Versailles was, at the very least, temerarious. That they described their province as a "major state equal to France" and dismissed the Plenary Court as a "foreign tribunal" shows that by 1788 even jurists noted hitherto for their relative docility in public affairs were taking up the most extreme provincial and particularistic pretensions.

And they did not hesitate to rub the salt of such pretensions into the government's wounds after the capitulation of Lamoignon and Brienne later that year. In calling on 21 October for registration of the royal declaration of 23 September reinstating the old judiciary and the old justice, Procureur-Général Leblanc de Castillon stipulated that such action must conform not only with "the constituting Laws of the French Monarchy" but also with those of Provence. In this latter connection he dilated upon "the rights acquired by the said region of Provence and by its representatives convened in its estates general." Faithful to the end to the parlementary tradition, Leblanc de Castillon evoked the "treaties, statutes, liberties," and "customs" of Provence, reaffirmed that it had been joined to the French crown as an "equal *and not subordinate* state," and applauded "the ordinances emanating from the Kings of France in their capacity as *counts and sovereign lords of the said region.*"[109] True, the *procureur-général* went on in a vein of French patriotism to augur great benefits to flow to all Frenchmen (including Louis XVI) from the upcoming Estates General at Versailles. Nonetheless, the language underlined deliberately in this address of 21 October, like that underscored just as pointedly in the protests of 7 June, reminds us once more that our judges were *provinciaux* as well as *français*, and flaunted this fact even after the detested reforms of Brienne and Lamoignon had been rescinded.

The story of provincialism as mirrored in the high magistracy on the eve of revolution has been told in especial detail for the Provençal *parlementaires*, but in reality it was much the same everywhere. As early as 1 September 1787, Droz des Villars and his intractable fellow jurists at Besançon were averring to Louis XVI that the inhabitants of Franche-Comté had through their Estates exercised "the right to administer their own affairs under the sole and immediate authority of their Sovereigns" long before those sovereigns had been of French blood. If, in much later times, Franche-Comté had pledged "fidelity and obedience" to Louis XIV, and Besançon in particular had "abdicated" its proud "sovereignty," this could in no way efface the memory of the heroic epoch antedating the sway of France—nor dispense the current French monarch from acknowledging that past by reviving the local Estates.[110] The *parlementaires* at nearby Dijon, like those at Aix, ridiculed the ministers' attempt "to present the Court of Justice of Philip the Fair as the prototype of the Plenary Court." The Capetians' Court "had never had any authority over the provinces joined in later days to the Crown."

Burgundy's union with "the kingdom of France" had been "voluntary," and contingent upon the existence of "a Parlement, whose preeminence and authority would be the same as that of the Parlement of Paris." Such a concession was no more than recognition of the prescription of the past, for the Burgundians' laws had always required "verification" in both the "Court of Parlement" and the Chambre des Comptes at Dijon.[111] Parlement, Chambre des Comptes, and Estates must share the signal honor of speaking for the Burgundian "nation" in unavoidable dealings with the authorities at Versailles.[112]

Even the lesser *parlements* hurled this challenge of rampant provincialism in the teeth of the centralizing French monarchy. As early as 3 September 1787 the judges at Perpignan were maintaining that no French sovereign had ever rightfully exacted, or could now or in the future exact, any monetary tribute from the "nation" of Roussillon. This "nation," after all, "shared the legislative power with the Sovereign," and thus must freely consent to "French" taxation.[113] By the following May the high tribunal at Perpignan was proclaiming that "neither its foundation nor its constitution" had "ever emanated from the royal authority," but derived instead "from the sanction and authority of the nation assembled at Barcelona in 1589 in the form of the Estates General of Catalonia and Roussillon."[114] Even the high court at Nancy, so recently indebted to the crown for its prestigious designation as a "parlement," made bold to lecture the king on the antiquity of sovereign tribunals that allegedly owed nothing to "positive acts of the authority of the Kings of France." A wise administration, intoned Nancy's judges very much à la Montesquieu, would enthusiastically endorse the *parlements'* championship of local "rights and privileges," perceiving in those rights and privileges the august glory of the French monarchy.[115]

Obviously, *parlementaires* from Provence to Lorraine had always been motivated by a complex of considerations, selfish and otherwise, to preach a gospel of provincialism. Such a philosophy, everywhere rooted as deeply as it was in a parochial past, could not help but figure prominently in magisterial pronouncements upon public matters. However, in the course of the eighteenth century a newer patriotism envisioning the greater community of France appeared with increasing frequency alongside the older Norman or Burgundian or Provençal patriotism in parliamentary polemics and correspondence.[116] It is no surprise to discern in the universal parliamentary outcry of 1787–88 a patriotism whose duality was brought into sharper focus than ever before. For the same magistrates so enamored of the "national" franchises and immunities of Normans and Burgundians and Provençaux were also demanding government recognition of the "national" rights of Frenchmen. They attested the growth of this more novel variety of patriotism by declaring Calonne and Lamoignon guilty of *lèse-nation* as well as of *lèse-majesté*, by excoriating certain intendants for their "antinational" abuses of royal authority, and by portraying *lettres de cachet* and *lits de justice* utilized against refractory judges as a menace to all Frenchmen. But of course the *parlementaires* most dramatically invoked this "French" patriotism in the provinces during the prerevolutionary crisis by calling for the Estates General and praising its good works in advance.

At least one of the major *parlements*, that of Bordeaux, regarded the perils of the provincial assemblies as sufficient in themselves to necessitate this drastic recourse. By the close of October 1787 the Bordelais were maintaining that the act establishing the provincial assemblies changed "absolutely . . . the form in which the divers orders of the State must acquit their tax obligations," and, as such, "obviously and essentially" concerned "the interests of all France." History attested that "the august and authentic assemblies of the nation not only regulated everything involving the Sovereign's glory, the people's security and liberty, the necessity of taxes and the form of their assessment, but also . . . drew up the rules and regulations requisite for public order." Hence, concluded the Bordelais, it was now "very much the Nation's right" to "form the provincial assemblies, [and] to convene them."[117] In reality, the magisterial exiles at Libourne heartily detested the government's provincial assemblies, and they would have liked nothing so much as to see them dispatched to infamy by the kingdom's Estates General.

The Bordeaux Parlement's repeated references to taxation upon this occasion indicate that financial matters were (as usual) uppermost in judicial minds in the southwest. And this was unquestionably the case everywhere in provincial France. Judges in all the jurisdictions passed swiftly beyond the issue of provincial assemblies to confront the problem that could most compellingly justify calling for the Estates General: the frightful mismanagement of royal finances as revealed at the Assembly of Notables. As early as 21 August 1787, the Grenoblois spoke for their fellows all over the realm on this matter, declaring

> that the critical situation of affairs imperiously demands the convening of the Estates-General, that it is only in the assembly of the nation that one can substitute a fixed and permanent plan of conduct for the vague and incoherent ideas of the administrators, who seem in succeeding each other so rapidly only to destroy, one after another, the edifice so swiftly raised by predecessors, and who, caught up one after another in contrary systems, concur only on a single point, which is to burden the people unceasingly with new taxes.

Only the nation's assembled representatives could "adopt sure measures to determine the quality and use of monetary tributes," could "guarantee the soundness of debts contracted in the name of the State," and could "deliberate legally upon the most advantageous disposition of the domain of the Crown."[118] As if revenue garnered from this last source could somehow count for very much when measured against the overall fiscal requirements of government policy. Indeed, the provincial law courts were as insistent as the Cour des Pairs itself on this condition: failing parlementary sanction, all additional taxation must be approved by the Estates General. It was "a public and acknowledged principle," a "national truth," asserted the Rouen Parlement typically in December 1787, "that from the concurrence of the three orders of the State alone can come the consent to a new impost." Such a "truth" was "all the more sacred in that, having been courageously defended by the Parlement in session at Paris," it had "survived the persecutions" which the Paris Parlement, too, had endured "on its behalf."[119] The Parisian jurists had grudgingly gone along with reinstated and extended *vingtième* taxation in the place of the accursed and stillborn *subvention territoriale*, but only after having extracted from the ministry the capital concession of the Estates General. If, now, the judges of provincial France, alive to their "constitutional" responsibilities, should balk at the prospect of five more years of the *vingtièmes*, would this not happily expedite that historic convocation of the Estates so recently promised by the sovereign to his subjects? So must have calculated those magistrates who, at Rouen and elsewhere, rejected the act of October 1787 reimposing and extending the *vingtièmes*.

Ideally, we must suspect, the *parlements* would have preferred not to open the Pandora's box represented at least potentially by the Estates General. Unfortunately for them, state policy and its fiscal requirements precluded that option. In the provinces as surely as at the French capital, the *parlementaires* by 1787–88 found the inexorable logic of events forcing them into an open and ever more vocal espousal of national consultation on the great issues of the day. It was for this reason that several of the tribunals went so far as to upbraid Louis XVI and his regal ancestors for having so long overlooked the possibilities of truly representative government in France. Perhaps the most memorable statement of this kind came from the Toulousains in remonstrances of 12 January 1788:

> Why was it necessary for your august Predecessors, hidden away, so to speak, in the depths of their Palaces for nearly two centuries, to neglect those touching contacts with which even Charlemagne, for all his genius, could not dispense . . . ? Why did they find it neces-

sary to cover their administration with a veil of mystery, and prefer forced tributes to voluntary gifts? Trusting but a small number of men, and seeing only through those men's eyes, they could hardly glimpse the truth save through flattery's distortions. Soon they accustomed themselves to bringing the finest display of the Provinces to the Capital, and of the Capital to the Court, and thought they saw the comfort and prosperity of the People in the luxury and pomp that surrounded them.[120]

Although none of the other courts were quite this forthright, they all had occasion in 1787 or 1788 to review the history of representative institutions in France, and they all stated, or implied, that the atrophy of the Estates General had been a great national tragedy—as the judges of Dauphiné put it, "a change contrary to the nature of things and to the imprescriptible rights of the nation."[121] Was this stance partly hypocritical, coming as it did from jurists long wedded to the business-as-usual of registrations and remonstrances? Most certainly it was, but it was also the *parlements'* only logical position once a desperate and determined ministry had denied them the customary avenues of protest. The magistrates' commentary, moreover, constituted an indictment of isolated absolute governance that would be returned by ever wider circles of French citizens in the near future.

With whatever degree of sincerity the *parlementaires* handed down this inflammatory indictment, they had to follow it up with rosy predictions of the benefits that would accrue to France from the resurrection of the Estates General. And, indeed, they were nearly unanimous in doing so. The Bordelais prophesied that "Patriotism will furnish resources, order will be restored in finances, confidence will resuscitate credit, the national debt will be guaranteed, the people will no longer fear to see the government go back upon its engagements, Commerce will no longer be ceded to a rival power . . . the nation will be respected at large, the manufactures of the Kingdom will resume their former activity, peace and abundance will reign."[122] The Toulousains spoke in a similar vein of "flourishing agriculture, commerce freed from its shackles, industry taking flight anew, imposts simplified, destructive luxury suppressed, virtue honored; talents assigned their proper place, the system of laws perfected, patriotism quickened in all hearts."[123] The Rouennais summed it all up: "This moment, upon which all the nation's hopes are fixed, will no doubt bring forth a new order of things, a new regime of taxes, a new system of finances." The Normans went so far as to predict an "imminent revolution."[124] The Toulousains just as confidently forecast "the most brilliant revolution" about to convulse France.[125]

The sovereign courts insisted, predictably enough, that the king would profit as substantially as would his subjects from convocation of the Estates General. There was no medieval constitutional scholar, no recent jurisconsult the *parlementaires* were unprepared to quote in support of this contention. How, they queried, could royal prestige and authority fail to be augmented once the sovereign, liberated from the pernicious influence of sycophantic courtiers, parasitic financiers, and despotic ministers, consulted trustfully with the nation's deputies upon the nation's problems and needs? How could a "national assembly" not render honor unto the "king of the French" in such circumstances?[126] Such phraseology may strike us today as eerily anticipatory of revolutionary times soon to come. Of course, this was the judges' propaganda, their rhetorical attempt to put the best possible face upon a turn of events resulting ineludibly from the crown's financial plight. Yet it is natural to wonder how many of these provincial magistrates may have privately suspected, as did Etienne Denis Pasquier's apprehensive seniors at Paris, that dangerous times lay immediately ahead for both monarch and high judiciary. Perhaps not too many of them did; perhaps the majority chose to regard the future, if they regarded it at all, with a modicum of tempered optimism. Perhaps, but we shall likely never know.

We do know, however, that contumacious jurists willing to vaunt provincial and French patriotism were not going to abandon their own profession's political pretensions. Whether extolling the magistrate's civic virtues, preaching parlementary solidarity, or campaigning for membership in provincial assemblies, local Estates, and Estates General, the high justices betrayed their own ambitions as absolute monarchy in France began to collapse. These custodians of the "constitution," in other words, revealed themselves for the very deeply "involved" politicians they were.

Exaltation of the robe had naturally been a staple in parlementary literature and polemics over the years; here it is necessary only to note how far in this direction some of the judges went during 1787–88. The Grenoblois waxed typically rhapsodic on the subject in remonstrances of 20 December 1787:

> The divine laws order the Magistrate to descend from the Tribunal, if he is not sufficiently steadfast to make the Law triumph and to shield innocence from the sword of the powerful. Says the illustrious d'Aguesseau: *Such is the honorable rigor of the Magistrate's condition, that it tolerates no admixture of weakness. He who does not reckon himself courageous enough to master the vicissitudes of fate, and storm the ramparts of iniquity, is unworthy to*

*bear the name of judge; the Magistrate who is not a hero is not
even an honorable man.*

The "inestimable honor of having fulfilled all his duties to the Sovereign and the Nation" must be for this public paragon "an impenetrable
shield against the fear . . . so often inspired by deceitful stratagems,
Court intrigue, or obscure innuendo."[127] Thus, months before the coup
of May 1788, the Grenoblois were not so subtly contrasting magisterial
righteousness to the machinations of the *parlements'* adversaries at
Versailles.

Among the other provincial *parlements* declaiming similarly in the
late months of 1787, that of Bordeaux sought to portray its own banishment to Libourne as just such a heroic testing time for judicial virtue.[128]
By the next spring, adversity prompted even the normally docile judges
at Nancy to laud the magisterial virtues that must sooner or later topple
the "vain edifice of ministerial ambition and despotism."[129] Events thus
elicited from the provincial judges paeans to their vocation rivaling in
fervor those of Séguier, Lefevre d'Ormesson, and other Parisian *parlementaires* in 1788.

Perhaps more significant, however, because more worrisome to the
crown, were manifestations of parlementary solidarity in 1787–88. The
ministers were particularly sensitive to this development due to a particular precedent. The sovereign courts, continually at daggers drawn
with Louix XV's government during the 1750s and 1760s over financial
and other public issues, had frequently concerted their protests and had
justified doing so by invoking the principle of *union des classes*, or
"union of *parlements.*" According to this concept, the Parisian and provincial *parlements* were merely the constituent "classes" or "members"
of a single nationwide body. Understandably enough, Louis XV's ministers had flatly rejected this thesis.[130] In the years that followed, the issue
had lain dormant, not only because of the crown's attitude but also because the high courts, proud embodiments of provincial independence,
had preferred to go their separate ways. In 1787–88, however, the
Damoclean sword hanging over all the *parlements* provoked another
magisterial revolt and imparted new life to notions of judicial solidarity.

Jean Egret's survey of parlementary polemics in the prerevolutionary
crisis yields an impression of solidarity varying more or less in proportion with the general importance of the specific incidents being protested.[131] At least eleven of the law courts (including the "primary"
eight) rallied to the Paris Parlement in exile at Troyes between 21 August and 3 October 1787, whether by "fraternizing" with the Parisians
by letter, issuing *arrêtés* announcing protests to come, or appealing directly to Louis XVI. At least nine of the tribunals (including all the

"primary" courts save for that at Aix) stood by the embattled Parisians again in manifestations from 6 December to 28 January criticizing the disgrace of the duc d'Orléans and the arrest of Fréteau de Saint-Just and Sabatier de Cabre in November. The Paris Parlement and nine of the provincial *parlements* (this time including that at Aix) condemned the exile of the Bordelais judges to Libourne by varying means between 24 September and 13 February. In addition, several lesser incidents involving officers of the courts at Toulouse, Grenoble, and Metz drew expressions of support for those tribunals from smaller numbers of their sister institutions throughout France. At one extreme, the minor tribunals at Douai, Colmar, and Perpignan engaged themselves little or not at all in these matters; at the other extreme, the *parlements* at Pau, Grenoble, and Rennes braved the ministers' wrath repeatedly by invoking the cause of parlementary solidarity. The undoubted champions of the judicial resistance, the Parisians and the Bordelais, preoccupied as they were with combating royal fiscal policies, had little time to devote to parlementary tribulations elsewhere—although the Bordelais did betray some irritation over the Paris Parlement's willingness to ratify the legislation on the provincial assemblies and the extension of *vingtième* taxation.[132]

All in all, despite occasional traces of resentment in other provincial parlementary quarters over the Parisian judges' supposed complaisance in dealings with the crown, the evidence points to a substantial revival of judicial solidarity in the face of Brienne's and Lamoignon's campaign of reform. Indeed, at least two of the law courts (those at Rennes and Besançon) went so far as to disinter the dusty old theory of "union of *parlements*," thus raising in their remonstrances the specter of the intransigent judicial opposition of Louis XV's times.[133]

Finally, participation in provincial assemblies, provincial Estates, and (ultimately) the Estates General was a concrete issue. Signs were abundant that the provincial judges wished to take advantage of such institutional innovations and revivals in 1787–88 to expand their role in public affairs. For example, President Desenaux of the Toulouse Parlement wrote to the government on 25 July 1787 to suggest that the newly created provincial assembly of Auch should include his colleagues "in a number proportionate to the number of substantial landowners belonging to [the *parlement*] in that part of its jurisdiction." This *président à mortier* of Languedoc argued that "the talents, the zeal and the insight of the Magistrates," their "fund of knowledge," and their exemplary decency and honesty, "so essential in deliberative bodies," would be sorely needed by the fledgling assembly at Auch. Moreover, to place Toulousain *parlementaires* in the new assembly would "also be a sure means of establishing between the *parlement* and that new administration a harmony and confidence that will insure the general happiness of that province."[134]

The government was unlikely to countenance such an ambitious proposal, but we do know of individual *parlementaires* actually nominated to provincial assemblies in their respective jurisdictions. For example, the clerical counselor Gérard of the "sovereign council" at Colmar participated in the provincial assembly of Alsace; Avocat-Général Lucia apportioned his time between the tribunal at Perpignan and the assembly in Roussillon; two counselors of Lorraine, Fisson de Montet and Bouteiller, entered the assembly at Nancy; and President Couvert de Coulons in Normandy was admitted into the assembly at Rouen.[135]

As for the provincial Estates, they, too, might in some cases afford new political opportunities to the king's magistrates. At least we can point to the example of Provence, where President Fauris de Saint-Vincent could contentedly observe in his journal not only that "Estates have been granted to the province," but also that "Magistrates have had entry into them without difficulty from the government." It was on the basis of these concessions by the authorities that Fauris de Saint-Vincent counseled nonintervention by his company in the affairs of other *parlements*.[136] In communities such as Dijon and Toulouse, where the traditional Estates had never ceased to function, the *parlementaires'* "will to power" expressed itself in relentless attacks upon these institutions whenever they were deemed too amenable to Versailles. We cannot forget how, in the Burgundian capital, the Prince de Condé viewed the *parlement* as striving to become "the absolute master of the province as it is now the [master] of the Estates."[137] At Toulouse, nothing less than a new system of representation in the Estates would do for the judges.[138] In Dauphiné and Franche-Comté, too, the justices evidently hoped to wield increased influence through restored Estates.[139]

Everywhere, then, magisterial ambition revealed itself in connection with the immediate issue of the provincial assemblies and Estates. But the *parlementaires* plainly had the future on their minds as well: a future whose institutional arrangements in France could secure the high judiciary's political role in perpetuity. Hence, the Rouen Parlement's prediction on 4 March 1788 that Estates General, sovereign courts, and provincial assemblies would cooperate in determining taxation in the new France. Hence, its insistence that such "cooperation" must not assign the magistracy a role constitutionally inferior in any way to that of the regularly convening Estates of the kingdom.[140] (Duval d'Eprémesnil, of course, was making precisely the same points at Paris.) Given these convictions, it was not at all surprising that some of the provincial justices, like some of the Parisian jurists, should have offered themselves as candidates for the Estates General in the early months of 1789.

After all, an influential parlementary contingent in this national convocation could have looked after the sovereign courts' interests in the critical days that lay ahead. Just as foreseeable, however, was the general frustration of such designs.[141] Magisterial politics had had their day; genuine revolutionaries would now sow and reap where insubordinate royal judges had broken ground.

Analysis of constitutional and political attitudes in the provincial *parlements* during 1787–88 shows us that the members of these institutions were as unprepared as were their Parisian counterparts to serve their regal master in the most crucial ways at a most crucial time. The provincial judges remained incontrovertibly loyal to their sovereign in traditional ways. They defended him against the perceived machinations of Rome, they criticized the perceived spoliation of his domain, and they condemned the perceived malevolence and malversation of his advisers and administrative agents. But because of their other advocacies—of clergy and noblesse, of taxpayers of all classes, of their own profession, of provincial customs and privileges—and because they genuinely if quixotically preferred to think of the French monarchy as largely reducible to the monarch, they could not brook the ever-mounting fiscal and administrative demands of late eighteenth-century royalty as posited by the likes of Calonne, Loménie de Brienne, and Lamoignon. And precisely because they could not suffer such demands, they found themselves refurbishing old and not-so-old challenges to historic monarchical governance in France. They summoned up from past centuries hoary specters of regional and magisterial insurrection against the writ of royalty; furthermore, they associated the medieval institution of the Estates General and the medieval notion of representative and restrained government embodied in that institution with the more modern stirrings of national popular patriotism. These magistrates thereby helped formulate constitutional issues whose implications would be revolutionary for both the governors and the governed in this land.

That these events came to pass in provincial France was every bit as ironic as was the analogous process at Paris. No less than the jurists of the French capital, those of the French periphery had in so many ways so much to lose and so little to gain from the dissolution of the absolute monarchy. In the near future they (like their Parisian counterparts) would have to reckon with national policymakers far more powerful than those they had so bitterly opposed in the past. And the successors of Calonne, Brienne, and Lamoignon would pay even less homage to the *parlementaires'* cherished privileges and convictions than had those "despotic" ministers of the prerevolutionary crisis.

FOUR

Provincial Magistrates, "Prayers," and "Fighters"

In the twilight of the *ancien régime*, so the luminous Georges Lefebvre assures us, "the nobility no longer thought of recouping power through armed force: it now challenged and undermined the king's rule with bourgeois methods, opposing him through sovereign courts and appeals to public opinion."[1] By the 1780s, Albert Soboul avers, the French nobility "firmly controlled" the *parlements* and proceeded from such "bastions of aristocratic power" to besiege the crown.[2] Even Jean Egret, although suspecting that "the revolt of the nobility" had heretofore been "so frequently exaggerated in both its extent and power," affirms that "those who wanted to put the king under the joint tutelage of the parlements and the Estates General were in effect attempting an aristocratic revolution."[3]

Testimony from such historians merits respect. Yet, whatever may have been the purposes of nobles "using" the magisterial opposition at this time, we already know that the Parisian *parlementaires* of the prerevolutionary crisis were far less eager to foment or even endorse "aristocratic revolution" than they were to defend long-standing privileges of "aristocrats" *and* their social inferiors in France. But what of the high justices in the provinces? Is it not at least plausible that noble magistrates at Rennes and Toulouse and Aix, far removed from the French capital and consequently from their Parisian cousins' sense of proximity to and responsibility toward the crown, and faithful to the prejudices and aspirations of the provincial noblesse, were likelier to sympathize with "aristocratic" insurrectionaries in the crown's most dangerous hour?

Closer investigation suggests, however, that the provincial magistrates' attitudes toward the social elite, like their opinions on political and constitutional questions, did not really differ all that much from those of their Parisian counterparts. Indeed, constitutional and social issues and attitudes were ultimately as interrelated at, say, Grenoble or Bordeaux or Pau as they were at Paris. If (as we have just seen) such provincial jurists continued on the eve of the Revolution to espouse monarchism, in however quixotic a fashion, was it probable that they could reconcile this commitment (which served their own professional interests) with a clarion call for "aristocratic" rebellion? We shall see now that the judges of provincial France desired fundamentally to remain social conservatives even as their comfortable world was starting to disintegrate in 1787 and 1788. Careful analysis of their attitudes toward the traditional social elite to which they nearly all belonged yields three principal conclusions: first, that they were profoundly antiegalitarian, profoundly wedded to the existing social hierarchy; second, that they found many ways during the prerevolutionary crisis to champion accepted privileges of the elite; and, third, that they also found many ways to express their disinclination for any "aristocratic" political resurgence that could radically alter public affairs in France.

In Defense of Social Inequality

It would contravene everything we have so far learned of our provincial *parlementaires* to depict them now as receptive to fashionable notions of social equality. True, very few if any of them envisioned turning the clock back to those distant and dangerous times predating the existence of a Third Estate counterbalancing clergy and nobility in the magistrates' beloved "constitution." Yet at the same time, relatively few of the justices proved radical in the opposite sense by embracing the cause of an insurrectionary "commons" in 1787–88. Brief visits with the *parlementaires* at Besançon, Grenoble, Rouen, and Aix can provide us with convincing examples of the safe conservatism on social issues far more typical of the provincial judiciary in the *ancien régime*.

At Besançon, François-Nicolas-Eugène Droz des Villars held forth with avuncular good humor upon the follies of the eighteenth-century egalitarian philosophy. As he confided to an acquaintance in a letter of 26 February 1789:

> After having spent my entire life collecting 100 volumes of charters and ordinances and reading through thousands of others, I cannot make myself believe that our ancestors were imbeciles and that we should be on guard against imitating them. Equality, uniformity, liberty: these are grand words, but how to apply them and reconcile them with the monarchy, subordination, customs founded upon local circumstances, climates, production . . . I leave all these grand views to more clever minds, they must simply say of me . . . he compiles.[4]

About a month later Droz des Villars brought out his *Mémoires pour servir à l'histoire du droit public de la Franche-Comté* wherein he candidly reiterated his belief in social inequality:

However much compassion may be merited by those persons whom fate has placed in the inferior classes, this Court, charged with maintaining the rights of all the orders, cannot dispose of the property of the rich in favor of the poor; and even in exercising its high administrative role, it can strive to alleviate the situation of the miserable classes only with circumspection.

"Views influenced by politics, ambition or personal interest," continued this *parlementaire*, "cannot be allowed to trouble the established order."[5] Social order, then, was everything; and there could manifestly be no order without the inequality that society had always known.

By the time Droz des Villars penned these words, of course, he and his associates were witnessing the collapse of "order" all around them. Yet they could hardly reproach themselves with having failed throughout the preceding two years' crisis to champion the old values in official letters, *arrêtés*, and remonstrances. In their remonstrances of 1 September 1787, to cite just one example, Besançon's magistrates had intoned darkly that "those who oppress the Third Estate . . . issue from the bosom of the Third Estate itself." Who were these villains? The court had not said; nevertheless, Swiss commoner Jacques Necker in his earlier capacity as finance minister seems indicated here, for the Comtois had spoken of "that individual" who in "so-called provincial assemblies" had "claimed to nullify the suffrage of the nobility and that of . . . the Church, and prohibited them from deliberating in any instance separately, on the pretext of their being prejudiced against the Third Estate." Added the judges: "He sought only to ensure that there would be opposition to Your Parlement's representations, and to extinguish the influence of the first two orders, who could apprise you of the needs of the People."[6] Thus, let no "individual" presume now to challenge the ascendancy and asperse the motives of magistrates, nobles, and clerics in Franche-Comté.

Such strictures in September 1787 make it wholly understandable that, in their notorious *arrêté* of 27 January 1789, the apprehensive judges of the Besançon Parlement should have expounded on the need for social deference and on the anarchic implications of unchecked reform in France.[7] The magistrates bewailed "the fermentation reigning in the Kingdom, principally in the Cities," agitation fomented by "a multitude of writings likely to lead the People into error." Could such "audacious opinions and assertions, brazenly advanced by Individuals without character and without authority" fail to "destroy all kinds of subordination, raise insurrections against legitimate authority, engender a civil war, and shake, perhaps even overthrow, the Monarchy"? In all ages, the jurists maintained, their institution had done all that reasonably could be done to succor the commonalty; but it could never "sanction pretensions that tend to confound all Orders of Citizens together, and to plunder some, upon the pretext of helping the others." Inequality was "inherent in the decrees of Providence and in the nature of the social order." Moreover, as if challenging the wrath of aroused commoners in the province, the judges insisted in their *arrêté* that the local Estates "deliberate only by Order and by chamber," and that "in all matters," two orders, voting, could bind the third—although admittedly in the area of taxation the unanimity of the three orders was required.[8]

Critical contemporaries were wont to characterize Besançon's magistrates as unusually selfish and "reactionary" even by parlementary standards; certainly the judges' rejection of reformist legislation throughout the 1780s went far toward confirming that assessment. But were *parlementaires* elsewhere noticeably more flexible when inequality in society was at issue? No sovereign court showed itself more open-minded and humane in connection with a variety of constitutional and social questions on the eve of the Revolution than did the *parlement* at Grenoble.[9] Yet when the Dauphinois magistrates displayed some of that openmindedness and humanity in protests of 10 March 1787 directed against the crown's policy on the *corvée royale*, they also served notice that social compassion must not be permitted to jeopardize the social order.

> There are privileges that one cannot abolish without altering the very constitution of the Monarchy, whose strength and continuation depend upon the preservation of the intermediary ranks that compose it. One cannot subject to an impost representative of the *corvée* either the Clergy, exempted in all ages from obligations of that nature by the eminence of its functions, or the Noblesse, always ready to shed its blood for the defense of the State . . . or Magistrates, all of whose hours are devoted to maintaining domestic order and tranquillity.[10]

Thus, the standard mixture of Montesquieu, social conservatism, and professional expediency, utilized on this occasion to prevent administrative reform in Dauphiné (or the magistrates' suggested alternative to that reform) from calling into question certain preordained inequalities. It was only within this framework that (as we shall see later) the Grenoblois proceeded to argue against taxing the *corvéables* of the province more heavily in lieu of their continuing to labor upon Dauphiné's roads and bridges.

We shall find the *parlementaires* at Rouen as inclined as any jurists in the kingdom to articulate perceived popular grievances at certain points in the late 1780s. Nonetheless, the Normans, too, left no doubt as to where their sympathies lay in the grand confrontation between the old and the new visions of society in France. In their spirited decree of 25 June 1788 riposting against the government's May Edicts, the Rouennais demonstrated how parlementary opposition to those reforms was rooted in the time-honored vision of hierarchy, privilege, and provincialism as well as in magisterial expediency.

> Not content with necessitating the entire cessation of distributive justice all over France, with depriving thousands of citizens of their livelihood and fortune at the same time, these rash innovators have dared to advance the fatal project of bringing everything into a system of *unity* which, no doubt rejecting the diversity of social ranks, of privileges, of prerogatives, of capitulations of provinces and cities, as it must reject the diversity of customary laws, will leave all France no longer with a cherished King and faithful Subjects but rather with a feared master and debased, cowering slaves.[11]

Avocat-Général Séguier himself could not have put the matter better in one of his storied diatribes at Paris. We sense here, as elsewhere, a touch of indebtedness to the author of *L'Esprit des lois*, though of course the Rouennais and *parlementaires* of other jurisdictions did not really need chapter and verse from Montesquieu to know where their interests lay and what their social vision must be. As noted earlier, future revolutionary Robert Lindet, taken aback like other contemporaries by the violence of the Norman judges' attack upon Lamoignon in their decree of 25 June 1788, quite understandably described it as "the grand finale of the parlementary fireworks."[12] From our present perspective, however, of social rather than political ramifications, this decree is chiefly interesting for its invocation of that society of inequality which at that very time was under assault by philosophes and reform-minded ministers alike.

In at least one sovereign court jurisdiction—that of the Aixois *parlementaires*—the old society of inequality was also reeling beneath the blows of affronted commoners delegated to the local Estates, and this as early as the winter of 1787–88. The government, we recall, had granted to Provence the restoration of her historic Estates in 1787 (thus facilitating parlementary acceptance there of the October legislation reinstating *vingtième* taxation). The resultant sessions of the Provençal Estates, however, became bogged down in disputes between assertive bourgeois seeking to use the Estates as a vehicle for reforms transcending equalization of the local tax burden and nobles and clerics ever on the defensive against the escalating demands and ambitions of the Third Estate delegates. On 1 February 1788, just as the 1787–88 session of the Estates was adjourning, twenty-one of the Third Estate delegates signed a manifesto complaining of unjust treatment accorded their order in the Estates and calling for convocation of a "general assembly of the communities" in Provence to further commoners' interests in the region. The manifesto was addressed to Louis XVI but was also widely discussed in municipal assemblages throughout Provence in the weeks that followed. In Provence, at least, the "bourgeoisie" was thoroughly aroused over serious political and social issues well before the government's promulgation of its May Edicts.[13]

Predictably, the custodians of the social order in the *parlement* at Aix took fright. At the plenary session of 27 February 1788, several of the magistrates denounced the preceding day's meeting of the Aix municipality at which (they indignantly alleged) talk had arisen over the needs to "reform" the Provençal Estates, to remonstrate to the king about wrongs supposedly done the Third Estate by clerics and nobles, and to agitate for concerted action on behalf of commoners in the province. Without even waiting to hear from its *gens du roi* on this matter, the tribunal condemned the reported assembly of the Aix municipality as "prejudicial to the authority and the rights of the Estates," as supportive of "the all too manifest scheme to augment the disorder and fermentation already existing in people's minds due to public proceedings, published memoirs sent to all the communities, and disseminated so pretentiously among the Public." The judges then heard a lengthy report upon the affair by the king's men, summoned and closely interrogated the chief officers of the municipality, and eventually issued a stern decree prohibiting such "illegal" discussions and activities in the future.[14]

But even at this relatively early date the *parlementaires* found themselves unheeded: the agitation among the communities of Provence continued to grow. The jurists returned to the attack on 12 March with a lengthy decree that diplomatically conceded the established prerogatives of the communities and communal assemblies and Estates of the province but also reiterated the earlier decree's strictures against the "illegal proceedings" of popular gatherings. That the emphasis in this decree lay upon the imperative need for harmony among the orders in Provençal society rather than upon the need for a more rigorous enforcement of law and order may in some measure reflect the magistrates' deteriorating relationship with the crown and their increasing need for the support of *all* ranks of Provençaux. Still, the Aix Parlement even in its admittedly more conciliatory *arrêt* of 12 March 1788 could not forgo citing "the urgent necessity to arrest the progress of errors, or of ambiguities, that a dangerous presumption has inspired and disseminated." Moreover, in their very invocation of the need for concord among the "three orders" of Provence, the magistrates were witnessing their continued adherence to the traditional structure of society.[15]

Several of the Aixois *parlementaires* betrayed in their private papers a much sharper anxiety over the evolution of public affairs in Provence than did their assembled company in its official decrees. President Fauris de Saint-Vincent commented in his journal that "the bad humor displayed by the third estate during and especially after the estates is rather remarkable. What has it lost through the reestablishment of the estates?" The president suspected that the unruly commoners were reaching for a tantalizing "shadow of exclusive authority."[16] First President (and Intendant of Provence) Gallois de La Tour and Procureur-Général Leblanc de Castillon corresponded frequently with the archbishop of Aix, the military commandant in Provence, the baron de Breteuil, and others in authority at Paris over the events unfolding in the Provençal communities in 1787–88.[17] Both men repeatedly criticized the "illegal" and fractious assemblages of aroused *roturiers*; both men repeatedly defended the parlementary decrees of 27 February and 12 March as essential if the clergy, nobility, and the Third Estate itself were to withstand the "intrigues," "maneuvers," and "conspiracies" of nameless demagogues risen from within the ranks of commonalty. The first two orders might voluntarily make concessions to the "commons" on fiscal matters, and perhaps on other matters besides, the two judges intimated— but let no subject question the traditional social hierarchy. Both Gallois de La Tour and Leblanc de Castillon harped upon the Aix Parlement's role as guarantor of social subordination and, hence, of social quietude in Provence—a reminder (if any were needed) of the natural marriage of social and constitutional principle with professional expediency in judicial minds at Aix and elsewhere. Exactly one year later, the 1788–89 session of the Provençal Estates and the burgeoning insurrection of municipalities and villages would spur the first president and *procureur-général* to renewed and even harsher denunciations of social insubordination in the province.[18]

The official decrees of the justices at Aix, the scoldings confided by Fauris de Saint-Vincent to his journal, and the alarms sounded by Gallois de La Tour and Leblanc de Castillon in their correspondence attested, as did the ruminations and decrees emanating from Franche-Comté, Dauphiné, and Normandy, to the *parlements'* identification with an imperiled social order. Attesting to that same identification were magisterial advocacies of some very specific interests of miter and sword on the threshold of the revolutionary era.

A Traditional Championship of the Elite

In his melodramatic rendition of events attending the imposition of the May Edicts upon Brittany, the *parlementaire* Amand Du Couëdic de Kergoualer predicted that "all Bretons will regard and treat as Enemies of the Fatherland, all those adopting such a system, all those concurring in its establishment. That Nobility, accustomed to providing the State with heroes and avengers, will know how to sacrifice everything to the defense of the People's interest and to the preservation of national harmony: it will be supported by the Citizens of all Orders."[19] Despite such braggadocio, however, the noblesse (in Brittany and elsewhere) was not about to abandon a host of "useful" and "honorific" privileges enjoyed since time out of mind. It was only logical, moreover, that Amand Du Couëdic de Kergoualer and others in the high judiciary, themselves nobles as well as men of the robe, should have continued to uphold those prerogatives of the social elite that were reconcilable with magisterial influence in public affairs. That the provincial *parlementaires* did so in the prerevolutionary crisis has always been common currency; that they exercised this role at times in relation to specific issues unconnected with the government's emergency agenda of reform, is less well known.

Of course, there were, to begin with, the causes célèbres of those years: the *corvée royale* and serfdom, "feudal" justice and other seigneurial survivals from the past, the *subvention territoriale* and the *vingtièmes*. The first two issues elicited from Droz des Villars commentaries pointing up the parlementary resolution to champion the "privileged orders" wherever possible. On Anne-Robert-Jacques Turgot and the controversy over the *corvées*, we have this from the learned Comtois: "For a long time individuals had been working underhandedly against the Noblesse and the Clergy. The Edict of 1776 abrogating the *corvée*, without talking of privileges, deceived no one as to the motives that had dictated it."[20] Defeat for Turgot's famous reform, in other words, had been vindication for a noble and clerical right unquestionable in parlementary eyes. As for the vestiges of serfdom (more significant in Franche-Comté than almost anywhere else), Droz des Villars had this to say:

> An Edict of August 1779 abrogated mortmain upon the royal domain, and abolished the right of pursuit. The King announced that he *would have preferred to abolish these vestiges of a harsh feudality unconditionally; but our finances not permitting us to redeem this right from the hands of Seigneurs, and restrained by the respect that we will have in all times for the laws of property,*

*which we consider to be the surest foundation of order and jus-
tice*: His Majesty confined himself to giving the example in the
matter.[21]

But the Besançon Parlement had adamantly refused to ratify even this
diluted reform. Why? Seemingly because of a suspicion that abrogation
of serfdom upon the king's lands within Franche-Comté would in some
fashion trench upon local lords' rights of mortmain. "Applauding the
Sovereign's benevolent views," the *parlement*—so explained Droz des
Villars—"witnessed with pleasure the alleviation of personal servitude,
but it considered itself obligated to respect the real and feudal properties
founded upon custom and possession."[22] The justices at Paris, hardly
social innovators themselves, had held their noses and gone along with
the crown's humanitarian gesture; but not the jurists in Franche-Comté.
Profiting as they did (or, at least, knowing those who did profit) from a
relic of lordly power over lowly human beings harking back to medieval times, the justices in this antique province would render only so
much "justice" and no more to luckless *mainmortables*. Serfdom was
no longer a thriving institution, even in benighted Franche-Comté; but
where it still survived, pronounced the legists, it must be respected, and
preserved.

Given this attitude, compounded of self-interest, social solidarity, and
legalism, the *parlements'* response to Lamoignon's curtailment of seigneurial justice in May 1788 could only have been a foregone conclusion. Few were the *parlements* protesting the May Edicts that did not
direct some of their fire at this particular reform. Several sovereign
courts went so far as to recapitulate and reject the offending ordinance
article by article. How, they inquired, could lords hope to retain their
tribunals, allegedly so useful in so many small ways to humble litigants,
if they must maintain in them all the legal specialists coolly required
by the legislation?[23] In any case, they indignantly pointed out, plain-
tiffs and defendants could henceforth ignore the seigneurial courts altogether, pleading their suits in the proximate royal tribunals. Whether
expatiating upon these or upon other aspects of Lamoignon's reform, the
provincial judges unfailingly rushed to the defense of long-established
seigneurial rights.

The Grenoblois were among the most forthright of the provincial
parlementaires on this issue—even if, for the life of them, they could
not help but place their advocacy of local lords in a classic constitutional context. As they declared on 20 May 1788,

> The statute on *the administration of justice* violates the sacred
> right of property in depriving the Seigneurs of the justice appertain-
> ing to their lands. . . .

. . . certain individuals have not ceased taking the Seigneurs' justice away from them in this manner upon the pretext of abbreviating judicial disputes, but with the actual intent of doing away with even the shadow of anything that could arrest the impetuous march of absolute power, . . . nothing leads more infallibly to despotism than the abolition of the prerogatives of the different orders in the state.[24]

Lest the reference to constitutionality somehow be missed, the following gloss, a citation from *L'Esprit des lois*, was inserted in the margin of the court's decree: "Abolish in a monarchy the prerogatives of the Lords, of the Clergy, of the Noblesse and the cities, and you will soon have either a popular state or a despotic state."[25] In arguing thus, and enlarging lovingly upon the myriad *libertés et lois delphinales* of ancient date supposedly violated by Lamoignon's statute, the judges at Grenoble undoubtedly regarded themselves as intrepid paladins of both the seigneurial elite and the "constitution" of the realm.

Elsewhere, the story was essentially the same. The magistrates at Dijon insisted that the government's judicial reform overthrew seigneurial rights guaranteed explicitly in "the treaty concluded on 24 January 1476 between the Estates of Burgundy and the agents of Louis XI for the voluntary union of this Province with his Kingdom."[26] The Burgundians, hidebound conservatives to the bitter end, spoke of "duchies" and "great fiefs," of "lords" and their "vassals" among the peasantry, and expostulated with the ministers upon the need to preserve these vestiges of a chivalrous past. Nancy's high magistrates held forth in similar fashion in protests of 11 June, save that they, like the *parlementaires* of Dauphiné, could not forgo exploring the constitutional implications of the ordinance on justice. The men of Lorraine averred that "it is thus that the leveling of social ranks, the abolition of the privileges distinguishing them, the extinction of the intermediary bodies, and of the subordinate powers, gradually sap the foundations of monarchical government and prepare the way for arbitrary rule."[27] Rouen's *parlementaires* proved notably adept at paying court simultaneously to seigneurs, proprietors of all classes, and magisterial interests. The Normans declared in their contumacious decree of 25 June 1788

that the King owes to these [seigneurial] jurisdictions the same protection he owes to all the properties of his subjects; however, the Keeper of the Seals has intended by virtue of the provisions of this same ordinance to remove from a great number of these jurisdictions one of their most prized prerogatives, that of being directly under the Parlement's own cognizance; . . . this enterprise of arbitrary power . . . makes manifest what kind of treatment will be accorded rights and properties of all types under the baneful "protection" of this destructive authority.[28]

The Rouennais would yield to no other *parlementaires* in their resolve to champion what remained of historic seigneurial justice, although they, like magistrates elsewhere, obviously had other "special interests" in mind as well. Would the judges of provincial France have been prepared the preceding year to support the first two orders as vociferously over the issue of the "territorial subvention"? Most likely, yes. As it turned out, of course, the Court of Peers spoke for the entire high magistracy on this question in the summer of 1787; Grenoblois and Rouennais and Aixois never had to confront the *subvention territoriale*. Still, the decree issued by the Chambre des Vacations at Dijon on 12 September 1787 may provide at least one indication of provincial justices divining in this proposed imposition a ministerial design to tax the rural elite more heavily. It stated that

> . . . the *subvention territoriale* . . . would injure in the most direct fashion the property rights of all orders of citizens; . . . a small number of administrators could render that taxation totally arbitrary, whereas the *vingtièmes*, fixed by their nature at a determined quota and amount, seem tailored to assure the taxpayers the free disposition of the remainder of their revenues.[29]

Not that the *vingtièmes* were above criticism: few issues, indeed, provoked more rancor in parlementary circles in late eighteenth-century France. Nevertheless, as *impôts de quotité* the *vingtièmes* should, at least in theory, tax affluent magistrates and other landed gentry no more heavily than less-favored proprietors, whereas with a dread *impôt de répartition* such as this newfangled "territorial subvention" there was no telling how much fiscal liability might devolve upon the "best" in rural society. There may have been no Burgundian counterpart of Duval d'Eprémesnil in Dijon's Chambre des Vacations on this occasion to fulminate on behalf of clergy and noblesse against the degrading *contrainte solidaire*; yet the Dijonnais were as quick as the Parisian justices to fathom the government's intentions regarding the lands of wealthy Frenchmen.

But it was not only nationwide controversies that exercised these provincial paladins of the elite during the prerevolutionary crisis. If we peer beyond *corvées* and *vingtièmes* and May Edicts we can make out obscure quarrels of purely local interest, wrangles between royal administrators and individual sovereign courts that have never appeared in standard histories of the period but that nevertheless reveal the multiplicity of ways in which the provincial judges articulated the concerns of the first two orders. In three of these cases we find the magistrates of Burgundy, Normandy, and Dauphiné, respectively, pitted against ministers and other agents of Louis XVI on the eve of revolution.

The dispute at Dijon was especially acrimonious in that here the *parlementaires* were once again combating their old local adversaries the Elus or "Elected Ones" (actually, crown-appointed leaders) of the Burgundian Estates. The Elus had long regarded the judges as pretentious and obstructionist politicians, whereas the magistrates had long derided the Elus as tools of the ministers and as upstart challengers to legitimate parlementary ascendancy in local affairs.[30] At issue in the present imbroglio were rights of surveillance over the passageways of the province: the king's highways, the so-called *chemins finerots* or roads linking the Burgundian villages, the roads running from the villages to the rivers and streams of the province, and the towpaths and footpaths along those rivers and streams.[31] The magistrates had since time out of mind considered these arteries of communication and commerce to be exclusively within their administrative purview. The Elus predictably had contested this claim over the years. Great was the satisfaction of the current Elus, therefore, and correspondingly great the indignation at Dijon's Palais de Justice, when the crown had the Burgundian Estates (but *not* the Dijon Parlement) register letters patent of 11 December 1785 reconfirming the administrative rights of the Elus over the *grandes routes, chemins finerots,* and other roads and byways of the province.

What an opening for President Joly de Bévy and the other hotspurs of the magisterial opposition in Burgundy! The following months witnessed the sort of exchange between *parlement* and central government that had all too frequently marred the disposition of public affairs in the province. The justices issued decrees purporting to nullify the "unconstitutional" letters patent of 11 December 1785 and anathematizing the Elus; the government struck back repeatedly with its own decrees against the willful tribunal at Dijon. Before the close of 1786, Louis XVI's ministers would be meditating a more forceful response to the disobedient Burgundian *parlementaires*, even as the approaching Assembly of Notables increasingly occupied their thoughts.

The Dijonnais seem primarily to have been actuated in this affair by their professional egotism and by their animus against the Elus—though naturally this motivation came out in their decrees as a defense of the sacrosanct "law of registration" and of all "constitutional" prerogatives in Burgundy. Yet the *parlementaires* did go beyond this stance to define and champion specific social interests in their jurisdiction, and foremost among these interests were alleged rights of seigneurs. This advocacy emerged plainly in a letter of 22 August 1786 from Procureur-Général Pérard to one of the ministers. Parlementary ratification of all edicts affecting Burgundy was constitutionally necessary, argued Pérard, and "all the more essential" in the case of "the administration of the *chemins finerots*," which heretofore had always "belonged to the *seigneurs hauts-justiciers*" and been exercised "through their judicial officers." The *procureur-général* did not deny that the change announced in the letters patent of 11 December 1785 could be "useful," and in fact voiced his confidence "that all the interested parties would agree to it." Still, "a Law that deprives the principal Citizens of the State of a portion of their Patrimony, must be accompanied by all the requisite formalities."[32] Whether "all the interested parties" alluded to by Pérard and supposedly affected in their lordly rights by the contested legislation were indeed as amenable to its provisions as the *procureur-général* suggested remains unclear. Assuredly some of Pérard's own professional brethren must have figured among these "principal Citizens of the State," so deeply involved were the Burgundian judges (like magistrates elsewhere) in the seigneurial regime. But, again, the invocation of a specific social interest here was most probably subordinate to the jurists' complaint of being despoiled of a certain administrative role in favor of a detested rival institution.

Pérard and his associates remained irreconcilable in their opposition to the letters patent of 1785 and sought through their decrees to paralyze the Elus and their agents in Burgundy. The government, whose paramount authority in administrative matters was after all being challenged by this obstructionism, finally intervened more forcefully in the affair by summoning the entire *parlement* to Versailles in January 1787. The king and his advisers, already preoccupied with the impending convocation of the Notables, attempted in cursory fashion to mediate between the Burgundian Elus and *parlementaires* upon a host of contested matters but insisted nonetheless that the judges accept the new status quo regarding administration of the *chemins finerots* and other roads within their jurisdiction. The magistrates, however, remained unbowed in their opposition: they had scarcely returned to Dijon when they resolved to draw up full-dress remonstrances on the issue.

In the resultant protests of 27 February 1787 the *parlementaires* expanded upon the need for magisterial ratification of all royal acts affecting "public administration" in Burgundy, and once again upbraided the Elus for interfering in matters not concerning them. The Dijonnais furthermore invoked social interests as readily as had their *procueur-gé-*

néral in his letter of the preceding August. However, on the specific question of seigneurial rights the jurists manifested considerably less flexibility than had the chief officer of their *parquet.* They immediately joined battle on this last issue by reviving the vexed question of the *corvées:*

> The *corvéables* are only obligated to devote six days a year to the construction of the *chemins finerots.* The Elus can now compel the inhabitants of a village to labor upon the roads situated on the territory of another community; well, it is an established fact that if they exercise that option and force the *corvéables* of one village to spend their six days of *corvée* laboring upon the road of a neighboring community, the seigneur will no longer be able to oblige them to repair that road over which his own jurisdiction extends, and henceforth the exercise of his prerogative will always be subordinated to the will of the administration [of the Elus.][33]

Obviously this was not a plaint motivated primarily by sympathy for the luckless *corvéables* of the region. But what particularly incensed the Burgundian judges was a requirement unilaterally set forth by the Elus in session on 7 February 1786 that "when anyone wants to raise new structures on the principal streets of towns and villages or near the *chemins finerots,* all alignment work will be regulated according to the rules prescribed for the major royal highways." In effect, protested the *parlementaires,* the Elus were contravening the letters patent of 11 December 1785. Whatever their shortcomings, those letters patent had at least stipulated that "the Elus can only lay claim to jurisdiction over the *chemins finerots* in the event that the *seigneurs hauts-justiciers* fail to avail themselves of that jurisdiction." But here were the Elus, presumptuously brushing that seigneurial option aside and arrogating to themselves all authority in this area, much as they pretended to exclusive jurisdiction over the king's highways. Henceforth, if the Elus had their way, seigneurs and all others wishing to build in the designated regions would have to "apply to them for permission, to solicit an alignment and to conform to other formalities no less inconvenient than expensive."

The remonstrances of 27 February 1787 championed the rights of local lords on an associated front as well. The letters patent of 11 December 1785 had dealt with superintendence over passage by water as well as over passage by land in Burgundy. Yet another problem thereby arose in parlementary eyes:

> The Letters-Patent of 1785 confer upon the Elus unlimited powers of inspection and jurisdiction over the rivers Saône, Doux, Seille,

Arroux, Yonne, and those flowing into the former, that is to say over all rivers and even streams running through the province of Burgundy.

This immense jurisdiction which the Elus would like to possess belongs, nevertheless, either to the *seigneurs hauts-justiciers*, as a prerogative attached to their seigneurial domains, or to the ordinary royal tribunals.[34]

Should the royal act of 1785 remain in force, the judges concluded, the lords would in this sphere as in others be injured in their proprietary rights. Additionally, "a number of tribunals would be deprived of some of their functions, and the Elus, who would further develop amidst all that pillage powers that are already excessive, would not be obligated to compensate any of the injured parties."

That the Dijonnais waxed indignant over this affair on behalf of local lords was of course nothing new: some, perhaps quite a few of these magisterial remonstrants were looking after their own as well as others' interests, and had always done so. Still, we are struck by the ultimate reversion in the Burgundians' protests to the defense of sacrosanct parlementary powers. The judges pointedly reiterated that "jurisdictions have been instituted by solemn laws, verified by the Courts; to repeal them, the same formalities must be observed, and letters patent or letters of commission registered by the Estates are . . . incapable of replacing these formalities." The authorities at Versailles must have been galled by this latest display of judicial egotism at Dijon, especially in view of their recent effort at mediation between Elus and judges. Surviving documents suggest that this Burgundian wrangle was still unresolved at the advent of the Revolution.[35]

There were striking similarities between this jurisdictional quarrel over roads and rivers in Burgundy and the altercation over development of wasteland in Normandy. In both cases parlementary resistance to royal policy stemmed from a variety of motives—one of which, undeniably, was the determination to stand by the seigneurial class that counted many of the justices themselves among its number. The affair in Normandy, as discussed in chapter 3, originated in the government's decision to lease out to various *concessionnaires* (or speculators) certain wastelands in the province that were deemed to lie in the royal or "public" domain. Development of such *terres vaines et vagues* was expected eventually to benefit the financially pressed crown. However, this policy of "concessions" of lands, implemented in *arrêts du Conseil* of 25 June 1785 and 10 September 1786, aroused judicial opposition at Rouen. On 28 March 1787 Rouen's *parlementaires* issued a decree criticizing the ministers' initiative as violating (among other things) Norman law and custom and national principles of the inalienability of royal domain. Versailles swiftly responded with royal decrees of 7 June 1787 that not only reconfirmed the implementing decrees of 25 June 1785 and 10 September 1786 and quashed the Normans' decree of 28 March 1787 but also "evoked" or removed cognizance of the land-development policy from the Rouen Parlement altogether. Moreover, the government made a point of having these latest royal decrees of 7 June 1787 sent, not to Normandy's *parlement* as was customary, but rather to inferior tribunals in the province.

The ministers could not have more effectively ensured that they would hear again from Rouen's aroused *parlementaires* on their land-development initiative in Normandy. The judges, although following, like their provincial counterparts elsewhere, the great debate in the nation's capital between crown and Court of Peers, nevertheless found time to draft formal protests over the *concessionnaires'* exploitation of *terres vaines et vagues* in Normandy. In general, these remonstrances, dated 8 August 1787, advanced three complaints: (1) that leasing out waste from the crown's lands by simple decree not registered in parlement constituted illegal "alienation" of royal domain; (2) that allowing *concessionnaires* to exploit other wasteland in the province transgressed against local proprietors' rights as enshrined in local law, custom and usage; and (3) that signifying royal acts of any kind to inferior tribunals rather than to the sovereign court of Normandy usurped the authority of the latter and jeopardized the dispensation of justice throughout the province.[36]

Probably the magistrates were most exercised about the last of these three grievances. Even so, professional pride of function and proprietary self-interest could quite compatibly motivate a spirited defense of all rights of ownership purportedly threatened in Normandy. And, as a matter of fact, the remonstrances of 8 August 1787 were very specific in citing examples of proprietors aggrieved by usurping *concessionnaires* under contract with the government. Many of the interests the justices championed were genuinely "popular"—a fact that will require elaboration later on—but the *parlementaires* were resolved first and foremost to uphold the seigneurial regime. Thus they observed at one point in their representations that "it is a maxim in jurisprudence, and this principle has always been sworn to by Your Majesty, that the plots of ground lying in waste belong to the Seigneur of the fief in whose jurisdictional domain they are located, if the contrary cannot be demonstrated." In other words, even in remonstrances noteworthy otherwise for their invocation of commoners' documented proprietary rights, the burden of proof of ownership in *terres vaines et vagues* lay upon peasant "vassals" rather than upon their lords. Moreover, the jurists detailed the alleged grievances of seigneurs as readily as they described those of their social inferiors in the province. For instance:

> The Sieur de Calmesnil . . . has also gotten his hands upon a plot of ground known under the name of Bruyères de Clinchamp and has been audacious enough to attempt to enter fully into its possession, even though this land is situated at the center of the fief of Clinchamp and the proprietor of that seigneurie has held it at all times as a legacy from his forebears . . . explicitly included, in the acknowledgments rendered to Your Majesty, as part of the family domain.[37]

Here and elsewhere the Rouennais spoke in the anachronistic language of seigneurialism, a language that remained, on the very eve of revolution, dear to nobles' hearts all over the realm. Of course the dispute at Rouen was fated as surely as was that at Dijon to be swallowed up in the national crisis of those years; it is certain, however, that the Burgundian *parlementaires*, themselves remonstrants over seigneurial prerogatives in 1787, would have warmly applauded their Norman cousins' protests.

While the magistrates in Burgundy and Normandy were speaking out on behalf of fiefs and fiefholders, the high justices in Dauphiné were complaining about the government's treatment of daughters of the poor rural noblesse. In 1784 the Grenoble Parlement had registered letters patent establishing a local chapter of canonesses affiliated with the Order of the Knights of Malta.[38] Religious chapters, like military schools, could benefit many a less-than-affluent country squire with children to place in society, and consequently their foundation was avidly solicited by those lobbying at Versailles on behalf of the rural nobility.[39] In the case of the religious congregation founded in Dauphiné, however, what had seemed at first to be the answer to local gentry's prayers had turned out to be something of a nightmare. The grand prioress and her flock had been housed initially in the local Abbey of Saint Anthony, but in the following months the chapter had squabbled incessantly with the parent Order of Malta over disciplinary and administrative matters, and at one point the canonesses had been expelled from the abbey. Apparently what brought the Grenoble Parlement into the fray, apart from the resultant tribulations of these highborn *religieuses*, was the government's decision to "evoke" all present and future litigation arising from this imbroglio to the king's own Council.

Here, then, was yet another case of parlementary protests reflecting magisterial as well as noble interests. In the pertinent remonstrances of 11 April 1787 the Grenoblois launched into a litany of historic judicial privileges supposedly violated by the ministers' actions, citing notably the Ordinance of Abbéville, which "accords to Your Parlement cognizance of the lawsuits of Prelates, Chapters, and Commanders of Saint John of Jerusalem"—this last in reference to the Knights of Malta.[40] It was only appropriate, declared the judges, that they should have "expressly reserved" to themselves jurisdiction over the chapter of canonesses whose foundation they themselves had earlier ratified. Yet now the central government was endeavoring by virtue of unregistered royal decrees to deny parlementary cognizance of matters at the former Abbey of Saint Anthony, and thus to gainsay the magistrates a legal and essential role in local administration. On the subject of the canonesses themselves, the justices waxed similarly indignant. "The rich and powerful man invariably gains access to his tribunal," they complained, "but the weak could never be heard there. How are some canonesses, daughters as poor as they are noble, to maintain their rights against an Order that joins to the prerogatives of citizens the credit and the display of a foreign power?" The magistrates went on to depict in bleak terms a situation in Dauphiné that the ministers (according to these remonstrants) had only tardily decided to address:

> The Chapter is deprived of the administration of its own wealth; the grand prioress is without a priory, the nuns without prebends, the archivists without charters and papers, the librarians without books; the treasurers were, not long ago, without money.
>
> Some of the canonesses had sought refuge in the bosom of their families, the others were lodged in the religious house of Tullins, a crumbling structure, when [finally] it pleased Your Council to retrieve them from this ruination, and to order them to reoccupy the buildings at Saint Anthony's.[41]

"The sole means of ensuring the canonesses' enjoyment of the properties belonging to them," insisted the judges, "is to entrust them with the stewardship of those properties from this moment on." The *parlementaires* also alleged that the "pretexts" advanced to despoil the canonesses of their rights had been "dictated by the same motives that occasioned their eviction from the House of Saint Anthony in the first place."[42] The jurists did not expatiate upon those original motives (presumably of the Knights of Malta). They did, however, call for royal revocation of all edicts that left the noblewomen at the Abbey of Saint Anthony in a position of insecurity, or that denied ultimate parlementary jurisdiction over their congregation. The judges' protests closed with an exhortation to the sovereign to follow up his reorganization of government finances with "reforms . . . in the administration of justice." For the Grenoblois and for *parlementaires* elsewhere, "judicial reform" fundamentally meant two things, and two things only: namely, that the monarch should cease annulling the law courts' decrees, and that he should cease "evoking" their litigation to his own Council. We may safely assume, however, that the magistrates of Dauphiné would have been less eager to invoke the grand notion of judicial reform on behalf of noble canonesses in their jurisdiction in 1787 had they sensed the increasing fragility of their entire world of "justice."

The affair at Grenoble was overtaken as swiftly as were those at Dijon and Rouen by the governmental crisis. These obscure local disputes point up as effectively as do the more familiar national controversies the multiplicity of ways in which the high judiciary served interests of the elite in the prerevolutionary period. Yet the sovereign courts certainly betrayed no exclusive concern for the interests of the social elite. It is especially noteworthy that the robe could be stung to fury as surely by challenges to its own influence in public affairs as by any assault upon the first two orders in French society. And precisely because this was so, the provincial *parlementaires* were not likely to welcome an expanded "aristocratic" role in French politics, for that could conceivably jeopardize their own long-standing influence in the affairs of the realm.

Political Robe versus Political Sword

Power in political and administrative spheres—this was, indeed, the cutting issue, the rock upon which the alliance of robe and sword began to founder as the old regime itself began to fall apart in 1787–88. And here we have valuable witness from both partners in the failing alliance or (to put it more accurately) both parties to a burgeoning political dispute whose ramifications appeared ever more serious in the light of weakening royal authority. The provincial justices, like Duval d'Eprémesnil and his confederates at Paris, left little doubt that they wished their cousins of the sword to keep their place: that is, rusticating upon their estates or serving manfully in military ranks. Public and civilian affairs, they insisted, were the business of the king and his advisers, among whom the *parlementaires* plainly numbered themselves. Gentlemen of the sword, for their part, commented sourly upon these attitudes all over France and unfurled their own banners of political aspiration. Thus, robe ambivalence toward sword was more than reciprocated in the pronouncements of certain would-be politicians and administrators of military noblesse in the late 1780s.

Let us first turn to the men of the robe. Wherever we look, in this kingdom sliding toward revolution, we find our magistrates relating the staple parlementary tale of royal authority usurped in the bad old days by overweening sword and miter, or voicing updated misgivings about contemporary prejudices and pretensions in the nobility. When Avocat-Général Joseph-Louis de La Boissière addressed his colleagues at Grenoble during the plenary session of 17 November 1788 that celebrated the Dauphinois Parlement's return from oblivion, he recalled with distaste "those military parlements of the first race" dominated by "soldiers voting upon how to augment their conquests by force of arms." He manifested similar disdain for "those solemn assemblies of the second race, held under the influence of a clergy become powerful." The decrees emanating from those assemblages, he continued, "seemed rather to be the acts of an ecclesiastical council, than laws agreed to by the people and constituted by the sovereign." Charlemagne, of course, had set matters right for a while, but then had come the trials of late Carolingian and early Capetian times. The kings of the "third race" had managed gradually to "gather together the diverse branches of their authority," but as the realm they inherited from their predecessors came to them practically "in tatters," the new, post-Frankish polity they fashioned ineluctably preserved some of the flaws and abuses of earlier periods. As de La Boissière put it: "the feudal laws instituted by the seigneurs, the customs introduced by usage, the privileges that habit and the hazards of war had sometimes sanctioned and sometimes abrogated, the pecuniary obligations that these privileges and manumissions had necessitated, the resort to acts of fiscal extortion, all were incorporated into the regime of France." To be sure, some of the later monarchs in their turn had become prodigal and lax, had entrusted too much power to corrupt "courtiers" and ambitious ministers; but all the more reason now for Frenchmen of *all* ranks and estates to pull together and make of the upcoming Estates General a means to inaugurate the regeneration of France. Particularly revealing was de La Boissière's expressed hope that "the minister of the altars, the warrior, the magistrate, the financier, forgetting in unison their ancient prerogatives, jealousies and hatreds" would join together in the great work of regeneration.[43] Here was no call by the officer of the *parquet* at Grenoble for "revolution" by any class in society, but rather an acknowledgment of past competition among "estates" and professions (including, naturally, the robe) and an exhortation to such ancient rivals to labor side-by-side in the vineyards of the new commonwealth.

At Aix-en-Provence we find no animadversions upon ecclesiastical and noble mischief making in medieval days, but we do find a typical mixture of criticism of contemporary nobles and lionization of contemporary "robins." President Fauris de Saint-Vincent betrayed as much impatience with members of the first two orders as with members of the third when remarking in his journal upon Provençal politics in 1788.

The Third Estate, he conceded, "has several legitimate grievances against the two other orders." He cited as one example "the smallness and the shabbiness of the sums offered by the latter as their contribution for upkeep of roads and for bastards" in the preceding year's Estates. Then, again, the president saw no reason why all Provençal nobles "possessing fiefs" need flock to the local Estates of 1788–89. Apparently these overly zealous gentlemen were under the impression that they were to choose their delegates to the Estates General in the local assembly of the orders, but this, according to Fauris de Saint-Vincent, was not so: each order, in separate convocation, was to designate its national deputies and charge them with appropriate "instructions." Consequently, "nothing necessitated a plenary convocation" of nobles holding fiefs in the Estates of Provence. Admittedly, "the third estate is impetuous, hot-headed, does not faithfully observe forms and procedures. But the noblesse of Provence is rather arrogant. It is every bit as attached to its prerogatives and privileges now as it was in the fifteenth century."[44] It is not surprising, in light of this studied impartiality toward clashing pretensions of nobles and commoners, that the president could even confess some grudging admiration for one of Mirabeau's inflammatory tracts arguing for broader representation in the Provençal Estates. "There are doubtless some good ideas in this memoir," he admitted. "The new constitution of Dauphiné has been established in great part along these lines. But [in Provence] minds are too embittered, too stubbornly attached to the old ideas to permit such a plan to succeed."[45]

President Fauris de Saint-Vincent and his fellows in the Aix Parlement deemed themselves mediators among the contending social orders in much the same fashion as they regarded themselves as impartial arbitrators of all disputes in law. After all, were not clergy, nobility, and commonalty essential components of that "constitution" over which they so jealously mounted guard? And was their stewardship of the "constitution" any less crucial to their self-esteem than their immensely influential role in daily justice and administration? When the celebrated *procureur-général* at Aix, Leblanc de Castillon, addressed his assembled company on 21 October 1788, his words revealed how much more encompassing than advocacy of any specific social aspiration was the *parlementaire*'s sense of the magistracy's role in the commonwealth of France:

> The force of the Constitution, the wisdom of the maxims of State and of the parlements' conduct, have not only warded off all troubles, but have procured the greatest advantages from bringing together in the same hands the judicial power, the right to receive judicial appeals, . . . the right to be, according to the laws' expression,

the *last refuge* of Citizens of all the classes of society, [and] *the power to verify the laws, superior to the right of judging.*[46]

The *parlements* and their justice, maintained Leblanc de Castillon, linked all the classes together, negotiated among them and between subjects and sovereign, and reaffirmed the grandeur of both king and nation. Certainly, he conceded, the *parlements* would have to cooperate with the resurrected Estates General in the months to come—yet in saying this the eminent Provençal was only evincing anew the magisterial sense of standing somewhat apart from clerical and noble as well as "bourgeois" aspirants to power.

It is nevertheless incontrovertible that by late 1788 and early 1789 growing numbers of Frenchmen of high and middling status were beginning to think of wresting unprecedented political concessions from the discredited royal government. There are, however, some explicit indications that the provincial judges wished this no more for the noblesse than for commoners.

Most fascinating in this regard are the *Réflexions sur les inconvéniens et les dangers des nouveaux systèmes d'administration relativement à la province de Franche-Comté* put out, apparently in December 1788, by Besançon's Droz des Villars.[47] In this lengthy essay (which preceded by several months the *Mémoires* already cited extensively) the genial *érudit* who so often spoke for his fellows in the Besançon Parlement voiced his misgivings over the tendency toward administrative innovation in France exemplified by provincial assemblies, revived provincial Estates, and resurrected Estates General. And much of his apprehension focused upon the way such experimentation in government, as he saw it, would "denature" the nobility, drawing it from its appropriate military vocation to an administrative career that could endanger the polity and its citizenry.

> For a long time we have had writers incessantly advocating a commercial career for the Noblesse . . . today, we are told, an administrative career is similarly fitting for the Noblesse in France. . . .
>
> It is thus that [such authors] want by force of public opinion to alter the Nation's spirit, and they do not see that the authority of gentlemen administrators could weigh more heavily upon the people than the vestiges of their former privileges . . . they do not see that the moment the noble, disguised in a counting-house, a bank, a receiver's office, speculates, reckons, expounds his ideas, new hordes of tartars will seem to menace Europe. . . .
>
> Let us guard against destroying the warrior spirit of the French noblesse, by turning it away from its primitive destination; the

shocks sustained by the Government are perhaps due only to this change of destination.[48]

Although he could not know it at the time, Droz des Villars was repeating almost verbatim what the leading Parisian *parlementaires* had said eight years before in a confidential memorandum to the ministry.[49] Like the Parisian jurists of 1781 (whose specific complaint had concerned Necker's provincial assemblies), Droz des Villars in December 1788 could not favor any novel concession of authority to the noblesse.

Moreover, like the magistrates in the French capital, this *parlementaire* of Franche-Comté left no doubt in whose hands governmental responsibilities should lie. *Magistrats* rather than *militaires* should always counsel the king.

> As long as the Ministry has been staffed by Magistrates accustomed to holding the scales of justice, favors and rewards, suitably distributed, have never overburdened the State; the remonstrances of the Courts, maturely weighed, have for the most part had the success they deserved; but as soon as Generals, trained in principles of blind subordination required in military life, have proven incapable of distinguishing between the enlightened obedience of Magistrates and the passive obedience of soldiers, as soon as an arbitrary will has been substituted for lawful rules, each Minister, governing in his own fashion, has more or less brought the peremptory spirit of the Soldier into the civil Government, and without desiring to do so, perhaps even without becoming cognizant of it, such individuals have most violently injured the Constitution.

Public affairs required an *esprit d'état*, an *esprit de corps*, an *esprit de famille*, and an education found only in the robe. "The *Militaire* cannot guide his children through the studies of the Magistracy, still less along the mercenary path of commerce and finance; . . . thus it is necessary to leave each individual in the station of life where Providence has left him."[50] With this last assertion, Droz des Villars demonstrated once again how the magistracy's vision of social hierarchy could be as little reconciled with political insurgency in the noble elite as with analogous insurgency in the Third Estate.

At certain points this provincial jurist's observations upon the French noble elite are uncannily reminiscent of sentiments voiced by his contemporaries at Paris. For example, his hope that the typical nobleman would "find in his château a rallying-point" that would "keep him from the cities" so that he might bend all his efforts toward "reviving the countryside" resembles nothing so much as (and indeed may have been inspired by) Duval d'Eprémesnil's vision of the quiescent rural seigneur cultivating his lands and his rustic virtues (see chapter 2). Again, his fear that "the paternal government of a good King" was about to give way to either "the tumult of a popular administration or the horrors of the despotism of society's Grandees" recalls the thoroughgoing social conservatism of the Joly de Fleury brothers in 1787 (see chapter 2). There are the inevitable historical passages that dilate upon "the horrors of the despotism of society's Grandees" in the dark times of early Capetian kingship. President Joly de Fleury would have heartily endorsed this rendering of the past in 1787–88, though his ambitious cousins of the sword would no doubt have preferred Fénelon's and Boulainvilliers's nostalgic approach to the subject.[51] In sum, Droz des Villars, oracle though he was of a notoriously obstructionist and conservative *parlement*, rejected as resolutely as any Parisian magistrate the notion of a politicized "aristocracy."

This judicial conception of a French noblesse that must, as surely as any other class, know its proper place manifested itself elsewhere on the eve of the Revolution. When Bordeaux's fractious *parlementaires*, in exile at Libourne, remonstrated on 15 April 1788 against the government's incarceration of Toulousain Avocat-Général Catellan de Caumont, they characterized those who had arrested this judge in broad social terms:

> Let it be permitted to Your Parlement, Sire, to signify its astonishment at seeing the nobility, which serves as bulwark of the fatherland and dedicates itself in all its actions to glory, employed to deprive submissive and loyal magistrates of their liberty: is it possible that your ministers turn these triumphant hands which were destined to put only enemies of the State in irons against the defenders of the laws and of the national constitution, and that a French officer is ordered to arrest, guard, and imprison a peaceful Citizen?[52]

The exiles at Libourne did not, it is true, explicitly condemn the forays of gentry into administration and politics. Nonetheless, their portrayal of the nobility as ideally devoting itself "in all its actions to glory," and their apotheosis of "submissive and loyal magistrates" as "the defenders of the laws and of the national constitution," suggest plainly enough a conviction that robe rather than sword must wield influence in the domestic affairs of the realm.

The unruly judges at Pau articulated a similar viewpoint in the spring and summer of 1788. Their protests of 21 April, though primarily alleging specific ministerial violations of individual rights in the 1787–88 crisis, chronicled as well the waning of military power and the waxing of the robe's influence over the centuries in France:

When, after the last convulsions of the feudal regime, France was torn by civil wars, disregarded royal authority needed the support of arms. The laws had willy-nilly to invoke the dangerous assistance of military power. . . .

But since all rival powers have disappeared before that of Your Majesty, since the domestic peace, reestablished in all provinces, has progressively unified the diverse parts of the state . . . the laws have sufficed to maintain public order. From one extremity of the kingdom to the other, the weakest organ of these laws can now make them respected. . . . For a long time the military power, become foreign to the domains of the Government, has been essential only for the defense of our frontiers.[53]

Once again, the sword was being assigned its proper place. Unfortunately, however, the modern nobility had other, more sophisticated weapons in its arsenal wherewith to challenge the high judiciary's role in affairs of state. So felt these magistrates of Béarn and Navarre scarcely two months later as they lashed out in protests of 26 June against the ministers' projected Plenary Court. At one point in their remonstrances they apotheosized the historic Court of Peers (in both its Parisian and its provincial versions) and excoriated certain nobles who, through membership in the Plenary Court, would usurp the former tribunal's role:

What an appalling project, to substitute for an antique and unalterable body, recognized by the Nation, an assembly composed in an uncertain manner, by the selection of transitory agents of royal authority, where the Princes and Peers . . . will share their legal right of suffrage with courtiers designated by special favor, where the Parlement's prerogative, acknowledged by the very authors of the scheme, would be ignored . . . even though it is . . . the King's legal council, established in different seats with common duties.[54]

"Established," the jurists meant, in "different seats" ranging from Paris to their own Pau. These *parlementaires*, like their counterparts in other jurisdictions, heartily detested noble sycophants at Versailles and probably had little use for the lordly Princes and peers—especially as they were to participate now in this blatant usurpation of sovereign court functions.

But the most impressive manifestation of corporate robe animus against the military noblesse in 1787–88 involved the notoriously noble magistrates of the notoriously noble province of Brittany.[55] Here, a jurisdictional dispute of eleven months' standing culminated in parlementary remonstrances of 20 August 1787. It seems that, the preceding September, the municipal police at Nantes had arrested two men suspected of having stolen several bars of iron found in their possession. Investigation had revealed that the bars had come from an old brick oven near the military château de Nantes. Both the presidial court at Nantes and the *corps d'artillerie* at the fortress had claimed exclusive cognizance of the case against the two alleged thieves. The presidial court had wished to try the suspects as civilians subject to the "ordinary" or civil tribunals; the army officers had proclaimed their right to try them "militarily" in a "council of war" for having allegedly stolen artillery matériel. The *corps d'artillerie* may have considered itself an easy victor in the affair, for it had taken or been granted custody of the two suspects soon after their arrest. The presidial judges, however, had continued to press their own claim in the matter by delegating several *huissiers* and other functionaries to obtain further information at the fortress concerning the brick oven, the items stolen from it, and the suspects themselves. When the presidial's men were, upon their own account, threatened and insulted by the guard at the château de Nantes, the presidial court retaliated by accusing three of these *militaires* of having outraged officers of the king's justice! The commander of the fortress predictably refused to hand his men over to the royal tribunal for judgment and continued in addition to assert full jurisdictional rights over the two men apprehended in September 1786. The two sides hurled decrees and counterdecrees at each other throughout the early months of 1787. Then, on 4 May, a royal decree seemingly resolved the squabble in favor of the *corps d'artillerie* at Nantes by quashing all pertinent *arrêts* issued by the presidial court there.

At this point, however, the Breton *parlementaires* took up the cudgels on behalf of their subordinates at Nantes. After versing themselves in the details of this dispute, the judges at Rennes voted to remonstrate to the king on the matter; the resultant protests were approved by the membership and sent off to Versailles on 20 August.

To today's historian, the affair at Nantes might seem but another unedifying instance of trivial contention between two courts of law in the old regime.[56] For the jurists at Rennes, however, vital principles were at stake, beginning with the crucial distinction between civilian and military justice. "In all cases other than those . . . immediately concerning military functions, and the discipline of the camps," intoned the Bretons, "the soldier, the officer always remains subject in civil or criminal litigation to the regular tribunals which the law has established for the preservation of public order." And under no circumstances whatsoever could "the citizen, the resident, the *père de famille*, in a word the man not serving under the colors be . . . judged by a council of war." But the Bretons intended to do more than drive a legal point home, as crucial as they might conceive it to be. In vintage parlementary fashion, they insisted upon arraigning the pretensions mirrored in military tribunals:

> In a State governed by laws, . . . all would be lost, if ever the time came, when the constant and steady course of civil and ordinary justice was no longer [shielded] from the injuries, the enterprises, and the extravagant pretensions of the sword. . . .
>
> Let the *puissance militaire*, designed solely for foreign action against the foes of the State, remember that it must, like all other interests acknowledging your sway, respect the general administration within your realm, respect the forms that protect the citizen, respect the judges charged with observing the laws and making all others observe them.[57]

Military men, pursued the Bretons relentlessly, must not be permitted "to forget for a single instant" that the king's subjects were not to be entrusted to them; that "impunity" was not one of their privileges; that, however grand their prerogatives, they would never include "that of judging a citizen or flaunting justice." Men of the sword, kept firmly in their place "starting with Louis XII, father of his people," must continue to know their place.

The *parlementaires* probably intervened in this affair all the more readily in that they saw it as closely resembling an earlier dispute pitting the presidial at Nantes and their own court at Rennes against the men of the sword at the château de Nantes. In 1778, averred the Bretons, a "resident of Nantes, a *père de famille*, a metal-worker" had been imprisoned at the fortress for having allegedly appropriated for his own use a sheet of copper intended initially for the *corps d'artillerie*. Notwithstanding the protests of the presidial court (whose deputies had also upon *this* occasion been insulted and abused at the château), a seven-man *conseil de guerre* "whose incompetence was obvious" had summarily condemned the unfortunate suspect to death. What was more, asserted the judges, the men of the sword had not even bothered to apprise the king's minister of war of their "barbarous judgment" before executing the prisoner. The *parlementaires'* representations concerning this earlier miscarriage of justice had been unavailing; now, the Bretons queried, was yet another outrage to be laid to the account of this "sanguinary" jurisdiction at Nantes?

The latter squabble, stemming from the two arrests in September 1786, dragged on indefinitely: the Rennes Parlement wrote again to the king and ministers on 15 April 1788 soliciting a response to their so far unheeded protests, and Lamoignon's answering letter of 5 May, stating the king's desire "that there be no further sequel to that affair," is the last we hear of this incident.[58] By the time the Bretons received this injunction from the keeper of the seals, of course, more urgent matters were claiming their attention. It is intriguing nonetheless to note a telling similarity between the Bretons' remonstrances of 20 August 1787 and protests presented to Louis XVI just two years before by the Parisian *parlementaires* in connection with a controversy involving the mayor of Bordeaux and the tribunal of the Marshals of France.[59] The Parisians, too, had seized upon a specific application of martial law in a military tribunal to proclaim the subordination of sword to robe in justice (and, by implication, in all public affairs) and had ridiculed the historic pretensions of a military noblesse grown too powerful over the centuries.[60] That such similar jurisdictional altercations should have evoked such similar responses from magistrates close to royalty and government in Paris and jurists renowned for venerable pedigree in noble Brittany suggests once again the solidarity of robe interests and of judicial defiance of sword in this twilight of the old France.

There was another, rather curious way in which at least several of the provincial *parlements* subordinated the interests of the well-born to magisterial concerns in the prerevolutionary crisis. Historians have tended to view the sovereign courts' outcry in 1787–88 against the Bourbons' *lettres de cachet* with skepticism, discerning in it little more than a cynical use of humanitarian rhetoric to champion individual judges and nobles and thus further the magisterial-aristocratic "cause."[61] Some truth to this there may be. Yet it is also true that the provincial justices in some instances explicitly founded their opposition to the hated *lettres de cachet* upon their refusal to see society's high and mighty spared the application of these notorious "administrative orders." For two examples, we need only return to the judges most recently cited, at Pau and Rennes.

In their remonstrances of 21 April 1788 the magistrates of Pau showed how unimpressed they were by the argument of those in government that *lettres de cachet* were sometimes necessary to prevent the reputations of the "best" families from being smirched by the misdeeds and public trials of their black sheep:

> But has the interest of society been considered in that partiality of a government invariably eager to save culpable persons of favored circumstances? Why must the law's rigors necessarily be reserved for the weak and the indigent, while legal impunity is added to all the other advantages of the most favored classes? Since the shame and disgrace associated with punishment constitute the most effective bridle upon action among men whose sentiments have been exalted by education, let them no longer be encouraged to commit

crimes by assurances of favored treatment, by promises that they will be spared stigmatizing punishments.[62]

"Stigmatizing punishments" should indeed be meted out to such offenders; why let them off without public prosecution, with only the quiet and comfortable confinement accorded so easily by the government's *lettres de cachet*? On the other hand, the magistrates observed, such "orders" sometimes served the private purposes of vicious grandees:

> The alleged criminal whom one will appear to be rescuing from the severity of the laws, will often be a victim sacrificed to the interest of a favored relative. Thus your very beneficence will second the designs of iniquity, will consummate its transgressions. Believing that you have dispensed mercy, in actuality you will have condemned an innocent person to the despair of an eternal captivity.[63]

Of course the judges at Pau were themselves "favored" Frenchmen who obdurately defended "all the other advantages of the most favored classes." Still, they were induced by their hearty detestation of *lettres de cachet* to portray some individuals in those "most favored classes" in unflattering colors on the eve of revolution.

In Brittany, at the other end of the kingdom, precisely the same reaction was provoked by the government's recurrence to these "administrative orders." In remonstrances of 2 May 1788 the Bretons bewailed "the assertion that families have often owed the preservation of their honor to *lettres de cachet*." They declared themselves "revolted by that absurd opinion that places the disgrace in the punishment and not in the crime, that opinion destructive of all equity, that ever results in the deliverance of the rich and powerful man from the vengeance of the laws, while the *malheureux sans crédit* is the sole individual the tribunals are permitted to prosecute and punish." Such a "barbarous" state of affairs might exist "in a century of ignorance"; it was, or ought to be, unthinkable in an age of "enlightenment." The time was fast approaching, foretold the Bretons grandly, "when the French will finally realize that the sole, the true honor, consists of serving the state, obeying the laws and cherishing the fatherland."[64] In that happy hour, perverted notions of "honor" and *lettres de cachet* alike would be but unpleasant memories from a benighted past.

No doubt the sovereign courts' many critics would have found such invocations of "enlightenment" and such prophecies of more equitable times to come sorting very ill indeed with parlementary pronouncements and actions on other issues. Certainly in hindsight such language, so closely preceding a genuine revolution, appears ironic in the extreme. The magistrates declaiming against *lettres de cachet* at Pau and Rennes were to get more "enlightenment" and equity than they had bargained for, and very soon. Nonetheless, their willingness to criticize courtiers and military nobles on other, unrelated grounds suggests that, when it came to *lettres de cachet*, their unflattering commentary upon iniquity and favoritism in society's upper ranks was no less sincere than their proverbial hatred of the government's "administrative orders" themselves. What is more, magisterial dudgeon over the utilization of *lettres de cachet* in the cases of wealthy and noble Frenchmen was by no means limited to Pau and Rennes in 1787–88. *Parlementaires* all over the realm held forth vociferously on the issue, and not surprisingly so, given the apparently general judicial refusal to endorse novel political pretensions in the first two orders.[65]

What about the attitudes of the nonjudicial nobles toward the high robe? This complex subject is of course not our primary concern in these pages; yet in the cases of at least five of the major provincial *parlements* we have strong evidence of military noblemen's indifference or hostility toward the men of the robe. A brief review of this evidence tentatively indicates some conclusions about the state of robe-and-sword relations in the final political crisis of the *ancien régime*.

In chronicling the events of the prerevolutionary crisis in Franche-Comté, Jean Egret was struck by the tardiness and feebleness of "aristocratic" manifestations of support for what was commonly perceived as a "despotic" and "haughty" *parlement* at Besançon.[66] Only on 4 June 1788, nearly a full month after the ministerial coup against the sovereign courts, did 101 nobles of the province gather to sign "a timid request" to the authorities for reinstatement of Besançon's *parlementaires*. Timorous attempts to form other assemblies for purposes of protestation were quickly squelched by the king's lieutenants in Franche-Comté. True, on 10 September—more than two weeks after Loménie de Brienne's fall from power—145 nobles, assembled surreptitiously at the Priory of Saint-Rénobert near Quingey, petitioned Louis XVI for the *parlementaires'* recall. Significantly, however, they had come together on this day primarily to formulate a request to the central government for the revival of their beloved provincial Estates, suspended since the preceding century.

Only on 1 October—on the eve of the *parlement's* reinstatement at Besançon—did another convocation of nobles at Quingey "decide to present a long and vehement critique of the judicial and political reform attempted by the principal minister and by the keeper of the seals, both of whom were now in disgrace." An observer of these events, the celebrated Benedictine dom Grappin, noted three days later "the meager interest shown by the greater part of the Nobility and almost all the people" in the fate of the stricken law court throughout the crisis.[67] Most of the *parlementaires* entitled to attend the sessions of the Estates of Franche-Comté that ran from November 1788 to January 1789 reportedly stayed away.[68] In the end, their decision to do so must have gratified the most reactionary gentlemen in the province. The latter could only have been incensed when the judges, in their controversial *arrêté* of 27 January 1789, came out against efforts by some of the oldest families in the province to exclude nobles "without fiefs" and other nobles of recent extraction from the local Estates.[69] In sum, there appears to have been little love lost between robe and sword in Franche-Comté in 1788 and 1789—and there might have been even less had the local military noblesse gotten wind of Droz des Villars's thoughts upon the need to keep the sword out of politics and administration.

While Besançon's highest justices for the most part held themselves aloof from local politics, Bordeaux's *parlementaires*, recently emerged triumphant from their long banishment at Libourne, threw themselves with a will into electioneering and other political activities on behalf of Guyenne's nobility in the early months of 1789.[70] In the process of doing so, however, they seem to have exposed a raw nerve of local nobles' resentment toward the robe. When the preliminary assembly of the nobility adopted on 10 February a document establishing guidelines for the *cahier de doléances* of the Second Estate in the *sénéchaussée* of Bordeaux, twenty-seven dissenting nobles immediately drafted a "minority" document. They apparently did so because the majority's project, calling as it did for such actions as an end to *lettres de cachet* and the preservation of the parlementary functions of registration of and remonstration against royal acts, bore unmistakable signs of magisterial authorship. As William Doyle has appositely observed, "Thus, even before the elections began, the nobility was divided, and beneath the apparent principles professed by the opposed sides, lay the more real issue of the political role of the parlement. The traditional hostility between robe and sword, long since without significance socially, was reawakened by the opening of access to wider political power; as it was elsewhere at the same time."[71]

To some extent, the schism within the elite at Bordeaux pitting robe against sword reflected a clash of personalities: specifically, the leaders of the twenty-seven dissenting nobles, the duc de Duras and M. A. Dupérier de Larsan, grand seneschal of Bordeaux, opposed J. S. de Laroze, honorary counselor in the Bordeaux Parlement, on a number of matters relating to the drafting of *cahiers de doléances* and elections of deputies to the Estates General. But personalities and substantive questions could not be easily kept apart, as was demonstrated by Dupérier de Larsan's charges in subsequent weeks that most of the *parlementaires* were neglecting their judicial duties and concentrating instead upon influencing the three orders' *cahiers* and selections of delegates to the Estates General. Although in actuality the judges seem to have exerted little influence in the assemblies of the First and Third Estates, they certainly did play a prominent role in the assemblies of the noblesse: the *cahier de doléances* of the Guyenne nobility bore the imprimatur of the judiciary, and a number of the order's representatives at Versailles were to be Bordelais *parlementaires*.[72] Dupérier de Larsan, Duras, and the other dissenting nobles endeavored unavailingly to have the ministers replace the majority *cahier* and slate of representatives with their own *cahier* and slate of delegates. That they remained irreconcilable on these interrelated issues testified as effectively as did their sour commentary upon the Bordelais judges to the survival of tensions between robe and sword in southwestern France.

Political issues seem similarly to have driven a wedge between robe and sword in Dauphiné.[73] The magistrates at Grenoble aroused the hostility of the military noblesse as early as the summer of 1787, when, in an effort to head off the imposition of a provincial assembly upon the province, they proposed restoration of Dauphiné's historic Estates in a memorandum to the ministers. The judges' project would have accorded as many deputies to the Third Estate as to the first two orders combined and would have permitted voting "by head" in all substantive deliberations, but at the same time the Grenoble Parlement and Chambre des Comptes, through their role of registration, would have held veto power over the envisioned Estates in all areas of policy. In effect, no taxes could have been levied, no funds lent or borrowed, no "treaties" or "transactions" of any kind concluded without magisterial approval, which might have been secured first of all by the presence of the first and second presidents of the *parlement* and first president of the Chambre des Comptes at all deliberative sessions of the Estates.

Although the ministers rejected this plan and insisted upon the establishment of a provincial assembly in Dauphiné, there were those in the Grenoble Parlement who urged defiance of the government on the issue, and even the majority who voted grudgingly to accept the pertinent royal legislation stipulated in their decree of registration that the new administrative body "could assess no tax whatsoever nor agree to any loan whatsoever without a law registered in the Parlement."[74] By this time, however, some nobles of the sword were beginning to signify their irritation at the magistracy's political pretensions. The marquis de Berenger, attending a reception at the Grenoble townhouse of First President de Bérulle in June 1787, raised his voice somewhat tactlessly against the *parlement*'s preference for its conception of provincial Estates over the government's vision of provincial assemblies.[75] The marquis de Marcieu, in a letter to the comte de Brienne, secretary of war, suggested what many nobles felt was really at stake in this controversy:

> The Noblesse attached to military service and ranked as general Officers, upon return to the Fatherland, cannot hide from itself its absolute nothingness, even in the bosom of its estates. That Noblesse which, not having attained the officered ranks, has returned to its domestic habitations, decorated with the Cross of Saint-Louis, is and remains astounded at seeing no esteem associated with its rank and station. Even the Church no longer has extensive prerogatives. The King in his beneficence having granted provincial assemblies to his provinces, everyone has flocked to them, because they have seen in them a means for escaping the authority of the Parlement.[76]

Or, as Marcieu put it even more bluntly in a slightly different context,

> For a very long time, the Parlement of Grenoble has been sole and unique administrator in Dauphiné . . . The Church, the Noblesse, the Third Estate have never played up to the present day any kind of role whatsoever in administrative matters. People are tired of counting for nothing and of depending upon a Parlement that no longer draws its members, as it did in earlier times, from the oldest Houses in the Province.[77]

The rancor of the marquis, fueled as obviously by the old social snobbism as by frustrated political aspirations, was no more pronounced than that manifested by the comte de Virieu, commandant of the Royal-Limousin regiment, when speaking of a conversation he had had with Loménie de Brienne concerning the upcoming provincial assembly in Dauphiné:

> Monsieur the Archbishop, responding to fears and objections that if Nobles wishing to represent the Nobility were not adequately examined as to their pedigree, the Assembly would end up being filled with Magistrates from all the Courts, recognized the ill consequences that could follow and promised that if matters were not set right in the implementing rules and regulations the authorities would grant the Assembly's wishes upon its request. . . . In like fashion he assured us that in the event that holding the Assembly's sessions at Grenoble, amidst all the influences of the Bar, brought vexations and turmoil upon our heads, he had not engaged himself to leave the Assembly there forever and could very well transfer it elsewhere.[78]

In later months marked by parlementary censure of Dauphiné's provincial assembly, the comte de Virieu was to continue fulminating in his correspondence and in various private memoranda against the pretentious justices at Grenoble. "Lawmaking and administration," he was to declare, "belong as rights to all, and consequently a few isolated individuals cannot scheme to arrogate those activities to themselves without injuring the most sacred rights of the people and all the proprieties of justice and reason."[79] Not a few thoughtful Dauphinois happened to agree with the "isolated individuals" in the Grenoble Parlement that the ministers' administrative innovations, in their province and elsewhere, could very conceivably serve despotic purposes.[80] For the comte de Virieu and other restive gentlemen, however, it was the long-standing influence and undiminished pretensions of the robe, and not the possibility of despotic designs at Versailles, that galled the most.

Of course, tension between robe and sword deriving most fundamentally from the cutting issue of access to power could be, and was, reinforced by petty incidents involving individual nobles. When, for instance, the marquis de Belmont had a *huissier* at the Grenoble Parlement notify the judges in January 1788 about an *arrêt d'évocation* withdrawing this minor gentleman's minor lawsuit from their cognizance, the jurists riposted with a decree that stripped the *huissier* of his professional functions for a full year, fined the marquis himself, and threatened more rigorous action against both men should they attempt to revive the matter.[81] The magistrates' message was clear: let no man, whether of noble or common pedigree, challenge parlementary competence at law. This seemingly insignificant incident, along with so much else, must have rankled in noblemen's minds. A year later, in 1789, a Dauphinois noble in a letter to a deputy of the province at the Estates General commented upon the (by now) humbled magistrates: "It is impossible to deceive oneself about it: what rank in society, what institution, what individuals have they not vexed and abused? . . . What haughtiness . . . toward the Nobility and all the military! M. de Belmont was perhaps somewhat in the wrong but his [punishment] was revolting."[82] Thus, in the end, the misfortunes of a provincial marquis could not be disassociated from, and indeed were seen as illustrative of, the prevailing situation in this part of France.

And what was true in the southeastern and southwestern reaches of the realm seems to have been equally true in the great northwestern provinces of Normandy and Brittany. Moreover, evidence of the sword's hostility toward the robe is particularly interesting in these last two cases in that it comes to us in the form of statements purportedly representing the views of many or all military nobles in the two provinces.

In Normandy, a manifesto entitled *Mémoire des Députés du Clergé et de la Noblesse de la Province de Normandie* appeared during 1787. The "deputies" referred to in this title were apparently responding to the officers of the *bailliage* at Rouen on the issue of precedence of representatives of the various Estates and orders in the local assemblies of Normandy. A familiar attitude of sword toward robe appears immediately in the memorandum's introduction:

> By the manner in which they have cited the Edicts and Letters-Patent of 1764, 1766 and 1767 concerning the assemblies of Notables in the cities of the Kingdom, the officers of the Magistracy, even the most inferior, have aspired to preeminence and priority of suffrage over the Clergy and the Noblesse. These two orders, in the province of Normandy, have beseeched the King's Council to maintain their prerogatives. The officers of the Bailliage in the Capital of this Province have sent a Memorandum against that petition to the Ministers. The method of replying to this Memorandum that has seemed most appropriate has been to discuss it article by article and expose . . . all proofs of the rights of the Clergy and Nobility, from the Monarchy's origins to the present, and determine the proper rank of the Judiciary in general.[83]

This manifesto announced candidly that it would be settling the quarrel over precedence in Normandy "in favor of the Clergy and Noblesse." Certainly its authors went at their work with a will: the prodigious length of their manuscript (more than 250 pages) attests to their industry. Examination of the main body of the text reveals that for the most part these spokesmen for the first two orders were sufficiently diplomatic to laud the magistracy for its dispensation of the king's justice and to focus upon the political pretensions of the presidials, *bailliages*, and other inferior courts rather than upon those of the *parlement* at Rouen. Nevertheless, a submerged noble and clerical hostility toward the high judiciary in political matters occasionally surfaces. For example, the treatise recalls

> the singular epoch during which the principal Magistrates of the entire Kingdom attempted to attain precedence over [the nobility] in an Assembly of Notables held at Rouen. It is not without astonishment that citizens have seen the moving force behind such an enterprise renewed several times since, and seen how the slightest innovations in the matter of prerogatives sooner or later lead to their destruction. But a noble resistance and the force of National Law have always, by reaffirmations, maintained the preeminence that belongs to the Noblesse.[84]

And what of the current tempest blowing up around the ship of state? To this the nobles' and clerics' manifesto seems to make pointed allusion:

> As unreasonable as it would be . . . in assemblies of the Estates, or in assemblies of notables composed of deputies of the divers classes of citizens, to place the high magistracy in the Third Estate, it would be just as contrary to the fundamental Constitutions to place it above the Clergy and the Nobility. If there are examples of members of Superior Courts attempting in several past assemblies of notables to achieve precedence over the Nobility, they did so only because they had momentarily forgotten their place. . . .
>
> In the Constitution of our Government, the Magistracy can be ranked only beneath the Clergy and Nobility.[85]

There were no overt attacks here upon contemporary *parlementaires* at Rouen or, for that matter, anywhere else. But in a sense that was quite unnecessary: it was fairly obvious that these spokesmen for clergy and noblesse in Normandy felt, as their social counterparts felt elsewhere, that the entire order of the robe, from *parlements* down to *cours prévôtales*, should administer royal justice and stay out of politics altogether, or at the very least defer to miter and sword in all realms of action outside the safely apolitical world of litigation.

In nearby Brittany, meanwhile, a similar incident exposed a similar attitude. Surely if there was a single province in late eighteenth-century France that should have provided fertile ground for a political alliance between robe and sword, that province was Brittany. Here, after all, nobility was notorious for its numbers and its ancientness of pedigree, and *parlementaires* were famed for their recruitment from that storied old noblesse. Yet, here again, we can find no such coalescence of sociopolitical forces on the eve of the great upheaval in France. Quite the contrary. The judges at Rennes, we have already noted, were every bit as prepared to castigate noblemen who encroached upon "ordinary" courts' domain or who availed themselves of hateful *lettres de cachet* as they were to champion well-born seigneurs against the "administrative monarchy" or against social pressures from below. Nonparlementary nobles in Brittany, for their part, did not exactly warm to the idea of a "political magistracy" in 1788. On 2 October of that year, a certain M. Georgelin, "permanent secretary" of the Académie de Bretagne, signified to Necker the "secret but unanimous will of all the intermediary commissioners" of the noble-dominated Estates that they be "preferred over the parlement for registering edicts, so that a free nation would not be under the tutelage of the imperious and despotic magistracy."[86] Here, indeed, was a deadly turning of the word "despotic," that most cherished polemical adjective of the judges.

Actually, friction between *parlement* and Estates was an old, old story in Brittany, as it was in several of the other provinces still boasting historic convocations of the three orders.[87] Whether Loménie de Brienne should have endeavored to capitalize politically upon that tension in Brittany as he did elsewhere in the critical summer of 1788 by playing judicial and military noblesse off against each other remains moot.[88] What appears undeniable is the reciprocity of suspicion and frank hostility between provincial *parlementaires* and provincial men of the sword in the arena of prerevolutionary politics.

To be sure, the provincial magistrates for the most part must have welcomed the Paris Parlement's call on 25 September 1788 for the 1614 form of the Estates General, even if their desire to avoid anything like the Parisian judges' consequent loss of popularity made them, in some cases, less than forthright about this in their own decrees. (As we have seen, Besançon's jurists, at least, candidly endorsed the Parisians' position upon this question in their controversial *arrêté* of 27 January 1789.) Yet there is no evidence that, in the provinces any more than at Paris, magisterial favoritism for the precedent of 1614 betokened solidarity with a politically resurgent nobility. Thus, the *Gazette de Leyde* commented that those in the know in France were convinced that the sovereign courts insisted upon the precedent of 1614 only "to ward off all discussions and debates about the pretensions of *Corps particuliers*, that could make the . . . Estates-General miscarry, or render it useless for the principal object, upon which the Nation is unanimous, which is to end Ministerial Despotism in France."[89] And assuredly from what we already know of the judges, whether Parisian or provincial, obsession with "ministerial despotism" motivated them as much as or more than any other consideration in 1787–88.

In concluding this discussion we would do well to bear in mind that gentlemen of the robe and gentlemen of the sword were not that frequently at cross-purposes, let alone mutually antagonistic, in the provincial France of the prerevolution. The magistrates, after all, had every possible reason as noblemen, as defenders of tradition, and as guardians of law and order to uphold the ancient hierarchy of orders and to protect in general terms and upon specific occasions the age-old socioeconomic privileges of highborn and clerical Frenchmen. The beneficiaries of that magisterial policy, for their part, had every reason to be thankful that the provincial *parlementaires* were speaking out with undiminished resolve as conservators of the old society. In all this, provincial France could have been Paris. Thus, the socioeconomic interests of robe and sword were mutual interests everywhere in the kingdom as 1789 approached.

Equally unmistakable as a national phenomenon at this time, however, was the bad will between robe and sword in the domain of politics. Like their counterparts of Paris, the provincial justices were pretentious administrators and politicians, and in those capacities could scarcely approve of the nobility as a resurgent political elite. Moreover, the closer the nobility might seem to come to a reassumption of power in the political vacuum left by the spreading paralysis in government, the more apt were the *parlements* to censure such a development. The magistrates' fears on this score did not go unnoticed by their cousins of the provincial sword, who, harboring long-felt grievances against the sovereign courts even as they held out bright hopes for an enlarged future role in public affairs, quite naturally returned the jurists' hostility and criticisms with interest.

Of course to raise this last point is to acknowledge that some of the stuff of "aristocratic revolution" did undoubtedly exist in the form of political aspirations of nonjudicial nobles all over the realm in 1787–88. Furthermore, it is at least arguable that such ambitions found institutional voice in the two Assemblies of Notables, the Assembly of the Clergy, and the various Estates of provincial France. As we have seen, however, such aspirations did not find institutional expression in those bodies most instrumental in raising the lethal nationwide insurrection of 1787–88 against Louis XVI and his government—namely, the *parlements* of Paris and the provinces. Insurrectionary the *parlementaires* assuredly were—but not exclusively on behalf of the first two orders, and certainly not at all on behalf of politically overweening clerics and nobles. Accordingly, as we seek to characterize the situation in France on the eve of 1789 we may have to abandon the term "aristocratic revolution" altogether and cast about for words that describe more faithfully the complicated and evolving social dynamics of the prerevolutionary crisis.

Provincial Jurists and
the Third Estate

In the national disputation over the May Edicts of 1788 the provincial *parlements'* myriad critics delighted in pointing up the expediential nature of magisterial protest against government reforms.[1] They could so very easily argue, for instance, that the high justices resented the prospect of losing commoners' litigation in major affairs to *grands bailliages* and losing their cherished roles of registration and remonstration to the ministers' Plenary Court; they could so very easily demonstrate that it was the *parlementaires* themselves (or their relations or social peers in the countryside) whose seigneurial jurisdiction was to be curtailed or abolished altogether.[2] One royal partisan gleefully remarked that the men of the *parlements*, false paladins of popular interests that they were, could not help but be in a dither over these and all associated points in Lamoignon's judicial statutes, because they knew perfectly well that systemic improvements in justice must necessarily "humble their pride and shackle their greed."[3]

Yet it would be as simplistic to deny all humanitarian motivation to the provincial judges in the late 1780s as to deny that attribute to their Parisian counterparts in the same period. Reality was more complicated than that, as provincial and Parisian archives eloquently testify. That the provincial magistrates continued to lump all secular *roturiers* together as constituting the "Third Estate," and that they continued to subordinate the Third Estate to clergy and nobility in their beloved "constitution," we have already seen. What we have yet to explore are the numberless ways in which these *parlementaires* ventilated the grievances and aspirations of lay commoners—at least as they perceived those grievances and aspirations—on the very eve of revolution in France. Once again, as with reference to noble and clerical interests, those "numberless ways" comprehended judicial reactions to purely local altercations as well as to the great national controversies of the prerevolutionary period. And once again, the pride and pretensions of these great officers of the robe potently reinforced their efforts to bring matters momentous and trivial to the attention of the king and his agents. In some of the cases discussed in this chapter, commoners' and nobles' interests were so closely intertwined as to suggest the expediency of parlementary champions of the former. In other situations, however, the judges addressed themselves to issues that they seem genuinely to have regarded as concerning primarily (if not exclusively) "common" French people of town and countryside.

In Defense of "Classes and Masses"

Only the magistracy's most uncritical adherents in the late 1780s could have gainsaid the role expediency played at times in parlementary invocations of presumed "popular" interests. To be sure, the issue was seldom as clear-cut as in the matter of the May Edicts, which called into question parlementary justice itself. Still, the judges were members of a proud propertied class in the country as well as town practitioners of justice; they were therefore especially likely to speak out for humble folk whose proprietary interests were unavoidably caught up in their own. The outstanding issue at any time in eighteenth-century France involving landowners of robe, sword, and commonalty in a shared complex of interests was naturally royal taxation, and in the final crisis of the old regime this issue took the form specifically of the government's reimposition of the *vingtièmes* following its revocation of the ill-fated *subvention territoriale*. From Dijon, Toulouse, and Rouen to Douai, Nancy, and Perpignan arose parlementary complaints on behalf of fiscal interests cutting across the strata of society. The more localized quarrels—as over the *chemins finerots* in Burgundy and *terres vaines et vagues* in Normandy—are additional illustrations of the judicial advocacy of "common" interests bound up with those of the elite.

Of all the provincial *parlements* taking the ministers to task for the legislation of October 1787 reimposing the *vingtièmes*, none enumerated the various social interests adversely affected by the government's action more forthrightly than did that of Dijon. The Dijonnais, however, in their lengthy remonstrances of 4 April 1788, declared themselves and their fellow Burgundians to be aggrieved not only by the reimposition of the *vingtièmes*, which policy applied to other provinces as well, but also (and especially) by the letters patent of 16 February 1788 fixing this taxation at a much higher level in Burgundy than had ever been the case before. For the justices at Dijon, the situation in the countryside was already bleak:

> The excess of the imposts known as *tailles* and of those associated with the *taille*, has discouraged the farmers in Burgundy; agriculture here is languishing to such an extent, that the exploitation of many leases remains an expense upon the proprietors for lack of

tenant farmers: almost all those [lands] leased over the past two years have depreciated considerably in lease value. The proprietors, who have no resources other than their rents from which to pay their own taxes, are forced to the desperate recourse of seizures and warrants against their tenant farmers; arrests and imprisonments multiply day by day and consummate the inescapable ruin of the farmers.[4]

Let the sovereign remember, intoned the Dijonnais, that his realm could "prosper only insofar as prosperity generally reigns in the two classes of men which between them constitute the sole genuine resource" of France. We may be sure that the "two classes of men" the Burgundians spoke of here included noble proprietors directly or indirectly affected by the misfortunes of *taillables* as well as the woebegone *taillables* themselves. And to "order in such circumstances an augmentation in the two *vingtièmes* that would make them exceed the level of the three *vingtièmes* levied during the [last] war . . . would deliver the ultimate blow to all properties."[5]

Consequently, these judicial remonstrants at Dijon, noble harvesters of rents themselves, were well advised to display concern for the harried peasantry of their province. Their concern focused momentarily upon two recent grievances or alleged grievances of Burgundian *taillables*. First, the *parlementaires* complained that the royal legislation of February 1780 "providing that the . . . *taille* would remain definitively fixed at the level set as of 1 January 1781. . . . was never sent to your Parlement of Dijon." As a result, while "the farmers of the Pays de Généralités benefited from that Law," the weight of the *taille* continued to increase in Burgundy "at the most fearsome rate." Second, Dijon's highest tribunal had also failed to receive from the government for registration its act of 1 January 1775 abrogating "the solidary or binding contribution of *taillables* to the payment of the assigned quota of taxation in each community." Thus, in contravention of "the Privilege that the residents in a Pays d'Etat ought to enjoy . . . the payers of the *taille* in Burgundy are still subjected to the rigor of binding contributions condemned as odious by Your Majesty everywhere else in your Realm."[6] Significantly, the Dijonnais were not to be the only magistrates in 1788 reminding monarch and ministers about Necker's famous pledge of February 1780 not to raise the *taille* without the sovereign courts' consent. Again, the Burgundians' invocation of Turgot's equally celebrated legislation of January 1775 abrogating the notorious *contrainte solidaire* as traditionally applied to rural communities is similarly telling, for it shows that judicial noblemen of Dijon were as willing to defend peasants against the *contrainte solidaire* as, say, Duval d'Eprémesnil was at Paris to defend clerical and noble taxpayers against such an administrative abuse. Furthermore, the Dijonnais did not stop with these allusions to notable recent reforms designed to alleviate the popular misery. Utilizing the accounts submitted by the treasurer of the Estates of Burgundy to the Chambre des Comptes at Dijon, the judges calculated that the yield from the *taille* and associated imposts in Burgundy had increased from 2,161,252 livres in 1785 to 2,312,538 livres just two years later. They also complained that the *capitation* paid by the *taillables* had "been augmented in the same proportion."[7] Finally, the jurists maintained that "according to a new tax-rate illegally introduced [into the province] by the Elus of the Estates of Burgundy," commoners were to be burdened further with "a *taille d'exploitation* imposed upon sharecroppers and equivalent to 5 percent of the product of their lease" and "another *taille* assessed upon the proprietor of the sharecropper's lands if that proprietor is a Commoner and . . . equivalent . . . to 5 percent of the yield of his lands." In effect, the magistrates alleged, Burgundian *roturiers* would be groaning under the weight of no fewer than five *vingtièmes*, quite apart from the onus of their "normal" or traditional *taille*.[8]

The *parlementaires'* jab at the detested Elus reminds us that motives at Dijon's Palais de Justice were complex. And indeed, at most points in their protests of 4 April 1788 the Burgundians articulated plaints that could not have issued exclusively from any one stratum of rural society. These comments, for instance, concerned the matter of new highways cutting through provincial France:

> One cannot think of any province in which the Grands Chemins have been so multiplied as in Burgundy, especially in view of the smallness of that province. It is crisscrossed by more than five hundred leagues of highways. Nonetheless the proprietors of the lands over which these new highways are established have never received any indemnification whatsoever for the losses they have sustained.[9]

Obviously, this was an issue that could concern rich and poor, mighty and humble alike. So, too, could any controversy over that most renowned of Burgundian products, wine. All experienced ministers, the judges declared, had realized over the years

> that the principal resource of Burgundy consists in the harvest of its wines, whose fickleness often nullifies any product for the proprietor during stretches of several years, [and] that the cultivation of vineyards requires considerable investments of capital that nev-

ertheless result all too often in a dead loss for the proprietor, if only because of the sheer misery and insolvency of the workers in the vineyards.[10]

Given, then, the chronic and severe difficulties of those who owned the vineyards, and the abject poverty of those who labored in them, how could the government possibly expect to extract an additional 250,238 livres on each *vingtième* from Burgundy's *contribuables*? Such was the augmentation of *vingtième* taxation announced for the province in the letters patent of 16 February.

In truth, Louis XVI's ministers (and, perhaps, taxpayers in the *pays d'élection* as well) could have responded to this barrage of complaints by reminding the Dijonnais that their province, as a *pays d'état*, had long escaped its fair share of monetary and other forms of tribute to the central government. Somewhat belatedly, Loménie de Brienne and his associates were striving to equalize direct taxation for all Frenchmen as best they could within the limits imposed by the ramshackle institutional arrangements of the *ancien régime*. The *parlementaires* at Dijon, however, as parochial in their outlook as provincial magistrates elsewhere, would have none of this: indeed, their remonstrances of 4 April 1788 resoundingly championed Burgundians of all social ranks against Frenchmen of other provinces. In fact, the Dijonnais claimed that their province was being taxed first as a *pays de généralité* and then again as a *pays d'état*, and was consequently being forced to shoulder the burdens of the two different administrative regimes within France.[11]

There is no denying that the authorities at Versailles were setting an unprecedentedly high *abonnement* for the *vingtièmes* in Burgundy, nor that the judges at Dijon combated this policy in part by invoking genuinely "popular" interests in their formal protests. But these realities were in no wise unique to Burgundy in the troubled early months of 1788. In the much vaster *pays d'état* of Languedoc in southern France a very similar situation obtained. Here, too, the government was determined to extract a larger lump sum (*abonnement*) in *vingtième* taxation from the provincial Estates than had ever been extracted before; here, too, the *parlementaires* intervened against what they regarded as collusion between the Estates and the king's agents. The judges might have had good reason to regard cooperation between Estates and ministerial representatives as particularly menacing to *privilégiés* like themselves in Languedoc, for a move was on foot to conduct a new survey of all taxable rural properties so that in the future the burden of taxation might be shifted somewhat from the luckless *taillables* to nobles and other privileged landowners.[12] On the other hand, long and bitter experience had taught commoners as well as *privilégiés* in Languedocien rural society to view government reforms of taxation with skepticism and distrust: projects for fiscal reform had come and gone, but exactions from the north had never seemed to decrease. Thus, when the Toulouse Parlement protested formally against the *vingtièmes* on 12 January 1788, it could probably claim with about as much justification as its sister institution at Dijon that it had the interests of all taxpayers of the province, and not merely those of the privileged, in mind.[13]

In their remonstrances of 12 January 1788 the Toulousains wasted no time in sounding a popular note of protest as they advised the king not to apply the royal legislation of the preceding October:

> We could first of all conjure up before your eyes the misery that devastates our countryside and that has, so to speak, cursed it with sterility, but we will spare your sensitive heart such a distressing portrayal. We will say to you in all simplicity, as witnesses making deposition concerning what they have seen, that the majority of small landed proprietors, constituting a class that is infinitely precious to the State, are reduced to the most straitened circumstances. Even assuming they could wait yet a few more years for the relief they so desperately desire, all efforts should be made to avoid aggravating their situation by adding anew to the weight that is already crushing them.[14]

Like the judges at Dijon, the judges at Toulouse approvingly cited Necker's legislation of February 1780, with its implied ceiling upon the *taille* and associated imposts, and reminded Louis XVI that they had ratified that edict "without signifying approbation of any increases in the *vingtièmes* that could be arbitrarily decreed."[15] Yet here, now, was the October 1787 legislation that seemingly augured everlastingly increasing *vingtième* taxation reflecting all increases in values of rural lands. Would this imposition, then, never be repealed? Was it fated, instead, to weigh ever more oppressively upon the *contribuables*? And if this were indeed the case, would not all incentive and enterprise in the countryside be crushed?

> What a terrible scourge must be a tax that strikes the imagination and causes torment more through the apprehension of the evil to come than through the evil event itself! The farmer, disgusted at seeing the fertility of his harvests punished by an increase in taxation, will not bother to improve his lands; and the fiscal regime will only have defeated its own purposes by exhausting the essential source of revenue through greed. Nature is just toward men, and compensates them for their pains; nature renders them hardworking by associating the most handsome rewards with the most

arduous labors; but if an arbitrary power snatches away nature's rewards, the old disgust for honest work will reassert itself, and idle-
ness alone will seem desirable.[16]

This was an accurate enough analysis of the "psychology of overtaxation" in the French countryside that had for so long stymied the efforts
of those in authority to stimulate the crucial agricultural sector of the
economy.[17] Whether the *parlementaires* at Toulouse, or anywhere else,
would have been willing to do their part toward breaking the vicious
cycle of overtaxation and underproduction in the countryside by ratifying a shift in the incidence of taxation toward *privilégiés* like themselves was, of course, another matter altogether. Across-the-board reduction in government expenditure (and thus in government taxation)
plainly had the highest priority in magisterial eyes.

The remonstrances of 12 January 1788 were followed by "reiterated
remonstrances" of 1 March in which the Toulouse Parlement refused
once again to register the legislation of the preceding October. The ministers attempted to enforce their will through a *lit de justice* held at
Toulouse on 10 March, but the fractious jurists struck back immediately
by declaring the forced registration of the October statute "null and
void."[18] In the meantime, the Cour des Aides at nearby Montpellier had
been excoriating the Languedoc Estates for their alleged docility toward
Versailles in fiscal matters, and on 11 March, the day after the *lit de
justice* at Toulouse, this tribunal forbade the communities in its jurisdiction to cooperate with the agents of the government and Estates in
the new land survey. On 27 March the Toulouse Parlement issued its
own condemnation of the Languedoc Estates and of the recently initiated survey of taxable rural properties in the province.[19] In its decree the
parlement upbraided the Estates for having failed to remind the king of
his purported assurances in 1780 that the *vingtièmes* would not be increased at least through 1790. The court also brushed aside the possibility that a thoroughgoing inquiry into land values in Languedoc might
in fact facilitate a more equitable assessment of taxation in the future,
insisting that the inquiry was motivated solely by the government's in-
satiable desire to raise the imposts levied upon *all* individuals. The
parlement again implored Louis XVI to "take into consideration the
misery of the People, which has been consummated since 1780 by the
stagnation of agriculture, a recession in trade, and a host of other circumstances," and requested that Languedoc be entirely exempted from
increases in the *vingtièmes*. Moreover, pleading the urgent necessity "to
allay the fears and anxieties" spread throughout the province by the
publication of the statutes mandating the new land survey, the *parlement*, in imitation of the Cour des Aides at Montpellier, prohibited all

officials and communities within its vast jurisdiction from cooperating with the government in its "verifications" of properties.

The actions of the jurists throughout this controversy certainly implied as much concern for *privilégiés* like themselves as for taxpayers of humbler status, but their protests were no less popular for all that. The syndics (trustees) of the Languedoc Estates as much as admitted this themselves by regretting that the ministers (in a royal decree of 22 March) should have incorrectly attributed to the Estates a formal acceptance of the major increase in *vingtième* taxation proposed for the province.[20] One of the syndics observed apprehensively to an associate in late April,

> In the present situation there is no doubt that if I send a copy of this decree to the dioceses, the inhabitants of the province will see in it a validation of the parlement's complaints in its decree of 27 March. . . . Concluding, with reason, that the *abonnement* is permanently fixed, they will therefore not consider the new inquiry as anything but a means of worsening their lot.

The last thing the Estates needed to do at such a critical juncture, this individual continued, was to augment popular fears "and give the courts new means [and] new ammunition for renewing their charges."[21] Apparently, the popular "fears and anxieties" cited by the Toulousain *parlementaires* in their decree of 27 March were no mere figments of the magisterial imagination. In Languedoc as in Burgundy, parlementary opposition to the *vingtièmes* cast light upon problems common to Frenchmen of widely varying rank and station.

This was the case in Normandy as well, although in the course of dueling with the crown over the *vingtièmes* the Rouen Parlement threw down something of a novel challenge to the ministers. The Rouennais had issued a stinging *arrêté* against the reimposition of this form of taxation as early as 20 December 1787.[22] They returned to the attack with full-dress remonstrances of 5 February 1788.[23] In most respects these latter protests resembled those drafted at Toulouse and anticipated the protests that soon thereafter emanated from the court at Dijon. In their remonstrances, the Rouennais magistrates commended Necker's legislation of February 1780 for making any increases in the *taille* and *capitation* subject to the sovereign courts' approbation. They sourly characterized the *vingtièmes* as "unlimited" taxation of indefinite duration and lashed out at agents of the government charged with surveying and evaluating taxable properties in Normandy. Again, the Rouennais, like their counterparts at Toulouse and Dijon, argued that the *vingtièmes*, by confiscating from the *cultivateur* the fruits of careful planning and hard labor, must necessarily discourage all rural initiative and depress agriculture further. But with a candor that did not usually attend the protestations of the provincial judiciary, the *parlementaires* at Rouen also confronted the fundamentally inequitable nature of *vingtième* taxation.

> Vicious in its principle, and dangerous in its effects, that impost attacks property more directly than does any other levy. Though ostensibly affording a proportional equality, in reality it falls inequitably upon the tax-payers; while taking from the affluent proprietor nothing but a portion of his superfluous wealth, it deprives the indigent of a part of what is absolutely essential to him, not the least bit of which can be extracted from him without destroying the principle and the justification of all property, namely the subsistence of the proprietor.[24]

There was all too much truth to this analysis—indeed, the judges' words might have come very easily from the lips of those agronomists and reforming ministers who for years had envisioned replacing the "flat" rate of the *vingtièmes* with a graduated and thus more equitable mode of rural taxation. (The ill-fated *subvention territoriale* of the preceding year had derived from just such calculations.) As the Normans themselves admitted in their remonstrances of 5 February 1788, the *vingtièmes* had always fallen most heavily "upon a particular class of Citizens, who are no less subjected to all the other impositions."[25]

Having offered such trenchant observations, the jurists at Rouen did not fall back upon the standard parlementary position of merely commending the ministers for abiding by the royal promise of 1780 not to raise the *taille* and counseling them to "freeze" or if possible repeal the *vingtièmes*. Instead, they put forth a proposal for overhauling the entire system of direct taxation upon rural properties in Normandy. Anticipating their critics, the judges indignantly rejected all attempts to construe their solicitude for the popular cause as but "an unreasonable opposition to a more equitable assessment and allocation of taxes." As "Ministers of Justice," they protested, how could they *not* wish to promote the reign of justice in society at large? With much fanfare, the *parlementaires* unveiled a project for tax reform whose main outlines, they claimed, had been confided to the government on an earlier occasion. Why, they asked, could not His Majesty commit himself annually to a *specific* and *irrevocably fixed* amount of revenue to be raised (in this case, in Normandy) entirely through the levying of one basic tax? All direct taxes—*taille, capitation, vingtièmes*, and the like—could be lumped together in an *impôt unique* to be assessed *solidairement* by local officials upon the rural properties of all nobles and commoners. All members of the Second and Third Estates, in other words, would have to pay this tax, and pay it "proportionally to their means." Naturally, the *parlementaires* in speaking of "local officials" were thinking of themselves first of all, if not exclusively. They detailed the procedures through which this wonderful *impôt unique* was to be raised:

> Order, Sire, that we be given exact and sincere accounts, affirmed as such, of what each city or town or outlying *arrondissement* furnishes in net revenue to your Royal Treasury in each form of taxation, . . . whose total yield, including the reasonable augmentation in revenue that will be offered to you, will constitute for the given community its unique tribute fixed in solidary fashion upon all tax-payers and payable on a specified day, in part to your Royal Treasury and in part . . . to the other *caisses* of the navy, of war, of bridges and highways, of *hôtels-de-villes* and so forth.[26]

The sovereign could in all confidence rely upon the *parlementaires*, "working in concert with your Cour des Comptes, Aides et Finances de Normandie to lay the foundations for this new tax." After all, the high judges, and they alone, could "confer upon that operation both the credibility that flows from the justice motivating us and the requisite activity of the sufficient number of Commissioners we will deputize to that effect."[27]

Warming to their subject, Normandy's imaginative *parlementaires* endeavored to explain how the annual predetermined quota of taxation, once "divided up among the trustees of the different parishes and communities," could then be assessed *within* each parish and community upon "the Citizens of the two orders subject to taxation." At this point the jurists became vague as to how, exactly, the landowners were to determine their fair contributions to their communities' tax quotas. They stated only that such determination would reflect the "knowledge" the proprietors had "of each other's properties, whatever their precise nature and composition." The judges did entertain the possibility of disputes arising among the taxpayers, and stipulated that such wrangles would be "adjudicated summarily in the Cour des Aides, where the tax-rolls would be definitively verified and thus rendered executory." In general, however, they regarded their *impôt unique* as likely to breed very little local controversy, above all because of its provision for local participation in the tax-assessment process. "The inhabitants of a given parish are perfectly familiar with their respective possessions," the judges reiterated. "They are even well versed in the values of properties in neighboring parishes. There you have, consequently . . .

certain, unquestionable facts at hand, acquired without expense, without surveys, without inquisitions."[28]

It is, of course, highly unlikely that the policymakers at Versailles (or the intendants in the provinces) could have ever viewed such a scheme as administratively feasible. The *parlement's* project nonetheless was symptomatic of the widespread magisterial obsession with the need to put a ceiling upon the taxation of all Frenchmen and to curb the vexatious activities (or "inquisitions") of surveyors and tax assessors. Characteristically, the Rouennais insisted in their remonstrances that the *impôt unique* every year be "stamped with the seal of registration: without this check, sometimes feeble, but always restraining, the impost would vary according to the caprice or avidity of each Administrator."[29] Although in later protests the Normans were to abandon this proposal and revert to more customary invocations of provincial and General Estates, their brief advocacy in February 1788 of a decentralized administration of direct taxation foreshadowed in some respects the fiscal reforms so soon to be undertaken by the Constituent Assembly.

The tendency to rail against royal taxes on behalf of commoners as well as nobles in 1787–88 may have been especially pronounced in the *parlements* at Dijon, Toulouse, and Rouen, but it was hardly limited to those major tribunals. The high justices of communities such as Douai, Nancy, and Perpignan were also eloquent upon the subject. Belying their reputation for quiescence and docility, the *parlementaires* at Douai in the far north unleashed an assault upon unnamed *agents du fisc* on 30 November 1787 that doubtless would have found favor among many taxpayers in French Flanders, Cambrésis, and Hainaut:

> These cruel bloodsuckers of the People do not for the most part take into account either deductions made for maintenance and rebuilding expenses, or hazards of the harvest, or lack of productivity, or in general all the losses that lands sustain; they compel the Proprietor to pay the *vingtièmes* upon revenues of which he is often deprived for several years at a time, and they thereby deny him the means of improving his property; they deliver a mortal blow to agriculture, compass the devastation of the countryside, hasten its depopulation and discourage the Farmers.

Yet it was precisely the farmers, "that precious and essential class," that must "in all times merit the attention, the protection and the favors of any wise and enlightened Government."[30]

In a special memorandum addressed to the king in February 1788, the *parlementaires* at Nancy complained in a like vein that tributes of every imaginable kind levied upon citizens of all social ranks in Lorraine were increasing at frightening rates; they, too, painted a distressing picture of the effects of all this upon those who owned the lands and those who worked them:

> There is no Province that, with a territory uniformly capable of being rendered fertile, has such a languishing agriculture; or lands so stripped of their value. One seeks the cause of all this. The cause lies in the Proprietors' and the Farmers' utter inability to afford the investments required for the proper cultivation of a naturally difficult soil, a cultivation involving a major expenditure in labor, livestock and fertilizers. The Farmer is poor; the landowner is exhausted. The payment of the *Vingtièmes* . . . of the tithe, of the *droit de terrage*. . . . the expense of repairs and of unproductive lands, absorb the better part of the produce from his properties.[31]

The conclusion drawn from these harsh realities by Nancy's *parlementaires* was that their province could not conceivably tolerate higher taxes.

What held for Lorraine apparently held with equal force for France as a whole. Certainly the jurists at Perpignan in the eastern Pyrenees did not hesitate to cast their nets of concern and condemnation over the fiscal regime as it burdened taxpayers in all the provinces of the realm. The inexorable increase in tributes to the crown "leaves all the orders of the State in consternation," asserted Roussillon's highest magistrates. Taxes "snatch from the Farmer's hands what is indispensable for obtaining Nature's rewards, deprive the day-laborer, shackled by misery, of what is absolutely necessary to him, and, thus leaving the Provinces in a torpor, dry up the sources of genuine State prosperity."[32]

Contributing thus from many quarters to the national debate over taxation in prerevolutionary France, the provincial magistrates proved to be tireless paladins of parochial interests shared by folk of high, middling, and low estate. But the *parlementaires* did not exercise this role solely with respect to great issues agitating many Frenchmen on the eve of the great upheaval. Countless matters of a purely local nature allowed the judges to intervene as champions of classes and masses—not to mention their own professional prerogatives. For two outstanding examples in point, let us return briefly to the controversies over the roads and rivers of Burgundy and certain *terres vaines et vagues* in Normandy.

The former affair involved the competing claims of Dijon's *parlementaires* and the Elus of the Burgundian Estates to jurisdiction over the community-to-community roads (*chemins finerots*), various other passageways by land, and rivers and streams within the province (see chapter 4). If the tribunal at Dijon, motivated in part by an ancient animus against the Elus and by its own political pretensions, spoke up for local seigneurs in connection with the *chemins finerots*, it also championed the rights of much wider circles of Burgundians whose holdings in land abutted the waterways of the province. Procureur-Général Pérard signaled his company's attitude on this question in his letter of 22 August 1786 to the ministers.

> In regard to the Rivers and major Streams that can accommodate barges and various commodities, proprietary rights are involved that overshadow the *chemins finerots* themselves. This latter object is only a right of justice; but the Rivers and Streams involve a useful right. The Proprietor can exploit it either by leasing it out to another or by having his own mills constructed there.

Just as the "Administrators of the Province, given free rein over the Highways, could decree the destruction of all Buildings they deemed obstructive to commerce upon those Highways," continued Pérard, "so they could do with respect to all mills [upon the] Rivers and Streams."[33] By "Administrators of the Province," of course, the *procureur-général* meant the abhorred Elus of the Estates.

The full tribunal at Dijon took up this argument in elaborate detail in its remonstrances of the following February, drawn up after the crown's unsuccessful attempt at mediation in the dispute. "By the letters-patent of 1785," complained the Burgundian jurists, the Elus were authorized to "determine the proximity of the mills to sources of water," to "carry out all the operations and alterations they deem necessary, as much for the repairs of the river-beds, in order to conserve, facilitate and establish navigation and the floating of wood, as for the restoration of the tow-paths upon the river-banks," and also to "have all trees standing within a certain proximity to the river-banks cut down and uprooted." Such an attribution of powers could not but bode ill in parlementary eyes:

> In view of these concessions, is there a citizen who does not tremble for his properties? Empowered to fix the proximity of the mills to river-water, the Elus will be able to diminish their value, and even rob those mills that are at present most productive of all value whatsoever; in their initial efforts to facilitate the floatage of wood, they will be able to do whatever they want to do with the rivers, alter their beds and their flow, denature the estates situated upon their banks, deprive the landowners of the water to which they are entitled for the irrigation of their soils, and, on the pretense of achieving benefits that are not chimerical, will bring about ills that are only too real.

The *parlementaires* were willing (momentarily) to concede that the trustees of the Burgundian Estates *might* not be deliberately abusing their unlimited powers. Even at the very best, however, the Elus were being duped by "the persons to whom they accorded their confidence," seduced by "brilliant speculations" that could but produce disastrous policies.[34]

Why, the jurists persisted relentlessly, should anyone insist that towpaths be restored where they would not facilitate river commerce, where they could only damage proprietors' lands? Why permit horses drawing river-barges to trample upon some of the richest meadows and grasslands in Burgundy, as could not fail to happen with the establishment or restoration of towpaths? Had not the Elus of ten years before abandoned plans for a new towpath upon the banks of the Saône in the face of protests by all the landowners along the river? Why, then, resurrect and generalize a policy now that could only jeopardize "the most precious lands in the province?" The magistrates then came to the judicial gravamen of their complaint:

> Finally, the letters-patent of 1785 authorize the Elus to summon and fine at their own caprice individuals held to have interfered with the operations they have ordered: [namely] the seigneurs, proprietors, farmers and . . . peasants who refuse to fell and uproot trees and take down hedges planted close to navigable rivers, or who are dilatory about it, and millers who, dissatisfied with their mills' accessibility from the rivers, endeavor to do something to better their situation.[35]

But this, the *parlementaires* objected, was to concede "arbitrary power" to the Elus that could set at naught the right of lords and peasants alike to avail themselves of parlementary cognizance of their proprietary affairs. Things had come to a fine pass indeed, if these remonstrants of the robe were to be believed in February 1787.

There were, it seems, many Burgundians who did believe the various magisterial pronouncements upon this controversy. The *parlementaires* had been issuing decrees against the Elus regularly during the preceding months, and in a letter to Calonne of 6 January the intendant in Burgundy, Amelot de Chaillou, complained that one of those decrees was "more and more arousing the inhabitants of that Province and especially that element of the people incapable of divining and guarding against the illusion of fine-sounding language." The judges, he warned, were proving dangerously adept at "presenting the administration of Messieurs the Elus as ruinous for the Province, as financially straitened and as capable of escaping that supposed embarrassment only by overtaxing the People."[36] One of those abused Elus, Abbé de La Fare, wrote to the ministers in much the same vein, fuming against "the seditious principles of the Parlement of Dijon" and voicing the hope that the timely arrival of royal troops in the Burgundian capital would mean the prompt cessation of local agitation.[37] Both men spoke of the imperative need to muzzle the *parlementaires*—counsel that the authorities at Versailles must have appreciated but never really had the chance to follow.

Later that same year, the Dijonnais jurists' counterparts at Rouen likewise championed what they perceived to be the rights of local proprietors of all classes. We have already seen how the Norman *parlementaires* remonstrated on 8 August 1787 against the crown's policy of leasing out various lands designated as waste (*terres vaines et vagues*) to *concessionnaires*—that is, speculators (see chapters 3 and 4). The judges assailed the notion that such lands necessarily belonged to or "depended upon" the royal domain and excoriated the ministers for insisting upon removing cognizance of litigation arising from this policy to the king's Council at Versailles. But it was not only the seigneurial class in Normandy that received magisterial support upon this occasion. As a consequence of the government's decrees, the Rouennais argued, it would

> suffice henceforth to be a speculator to have the right . . . to despoil the honest citizen who cultivates his ancestors' land, entire parishes whose inhabitants subsist and pay their taxes only by virtue of the resources they derive from their communal fields, and, finally, the unfortunate proprietor to whom the sea and rivers seem only grudgingly and slowly to restore even a sterile soil as indemnity for fertile pastures engulfed in their tides.[38]

Elaborating upon this theme, the *parlementaires* described various "invasions" of villagers' commons, sea marshes, and adjoining alluvial lands by unscrupulous *concessionnaires*. The projects of these individuals, the judges maintained, had caused extensive damage to lands of seigneurs and peasant communities by allowing them to be inundated by high tides and battered by winds and waves at all times. And what legal recourse did the unfortunate citizens of Normandy have? None whatsoever, in effect, as the same royal decrees that arbitrarily leased out to speculators lands that did not lie in the crown's domain in the first place also stipulated that aggrieved parties must bring their suits, not to the ordinary courts in Normandy, but rather to the king's own Council. This was tantamount to entrusting the lambs to the lion, the jurists protested. The "privileges of Normandy" entitled all Normans, whether of high or humble station, to have their affairs adjudicated in "the Tribunals of the Duchy"—meaning, of course, the hierarchy of "ordinary" courts headed by the *parlement* at Rouen.

An attentive observer noted at the time how closely the dispute in Normandy resembled one of very recent date in the jurisdiction of the Bordeaux Parlement.[39] There, too, the crown had clashed with noble and nonnoble proprietors over the ownership and exploitation of certain alluvial lands and marshes, and in that case parlementary intervention had proven successful.[40] The Norman judges' quarrel with the ministers over local proprietary issues soon gave way to the greater confrontation between crown and robe over national reforms, but there is no reason to believe that the Normans' advocacy of local proprietary rights in August 1787 was any less sincere than that recent campaign of their Bordelais cousins. At the same time, however, it is noteworthy that Rouen's magistrates had been provoked to action as much by perceived insults and threats to their own judicial-political role as by the perceived despoilment of lords and peasants in the Norman countryside. Admittedly, the *parlementaires* in their remonstrances hinted at the possibility of a fruitful working relationship between their company and newly established provincial assemblies in Normandy to ensure royal exploitation of what was truly royal domain, and private proprietary enjoyment of what was not. Such a suggestion, however, designed as it probably was to render these combative magistrates somewhat accommodating in royal eyes, could in no way obscure their determination to retain their powers of sovereign justice, registration, and remonstration.[41] Clearly, pride of professional function could complement proprietary considerations in motivating the Normans, like *parlementaires* elsewhere, to speak out on behalf of all ranks of landowners.

In a variety of forms, then, expediency helped inspire magisterial acknowledgments of commoners' interests in the provincial France of the prerevolution. Of course, that did not necessarily make such acknowledgments any less valid—or any less appreciated by the commoners in question, as worried royal administrators from Burgundy to Languedoc had occasion to note. Furthermore, there were numerous instances of parlementary support for affluent and not-so-affluent Frenchmen in the Third Estate during this fateful period that owed somewhat less to considerations of self-interest.

An Advocacy of Entrepreneurial Commoners

Could provincial magistrates deriving most of their income (and many of their greatest pleasures) from the countryside evince any great sympathy for men of entrepreneurial pursuits, quite a few of whom certainly were *roturiers*, abiding in towns, cities, and overseas colonies? Magisterial attitudes toward such Frenchmen were, at times, ambivalent; yet the sovereign courts did espouse certain causes involving, primarily if not exclusively, entrepreneurial commoners in the late 1780s. Traders upon the high seas, settlers beyond those seas, and merchants trafficking upon the soil of the homeland were, knowingly or unknowingly, beneficiaries of judicial protest in the waning months of the old regime.

That there was incontrovertibly some parlementary ambivalence regarding the activities and aspirations of such commoners is demonstrated most strikingly upon the pages of Droz des Villars. Besançon's erudite jurist conceded that "one finds in the Third Estate bravery, generosity, intelligence, and perhaps less corruption" than in the upper strata of society. "The employments of the bar, the very creation of a multitude of posts that might appear superfluous, have multiplied the class of persons living nobly in the Kingdom," he continued. Moreover, it was by ennobling "the distinguished subjects of that part of the Third Estate that borders upon the Noblesse" that one could "regenerate the families that are dying out." At the same time, cautioned this *parlementaire* of Franche-Comté, let us not encourage *every* commoner to aspire to noble status: where, in that case, would be the commerce, the "manufactures" and the agriculture of provincial France? Apparently this influential magistrate believed very firmly that entrepreneurs had and should always have as much of a role to play in the prosperity of the realm as barristers and *officiers* of various descriptions. Yet none of this could save unnamed traders and moneylenders from the censure of Droz des Villars. He referred scathingly to "tradesmen, whose enormous profits, founded upon fashion, luxury, and all the dissipations that lead youth astray, return nothing to the State." It said much about the injustice of the world's ways that such individuals found "in this sort of wealth a source of good fortune and comfortable living." Again, he anathematized "capitalists and *rentiers*, who suffer no levy of *vingtièmes*," and "bankers who loan at excessive rates of interest, without being taxed." The ordinarily genial and judicious Droz des Villars went so far as to charge that the government, "upon the pretext of maintaining public confidence, . . . still wants to pamper the parasitical class of *rentiers*." In this fashion, he grumbled, "the debtor in distress is at the mercy of the usurer who lends him money."[42] This justice of provincial France might admit to the existence of "bravery," "generosity," and "intelligence" in the "distinguished" upper reaches of the Third Estate, but he just as plainly betrayed the local landowner's prejudice against men who dealt primarily in trade, annuities, and capital rather than in land. For that matter, the conviction that the taxes wrested from landed proprietors of all classes in rural France were subsidizing the peculation and extravagance of "capitalists" of all stripes in the kingdom's cities and towns (especially Paris) ran like a leitmotif through the provincial *parle-*

ments' pronunciamentos of 1787 and 1788. (In much the same fashion, courtiers of the sword were viewed as some of the principal sycophants at Versailles. Terms such as *capitalistes, rentiers, financiers, traitants,* and *courtisans* were employed almost interchangeably in the provincial judges' philippics against the central government during this period.)

The conservative landed magistrates never denied the importance of commerce in the economic scheme of things, however. They often defended mercantile interests in the prerevolutionary years. True, the Parisian judges alone had to confront Loménie de Brienne's stamp tax legislation in the summer of 1787, but even in the outlying regions of the realm there were signs of judicial opposition to this measure. At Perpignan in the Pyrenees, for example, the magistrates insisted "that the enormous extension of the Stamp Tax" would be "irreconcilable with the Liberty that quickens Commerce, with the tranquillity of Citizens who ever act in good faith, and with public safety, menaced at every step by all the rigors of the arbitrary system of government fiscal agents."[43] But it was the Dijonnais who dilated at greatest length upon the ominous commercial and "industrial" implications of the stamp tax legislation. Burgundy's *parlementaires* asserted

> that the Declaration concerning the stamp tax ... is as destructive of commerce ... as that concerning the *subvention* is of property; that the manifold fetters that are already encumbering French trade and manufactures barely allow them to sustain competition with neighboring nations; that in this situation of precarious equilibrium, the slightest weight can tip the balance against us, and, destroying all commerce with foreigners, exhaust forever this source of public and private prosperity, diminish the yield from the established taxes and the number of inhabitants, and cause damage that a century of thrift and encouragement of economic activity could not repair.[44]

Thus did the Dijon Parlement's Chambre des Vacations echo, on 12 September 1787, the fiery sentiments expressed a month earlier in Duval d'Eprémesnil's decree at Paris. There is no reason to believe that a full chorus of provincial parlementary complaint against the extension of the stamp tax would not have immediately followed the judges' resumption of ordinary judicial business in November had the offending legislation not been withdrawn by then through temporary compromise in the kingdom's capital.

Even before the Parisian magistrates had to consider Brienne's extension of the stamp tax, however, *parlementaires* in provincial France were already articulating what they perceived as mercantile interests on an associated if less publicized front. In December 1786 the government had promulgated regulations affecting the transportation of passengers, merchandise, and correspondence and papers between France, on the one hand, and the French Caribbean and Indian Ocean colonies and the United States, on the other.[45] Whereas, in the past, individuals wishing to travel to these overseas destinations, or to send to them or receive from them merchandise and/or private and commercial correspondence, had customarily made their own arrangements in various French ports, now they were to abide by certain procedures laid down at Versailles. Henceforth, there were to be twenty-four *paquebots* (packets) regularly carrying passengers, merchandise, and private and business documents at specified rates between two designated ports—Le Havre and Bordeaux—and overseas areas in the Americas and the Indian Ocean. Furthermore, all objects so transported were also to be subjected to prevailing postal rates *within* France; that is, moved *within* the home country, to or from Le Havre or Bordeaux, by the postal service.

The government's regulations, it is true, left individuals the option of making their own arrangements, as before, with independent *vaisseaux marchands* plying the seas out of seaports other than Le Havre or Bordeaux; but even in these cases, all transported goods and papers were to be taxed by the postal authorities within France. As all services rendered by the designated packets were to incur charges and all postal rates within France were to be substantially increased over earlier rates according to a schedule published as part of these regulations, it was patent that the ministers expected thereby to secure a considerable increase in badly needed revenue.

Naturally the authorities did not present their case in these latter terms. They spoke instead of the commercial benefits and sheer convenience to accrue to Frenchmen with overseas connections, and to the colonists themselves, from these measures. But apparently a goodly number within trading and colonial circles were unimpressed, for in the months that followed at least three of the major provincial *parlements*—those at Bordeaux, Rennes, and Aix—were moved to protest to one degree or another against what the ministers had wrought.

The Bordelais broached the issue well before their more notorious collision with the government over the provincial assemblies.[46] At the court's plenary session of 5 May 1787, one of the judges denounced the royal legislation of the preceding December to his colleagues, who speedily instructed the *parquet* to look into the matter. Nine days later, Procureur-Général Dudon *fils* (who had the post *en survivance avec exercice* from his father) took the floor to address his company. Dudon alluded darkly to "that clamor that has arisen in the world of Commerce, and from there has spread into all classes of citizens" as a result of "the surtax imposed recently upon all letters coming from the Colonies." The crown's establishment of the overseas packet-boat service, Dudon asserted, was merely "the pretext for that surcharge that is going to shackle Commerce, strike at all those who have any kind of relations whatsoever with the colonies, and sooner or later affect all the King's subjects adversely." The *procureur-général* expatiated upon the need to keep correspondence dealing with maritime matters free from administrative fiat:

> Maritime activities are subjected to too many variations to permit the correspondence they engender to be confined in a maze of inland postal regulations; the decisions and the orders of the speculator must of necessity vary as do the winds that determine their fate. If that freedom is denied to him, his calculations must go awry; fortunate he is if he can escape the baneful effects of the delays imposed by over-regulation! Some transactions, whose results have proven astonishing, have depended entirely upon timely advice brought on board a vessel just as it was slipping away from its moorings; such advice ordinarily consists either of orders for purchases that must be made by a certain time, or of orders for insurance upon which that individual relies who entrusts a considerable cargo to the hazards of the sea; often, new information can mean a change of destination.[47]

Furthermore, Dudon continued, to tax the business correspondence of the entrepreneur with overseas interests might very well ruin him—especially if that correspondence was in duplicate or triplicate, and accompanied by such essential documents as nautical bills of lading, letters of exchange, letters according power of attorney, testaments and bequests, and so on. Procureur-Général Dudon complained that the authorities at Versailles were even applying the higher postal rates to letters sent from the French colonies to other European countries and then forwarded by land to France. To make matters even worse, the king's administrative prerogative in commercial affairs (whose constitutionality this officer of Bordeaux's *parquet* did not challenge) was being abused by one Sieur Lecouteux de la Noraye, who had been given "exclusive" control over the envisioned *paquebots* and the levying of duty upon their freightage. If the king truly deemed the changes outlined in the *règlement* of December 1786 to be necessary, concluded Bordeaux's *procureur-général*, let him promulgate those changes in the form of legislation "duly registered" in his sovereign courts. Pending that development, the magistracy must continue to recognize only those past edicts that bore the imprimatur of *enregistrement*—past edicts that guaranteed the individual's right to manage his overseas affairs as he best saw fit. Accordingly, upon Dudon's recommendation the Bordeaux Parlement issued a decree reconfirming the pertinent legislation most recently ratified by the company, the letters patent of 1759. The jurists strictly forbade all postal authorities throughout their company's jurisdiction to "collect taxes other than or higher than those allowed for in the said Tariff of 1759," and pointedly ordered their decree to be signified to all postal officials in the subordinate *bailliages* and *sénéchaussées*.[48]

No immediate response to this unilateral action was forthcoming from Versailles, where the ministers were preoccupied in May 1787 with the Notables' rejection of their reform program. Furthermore, they had soon to recognize that opposition to the new regulations affecting internal and maritime commerce was not limited to southwestern France. In Brittany, too, resistance was afoot. On 27 June, the *gens du roi* of the Rennes Parlement submitted to their assembled colleagues a variety of documents germane to the issue, including copies of the regulations themselves and protests of merchants at Saint-Malo and Nantes against the government's new policy.[49] The court ordered the commissioners habitually entrusted with the drafting of remonstrances "and all those would like to join them" to meet "without any delay" to review the matter, and instructed them to report back to the assembled chambers the following day. The hastily convened conferees pored over the royal acts of December 1786 and the plaints registered against them by merchants trading out of the ports of the province. Their conclusions were reported the next day in plenary session by the court's senior *avocat-général*, Saturnin Marie Hercule du Bourgblanc.

> The provision for 24 packet-boats of 300 tons each has provoked protest in the principal places of commerce. As a maritime and mercantile province, Brittany could hardly close her eyes to the injury done to her by this new order of things; as trustees and conservators of the rights of this great Province, charged with watching out for anything that could diminish the happiness of its inhabitants, interfere with their commercial transactions, and overburden them with new taxes, we come today, Messieurs, to portray to you, on the one hand, . . . the real ills that commerce is suffering, ills concerning which your good offices are implored, and on the other hand, the harm done to public order by taxes contrary to the laws registered in the Kingdom.[50]

There followed a long litany of grievances of maritime traders, of shipowners and captains of vessels, and of intrepid colonists struggling to do business with entrepreneurial Bretons back home. Avocat-Général du Bourgblanc's presentation differed in no essential respects from Bordelais Procureur-Général Dudon's denunciations. It is no surprise, then, that the Breton judges reacted on this occasion precisely as the judges at

Bordeaux had reacted the preceding month. Invoking "His Majesty's declaration of 8 July 1759 . . . registered in the Court," the Bretons decreed that under no circumstances should postal rates be set higher than they had been in the 1759 legislation—such stipulation applying to merchandise and documents carried on the high seas as well as to commodities and papers transported within France. The justices at Rennes ordered that their *arrêté* be signified to the postal authorities within the province, and threatened prompt chastisement of all who should abet the government in implementing its ill-conceived regulations of December 1786.

The *parlementaires*, from what we know of them, may have been exercised somewhat less by "a description of the real ills" afflicting mercantile interests in Brittany than by reports concerning "the harm done to public order by taxes contrary to the laws registered in the Kingdom." Few of the Breton jurists (and not even all judges of the wine-growing Bordelais) were deeply involved in overseas or domestic trade, whereas all jurists were by training and/or sheer self-interest keenly concerned for the maintenance of "public order" and the parlementary prerogative of registration. Still, the Bordelais and Bretons obviously regarded themselves as tribunes of the trading classes as well as of all other elements in society—and who, among these judicial proprietors, would deny the ultimate significance of commercial prosperity for all holding lands near the sea?

If the high justices at Bordeaux and Rennes were unlikely to make this latter denial, so were their counterparts at Aix-en-Provence. The story of magisterial defiance at Aix over royal policy on international trade and travel actually began at a time when most of the Provençal judges were on vacation in 1787. Whether because of its reputed political tractability or for some other reason, the Aix Parlement had initially raised no objection over the government's promulgation of the mercantile regulations of the preceding December, despite the presence of a considerable trading community within its jurisdiction. On 2 October 1787, however, the tribunal's Chambre des Vacations received royal letters patent dated 15 June that called in effect for formal parlementary ratification of those regulations.[51] The jurists in session on this occasion decided to refer the legislation of 15 June to "commissioners," but the court's full membership, when reassembled after the vacations, took no immediate action on the matter. (This may have been due in some measure to magisterial preoccupation with the convocation of the Provençal Estates and with the resultant politicization of the commonalty during the winter of 1787–88.)[52] Eventually, however, the Aixois resolved to remonstrate formally to Louis XVI over the establishment of the overseas packet-boat service and the assessment of higher freightage duties. The Provençal *parlementaires* approved their commissioners' protests on 13 February 1788 and sent them off forthwith to Versailles.

The burden of the judges' complaint against the royal policy enunciated initially in December 1786 was essentially at Aix what it was at Bordeaux and Rennes: that the overseas commerce of the French would unavoidably suffer.

> The fetters placed upon Commerce by the letters-patent of 15 June past, the delays with which they encumber commercial transactions, have caused alarm and consternation among the wholesale merchants of this province.
>
> The freedom to act is essential to the speculations of Commerce, action itself insures their success, [and] all obstacles that destroy those speculations, or arrest their success, sap commerce and overthrow it by degrees. First, business transactions are less numerous. Soon, one dares no longer to undertake anything. Finally, essential branches of Trade are abandoned altogether, since the roads to success have become more treacherous.[53]

The magistrates were prepared to concede that the establishment of service by packet between Bordeaux and Le Havre and overseas ports would prove useful to the sovereign and to some of his subjects. "Your Majesty's orders," they allowed, "will be conveyed swiftly and with regularity to all the countries under your sway. Secure communications will reign among all your possessions, [and] passengers will have easy and convenient means of transportation to the Colonies." Nonetheless, the legislation of 15 June posed crucial problems for trading interests in Provence. How, the Aixois queried, were Provençal merchants with overseas commitments to avoid serious financial difficulties, and perhaps utter ruin, if henceforth all of their business papers and outgoing and incoming shipments had to endure the delays and bureaucratic bungling and "enormously" increased duties of the French postal service? Like their judicial cousins at Bordeaux and Rennes, the *parlementaires* at Aix emphasized that subjecting the merchants' affairs to postal procedures in the French ports would be especially injurious in that it would deprive the entrepreneurs of the ability to respond flexibly to all the political, financial, and meteorological vagaries of international trade. In addition, however, the judges protested that the letters-patent of 15 June discriminated specifically against maritime traders of Provence. Should those entrepreneurs decide that overseas transportation of their correspondence and goods by packet was *in itself* more advantageous than any analogous service offered by independent "merchant vessels," they would still have to defray the expenses of transportation across France between Provence and Bordeaux or Le Havre—expenses that, in view of the steep increase in postal rates, must necessarily weigh much more heavily upon them than upon *commerçants* to the north and west.

The government's legislation, in other words, was a sham as far as the Provençaux were concerned. The opportunities it claimed to offer them were at best illusory; they were a devious means of augmenting royal revenue in the name of facilitating enterprise on the high seas. The *parlementaires* predicted that shipowners, captains, and wholesale merchants would evade the provisions of these letters patent and any associated decrees in their efforts to avoid financial ruin. Arbitrary penalties assessed against such transgressions, they warned, would only prove counterproductive. In concluding their remonstrances, the Aixois challenged the authorities at Versailles to remove all elements of "coercion" from the arrangements set forth on 15 June, so that the maritime traders of all provinces, no longer subjected to vexatious postal charges, bureaucracy, and delays, could freely ascertain the relative merits of government *paquebots* and independent *vaisseaux marchands*.

And, remarkably, in the hurly-burly of national debate over the May Edicts, the stricken *parlementaires* of Bordeaux, Rennes, and Aix—and perhaps other communities—received satisfaction on at least this matter. Or possibly those aggrieved entrepreneurs whose interests were ventilated in magisterial addresses, decrees, and remonstrances in provincial France lobbied effectively on their own behalf at Versailles. For whatever reason or combination of reasons, on 5 July 1788 the ministers promulgated a decree rescinding the pertinent acts of the preceding two years.[54] No government-sponsored packets would ply the waters of the Atlantic and Indian Oceans and Caribbean Sea; moreover, captains in the private merchant marine would transport correspondence to and from overseas ports free of all charges previously assessed. The trading classes of maritime France would be left, as before, to their own devices.

In speaking out upon *paquebots* and postal rates during 1787–88 the provincial judges were not altogether neglecting their own interests. As landowners they had a stake in the operations of the commercial economy—this was most notably true, perhaps, of the wine-growing justices of Bordeaux—and they were acutely aware that excessive regulation could adversely affect a sector of the economy that was at once dynamic and fragile. Nevertheless, specific commercial interests had urged the Parisian *parlementaires* to protest against the stamp tax legislation, and several of the provincial law courts had followed suit. Moreover, the jurists at Rennes, at least, could document the grievances of merchants against government-sponsored packets and higher postal rates. It seems fair to conclude that, whatever their reservations about *gens d'affaires* of various stripes (especially, we suspect, those earning dubious livings in Paris), the provincial *parlementaires* believed they were articulating and in actuality did articulate grievances of entrepreneurs in the upper reaches of the Third Estate on the eve of the Revolution. In a like fashion these magistrates, as guarantors of law and order and as *privilégiés*, harbored serious reservations about the unwashed masses—and not only those humble folk resident in the national capital—yet they still championed the *menu peuple* of town and country on numerous occasions in the late 1780s.

The Magistrates and the Menu Peuple

For the last time in this study of prerevolutionary parlementary attitudes, we acknowledge the distinction between issues inhering in the national political crisis of 1787–88 and issues related only indirectly or not at all to that crisis. Questions in the former category that vitally concerned the lower classes and attracted the attention of the provincial justices included the commerce of grain and other basic commodities and the *corvée* and its associated impositions. Questions of the latter type engaged "popular" interests and their magisterial advocates in a number of communities, most notably Pau, Rennes, and Rouen. That the provincial *parlementaires* could take the government to task on the critical issues of popular subsistence and compulsory labor, and challenge the ministers as well over popular causes of purely local import, goes some distance toward validating the jurists' image of themselves as paladins of the humble folk in France.

Naturally, championship of the poor was never a matter of unalloyed altruism in magisterial minds (any more than it was in ministerial minds). This was most obviously the case where the circulation of foodstuffs and other vital commodities within the kingdom was at issue. Nothing haunted the judges in this *état policé* more constantly than did the specter of popular "sedition" in times of scarcity and high prices. This helps explain the mixed motives behind the hostility many of them evinced toward Calonne's and Brienne's grain trade reforms in 1787–88.

Droz des Villars told part of the tale as it applied to Besançon. The *parlement* there, confronted with the government's edict liberating the commerce in grain, had argued that "such a law, beneficial in certain times, can be inconvenient at a time when essential foodstuffs, become scarce, are only available at an exorbitant price." The ministers nevertheless had overridden the Comtois judges' sage opposition to this legislation, securing its ratification "by military means" on 8 May 1788. Over the ensuing summer, wheat had inevitably become more expensive, and half-hearted government attempts to reimpose some salutary restraints upon the grain trade in September had met with little success. The Besançon Parlement had been reinstated the following month, recalled Droz des Villars, and appropriately enough its "first thoughts" had been about "the subsistence of the People." In fact, "the day after its reinstatement" the high court had prohibited "all export of grain for an indefinite period." After all, said this annalist, "there are times when the din of politics must cease so that the cries of urgent need may be heard, whatever be the cause of that need."[55]

Indeed, the *parlement's* official minutes bear out this rendition of events in Franche-Comté. At the plenary session of 20 October 1788, Procureur-Général Claude-Théophile-Joseph Doroz, finding the Council's recent suspension of export of grain "inadequate," argued for a supplementary decree "which, being addressed to all officers of royal Jurisdictions and of vassals' Jurisdictions in the District, will better carry out His Majesty's wishes." Accordingly, the *parlementaires* expressly prohibited "all individuals from exporting grain or flour directly or indirectly to foreign markets." Those in violation of this decree would be fined 500 livres, would suffer confiscation of their grain and/or flour, and would perhaps be punished in other ways as well.[56] Procureur-Général Doroz sent a letter to the government later that day, apprising it of his company's action and citing in justification the cruel increase in the price of foodstuffs in the province.[57] The magistrates' efforts to defuse the explosive issue of subsistence at Besançon proved ultimately unavailing, as testified by their numerous decrees in the late winter and spring of the following year censuring the riotous gatherings and behavior of a hungry and desperate populace.[58]

A similar story unfolds in Burgundy, although the *parlementaires* in that province invoked their own corporate prerogatives more explicitly in connection with the subsistence question than did the judges of Franche-Comté. Unlike Droz des Villars and his associates, the Dijonnais grudgingly ratified the legislation freeing the commerce in grain in 1787, but "without approbation nevertheless of the declarations and letters-patent mentioned in the present declaration that might not have been verified in the Court." The judges assured Louis XVI in their *arrêt d'enregistrement* that their company, "never ceasing to watch over the interests and needs of the people in its jurisdiction and to be alert as to the advantages and disadvantages of the free exportation of grains, will always regard itself as essentially duty-bound to apprise him of the changes and modifications that the times and the circumstances could require" in the grain trade. New "regulations" might be called for "in such an essential matter," regulations that "could be applied only after having been sanctioned in the Court."[59] Talk of "changes" and of "modifications" betrayed the judges' suspicion that the physiocratic regime of free trade would have to be abandoned altogether; talk of "regulations" to implement such a sane retreat from untenable principle enabled them to reassert their company's traditional political role and thereby strike an oblique blow at the rival Burgundian Estates.

The Dijonnais must have derived smug satisfaction from the ministers' decision the following year to terminate once again all experimentation with a free commerce in grain. Like their counterparts of Franche-Comté, however, they found that reversal of policy at Versailles to be insufficient in light of provincial conditions. On 13 December 1788 one of their number rose in plenary session to sound the alarm on the subsistence question. He cited "the entire loss of the harvests in some parts of the Kingdom," "the poorness of the yields in other parts," "the rigor of the season," and "the difficulty of transportation" as "circumstances" that imperatively required from his assembled colleagues "precautions ensuring that the people in your jurisdiction will be adequately provided with all that is necessary to them, until a more prosperous time restores abundance to them." The speaker continued:

> Thanks to the active foresight of the Municipal Officers of Dijon, and of the other cities in the Province, the markets have been sufficiently provisioned up to now. But is it not to be feared that greedy persons will profit from panics arising from reports of conditions in neighboring countries, by throwing themselves into speculations that would price grains out of the reach of the most numerous class of Citizens?
>
> The Court has consistently honored the obligation to watch out for their happiness and their access to the necessities of life. . . . it could no more usefully employ its authority, or exercise the high policing and regulatory powers that lie within its preserve.[60]

This sounded very like Avocat-Général Séguier at Paris, belaboring unnamed "greedy persons" who battened off the misery of the small consumer and exhorting his colleagues to act on behalf of the latter. Expediency, of course, played its role in such jeremiads, at Dijon as at Paris: the speaker in the Burgundian *parlement* reminded his fellows candidly that "in looking after these matters, you assure the tranquillity of the people, and they will see that their interests are at all times the object of your solicitude." These observations had an immediate effect. After hearing a corroboratory report from the officers of the *parquet,* the Dijonnais, like their counterparts at Besançon and Paris, issued a decree designed to complement the recent policy reversal at Versailles.[61]

The Burgundians' decree, however, entered into details not encountered in the other tribunals' acts. It not only prohibited all export of grain or flour from the province but also forbade individuals to engage in any purchases or other market-related transactions "that could possibly be directed toward the transporting of said grain or flour outside the Kingdom." Moreover, it expressly forbade advance transactions involving "grain in the sheaf that had not yet been threshed." The judges' decree stipulated that this precious commodity was to be displayed only in those marketplaces and other areas designated expressly in regulations already on the books, and warned "Merchants and all others, whatever their rank and station," not to attempt to drive bargains in advance with "those bringing their grains to market." All transgressors against these arrangements were to suffer confiscation of any grain or flour in their possession and pay fines of 500 livres. Finally, this decree of 13 December 1788 designated not only "violations that could be committed against this present Decree" but also "all machinations that could be employed to boost grain prices" as matters to be brought immediately before the "ordinary judges" of the jurisdiction—all of this subject to "appeal to the Court" at Dijon. Such were the Burgundian magistrates' intentions, although similar strictures and anathemas in later decrees—for instance, of 19 January, 31 March, 13 May, and 18 July 1789—testify eloquently to growing parlementary impotence in the face of an aroused local populace.[62]

The men of justice at Rouen, too, found the urgent needs of the *menu peuple* pressing upon them in the twilight of the *ancien régime*. Well before the onset of the prerevolutionary crisis the Rouennais (like their professional cousins farther up the Seine at Paris) had to bend considerable effort toward providing sufficient wood to fire the ovens and warm the citizens of their community.[63] According to the outstanding chronicler of the Norman *parlement*, the magistrates went so far as to order the felling of a splendid stand of trees dating from 1672 so that some warmth might be provided those *misérables* shivering in the cruel winter of 1782–83.[64] Things were no better during the winter of 1788–89: the jurists in those desperate months invoked the "just severity" of the laws against agitators and "delinquents" even as they contributed 6000 livres toward the purchase of firewood and sought similar largesse from the municipal administrators and others in the Norman capital.

But at Rouen as elsewhere it was the issue of bread that could prove most explosive and that accordingly exercised parlementary minds the most. Throughout that terrible winter of 1788–89 the high tribunal of Normandy multiplied decrees aimed at "procuring prompt relief for those places that clamored for it incessantly, protecting intimidated farmers, disconcerting selfish speculators, terrifying malefactors," and so on. All this very typical parlementary activity and rhetoric culminated in a letter sent by the judges to the king on 5 July 1789.[65] This melancholy missive spoke of "the people crushed by misery . . . everywhere in the province of Normandy, and, being so unhappy, surrendering themselves, at Rouen, to all the excesses of despair." Characteristically, 'the magistrates hinted at conspiracy behind the popular tribulation:

> The majority of your subjects cannot afford to buy bread; and what miserable bread one gives to those who can make a purchase! Ah, Sire, we accuse no one; up to the present time, all our efforts have not enabled us to lift the veil that envelops this mysterious iniquity that victimizes your people today, and that victimizes your magistrates in that some individuals do not even blush to blame them for all attendant hardships. Despite all our efforts, prices have been relentlessly increasing, and are finally well above what most can afford.

The *parlementaires* implored Louis XVI to sell at as low a price as possible all grains that might be stored by government order throughout their province. "Then we will witness the return of calm and tranquillity, of which we have been deprived for so long, the return of order and the reign of law, conservator of property and protector of the poor."[66] In this petition sent off to the king just nine days before the storming of the Bastille, Rouen's *parlementaires* (who were never again to intervene in popular affairs) acknowledged as frankly as did jurists everywhere else the expediential uses of humanitarianism.

Of humanitarianism's uses to the magistracy there could never be any doubt. Furthermore, sympathy for the plight of the masses could be squeezed out of the picture altogether when powerful magisterial interests were at stake. Thus, the animus of most Parisian and provincial *parlementaires* against physiocratic teachings on free internal trade had traditionally not been shared by the judges at Toulouse, who were among the most prominent grain entrepreneurs in the vast province of Languedoc.[67] Yet, as a rule, it is difficult to avoid the conclusion that the *parlements* evinced real concern for consumers of humble rank within their jurisdictions. When, on 30 April 1787, the jurists at Dijon issued a decree warning all sellers of tobacco in Burgundy not to discriminate against their poorer customers by refusing to make this odorous temptation available to them in small measures and at low prices, they were hardly under mob siege or confronting the prospect of an imminent dissolution of social hierarchy.[68] They were dispensing "justice" in one of its traditional forms, exactly as *parlementaires* did elsewhere, and expected always to do.

We can observe a similar dispensation of traditional justice when we turn to that other national controversy primarily if not exclusively affecting humble Frenchmen in 1787–88, the renewed debate over the *corvée royale.* As noted earlier, Calonne's decree of 6 November 1786 tentatively converting the *corvée* into additional taxation over an initial three-year period had specified that only rural commoners (that is, *taillables*) were to pay this taxation. (Although it would seem that in provinces, such as Franche-Comté, boasting the so-called *corvée réelle,* nobles holding any lands designated *taillables* had traditionally been expected, and might still be expected, to contribute somehow to the discharge of this obligation.) The government, already contemplating reforms that would unavoidably infringe upon long-standing clerical and noble privileges, had no desire to antagonize the rural noblesse over this particular issue by resurrecting Turgot's plan of 1776 to make nobles as well as commoners fiscally responsible for upkeep of the kingdom's roads. Under the policy sketched out in Calonne's legislation of late 1786, members of the Second Estate would in most regions be affected by *corvée* commutation only insofar as the additional taxation assessed upon their peasants diminished the ability of the latter to render unto their noble seigneurs what had always been the seigneurs' by right. Obviously, it was the luckless *taillables* or *corvéables* who would in the future continue to bear the primary onus for the maintenance of highways in France.

Even so, the authorities could not have been altogether unprepared for magisterial opposition to their project: the *parlementaires* at Paris and Bordeaux had objected strenuously to Necker's implementation of a similar policy just a few years before.[69] And, in fact, a number of high courts in provincial France during 1787–88 signified their displeasure with an administrative experiment they portrayed as a fertile source of new miseries for the overtaxed folk of the countryside.

The magistrates at Besançon resolved almost immediately to protest against Calonne's initiative. They were able to approve remonstrances and send them to the crown on 5 February 1787. Significantly, one of the points they raised concerned the famous royal act of 13 February 1780. Louis XVI, "after having announced [in that legislation] that the rate of the *taille* and the *capitation* could only be changed by virtue of laws registered in the Courts," had further stipulated "in article 5 that with the exception of local fiscal obligations freely deliberated upon in the communities, *no impositions could be ordered or levied upon the taillables to defray expenses of any kind whatsoever save in the form of letters-patent ratified in the Courts.*" Yet this was precisely what was coming to pass now, the jurists protested. Peasants whose few days of work each year upon the highways and bridges of Franche-Comté constituted no great hardship were now to be compelled to exchange that manageable obligation for yet more taxation—and where would such taxation, once established, ever end?[70]

The judges differentiated between provinces cursed by the *corvée personnelle*, where the *corvée*-exempt status of all *privilégiés* meant that the poorest and most powerless shouldered the entire burden of labor upon the roads, and those provinces such as Franche-Comté blessed by the *corvée réelle*, where even nobles, if they held lands in the peasant communities, had somehow to contribute as much to the upkeep of local roads as to the payment of the local tax quota. And had not the government itself explicitly acknowledged the advantages of the *corvée réelle* in Franche-Comté? The *parlementaires* cited a minister's memorandum addressed to the intendant of their province on 11 September 1776 and stating in part that "since all landowners contribute toward the *corvée*, that circumstance has led the King to believe that no inconvenience would arise from letting things remain on the traditional footing in that Province."[71]

True, peasants had in recent years been given the option of paying additional taxation to defray the costs of relinquishing their assigned work to gangs of professional laborers upon the roads, but "over and over again the communities have preferred to discharge these tasks themselves." And why not?

> A farmer burdened down already by all the other imposts would find himself forced to pay 15 or 20 livres more to have someone else perform the tasks he could perform himself without much difficulty.
>
> He could do so during those times when he is occupied neither by sowing and cultivation nor by harvesting. If he has a wife and children, they can help him; he never has to worry about spending what little money he may have or about borrowing and thus going into debt; another tax, on the other hand, would plunge him into despair, . . . he would no longer have the wherewithal to feed himself and his family.[72]

Besançon's remonstrants also charged that any leeway still granted on paper to the individual peasant communities to retain the more traditional *corvée en nature* was illusory. After all, what village wanted to be the first in its province to defy the intendant and his agents by initiating an appeal against the very policy those powerful men were administering? No, the *parlementaires* insisted, the only remedy for these ills, the only redress for the innumerable popular grievances already arisen or likely to arise from implementation of this newfangled policy, lay in an unqualified return to the old *corvée* of personal labor. Let a law to this end be submitted to and registered in the *parlement*; let the magistrates ensure through their constant surveillance that no *corvéable* would be summoned from his fields when they needed his attention, or compelled to labor too far from home, or abused in any other fashion. Every *corvéable* would have "justice," the destitute would be spared altogether, and the sovereign's humane legislation of 13 February 1780 would be honored in the observance.

A ministerial response to these remonstrances eventually came in the form of a memorandum from Lamoignon dated 18 June 1787.[73] The keeper of the seals courteously but firmly rebutted the magistrates' arguments. The *corvée réelle*, he conceded, might in some respects be less abusive than the *corvée personnelle*, but it could never be as equitable as taxation substituted for labor. Government agents could more easily assign fiscal obligation fairly than they could assign labor duties fairly, and as in the present instance the former obligation was simply being substituted for the latter, there was in effect no "new" impost to infringe upon the salutary restraints announced in the declaration of February 1780. Lamoignon assured the *parlementaires* that all moneys earmarked for local road work would indeed be employed for that purpose and insisted that Franche-Comté, like other provinces, could only benefit from the labors of paid professionals. He concluded his remarks by reminding the judges that, however welcome their "advice" might be at Court, the king could never brook their "direct involvement" in "purely administrative" matters such as the construction and upkeep of his bridges and highways.

The tribunal at Besançon riposted with a "letter" of 9 July: tediously challenging the keeper of the seals on each of the points he had raised, it said essentially nothing new.[74] As late as 1789, however, Droz des Villars was still underscoring his company's historic role of succoring the overtaxed and at times overworked *corvéables* of Franche-Comté— within limits, to be sure, set by the fundamental parlementary adherence to social hierarchy and privilege.[75]

At Grenoble, judicial consideration of the same issue revealed a similar kind of prudent humanitarianism. Calonne's decree of 6 November 1786 provoked an even swifter response from the Grenoblois than from Besançon's judges.[76] Dauphiné's *parlementaires* had the audacity to issue a decree of 20 December prohibiting execution of Calonne's policy in their province. The government quashed this temerarious decree ten days later, but the undaunted Grenoblois returned to the attack with remonstrances of 10 March 1787.

No more than their Comtois counterparts were these magistrates willing to concede an inch on constitutional principles. "There are privileges that one cannot abolish without altering the very constitution of the Monarchy, whose strength and duration depend upon conservation of the intermediary ranks composing it." Neither clergy nor noblesse nor magistracy, the Grenoblois insisted, could ever be subjected "to a monetary contribution representative of the corvée." The judges nevertheless allowed "that it would be fitting to come to the aid of the people, to help them support such a heavy burden." Accordingly, they recommended that the tenant farmers of "ecclesiastics, nobles, and other privileged persons" be assessed for the *corvée* at a level of taxation one-third higher than the value of the lands they worked would otherwise warrant. Poorer peasants could thereby pay that much less in *corvée*-related taxation. The *privilégiés* themselves would (voluntarily, it was assumed) compensate their *fermiers* for the fiscal sacrifice they had made on behalf of the needier commoners of the province. The judges went on, in vintage parlementary fashion, to assail the greedy "entrepreneurs" upon the highways to whom Calonne's ill-considered policy would accord an abusive liberty:

> No longer having to unravel complicated issues directly with the peasant communities, and being thus liberated from the active and clairvoyant eye of peasant self-interest, they would conspire among themselves to increase the price of their roadwork at their whim, they would employ means in which they are all too well versed to ingratiate themselves with those charged with reviewing their conduct and keep any competition at a safe distance; they would inevitably succeed in monopolizing within one Company various roadwork assignments that, although ostensibly parceled out among several gangs of laborers, would in the end be awarded to themselves alone.[77]

The Grenoblois also complained that the new administrative regime would prove discriminatory in that it would compel some communities that had already discharged their *corvée* obligations through separate arrangements to pay the additional taxation legislated for the 1787–89 period. The jurists cited the specific example of "the market-town of Voiron" whose conscientious and farsighted provisions in this sphere would now be set at naught. Was this "justice," or was it not an odious species of "double indemnity"? At this point, the judges asked for restoration of the Dauphinois Estates—or, at the very least, establishment of a provincial assembly—so that local landholders might be able to exercise some degree of surveillance and control over all those involved in execution of this policy. Pending that desirable event, they continued, let each community remunerate the personnel charged specifically with performing its assigned task, and let each community carefully supervise that work itself. In that fashion, the villages of Dauphiné would "not have the misfortune to see their taxes needlessly increased through the exactions of the general and local Tax-Receivers of the Province," but would assure themselves instead that their appropriated moneys were used wisely and well.

The government's response to these plaints (which it no doubt deemed hopelessly impractical *and* self-serving) arrived in the form of the royal declaration of 27 June 1787 definitively establishing the new type of *corvée*, to be administered in provinces such as Dauphiné by intendant and provincial assembly. The Grenoblois judges could receive, at best, ambiguous guidance on this issue from their counterparts at Paris. The latter ratified the government's legislation promptly—but with the attached proviso that the additional taxation to be paid by *corvéables* in lieu of laboring upon the roads not amount to more than one tenth of their current *taille* (see chapter 2). Furthermore, the justices at Grenoble, like the justices of other provincial courts, knew very well how doggedly the Parisians had criticized Necker's very similar approach to the *corvée royale* just ten years before. Magisterial dissatisfaction on the issue at Grenoble remained intense, however. On 17 January 1788 the judges approved and sent to Lamoignon a "counterproposal" for administration of the *corvée* in Dauphiné.[78] They repeated in this memorandum their suggestion of the preceding March that tenant farmers of *privilégiés* be assessed for the *corvée* at a rate one-third higher than was warranted by the value of their holdings, and that the *privilégiés* themselves indemnify their *fermiers* for this sacrifice on behalf of the poorer peasantry.

The jurists' plan also stipulated that labor be undertaken only on "the most essential routes," and that the additional imposition levied upon the *taillables* should only amount to one-half of the *capitation roturière* rather than three-fifths as provided for by the government. Again, communities were ideally to be assessed only for road construction and improvements from which they would directly benefit, and credited for roadwork they had already performed or commissioned under prior agreements. The magistrates furthermore insisted that the entrepreneurs (*adjudicataires*) be closely "supervised" by the communities whose labor obligations they were assuming, that they not run into greater expense than was authorized for each task, and that they be held accountable for maintenance of their work for three years after certifying its completion. Finally—and, we suspect, most critically in parlementary eyes—the entire regime of construction and repair of roads and bridges in Dauphiné was to be placed under the control of the justices at Grenoble, rather than being entrusted to the intendant and provincial assembly.

The magistrates even in their most sanguine moments could hardly have anticipated adoption of their counterproposal. Predictably, it drew the fire of partisans of the fledgling provincial assembly in Dauphiné for its advocacy of parlementary supremacy in administrative matters. Others ridiculed it for its administrative naïveté or criticized its ungenerous insistence upon maintaining the principle that only commoners were responsible for the upkeep of highways and roads. The authorities at Versailles, viewing Grenoble's *parlementaires* all along as delinquent for having refused to ratify the enabling legislation of 27 June 1787, would never even acknowledge receipt of the project of 17 January 1788. They reserved their response for the hectic days of early May, when the royal declaration of the preceding June was, along with the May Edicts, "militarily" inscribed upon the Grenoble Parlement's registers. Thus the government, at least temporarily, had its own way. This did not, however, prevent the judges at Grenoble from conjuring up all the old arguments against the purported abuses of the *corvée par adjudication* in their general protests of 20 May 1788.[79]

Similar statements on this staple controversy of the old regime emanated from the sovereign courts of Alsace and Languedoc. Intriguingly, the same issue that drove a wedge between *parlement* and provincial assembly in Dauphiné actually drew magistrates and provincial assembly together in Alsace. So it would appear, in any case, from a memorandum prepared for the Alsatian provincial assembly during October 1787. The memorandum complained that ever since the promulgation of the enabling legislation of 27 June, the intendant in Alsace, Antoine Chaumont de la Galaisière, had been authorizing "vicious adjudications" of the *corvée*. He had gone so far as to approve the levy upon commoners of additional taxation amounting to approximately 680,000 livres "to defray the expenses of maintaining the highways." And this was only for 1787: comparable sums were to be extorted from the *corvéables* by the royal tax collectors in 1788 and 1789! Such sums equaled "the yield from the two *vingtièmes*." But herein lay the irony of the situation. The memorandum claimed that the tax collectors at present could not even gather in "ordinary" revenues; "their embarrassment on this point is notorious." How could local officials expect to extract even more monetary tribute from the oppressed *contribuables* "for the profit of voracious Entrepreneurs" upon the highways of the province? Indeed, the "simple announcement of that exorbitant impost" had "provoked a general unrest" in whose threatening shadow the judges at Colmar, although ratifying the legislation of June on 30 August, had "proscribed" all unjust and vexatious operations relative to the *corvée par adjudication*.[80] That proscription had proven inadequate, unfortunately, as the intendant had forged ahead with new, even more abusive operations upon the roads and bridges of Alsace. The magistrates at Colmar had intervened yet again with an *arrêt de défense* of 25 September, but that, too, had proven ineffectual. The provincial assembly asserted in its apologia that the peasant communities of Alsace desired "unanimously" to be left alone to maintain the roads in the traditional manner, not to be crushed under yet another "onerous impost." It entreated the government to reverse its policy in Alsace, and to do so as expeditiously as possible so that the Alsatians might get on with fortifying their routes of travel against the coming winter. The Alsatian provincial assembly, however, might have done better to avoid any reference to the judges at Colmar in their plea: during the past summer, the "sovereign council" had incurred the wrath of Intendant Chaumont de la Galaisière by remonstrating to Versailles over alleged abuses visited upon the peasant taxpayers in its jurisdiction.[81]

Trouble over the government's *corvée par adjudication* was, it seems, also threatening in Languedoc at this time. The archbishop of Auch informed the ministers apprehensively in a letter of 17 October that provincial "unrest" was growing as a result of the attempt by Intendant Claude-François Bertrand de Boucheporn to apply their policy on local highways and roads. "It will probably be necessary for him to suspend the awarding of labor contracts," the archbishop ventured to predict. He reported that the parlement at Toulouse had registered the enabling act of 27 June, but only "on the condition . . . that the impost substituted for the *corvée* which in accordance with article 3 will be assessed for the present year upon his Majesty's *sujets taillables*, on the basis of the *capitation roturière*, will not exceed 10 percent of the taxes mentioned in the said article."[82] Two days later the archbishop wrote again to Versailles and spoke more fearfully than ever of "a great wave of protest" against the local application of the government's *corvée par adjudication* and associated taxation.[83] If this ecclesiastic's observations upon the situation in Languedoc were at all accurate (and there is no reason to believe they were not), the magistrates at Toulouse could have maintained at least as justifiably as counterparts elsewhere that the peasantry's welfare as they envisioned it was one consideration behind their critique of royal policy on this long-debated question.

But if provincial *parlementaires* invoked what they perceived as popular causes in commenting upon issues of national political significance in the late 1780s, they did likewise with respect to purely local matters. We have only to return, briefly, to Pau, Rennes, and Rouen to discover excellent examples.

At Pau there was the broil over the Franco-Spanish convention of August 1785 providing for adjustments of the border between the two countries in the Pyrenees. We have already had occasion to note ironically how the *parlement* at Pau became in effect *plus royaliste que le roi* by repeatedly denouncing what it depicted as unilateral concessions of

French royal domain in Navarre to Spain.[84] The jurists, however, manifested even more concern over alleged violations of individual proprietary rights stemming from the exchanges of territories high up in the mountainous southern periphery of the jurisdiction. A running debate ensued between judges and crown. The judges came down especially hard upon the comte d'Ornano, delegated as royal commissioner to deal with Spanish representatives upon these exchanges, and the crown quite understandably defended all d'Ornano's actions. The remonstrances emanating from Pau in December 1786 and August 1787 must have seriously concerned the French government, however, for at some point late in 1787 one of the ministers (most probably Lamoignon) produced a memorandum of no less than seventy pages that vigorously contested every assertion made by the judges concerning the Franco-Spanish negotiations and castigated them for their criticism of the comte d'Ornano.[85]

Undaunted by this detailed and devastating counterattack, the magistrates at Pau drafted yet another set of remonstrances on the Franco-Spanish territorial exchanges and sent them to Versailles on 14 December 1787. These protests, like earlier ones, cited alleged grievances of the mountain folk of the jurisdiction. For instance, they spoke of "a very productive iron mine that belonged to the pays de Cize," which had been ceded to Spain "without the consent of the proprietors, without any indemnity in their favor." They spoke of "an immense forest whose ownership lay securely in the hands of the inhabitants of the pays de Cize and the town of St. Jean-Pié de Port," which had been "abandoned to the enterprises of the Spaniards who indeed seized it even before Your Majesty had authorized his Commissioner's plan, and who exploited most of its wood for their navy." The remonstrances depicted plebeian afflictions in more general terms as well.

> . . . your Parlement, Sire. . . . sees a pastoral population, without commerce, without industry, having no resource for subsistence other than its herds of animals, threatened with losing, through the demarcation of borders, the greater portion of the pastures requisite for their sustenance. It sees misery and despair suspended over the head of the luckless peasant farmer . . . who must make all his payments to the state before assuring his own subsistence.[86]

The judges also resumed their assault upon the comte d'Ornano, accusing him of "having had the municipal officers of the valley of Baigorry arrested and incarcerated without an express order" from the king, and indeed without any legitimate cause whatsoever, and of having committed other "acts of oppression and violence against submissive and faithful subjects." The jurists grimly reminded their monarch that "all the severity of the Laws is reserved for that individual who dares to abuse the sacred name of Your Majesty by perpetrating unjust and tyrannical acts" against the helpless citizenry. The magistrates furthermore voiced their disappointment that the comte de Brienne, deputized during that summer of 1787 to review the border adjustments in Navarre and to investigate local grievances arising from those revisions, had been charged with that function only in the region of Navarre known as the pays de Cize, and not in the valley of Baigorry. This was particularly unfortunate as, in the latter area, the readjusted Franco-Spanish border "epitomized error and injustice." Had not the tribunal been at pains to point that out to His Majesty in its most recent remonstrances, those of August? And had not it implored His Majesty to "familiarize himself with the illegal activities going forward in that section of the Pyrenees, and with the complaints unceasingly addressed by the local inhabitants to all His Ministers over the past two years"?[87] Any less scrupulous counsel tendered to the king (so the judges implied) would have ill become the Pau Parlement, obligated as it was to plead the subjects' causes at distant Versailles.

These were the remonstrances of 14 December 1787 from Navarre and Béarn. Were the magistrates at Pau justified in maintaining that "the cry which arose on all sides," the "plaints and objections of all constituted bodies in the Province" concerning the boundary alterations in the Pyrenees, had more than any other consideration motivated them to intervene in this matter, and had in fact merited their sympathy?[88] The Pau Parlement's historian has argued that the tribunal indeed made itself "the echo of aggrieved groups of people" on this occasion, and was only seeking that which was just and reasonable in the circumstances.[89] On the other hand, a late eighteenth-century memorialist, less friendly to the jurists and their course of action, asserted that in this instance the government, desirous as it was of settling a long-term border dispute from which much ill will and some blood had flowed, was in the right.[90] Both commentaries upon this obscure but rather interesting affair at Pau probably contain some truth. Yet the fact that a genuinely "popular" uprising the following summer drove the king's agents out of Pau and temporarily reinstalled the cashiered *parlementaires* in their professional quarters may lend some additional (if retrospective) credibility to the judges' protests of 1786 and 1787. Up to this point at least there seem to have been substantial bonds of sympathy between the quaint population of Navarre and Béarn and the high justices at Pau.

Over two years before events took such a dramatic turn in the far south, the magistrates of ancient noble lineage at Rennes were petitioning Louis XVI on behalf of their own unfortunates. Hard economic times were besetting Brittany as well as other provinces in the late 1780s, affecting all elements of the population directly or indirectly and taxing ordinary sources of charity to the utmost.[91] In a letter to the sovereign commissioned on 16 February 1786 and sent a week later, Rennes' *parlementaires* depicted the dolorous situation in their province and solicited government assistance:

> At a time when we have just ratified the extension of the third *vingtième* for the present year, we cannot refrain from calling Your Majesty's attention once again to the myriad calamities afflicting your province of Brittany. Each day we learn new details of the extreme misery under whose weight most of its inhabitants are groaning. The pastors who govern the city parishes, and even more those in the countryside, confide to each of us their alarm concerning the people's subsistence until the next harvest. Immense numbers of livestock have perished due to the universal dearth of fodder. The listless state in which individuals with difficulty maintain those animals they have been able to preserve, nullifies that branch of Commerce for the moment, and perhaps for several years, a crucial fact for this Province; the price of Wheat, whose last harvest yield was very poor, cannot be paid by the peasant farmer, and in this general situation of exhaustion, the poor man cannot even avail himself of a neighbor in more fortunate circumstances, to whom he could sell his pathetic patrimony to provide for his family the means of subsistence.

His Majesty already knew of these tribulations, the jurists continued, for Brittany had in the recent past benefited from royal largesse in one form or another. But, tragically, more assistance than ever was urgently needed: "we dare to assure Your Majesty that there could not conceivably be circumstances in which that aid could be more essential."[92]

And, as a matter of fact, some small assistance was promised from Versailles. Ministers Breteuil and Miromesnil, in letters of 18 and 24 March, respectively, informed the judges that the king had awarded Brittany another 80,000 livres to subsidize public works, most notably labor to enhance the navigability of the river Vilaine which flowed through the Breton capital. The ministers expressed their hope that the *parlement* at Rennes would deem this a not altogether inadequate response to its petition of the preceding month.[93] The magistrates may or may not have been impressed by this latest succor from the government, but they were soon drafting another letter to Louis XVI, this time on an unrelated and somewhat mysterious matter.

It appears that, in the spring of 1786, local rumor had the policymakers at Versailles resolving for whatever reason to transfer a number of administrative and possibly judicial services from Rennes to some other community within the province. One of the *parlementaires* alluded vaguely to these rumored "innovations" at the court's plenary session of 11 May. Although there was seemingly no substantiation for these reports, a committee of jurists actually drew up a missive to the king on the subject during the next several days. The letter, as read out and approved in plenary session on 15 May, assumed the imminent realization of the administrative changes being bruited about locally and depicted them as potentially most injurious to "that indigent and unfortunate portion of the citizenry at Rennes." It was primarily on behalf of these *misérables* that the judges claimed to be writing:

> Rennes is an important city; but lacking external commerce and external resources, it subsists only by virtue of the numbers and affluence of the consumers living within its limits. Most of them come here and stay here only because of their divers business affairs. The announced transfer of administrative facilities would therefore deprive Rennes of the sole resource upon which it can rely . . . and [this at] a time when the Municipality is exhausted by the efforts it has made over the past four months to feed its poor and needy; at a time when it has turned a major portion of the onerous *octrois*, levied upon consumers' goods, to the benefit of those poor and needy through the establishment of public works.
>
> These sacrifices are immense, and if the projected revolution takes place, those that it will still be necessary to make after a year of want will probably be beyond the capabilities of the Municipality.[94]

Moreover, the Bretons argued, there was the question of sheer convenience—the convenience, that is, of all residents of the province whose affairs drew them to Rennes. Such individuals found the city readily accessible from all directions, abounding in cheap and commodious lodgings and in reasonably priced wares of every variety and description, and offering every imaginable expertise in business and professional matters. Was any other community so ideally placed in Brittany? Could any other community provide such an array of services, goods, and amenities? Clearly not, the magistrates felt. Such was the substance of their second missive to the monarch in the first half of 1786, well before the onset of the central government's terminal crisis. To be sure, the Bretons' letter to Louis XVI of 15 May, unlike that of the preceding February, may have been inspired in part by concern lest the bruited "revolution" at Rennes jeopardize their own professional and political roles in the province. As it turned out, furthermore, nothing came of these rumors in 1786. Nonetheless, the *parlementaires'* behavior in this curious affair affords one more example of magisterial readiness to invoke the cause of humble folk (along with other, related causes, to be sure) very late in the *ancien régime.*

Even later in the old regime—a mere fourteen months before the storming of the Bastille—it was the turn of Rouen's *parlementaires* to descant upon the harsh lot of the *menu peuple.* On this occasion, too, expediential considerations may not have been altogether lacking. The day was 3 May 1788; the Norman judges were in the process of sending off to Versailles heated protests against the *séance royale* staged in the Paris Parlement the preceding November; and the government's heavy hand was about to fall upon the higher judiciary. The judges at Rouen assuredly could pay court to local opinion by agreeing with Rouen's Chamber of Commerce and Normandy's provincial assemblies that the recent Free Trade Treaty with England lay behind the current economic distress in the province. And that is precisely what they said in a letter sent off that day to Louis XVI.

The magistrates' depiction of the local misery embraced all social groups allegedly victimized by the 1786 treaty, but struck a popular chord throughout, as evidenced in the following excerpts from their missive:

> The most disheartening stagnation has suddenly overtaken such a flourishing commerce; the wholesale merchants' warehouses are bulging with unsold goods, the retail merchants cannot sell, the manufacturers have no orders: some of their workers have been let go. Of the latter, some languish in idleness and in misery after having spent what little advance wages they had earned through assiduous labors; others have given themselves over to disorders attendant upon beggary; a very great number have embraced expatriation. . . .
>
> The layoffs in the workshops have resulted in the collapse of spinning. That occupation, earmarked particularly for women, no longer provides them even the meanest salary. Reduced to holding on to merchandise without value or to selling it at a loss, they find themselves deprived of all means of subsistence.[95]

In more prosperous times, the judges averred, those manufactories turning out linen, woolen, and cotton goods had employed more than 40,000 workers in Rouen and its suburbs. But no longer. Moreover, the *écoles de travail* directed by the parish priest in the poorest and most populous quarter of the city and formerly providing additional employment for textile workers could now sell few of their goods and were consequently bankrupt. The *parlementaires* endorsed the prevalent tendency to ascribe these tribulations to the Anglo-French Treaty of 1786.

What was to be done to alleviate the situation? Mechanization of the processes "for preparing, carding, and spinning cotton" might enable French cotton goods to compete successfully with those of English provenance in the long run, but such mechanization would have the more immediate effect of throwing additional workers out of their jobs. Local charity undoubtedly had a role to play. The judges lauded those endeavoring to open new workshops, those who sold their wares to the needy at reduced prices, and all other Good Samaritans in the current hard times. Unfortunately, "the sources of private relief are drying up, and stark need is reborn every day. It is only in Your Majesty's beneficent heart that your unhappy subjects can find lasting and adequate resources. Momentary relief would be insufficient." The magistrates did suggest upon their own account that the government encourage the cultivation of hemp and flax: in this sector, they affirmed, France could hold her own with her insular rival and she could do so without the massive introduction of machinery that would cost jobs.[96]

Having discussed the "grievous state" of textiles in Normandy, and having characterized it as the "principal source of the present distress," the *parlementaires* hastened to cite other areas of the local economy purportedly suffering as a result of government trade policies.

> The earthenware establishments of Rouen employed a great number of workers whom they can now retain no longer. Price differences, occasioned by fuel cost differences, do not allow them to remain competitive with the earths of England. The wood that they use is infinitely more expensive than charcoal. . . .
>
> The Norman tanneries, formerly so renowned, but fallen away now from their former state of prosperity . . . cannot avoid total ruin due to the introduction of [leathern] merchandise into the country.[97]

Rouen's high justices beseeched Louis XVI to "look with commiseration upon all the cantons" of Normandy: there was not one of them, asserted the Rouennais, that had "not had to groan under the weight of some calamity." In some regions, "the persistent scarcity of those fruits providing the ordinary beverage of the populace" had "ruined the farmers." In other areas, "epizoötic diseases" had "killed off livestock whose numbers had already been reduced by earlier droughts." In nearly all Norman cantons, the jurists maintained, "the decline of commerce and industry" had "adversely affected the fortunes of those relatively well off, and taken from the poor what they could not spare."

The magistrates must have been aware that royal policy could be held accountable for only so many deleterious economic developments and no more: paucities of selected fruits and epizoötic diseases in Normandy, after all, were hardly to be deemed acts of man, even by credulous provincials within and without the Palais de Justice at Rouen. Nevertheless, Normandy's *parlementaires* did insist upon blaming local economic distress in general on the Anglo-French trade negotiations. "The first law of nature," they proclaimed, "is man's subsistence; the first law of the State is the citizen's subsistence. That obligation becomes all the more sacred, when the citizens' misfortunes stem from State policies, and especially when those policies contribute to the growth of State revenues." Let the ministers acknowledge this, declared the Normans, and let them turn the revenue raised from imported English goods to the profit and indemnification of "the workers wronged by the introduction of those goods into France."[98]

The king and his ministers would scarcely be inclined to accord any more favor to this petition of 3 May 1788 than to the more overtly political remonstrances of the same day against the *séance royale* of the preceding November. Indeed, even as the Normans were approving these representations upon two unrelated subjects, Loménie de Brienne and Lamoignon were preparing to apply their drastic solution to the impasse between the crown and the *parlements*. Partisans of the tribunal at Rouen, and of the parlementary cause in general, would nonetheless have made out some genuine concern for plebeian Normans in the petition to Louis XVI of 3 May 1788. And, truth to tell, Rouen's judges had been voicing what they took to be "popular" concerns too consistently over the years to be dismissed summarily as disingenuous champions of the poor in the late 1780s.

Analysis of the provincial *parlements'* behavior toward secular commoners on the eve of the revolutionary era will probably not convince us that the judges were either as selflessly humane or as knowledgeable in dealing with bourgeois and plebeian concerns as they and their partisans claimed they were. Neither the Parisian magistrates nor the high justices of provincial France could fail to perceive that many of their own interests were bound up with the causes of the urban and rural commonalty. At the same time, these jurists were acutely aware that an overly generous conception and espousal of "popular" rights would contravene the social hierarchy and order from which all *privilégiés*, judicial and nonjudicial, benefited. On the other hand, how could the *parlementaires* be confident upon any given occasion that they could, even if truly inclined to do so, correctly identify and faithfully articulate the aspirations and grievances of affluent and not-so-affluent members of the Third Estate? A particularly wide gulf must have yawned between the perspective of ultraprivileged men of the robe and the variegated perspectives of the most numerous and humblest folk of town and countryside. For all these reasons, we must take care not to exaggerate the significance of the high magistracy's advocacy of commoners' causes during the prerevolutionary crisis.

Yet our analysis also suggests that the sovereign courts' many critics were and have always been unduly severe in condemning them outright as bastions of elitist selfishness and hypocrisy. Indeed, we can affirm now that the provincial *parlementaires* of the late 1780s, in belaboring those who would have taxed the "people" more heavily and those who would have speculated upon the popular misery, actually anticipated the most radical tribunes of the masses in the Revolution. It was not at all ironic, then, that so many commoners of widely varying estate, from the mountains of Navarre and Dauphiné to the streets of Rennes and Rouen, should have rallied to the stricken *parlements* in May and June of 1788 and raucously celebrated their reinstatement several months later. The judges in the twilight of the *ancien régime*, for all their limitations, were assuredly not altogether wanting as sincere and informed spokesmen for underprivileged France—and many a Frenchman realized this at the time. What *was* ironic, of course, was the fact that the rapid politicization of these same folk in late 1788 and beyond should have engendered such heady expectations and so radically altered old perspectives that the very magistrates who more than any others had brought about that politicization were soon tarred with the brush of the old regime and consigned along with that outmoded world to oblivion.

The Demise of the Parlements
and Their World

There is little left to say about the *parlements* as functioning institutions once we leave the prerevolution of 1787–88 and venture forth upon the terrain of the revolution of 1789 and subsequent years. Magistrates here and there attempted sporadically to intervene in consumers' affairs and other public matters during the first six months of 1789; a few enterprising judges of Paris and the provinces involved themselves in the elections for the Estates General. For the most part, however, the jurists, chastened no doubt by the Third Estate's hostile reaction to magisterial invocation of the 1614 Estates General, and sensing their growing isolation in an increasingly politicized France, confined themselves to their traditional judicial and administrative duties. Yet worse was soon to follow. By decree of the National Constituent Assembly, only skeleton crews remained in the various Chambres des Vacations to mete out essential justice after the recess of September–October 1789. Over the following two years the Assembly abolished the *parlements* altogether and revamped the entire judicial system. Several of the sovereign courts protested their impending demise in one fashion or another during late 1789 and 1790, but they were preaching in a desert of universal indifference. Their France had already passed into history.

And what happened to the Parisian and provincial *parlementaires* once their companies were broken up? Indeed, we should touch briefly upon the revolutionary and postrevolutionary fates of these sovereign justices of the *ancien régime* before analyzing their contribution to the upheaval in France and reassessing the overall genesis and nature of that upheaval.

Although the parlementary diaspora after 1789 has by no means been exhaustively studied, we may safely make several general statements concerning it. First, more than 40 percent of the approximately two thousand judges of the *parlements* and other sovereign courts of Louis XVI's France left the realm, temporarily or permanently, during the revolutionary era.[1] The Rouennais seem to have been most prone to strike out for foreign parts, although we also find impressive numbers of émigrés among the personnel of most of the other major courts. Second, if the Terror and the lesser bloodlettings of the Revolution undeniably cut a broad swath of destruction through the erstwhile magistracy at Toulouse, and wreaked considerable havoc at Paris and Bordeaux, former justices elsewhere were much less likely to fall victim to the destructive furies raging within France.[2] Finally, if a number of former Parisian and provincial *parlementaires* pursued public careers during the 1790s and beyond, the majority of one-time magistrates, preferring discretion to valor, quietly rode out the revolutionary storm upon their rustic estates. Managing their family patrimonies as of old, and acquiring in some cases "national properties," they prepared the way for their landed posterity in the nineteenth century's reconstituted "society of notables."

Some interesting individual stories, nonetheless, engage our attention. Among our old acquaintances at Paris, the former First President d'Aligre, President Joly de Fleury, Avocat-Général Séguier, and influential counselor Lefebvre d'Amécourt emigrated and refused to have anything to do with the new France.[3] Among the names of other Parisian émigrés catching our eye are Le Coigneux de Belabre, Goislard de Montsabert, Outremont de Minière, and Sabatier de Cabre. Some *parlementaires* who absented themselves from France during the dangerous 1790s not only made their peace with postrevolutionary regimes but proved signally successful at carving out new careers under their aegis. Robert de Saint-Vincent returned to France financially ruined after the Revolution, but even he was able to retrieve at least the shadow of his old affluence as headmaster of the new *lycée* at Caen in Normandy. Other cases speak of more striking success. Antoine François Claude Ferrand, that would-be conciliator in the tumultuous plenary sessions of the Court of Peers in 1787, counseled Louis XVIII in the middle and late 1790s and eventually served him as minister of state during the Restoration. Huguet de Sémonville, as incorrigible in the Court of Peers as Ferrand had been conciliatory, found himself ambassador to Holland under the Consulate, a senator under the Empire, and still playing an influential public role under Louis XVIII and Louis-Philippe. The former Avocat-Général d'Ambray, whose youthful eloquence had so impressed onlookers at the Palais de Justice on the eve of the Revolution, served as chancellor, as keeper of the seals, and as president of the Chamber of Peers under the restored Bourbons. Guy Marie Sallier, that assiduous chronicler of events in the prerevolution, emerged from obscurity after 1814 as a *maître des requêtes* and as a *chevalier* of the Legion of Honor under the Restoration, continued to turn out historical writings on the side, and died toward 1840, aged nearly ninety. But perhaps Etienne-Denis Pasquier, among all the erstwhile Parisian *parlementaires*, savored the most durable success in postrevolutionary France: he held high office under Napoleon and Louis XVIII, became the duc de Pasquier under Louis-Philippe, and died in 1862 at ninety-five, three-quarters of a century after his brief but unforgettable tenure in the turbulent Enquêtes of the old regime's greatest tribunal.

At the same time, a few of Pasquier's former colleagues did choose to play with fire by forgoing emigration (or safe anonymity in the countryside) and involving themselves in revolutionary politics. Adrien Duport was probably the luckiest of these, or perhaps merely the most prudent: he gave up trying to influence public affairs with his constitutional monarchist and antiwar stance in 1792, emigrated, and could at least die peacefully in his bed, if not in his native France. Several of his former associates were not as fortunate. Fréteau de Saint-Just was elected president of the Constituent Assembly early in the Revolution and later served as a magistrate in the capital—but was nonetheless guillotined in Prairial of Year II (spring 1794). Former President Le Peletier de Saint-Fargeau became one of the great popular tribunes of the Revolution, but his ultimate apotheosis was posthumous: he was martyred by an assassin in the Palais-Royal in 1793. One-time Avocat-Général Hérault de Sechelles was a *vainqueur de la Bastille* in 1789, served later on the national Tribunal de Cassation, was elected to the Legislative Assembly and Convention and chosen president of the latter, and was one of the famed or notorious Twelve on the Committee of Public Safety in late 1793—but for all that he was dead at thirty-four, guillotined for having incurred Maximilien Robespierre's displeasure in parlous times. On the other hand, the resolution, courageous if not politic, to defend the crown and the *ancien régime* in the assemblies of the Revolution brought a conservative's martyrdom to that erstwhile chief of the parlementary opposition, Duval d'Eprémesnil. Other magistrates of note struck down by the Revolution included former First President Bochard de Saron and former Presidents Lepeletier de Rosambo and de Gourgue. Seventeen former Parisian *parlementaires* were guillotined at the Place de la Révolution on 1 Floréal of Year II (April 1794). Yet we should set against these cases of misfortune the incontrovertible and substantial fact that the vast majority of former justices of the Paris Parlement, like the majority of former judges elsewhere (and, indeed, like the majority in the noble class to which they all belonged or aspired) survived the vicissitudes of the Revolution, for the most part by lying low in the countryside.

In provincial France, too, some luminaries of the old judiciary would have nothing to do with the new regime, or at least with the new regime in its murderous infancy, while others enthusiastically welcomed it from the start.[4] Emigrés of whom, in their prerevolutionary careers, we have already heard, included the following: fiery counterrevolutionary essayist Du Couëdic de Kergoualer and Avocat-Général du Bourgblanc at Rennes; former First President des Gallois de La Tour and hot-headed oppositionist counselor d'André at Aix; former First President Legouz de Saint-Seine and President Joly de Bévy, that inveterate foe of government and Estates, at Dijon; former First President Perreney de Grosbois and Procureur-Général Doroz at Besançon; former Procureur-Général de Rességuier at Toulouse; former President d'Ornacieux and pugnacious oppositionist counselor Corbet de Meyrieu at Grenoble; former First President Camus de Pontcarré at Rouen; and one-time Procureur-Général Dudon at Bordeaux. Some of these men eventually came to terms with new realities and returned home; others died, irreconcilable, in exile. (Corbet de Meyrieu, to cite only one of these latter, expired in Savoy in 1790, utterly convinced to the end that the Revolution was but a foul "conspiracy" soon to be undone.)

Among those justices who did not choose exile was our indispensable witness at Besançon, Droz des Villars. This good-humored *érudit*, having authored his company's final apologia on public affairs in 1789, retired soon thereafter to Pontarlier, a smaller community in his native Franche-Comté, where, save for a brief incarceration as an "aristocrat" in 1793, he weathered the revolutionary tempest. He later worked tirelessly to reconstitute the shattered Académie de Besançon (of which he had been a member since 1765) as the Société d'Agriculture du Doubs; he died in 1805. Even today, Droz des Villars is remembered in Franche-Comté's picturesque capital as a distinguished eighteenth-century academician and man of letters.

Several other quondam *parlementaires* of provincial France, whether in exile or not during the upheaval of the 1790s, eventually made new names for themselves in public walks of life. Pierre-Louis Roederer, onetime author of parlementary remonstrances at Metz, was a journalist, professor, and member of that prestigious intellectual society the Institute of France under the Directory, played a role in the Bonapartist coup d'état of 18–19 Brumaire (November 1799), held a variety of conspicuous positions under Napoleon, and, following retirement under the Bourbon Restoration, resumed an active role in the Institute and in political affairs from 1830 until his death five years later. Former Provençal counselor d'André, undaunted by exile, founded a model farm at Vienna under the aegis of that city's Société Imperiale d'Agriculture; returning in later years to France, he held a number of important offices in Louis XVIII's government before his decease in 1825. Savoye de Rollin, erstwhile *avocat-général* at Grenoble, served in the Tribunate and as prefect under Napoleon, and was later deputy from Isère to the national legislature; his former colleague Jean-Pierre Bachasson de Montalivet served successively as prefect, councilor of state and minister of the interior under the Empire, and was made a peer in Restoration France.

One-time Grenoblois President de Barral de Montferrat not only managed to survive the vicissitudes of the revolutionary period but actually was mayor of Grenoble during the Terror of 1793–94 (thereby acquiring his permanent sobriquet "Citizen Barral"); he again took up the role of prominent man of the robe under Napoleon, who promoted him to the first presidency of the Cour d'Appel at Grenoble. The former Norman counselor Louis-Jacques Grossin de Bouville turned up as vice president of the National Assembly from 1820 to 1830; a former colleague, President Lambert de Frondeville, served as Napoleonic prefect and was later elevated to the peerage, while yet another former *parlementaire* of Rouen, President Le Cordier de Bigars de La Londe, was the mayor of Versailles in 1816. A former Bordelais president named (somewhat incongruously) Lynch was a Napoleonic mayor of Bordeaux and a count of the Empire; turning his coat in 1814, however, he handed Bordeaux over to the invading British and was awarded a peerage by a grateful Louis XVIII! Yet such noteworthy individual histories were the exception: most *parlementaires* of old wishing to resume public service settled for inconspicuous if honorable membership in the tribunals of the new regime (witness, for example, presidential memorialist Fauris de Saint-Vincent at Aix) or served in the bureaucracy or deliberative councils of government.

Of course, in provincial France as at Paris, there were cases of personal tragedy to set against sagas of striking or merely humdrum success. The Terror, we have already noted, struck capriciously at the personnel of the *parlements*. Judicial ranks at Toulouse were truly devastated: perhaps fifty-five magistrates, more than half of Languedoc's *parlementaires*, were dispatched by the "scythe of equality," most of them in three great "batches" in Prairial and Messidor of Year II (spring and summer 1794). The officers of the *parquet* were spared; it was above all the regular lay and clerical counselors, and to a lesser extent the *présidents à mortier*, whose ranks were so bloodily reduced. Most of the victims, it appears, had signed sundry collective protests against the excesses of the Revolution, slipped across the border into Spain, returned under amnesties, and been caught when the Convention had annulled those amnesties. About half as many former Bordelais *parlementaires* fell beneath the poised and unrelenting blade of the guillotine, twenty-five of these after the quashing of Bordeaux's Federalist revolt in 1793. Among the victims were former President Pichard, Avocat-Général Saige, and Procureur-Général Dudon the younger. (At least twenty-seven other Bordelais judges were imprisoned as "suspects" during the Year II.)

Elsewhere, the Revolution left a less sanguinary mark upon the old judiciary. Dijon apparently lost only ten of its former high justices among those "assassinated" or executed: they included two members of the Micault de Courbeton family and one member of the Richard de Ruffey family. As notable victims who had in earlier years dispensed justice in other provincial *parlements* we can indicate only First President de Bérulle at Grenoble, First President Hocquart at Metz, and Procureur-Général La Chalotais at Rennes. The Revolution may have spared the old parlementary ranks altogether at Douai, Nancy, Pau, Perpignan, Colmar, and Besançon.

Thus, if the new France conferred luminous careers upon only a minority of the erstwhile *parlementaires*, at least, in her bloody infancy, she proved equally unwilling (save at Toulouse) to strike down more than a minority of former jurists. Even if we add to those swept away by the revolutionary torrent the undoubtedly larger numbers of former magistrates who fled the realm, or were incarcerated as "suspects," or suffered in some other fashion during the perilous 1790s, we can still assert with confidence warranted by the substantial research cited earlier that the Revolution proved more devastating to the professional than to the personal lives of most men of the old regime's *parlements*. We can also reiterate—although more work on this subject remains to be done—that after 1789 most of these Frenchmen quietly went about the business of ensuring that they and their progeny would survive and in fact flourish within the comfortable elite of the new regime. Whether or not they ever again donned the somber robes of justice, these prideful former *parlementaires* and their descendants would lend stability to and derive a renewed status and security from the propertied society of "notables" in nineteenth-century France.

What can we say in reappraising the Parisian and provincial *parlementaires* and the revolution they helped to unleash in the late 1780s? We must first of all disagree with those who have been content to view the judges as irresponsible censors of the crown, or as sponsors of noble insurrection, or as politicians hypocritically mouthing popular propaganda. On all these counts, the magistrates, although hardly as blameless and disinterested as they might like to appear, may be viewed in a kinder light than their many detractors have ever been willing to allow.

There is no gainsaying the ambivalence of the parlementary attitude toward the monarch and his government during the prerevolutionary crisis. As sincerely as the judges championed the centrality of the monarchy in French history, law, and administration—and, after all, sheer self-interest alone would have made them do so—they just as sincerely (again, for partly selfish reasons) upheld proprietary and individual rights in such a fashion as to call into question the finances and administration and hence the practical continuation of that monarchy.

But in endeavoring to appeal directly to Louis XVI over the heads of his ministers, thus differentiating between what they regarded as the king's legitimate authority and what they unflaggingly condemned as "ministerial despotism," the *parlementaires* were only echoing the concern of many a thoughtful Frenchman over what monarchy had become in that century. It had become, to many, a depersonalized, bureaucratic colossus no longer responsive to anyone's will (including the monarch's) and more isolated than ever before from the governed. The magistrates in 1787–88 defined this fundamental constitutional issue more effectively than did any other Frenchmen. They did so, as we have seen, by conjuring up the specter of representative government, by celebrating individual and provincial liberties as "fundamental laws" of the kingdom, and by inveighing against *lits de justice* and *lettres de cachet*.

True, such commentary was in part self-serving. Both at Paris and in the provinces, the *parlementaires*, exercising as they did critical judicial, administrative, and quasi-legislative functions, acted and spoke at times as if their *métier* were exempt from the restraints supposedly operating upon all institutions in France—the crown not excluded. Responding to the inexorably growing pressure of events attending the governmental crisis, the judges began envisioning their profession as a sort of "fourth estate" in the "constitution" that must, henceforth, play an unprecedentedly influential role in public affairs. This was plainly what Duval d'Eprémesnil and his ideological counterparts in the provinces had in mind in 1788. Yet these burgeoning pretensions were themselves part and parcel of the constitutional crisis of the late 1780s. For the special interests (including those of the judiciary) that were rotting eighteenth-century France had been especially able to thrive in the absence of a national consensus upon common rights, obligations, and purposes that only a more representative government could have provided. In defining this issue, therefore, the more perspicacious magistrates had to be uneasily aware that they were digging perilously near the roots of their own traditional authority. Under the circumstances, however, and representing as they did so many different interests in society, the jurists found themselves with no choice but to persevere in a critique of Bourbon governance that would contribute to the demise of both the absolute monarchy and the old magistracy.

Ambivalence similarly characterized parlementary attitudes toward the nobility. If, on the one hand, the justices were moved by legal training, social interest, and sheer concern for law and order to uphold the traditional hierarchy of estates and the established privileges of gentlemen, precisely the same considerations precluded their endorsing, let alone sponsoring, any dramatic concession of political and administrative power to the noblesse as a class. All available evidence suggests that the high robe, Parisian and provincial, would have discountenanced such a novel turn of events—unless, of course, that same high robe had been accorded a commensurate increment of political influence. This is not to say that the *parlementaires* failed to have their "social" impact in the prerevolutionary crisis—far from it. Insofar as they continued to the bitter end to apotheosize their own role in public affairs and defend the world of *privilège* in which that role had flourished, they probably emboldened *all* social groups to flaunt their ambitions before the weakening crown. In particular, the Paris Parlement's fateful invocation of the Estates General of 1614 may have had its "social" effect in 1788 by crystallizing latent tensions within the developing if as yet unrecognized sociopolitical elite of "aristocratic" and "bourgeois" notables.[5] The magistrates, that is to say, played their part in transforming the largely political or constitutional crisis of 1787 and early 1788 into a struggle of social groups for political power and status recognition in late 1788 and 1789. All the same, the preponderant majority of judges would doubtless have preferred no crisis of any kind in 1787–88. They had always derived immense benefit from the balance of social and institutional forces composing the old regime, and wanted to see no challenge mounted to their comfortable world by nobles of the sword or by any other Frenchmen. As we noted earlier, some of their resentful "military" cousins realized this clearly at the time—much more clearly, in fact, than have certain subsequent historians.

In much the same fashion, the *parlementaires* could not always be of one mind in considering people of inferior social station during this critical period. They recognized and championed the Third Estate as an essential counterweight to the first two orders in their cherished "constitution," yet had increasing reason to fear that the *roturiers* themselves might attempt to take public affairs into their own hands. They defended entrepreneurs against Calonne's and Brienne's extended stamp tax and against the bureaucracy, bungling, and higher rates of the French postal service, yet they peppered their protests to the king with denunciations of *traitants*, *capitalistes*, and profiteering *adjudicataires* upon the roads and bridges of the realm. They looked askance at the *menu peuple* as potential disturbers of the peace in city and countryside, and refused in the clutch to go along with judicial reforms that might in some small measure have ameliorated their lot, yet they displayed genuine if limited sympathy for them as *taillables*, *corvéables*, and consumers. The magistrates' overall advocacy of the commonalty may have been found inadequate by the standards of a revolutionary and postrevolutionary France, but the rush of many literate and illiterate *roturiers* to support the stricken law courts in 1788 suggests a less harsh assessment of the *parlementaires* in the commoner's mind of even the very, very late *ancien régime*. Indeed, it is ironically true that when the judges spoke up for provincial rights in the face of an encroaching central authority, upbraided the ministers for their heavy direct taxation, and accused "hoarders" and "monopolists" of conspiring to starve the *menu peuple*, they were but anticipating the rhetoric of a thousand and one revolutionary tribunes.

And so the justices of the *parlements*, for all their shortcomings, were not altogether irresponsible in censuring the government, nor altogether wedded to the pretensions of the nobility, nor altogether disingenuous in styling themselves paladins of the "people." It is the second of these findings that is likely to arouse the most controversy among specialists in this period. Until quite recently it was unchallenged orthodoxy that the French Revolution's fundamental causation lay in the dialectical tension between a rising "capitalist" bourgeoisie and a resurgent "feudal" nobility in the eighteenth century, and that the upheaval began as a series of "class" revolts—aristocratic, bourgeois, urban popular, and rural popular—against a bankrupt government and (in the last three episodes) against the aristocracy as well.[6] Yet the plausibility of this celebrated thesis, at least insofar as the outbreak of revolution in the late 1780s is concerned, has always rested in large part upon the assumption that the *parlements*, as the most consistent standard-bearers and rallying points of antigovernment rebellion in 1787–88, were promoting the cause of a politically resurgent nobility. We can now say, however, with a fair degree of certitude, that this was not the case: not only did the magistrates, Parisian *and* provincial, fail to display any enthusiasm whatsoever about the prospect of political insurrection within the noblesse at this crucial point, but on more than one occasion they positively opposed what they could have interpreted as manifestations of such a development. For that matter, even when it came to upholding established socioeconomic privileges, one of the most prized of parlementary roles, the judges proved to be solicitous about French folk in every conceivable walk of life (including themselves, naturally) and not only about gentlemen of the sword. If, in displaying such solicitude, the *parlementaires* quickened political ambition within the nobility, they patently aroused commoners as well.

The conclusion therefore seems inescapable that there *was* no concerted "aristocratic revolution" in 1787–88, but rather a nationwide antiministerial uprising led most consistently by the *parlements* that articulated a multitude of social interests within the kingdom and which eventually emboldened individuals in whom those interests were vested to take matters into their own hands. This having apparently been the case, "revisionist" historians today seem justified in arguing that the long-standing socioeconomic explanation of the Revolution's genesis can no longer serve, at least insofar as the immediate origins of that upheaval are concerned, and perhaps with respect to long-term causation as well.

This is not to say that scholars casting about for a plausible alternative explanation of the Revolution's origins have been in all cases willing to jettison social causation. The distinguished English historian Alfred Cobban, for instance, endeavored to reconceptualize the Revolution's social causes by turning the orthodox interpretation upon its head. "The revolutionary bourgeoisie," Cobban averred, "was primarily the declining class of *officiers* and the lawyers and other professional men, and not the businessmen of commerce and industry." Rather than representing "a step forward in the direction of a more developed capitalist economy," the Revolution "at least in some fundamental respects. . . . may have retarded" and not accelerated "the growth of a modern capitalist economy in France." Cobban was able to adduce considerable evidence in support of his thesis. He could, for example, cite the crushing preponderance of erstwhile lawyers and *officiers* of the old regime in the assemblies and committees of the revolutionary era. More significantly, perhaps, he could also cite data suggesting stagnation or downright decline in the financial, commercial, and industrial sectors of the early nineteenth-century French economy.[7] Furthermore, our own statistics documenting the overall decline in the value of parlementary offices in the course of the eighteenth century may in some senses confirm, at least with regard to the high judiciary, Cobban's characterization of old regime *officiers* as a "declining class."

On the other hand, Cobban's enlightened and useful assault upon the orthodox school's misuse of terms such as "feudalism" and "bourgeoisie" unfortunately did not prevent him from speaking of what must now strike us as an outdated concept: namely, "that *révolte nobiliaire* against the royal government with which the revolutionary movement had begun in 1787-8, and which had been an attempt to set up or—it was believed—revive, aristocratic government."[8] Cobban's readiness to carry this element of the orthodox rendering of the Revolution's causation into an otherwise unorthodox analysis of prerevolutionary and revolutionary France may have reflected a major failing in his work. Cobban was so preoccupied with socioeconomic terminology and analysis that he could devote little attention to the political and constitutional dimensions of the crisis of the 1780s in France; hence his hasty attempt to bridge the gap between socioeconomic dynamics before 1787 and political dynamics after 1788 by invoking the hoary and simplistic concept of a "noble revolt" in 1787-88. Finally, Cobban himself admitted that the decline in the value of parlementary offices during the eighteenth century was less pronounced than the decline of office values in the inferior tribunals. In any case, we have found no connection between this phenomenon in the sovereign courts and their sociopolitical attitudes in 1787–88.

Cobban's countryman Colin Lucas has proved equally loath to abandon a primary emphasis upon social causation. The interpretation he has propounded, however, is considerably more sophisticated than Cobban's depiction of an "anti-capitalist" revolution precipitated by a *révolte nobiliaire* in 1787–88. Synthesizing a formidable array of studies of eighteenth-century French society, Lucas rejects "the premise that there existed in eighteenth-century France two distinct and antagonistic classes of bourgeois and nobles." Because, according to Lucas, nobles and bourgeois actually belonged to the same propertied elite and therefore betrayed no inclination to proclaim separate "class interests" in the *ancien régime*, the historian's challenge is to explain "why, in 1788–9, groups which can be identified as non-noble combatted and defeated groups which can be identified as noble . . . and why they attacked and destroyed privilege in 1789."[9]

Lucas finds the solution to this conundrum in the specific political situation of the late months of 1788. In September of that year the Paris Parlement invoked the forms and procedures of the 1614 Estates General, thus reviving what had long been an obsolete juridical distinction between "fighters" and "prayers" on the one hand and "workers" on the other. The increasingly homogeneous eighteenth-century elite of noble and bourgeois proprietors, that is to say, was suddenly split along anachronistic lines. Consequently, middling and lower elements in the propertied elite, already afflicted by various economic and social frustrations, now faced the prospect of permanent humiliation in the political sphere as well, as an aroused France prepared to reclaim her representative political institutions. "The revolt of the Third Estate" in 1788–89, if we may believe Lucas, "was a revolt against a loss of status by the central and lower sections of the elite with the approval of those elements of the trading groups which were on the threshold of the elite. It was this social group that became the 'revolutionary bourgeoisie.'" Moreover, by the summer of 1789 the Third Estate's leaders in what was now the National Assembly, facing the "combination of the counter-offensive of the Ancien Régime and anti-privilege pressure from below," were compelled to do that which they had not at all intended originally to do: namely, anathematize the "nobility" as a class and jettison the entire system of "privilege."[10] That many bourgeois themselves had up to now aspired to noble status, and that *all* bourgeois had up to now been "privileged" individuals, could count for nothing in the revolutionized political context of 1789.

It is characteristic of Lucas's emphasis upon social causation that he should speak of "a contraction of social promotion leading to social conflict" and of "various areas within this complex social structure where friction developed during the century, eventually sparking off a revolutionary conflagration." Although he does cursorily discuss noble and bourgeois attitudes toward the absolute monarchy of Louis XV and his successor, and touches upon the role played by the monarchy of earlier times in the evolution of the social elite, Lucas seemingly regards political and constitutional developments primarily as immediate rather than as long-term causes of the revolutionary upheaval in France.[11] Yet, even if we conclude that this English historian has provided us with the most sophisticated conceptualization of social dynamics in eighteenth-century France to date, we may still find his accentuation of the social origins of the Revolution to be somewhat extreme.

It is only fair to scholars like Alfred Cobban and Colin Lucas to note that other specialists have gone to the opposite extreme, envisioning the Revolution's causation almost exclusively in political terms. The U.S. historian George V. Taylor has arrived at particularly radical conclusions. After arguing persuasively that most nobles *and* bourgeois in eighteenth-century France displayed "noncapitalist" or "proprietary" forms of wealth and thus were of the same socioeconomic grouping, Taylor declared roundly that the cataclysm of 1789 and subsequent years "was essentially a political revolution with social consequences and not a social revolution with political consequences."[12] In this rendering, moreover, the "political revolution" was not only devoid of long-term socioeconomic causes, it was also devoid of long-term political causes. For Taylor, 1789 in France represented a fateful but largely fortuitous conjuncture of immediate factors: fiscal crisis in government, failure of the harvest, and so on. The Revolution, then, however profound its consequences for France and indeed for the entire world, was an event without long-term analyzable "origins," a "political crisis" that abruptly and unpredictably became sociopolitical upheaval in the precise context of the year 1789.

More recently, William Doyle, whom we have already encountered as the English historian of the Bordeaux Parlement under Louis XVI, has concurred in part of this. "Down to the spring of 1789," according to Doyle, "the forces pushing France towards revolution were almost entirely political. There was no underlying social crisis; . . . Nor did economic factors play an important part." Admittedly, this scholar, unlike Taylor, has accorded the Revolution systemic and long-term as well as fortuitous and immediate "political origins." Thus, he has conscientiously reviewed those factors (characterized as largely political in nature) whose confluence produced by late 1788 a paralysis in Bourbon governance and a resultant power vacuum that various politicized and competing social groups endeavored to fill. Those primarily political factors (or "origins") included a governmental financial crisis reflecting a surfeit of seventeenth- and eighteenth-century warfare, irresolute royal leadership, bureaucratic infighting and confusion, the unrelenting opposition of the *parlements* and other vested interests to ministerial reforms, an aroused and more "enlightened" public in the *siècle des lumières*, and critical ministerial miscalculations in 1787–88.[13] This kind of interpretation must necessarily prove more satisfactory than that of Taylor to those who assume that "great events" such as revolutions have "great causes." Moreover, Doyle's explanation of the revolution in France is all the more welcome in that it is apparently symptomatic of a growing desire among historians to examine anew the long-neglected political background of that upheaval.[14] It is nonetheless arguable that both Taylor and Doyle have exposed as inadequate an appreciation of the social dimensions of the crisis confronting eighteenth-century France as have Cobban and Lucas of the political and constitutional dimensions of that crisis.

At this point we might well ask whether a *via media* exists between predominantly social and predominantly political explanations of the coming of the Great Revolution? According to François Furet, the dean of "revisionists" in the French Republic, such a middle way does exist. Furet has maintained that "the fundamental crisis of the eighteenth century" involved the dynamic but increasingly dissynchronous relationship between the modernizing state and the evolving elite of noble and bourgeois "notables." On the one hand, the French monarchy was devoting "more money and attention to the great tasks of modernity, such as urban planning, public health, agricultural and commercial improvements, the unification of the market, and education." The provincial intendant, that stalwart embodiment of royal authority, was "at the center of an immense effort of information-gathering and administrative reform, multiplying economic and demographic investigations, rationalizing his operations with the help of the first social statistics ever assembled in France." The "monarchical State of the eighteenth century" was thus "one of the great agents of change and of general progress—a permanent camp of 'enlightened' reform."[15] But there was also profound ambivalence within ruling circles toward the "society of notables." The Bourbons and their servants endeavored to remain faithful to the superannuated ideal of a society of "estates" even as they found themselves acknowledging in a thousand ways the modern society of meritocracy and mobility that their ambitious policies and bureaucraticized procedures were in fact doing so much to create.

On the other hand, little consensus on sociopolitical questions existed within a propertied social elite that was largely excluded from government. Bourgeois "notables" aspired to nobility and (in some cases) to a greater role in public affairs; individual nobles dreamed variously of "decentralizing" the centralized monarchy and reasserting "aristocratic" influence on the local level, or of controlling the centralized "bureaucratic" power for their own purposes, or of participating in "constitutional" and somewhat "representative" government. The nobility as a whole "had only one unifying principle, namely, hostility toward the State in the name of a social identity whose secret it had lost and whose memory it was unable to rekindle." Given this deeply rooted ambivalence of elite society toward government, and of the latter toward the former, neither monarch nor noblesse could come forward "with a policy or a set of institutions that might have integrated the State and the ruling society around a minimum of consensus." In actuality, the "two antagonistic poles" of eighteenth-century France, "the State and society, became increasingly incompatible."[16]

Furet's analysis is provocative and undeniably helpful, for it seems to prepare the way for an explanation of the Revolution's genesis that can comprehend the political *and* the social dynamics of the late *ancien régime* and satisfactorily characterize their interaction. Nevertheless, it is questionable whether this postulation of a dysfunctional relationship between government and the elite among the governed enables us, in its present form, to bridge the prodigious chasm between eighteenth-century politics-and-society-as-usual and the revolutionary process of 1789 and beyond.

The chasm might be bridged, and the dynamic interaction between state and elite society more acutely understood, were we to lay much greater stress upon France's geopolitical traditions and role at this particular point in the history of international relations. Intriguingly, it is precisely this kind of historical factor—the role played by the state in international power politics—that U.S. sociologist Theda Skocpol has cited as crucial to explaining the onset not only of the French Revolution but also of the Russian and Chinese revolutions.[17] In particular reference to the French case, Skocpol notes accurately that the Bourbons and their ministers were inveigled by their realm's "amphibious geography" into endeavoring simultaneously to achieve and maintain supremacy over the continental European powers and to prevail over the English in the ever-widening struggle for overseas colonies and maritime commerce. Over the long run, the implications of such an ambitious foreign policy for the finances and, consequently, the sheer viability of the absolute French monarchy were catastrophic. The critical point, Skocpol avers, is not that the waging of war left Louis XVI's advisers burdened with enormous annual deficits and an astronomical long-term debt. The ministers of Louis XV and Louis XIV had necessarily grappled with the same problems and had ultimately been able (at least in the short run) to extricate the French state from its difficulties. The telling point is that the policymakers of the 1770s and 1780s, unlike their predecessors, could not resort to extorting moneys from the "accountants, tax farmers, and other financiers" in Chambres de Justice (extraordinary judicial proceedings). Nor could they streamline the administration of these increasingly parasitical fiscal agents. Such individuals were by now untouchable—untouchable primarily because they had in the course of the eighteenth century bought their way in large numbers into the nobility, into elite society.[18]

But this last insight brings us back to the notion of an increasingly dissynchronous relationship between state and elite society in the eighteenth century. As Skocpol remarks, in adopting and elaborating that postulation, the "dominant class" was "dependent upon the absolutist state and implicated in its international mission." Landlords "no longer controlled significant means of coercion at local levels" and hence "depended upon the absolutist administration as their protector of last resort" against the peasantry. Moreover, the social elite profited handsomely from "the various seigneurial, corporate, and provincial institutions that were preserved under the umbrella of absolutism." Such institutions "expressed and reinforced the advantages of the richer propertied against the poorer," for they conferred upon members of the elite "state-enforced tax advantages and opportunities for income." Again, the absolute monarchy's "capacity to promote the military success and to tax the economic expansion of the country" meant military employment and/or additional economic security for "nobles" and certainly the latter for "bourgeois." For all these reasons, then, the members of the "dominant class"—and most fatefully, if we accept Skocpol's thesis, the ennobled *financiers*—would have been well advised to remain faithful to the absolutist French state. Unfortunately, however, the "dominant class" that included the strategically situated financiers "was also economically interested in minimizing royal taxation of its wealth and capable of exerting political leverage against the absolutist monarchy through its institutional footholds within the state apparatus." Thus, Skocpol concludes, when the eighteenth-century crown's "unquenchable penchant for war" landed it in "an acute financial crisis, it faced a socially consolidated dominant class" that was not amenable to ministerial arguments invoking *raison d'état*.[19]

This is Skocpol's explication of the climactic confrontation of 1787–88 between the belligerent absolutist state and the "socially consolidated dominant class," which we know more conventionally as the "prerevolution" or "prerevolutionary crisis."[20] In the end, the reformist avatars of the absolutist tradition (Calonne, Loménie de Brienne, Lamoignon) could not convince the entrenched elite that a reduction of its privileges was unavoidable under the circumstances. The noblesse and the *parlements* rejected the state's modernizing legislation; the clergy and certain provincial Estates refused the state critical funds; army officers unwilling or reluctant to suppress insurrection in effect denied the state its wonted monopoly of the means of physical coercion; the equivocal attitude of many financiers toward the authorities powerfully contributed to the sudden collapse of state credit in August 1788; and certain bourgeois notables began in their polemical tracts and speeches to make the social elite's antigovernment cause that of "the nation." Once the "dominant class" started to splinter over the issue of how, precisely, political power was to be apportioned among social groups in postabsolutist France, the "old-regime administrative system" collapsed, and massive insurrection could well up from below. France was experiencing an unprecedented "societal political crisis" by early 1789; the unanticipated peasant revolt in the summer of that year would make a veritable "social-revolutionary transformation" of the kingdom possible.

Theda Skocpol's work, as it applies to France, arguably goes far toward furnishing us with a tenable alternative to the "Marxist" or neo-Marxist explanation of the French Revolution's origins. The cardinal strengths of this explanation are threefold. First, in keeping with the recent revival of interest in political history and in defiance of the long-standing socioeconomic bias of much historiography, it forthrightly identifies the "international mission" of the prerevolutionary French state as the key dynamic factor in the gestation of a revolutionary situation in France. Second, it "preserves" social causation by reconceptualizing it in a fruitful manner. That is to say, it posits an elite society (or "dominant class") that was in part formed by and became increasingly reliant upon the warring absolutist Bourbon state but whose obdurate defense of its privileged position helped doom that state; and it acknowledges the central role played by the peasantry in transforming the "societal political crisis" of 1789 into a genuine social revolution. Third, it provides a convincing transition from the traditional politics and society of the old regime to the revolutionary process of 1789–99 by treating the crisis of 1787–88 as a confrontation (in some ways classic) between Bourbon governance and elite French society that gradually got out of control.

At the same time, however, we would be inclined to modify some elements in this interpretation. In the first place, the "international mission" of the eighteenth-century Bourbon state looks even more problematical to us than it does to Skocpol when we recall both that the English adversary was in the midst of an agricultural and commercial revolution and on the brink of an industrial transformation and that

Russia and Prussia were in the process of joining the Hapsburg state as powerful and dangerous continental rivals of France. Given this conjuncture of international developments, the Bourbon state by the late eighteenth century was more hard pressed than ever before to maintain what it persisted in viewing as its rightful greatness upon both land and sea.

Next, in the wake of François Furet's analysis we need to place a special emphasis upon the gradual maturation of *dysfunction* in the dynamic relationship between state and society in eighteenth-century France. We may well wonder how state and elite society could have possibly failed to become ever more "incompatible" when, on the one hand, the modernizing state was increasingly torn between irreconcilable visions of social organization, and, on the other hand, the emerging "society of notables" was increasingly divided over the proper institutionalization of political power. If, moreover, France's geopolitical ambitions genuinely did constitute the prime force behind the modernization of French governance and of elite French society, and hence behind the growing incompatibility in relations between state and society, we may note with the percipience of hindsight that the persistence of those geopolitical ambitions into the future would cast a long shadow over revolutionary and postrevolutionary France.

Further, in modifying Skocpol's interpretation, we would recall, as students of the high magistracy, that the *parlementaires* in 1787–88 saw themselves as articulating "popular" as well as "dominant class" interests. In other words, rather than finding the postulation of a "dominant class" insurgency against the crown in 1787–88 altogether satisfactory, we would prefer to speak once again of "a nationwide antiministerial uprising led most consistently by the parlements that articulated a multitude of social interests within the kingdom and which eventually emboldened individuals in whom those interests were vested to take matters into their own hands." Patently, the crown from 1787 on had to reckon with a social phenomenon even more complex than a "dominant" or "elite" class of politicized French individuals.

Finally, we might question whether the peasant insurrection of the summer of 1789, as dramatic and significant as it undoubtedly was, played quite as pivotal a role in furthering the revolutionary process in France as did the analogous upheavals in Russia and China. The middle and lower bourgeoisie, more consequential in late eighteenth-century France than in early twentieth-century Russia and China, may have played a commensurately greater role in the first revolution than in the latter two upheavals.

We may wonder, in conclusion, how fully Calonne could have grasped the need for a reintegration of state and society, for a new consensus upon national purposes, rights, and duties, when he submitted his fateful memorandum on reform to his royal master in August 1786. He did at least recognize the need for some significant changes in government and society—and for some form of national consultation upon those changes. He had been driven to that act of recognition by government fiscal difficulties whose roots lay in the imperatives of international politics and in the derivative and growing estrangement between state and elite society. In the end, France's political and social requirements would somehow have to be meshed, brought together in a new dynamic harmony, were she to proceed with confidence upon the uncharted path of the future. The men of the *parlements* in 1787–88 were groping their way toward this central issue of government and the governed—even if, in doing so, they were unknowingly contributing to the cataclysmic demise of a world that most of them had never really wanted to abandon.

Notes

INTRODUCTION

1. This recapitulation of events is based upon Egret, *The French Prerevolution*.

2. The post of keeper of the seals was the highest in French justice when the chancellor, appointed traditionally for life, was in retirement. In this case, Miromesnil had held the seals since the disgrace in 1774 of Chancellor René-Nicolas-Charles-Augustin de Maupeou. In February 1771, Chancellor Maupeou had attempted to curtail the political role and ameliorate the justice of the sovereign courts. He had thoroughly reorganized the *parlements*, abolished venality (and thus secure tenure) of office, reduced judicial fees, and implemented many other reforms. In 1774, however, Maupeou had been abandoned by Louis XV's young successor Louis XVI, and the old parlementary personnel and ways of justice had been reinstated.

3. He did not, however, assume Calonne's title of controller general, which passed to several other individuals in succession. The archbishop was later to be named principal minister.

4. From, that is, several of the fourteen provincial tribunals officially designated as "parlements," "sovereign councils," or "superior courts."

5. The royal accounts had also been solicited by, and eventually submitted to, the Notables.

6. See, for example, Marion, *Histoire financière*, 1; Marion, *Le Garde des Sceaux Lamoignon*; Cobban, *A History of Modern France*, 1: 67; and Alatri, *Parlamenti e lotta politica*.

7. As examples, consult Tocqueville, *The Old Regime and the French Revolution*; and Flammermont, *Remontrances*, 3: xlvi–xlvii.

8. Mathiez, *The French Revolution*, pp. 7–8, 24, 31; Lefebvre, *The French Revolution*, 1: 88; Soboul, *The French Revolution*, pp. 28, 37, 91, 111; Ford, *Robe and Sword*, pp. 246, 251; Bluche, *Les Magistrats du Parlement de Paris*, pp. 138, 288–89, 382; and Palmer, *The Age of the Democratic Revolution*, 1: 458–65.

9. Although even those who concede to the *parlements* a legitimate "constitutional" role in eighteenth-century France have acknowledged the judges' selfish interests and their recklessness in advocating principles tending toward constitutional monarchism. See notably Carré, *La Fin des Parlements*, pp. 17–19; Carré, "La Tactique et les idées de l'opposition parlementaire"; Carcassonne, *Montesquieu et le problème de la constitution française*, chap. 6; and Bickart, *Les Parlements et la notion de souveraineté nationale*.

10. All citations of this work will be from its English translation by Camp, *The French Prerevolution*. All translations of quoted material from French documents and sources are my own.

11. Egret had done so as well in earlier writings. See Egret, "Les Origines de la Révolution en Bretagne"; "La Révolution aristocratique en Franche-Comté et son échec, 1788–89"; and "La Pré-Révolution en Provence."

12. Egret, *Le Parlement de Dauphiné*.

13. Doyle, *The Parlement of Bordeaux.*
14. Stone, *The Parlement of Paris.*
15. Among the leading salvos in this assault: Cobban, *The Social Interpretation of the French Revolution;* Eisenstein, "Who Intervened in 1788? A Commentary on *The Coming of the French Revolution*"; Taylor, "Noncapitalist Wealth and the Origins of the French Revolution"; Richet, "Autour des origines idéologiques lointaines de la Révolution française"; Doyle, "Was There an Aristocratic Reaction in Pre-revolutionary France?"; Lucas, "Nobles, Bourgeois, and the Origins of the French Revolution"; Furet, *Penser la Révolution française;* and Doyle, *Origins of the French Revolution.*

CHAPTER I

1. There was, in addition, a "superior council" at Bastia (Corsica) and a "provincial council" at Arras (Artois).
2. On the origins of the Paris Parlement, see Marion, *Dictionnaire des institutions,* pp. 422–33; and Shennan, *The Parlement of Paris,* pp. 9–28, 78–85.
3. Péguilhan de Larboust, "Les magistrats du parlement de Toulouse," pp. 18–20; and Forster, *The Nobility of Toulouse,* pp. 18–19.
4. Doyle, *The Parlement of Bordeaux,* pp. 5–6.
5. Egret, *Le Parlement de Dauphiné,* 1: 1–5.
6. Colombet, *Les Parlementaires Bourguignons,* p. 29; Wolff, *Le Parlement de Provence,* pp. 1–5; Robinne, "Les magistrats du parlement de Normandie à la fin du XVIIIe siècle," pp. 1–3; and Le Moy, *Le Parlement de Bretagne,* pp. 3–7.
7. Delmas, *Du Parlement de Navarre,* pp. 105–9.
8. Michel, *Histoire du Parlement de Metz,* Introduction and chap. 1.
9. Pillot, *Histoire du Parlement de Flandres,* 1: 1–2.
10. Gresset, *Le Monde judiciaire,* 1: 53–54.
11. Mahuet, *La Cour souveraine de Lorraine et Barrois,* pp. 25–111.
12. Pillot and Neyremand, *Histoire du Conseil souverain d'Alsace,* chap. 1.
13. Galibert, *Le Conseil souverain de Roussillon,* pp. 17–28.
14. These included the Chambre des Comptes, Cour des Aides, and Cour des Monnaies at Paris and Chambre des Comptes and Cour des Aides in most provinces. Several of the provincial *parlements,* however, discharged all the functions of these specialized courts, which involved surveillance over taxes and other financial matters.
15. Refer again to Marion, *Dictionnaire des institutions,* pp. 422–33, and to Shennan, *The Parlement of Paris,* pp. 9–28 and 78–85, for the following discussion of the law courts' judicial roles.
16. Shennan, *The Parlement of Paris,* p. 79.
17. On the *parlements'* administrative functions, consult the pertinent sections of Marion, *Dictionnaire des institutions;* Shennan, *The Parlement of Paris;* and the works on the provincial courts cited in earlier notes.
18. Shennan, *The Parlement of Paris,* pp. 159–60 and 185–86.
19. Consult Hanley, *The Lit de Justice of the Kings of France.*
20. On this point, see, for example, Péguilhan de Larboust, "Les magistrats du parlement de Toulouse," pp. 20–23; Egret, *Le Parlement de Dauphiné,* 2: 4; Doyle, *The Parlement of Bordeaux,* pp. 6–7; Wolff, *Le Parlement de Provence,* p. 272; and Robinne, "Les magistrats du parlement de Normandie," pp. 6–25.
21. That is to say, the senior chamber's presidents succeeded to the first presi-

dency in order of seniority. The presidents of this period customarily inherited their offices from fathers or uncles, or acquired them in some other fashion involving family connections.

22. This functionary should not be confused with the judicial *rapporteurs* appointed in litigation to evaluate the litigants' evidence and suggest judgments to their fellow jurists.

23. Bibl. nat., MS Nouv. acq. fr. 945, p. 238.

24. As, for example, in a controversy of 1783–84. See Stone, "The Old Regime in Decay: Judicial Reform and the Senior Parlementaires at Paris, 1783–84."

25. On the Enquêtes and Requêtes, consult Marion, *Dictionnaire des institutions*, p. 425, and the pertinent sections of the works on the individual law courts cited in previous notes.

26. The chamber of Requêtes was officially called the Chambre des Requêtes du Palais. Its members long insisted that they were simultaneously *parlementaires and* holders of special royal commissions to dispense the civil justice associated with royal letters of *committimus*.

27. Bibl. nat., MS Nouv. acq. fr. 945, p. 238.

28. The issue of vestigial serfdom in Franche-Comté helped to poison relations between the Comtois judges and the crown in the 1770s and 1780s when the *parlementaires* refused to ratify royal legislation abolishing *mainmorte* on royal domain. Gresset, *Le Monde judiciaire*, 2: 1161–95.

29. Wolff (*Le Parlement de Provence*) discusses this and some less widely known institutional peculiarities at Aix.

30. Egret, *Le Parlement de Dauphiné*, 1: 4–5.

31. See Robinne, "Les magistrats du parlement de Normandie," pp. 6–25, for this and other peculiarities at Rouen.

32. In the Paris Parlement and several provincial *parlements*, twenty years of service conferred nobility upon a previously nonnoble judge—who would then pass this nobility on to his son. This was the so-called *noblesse transmissible au premier degré*. Elsewhere, under the formula *patre et avo consulibus*, two consecutive generations of parlementary service would confer nobility upon the heir. Egret, "L'Aristocratie parlementaire française à la fin de l'Ancien Régime," pp. 6–7.

33. See Bluche, *Les Magistrats du Parlement de Paris*; and Egret, "L'Aristocratie parlementaire française," pp. 1–14. Also useful: *Almanach royal* for 1775–90; and Roton, *Les Arrêts du Grand Conseil*.

34. Presidents in these inferior chambers lacked the prestigious *mortiers* and were little more than counselors designated to supervise affairs in their respective chambers; they were not, as were the presidents in the senior chamber, executives of the whole tribunal.

35. For these statistics regarding the post-1774 personnel, see Egret, "L'Aristocratie parlementaire française." A few clerics also entered the Enquêtes and Requêtes under Louis XVI, but they were greatly outnumbered by the lay entrants.

36. Again, Bluche, *Les Magistrats du Parlement de Paris*; and Egret, "L'Aristocratie parlementaire française," are essential. Also of use: *Almanach royal* for 1775–90, and Roton, *Les Arrêts du Grand Conseil*.

37. Quoted in Meyer, *La Noblesse bretonne*, 2: 935.

38. Ibid.

39. Ibid., 2: 930.

40. Ibid., 2: 936, 957.

41. That is to say, of 52 lay counselors entering the court in these years, 17

issued from parlementary families, while the other 35 newcomers without exception boasted *noblesse ancienne.* I derive this information from Jean Egret's unpublished research.

42. Meyer, *La Noblesse bretonne,* 2: 957–59. Unions with daughters of the *haute bourgeoisie* could usually be explained at Rennes (as elsewhere) by the attraction of middle-class wealth.

43. Ibid., 2: 955–56.

44. I am again indebted to Egret's unpublished research for this information.

45. This very interesting decree is discussed by Wolff, *Le Parlement de Provence,* pp. 15–21.

46. Ibid., for this information.

47. For these data pertaining to the Toulousain magistrates, consult Péguilhan de Larboust, "Les magistrats du parlement de Toulouse," pp. 33–39, 48–51, 52–56.

48. Ibid., pp. 53–56.

49. Ibid., pp. 33–36, for these data.

50. Ibid., pp. 36–39, for these statistics concerning dynastic and marital tendencies at Toulouse.

51. The primary source for data upon the Grenoblois is Egret, *Le Parlement de Dauphiné,* 1: 20–24, and 2: 27–30, 34–36.

52. For the information specifically pertaining to the 19 lay counselors admitted to the court under Louis XVI, I am again indebted to the unpublished papers of Egret.

53. Gresset, *Le Monde judiciaire.* Gresset's dissertation has been republished under the title *Gens de justice à Besançon: De la conquête par Louis XIV à la Révolution française, 1674–1789,* 2 vols. (Paris: Bibliothèque nationale, 1978).

54. See Gresset, *Le Monde judiciaire,* 1: 407, 415–16, for the data in this paragraph.

55. Ibid., 1: 375–76, 468–69, 476–85, 543–58, for the following data.

56. Robinne, "Les magistrats du parlement de Normandie," pp. 36–108, for the data for Normandy.

57. Doyle, *The Parlement of Bordeaux,* pp. 12–22, for the following data.

58. For the following statistics, refer to Colombet, *Les Parlementaires Bourguignons,* pp. 37–64. A fine point: 117 of Colombet's 120 Burgundian judges actually served in the court under Louis XVI; the 3 others were active only into the 1760s.

59. The following information on the personnel of the lesser *parlements* is culled from Egret, "L'Aristocratie parlementaire française," and Egret's private papers.

60. Bluche, *Les Magistrats du Parlement de Paris,* pp. 151–52.

61. For the following examples and data, consult Carré, *La Fin des Parlements,* pp. 2–3; Bluche, *Les Magistrats du Parlement de Paris,* pp. 188–91; and Bluche, *L'Origine des magistrats du Parlement de Paris* under the appropriate names.

62. These comments concerning the levels of affluence in Brittany's *parlement* are based on Meyer, *La Noblesse bretonne,* 2: 962–67, 976, 978, 980–86.

63. Sentou, *Fortunes et groupes sociaux à Toulouse,* esp. pp. 84–92. Also useful: Sentou, *La Fortune immobilière des Toulousains et la Révolution française.*

64. Gresset, *Le Monde judiciaire,* 2: 653, 796–814.

65. Doyle, *The Parlement of Bordeaux,* pp. 52–64.

66. Consult Colombet, *Les Parlementaires Bourguignons,* esp. pp. 70–78, for some germane information. See also the comparisons drawn between Comtois and Burgundian parlementary wealth in Gresset, *Le Monde judiciaire,* 2: 812–14.

67. Wolff, *Le Parlement de Provence*, pp. 31–35.

68. The source of the following information is Egret, *Le Parlement de Dauphiné*, 1: 27–28, 32–35, and 2: 35.

69. On the degrees of parlementary affluence at Rouen, see Robinne, "Les magistrats du parlement de Normandie," pp. 139–56.

70. On the composition of parlementary fortunes at Paris, consult Bluche, *Les Magistrats du Parlement de Paris*, pp. 150–55.

71. Gresset, *Le Monde judiciaire*, 2: 772.

72. Sentou, *Fortunes et groupes sociaux à Toulouse*, p. 84.

73. Robinne, "Les magistrats du parlement de Normandie," pp. 156–58, 187–236, for analysis of these attributes of magisterial wealth at Rouen.

74. Meyer, *La Noblesse bretonne*, 2: 968–79.

75. Colombet, *Les Parlementaires Bourguignons*, pp. 98–151; Doyle, *The Parlement of Bordeaux*, pp. 65–101; and Egret, *Le Parlement de Dauphiné*, 1: 33–35 and 2: 53, 70 (for examples of jurists' obsession with the land in Dauphiné).

76. See, on the subject of the Toulousain judges' exploitation of their lands, Forster, *The Nobility of Toulouse*, pp. 31–101, and Sentou, *Fortunes et groupes sociaux à Toulouse*, pp. 103–6.

77. William Doyle discusses this in *The Parlement of Bordeaux*, esp. pp. 65–101.

78. For some other regional examples of how late eighteenth-century *parlementaires* exploited their rural holdings in land, see Gresset, *Le Monde judiciaire*, pp. 704–71; Robinne, "Les magistrats du parlement de Normandie," pp. 187–236; and Colombet, *Les Parlementaires Bourguignons*, pp. 98–151.

79. For some interesting commentary upon provincial magistrates as *rentiers*, see Doyle, *The Parlement of Bordeaux*, pp. 58–59, 105–6; Colombet, *Les Parlementaires Bourguignons*, pp. 75–77; and Sentou, *Fortunes et groupes sociaux à Toulouse*, pp. 84, 106–10.

80. For examples of computations of revenue from eighteenth-century parlementary office, consult Bluche, *Les Magistrats du Parlement de Paris*, pp. 168–72; Wolff, *Le Parlement de Provence*, pp. 227–41; Gresset, *Le Monde judiciaire*, 2: 664–78; Doyle, *The Parlement of Bordeaux*, pp. 40–42; and Colombet, *Les Parlementaires Bourguignons*, pp. 68–69.

81. Bluche, *Les Magistrats du Parlement de Paris*, pp. 160–68. Sources for the following provincial statistics: Gresset, *Le Monde judiciaire*, 1: 206–10; Wolff, *Le Parlement de Provence*, pp. 31–35; Meyer, *La Noblesse bretonne*, 2: 937–41; Colombet, *Les Parlementaires Bourguignons*, pp. 61–63; Robinne, "Les magistrats du parlement de Normandie," pp. 159–73; Péguilhan de Larboust, "Les magistrats du parlement de Toulouse," pp. 59–65; Doyle, *The Parlement of Bordeaux*, pp. 27–29; and Egret, *Le Parlement de Dauphiné*, 1: 18–19 and 2: 36–37. Omitted here are price calculations for offices of clerical judges of all chambers, lay counselors of Requêtes, and king's men. Parquet offices were, of course, very few in number; clerical and Requêtes offices were customarily worth less than those of lay counselors of Grand' Chambre and Enquêtes. The prices of all these offices, nonetheless, fluctuated in broadly similar fashion during the eighteenth century.

82. See Doyle, *The Parlement of Bordeaux*, pp. 29–31; Gresset, *Le Monde judiciaire*, 1: 206–10; Colombet, *Les Parlementaires Bourguignons*, p. 63; Péguilhan de Larboust, "Les magistrats du parlement de Toulouse," p. 59; and Bluche, *Les Magistrats du Parlement de Paris*, pp. 160–68.

83. These comments are derived from Doyle, *The Parlement of Bordeaux*, pp. 102–15; Gresset, *Le Monde judiciaire*, 2: 570–81, 742–72; Colombet, *Les Parlementaires Bourguignons*, pp. 75–77, 81–97; Sentou, *Fortunes et groupes sociaux*

à Toulouse, pp. 85–92, 103–10; Meyer, *La Noblesse Bretonne*, 2: 980–86; Robinne, "Les magistrats du parlement de Normandie," pp. 237–52, 265–78; and Bluche, *Les Magistrats du Parlement de Paris*, pp. 188–226.

84. For especially thorough and interesting discussions of magisterial life in town and country, consult the relevant sections of the works by Bluche, Doyle, Gresset, Colombet, Robinne, Meyer, and Péguilhan de Larboust, cited in earlier notes.

85. For an enumeration of the privileges (both "useful" and "honorific") enjoyed by the judicial noble in common with his cousin of the sword—as well as those privileges he held additionally—see Ford, *Robe and Sword*, pp. 27–29, 66–67. Consult the provincial studies (cited earlier) for enumeration of privileges unique to each provincial court.

86. On private libraries of provincial judges, see Gresset, *Le Monde judiciaire*, 2: 948–58; Doyle, *The Parlement of Bordeaux*, pp. 136–38; Colombet, *Les Parlementaires Bourguignons*, pp. 194–200; Meyer, *La Noblesse bretonne*, 2: 1004–7; Robinne, "Les magistrats du parlement de Normandie," pp. 311–17; and Péguilhan de Larboust, "Les magistrats du parlement de Toulouse," pp. 153–63.

87. On the former, see Carré, "Un Précurseur inconscient de la Révolution"; on the latter, see Somerset, "Le Correspondant français à qui Burke adressa ses Réflexions sur la Révolution française"; and Robert Forster, *Merchants, Landlords, Magistrates*, pp. 177–206.

88. Gresset (*Le Monde judiciaire*) touches upon the professional and social talents of this fascinating Comtois *parlementaire*.

89. President Dupaty's tribulations at Bordeaux are chronicled by Doyle, *The Parlement of Bordeaux*, pp. 177–90.

90. Colombet, *Les Parlementaires Bourguignons*, pp. 208–16.

91. Egret, *Le Parlement de Dauphiné*, 2: 43, 47–48.

92. Meyer, *La Noblesse bretonne*, 2: 1004–7.

93. Robinne, "Les magistrats du parlement de Normandie," pp. 306–10, 317–18.

94. Sentou, *Fortunes et groupes sociaux à Toulouse*, pp. 109–10; and Forster, *The Nobility of Toulouse*, pp. 152–77.

95. Krug-Basse, *Histoire du parlement de Lorraine et Barrois*, p. 376.

96. Pingaud, *Le Président de Vezet*, pp. 11–12, 46–47.

97. Supposedly one had to be twenty-five years old to be a counselor, thirty to serve in the *parquet*, and forty (with ten years of parlementary experience) to be a president. Candidates for office must not have fathers, sons, nephews, uncles, brothers, or in-laws in the court. Candidates also must not hold other offices. But dispensations from all of these requirements (and from legal studies too) were common in most of the courts. See, for example, Wolff, *Le Parlement de Provence*, pp. 39–42; Gresset, *Le Monde judiciaire*, 1: 309–15; Doyle, *The Parlement of Bordeaux*, pp. 24–25, 31–33; and Colombet, *Les Parlementaires Bourguignons*, pp. 54–59.

98. Stone, *The Parlement of Paris*, p. 23. On the Parisian *parlementaires* in the prerevolutionary crisis, see Stone, *The Parlement of Paris*, pp. 22–28, 31–32, 154–55.

99. On Duval d'Eprémesnil's involvement in the mesmerism craze that swept the capital in the 1780s, see Darnton, *Mesmerism and the End of the Enlightenment in France*.

100. Stone, *The Parlement of Paris*, pp. 154–78, for a discussion of the political dynamics within the Paris Parlement in 1787–88.

101. Bachaumont et al., *Mémoires secrets*, 34: 189–94.
102. On these other Provençal *parlementaires*, see Egret, "La Pré-Révolution en Provence," pp. 100, 112–13; and Clapiers-Collongues et al., *Chronologie des Officiers des Cours Souveraines de Provence*, pp. 31–34, 153–58, 167–69.
103. *Journal du Parlement, du Président Fauris de Saint-Vincent*, Bibliothèque Méjanes, MS 1001.
104. Egret, "La Pré-Révolution en Provence," p. 113.
105. Doyle, *The Parlement of Bordeaux*, pp. 144–263, for a detailed treatment of these matters.
106. Bachaumont et al., *Mémoires secrets*, 34: 189–94; and Doyle, *The Parlement of Bordeaux*, pp. 44–46.
107. Bachaumont et al., *Mémoires secrets*, 34: 189–94; and Doyle, *The Parlement of Bordeaux*, p. 45.
108. See Doyle, *The Parlement of Bordeaux*, pp. 43, 45, for portrayals of these judges.
109. On this subject, of course, Jean Egret (*Le Parlement de Dauphiné*, esp. vol. 2) is the acknowledged authority.
110. Ibid., 1: 34–35 and 2: 160. In the books of his library, "the fawning which emboldens despotism and the supineness which allows it to reign peacefully" were "combatted with an equal force." Ibid., 1: 34–35.
111. Ibid., 1: 35–36 and 2: 160.
112. Ibid., 1: 35 and 2: 160–61, for characterizations of Chaléon, Garnier, and Anglès.
113. Ibid., 2: 161. Procureur-Général de Reynaud apparently harbored quite a "liberal" streak himself, having protested repeatedly to Keeper of the Seals Miromesnil and others about the rigors and abuses of the French criminal justice system during the 1780s. Ibid., 2: 44–45.
114. For portrayals of these two *parlementaires*, see Duboul, *La Fin du parlement de Toulouse*, pp. 262–64.
115. On these men of the *parquet* at Toulouse, consult Egret, *The French Prerevolution*, pp. 137–40, 165; and Duboul, *La Fin du parlement de Toulouse*, pp. 322–31.
116. Duboul, *La Fin du parlement de Toulouse*, pp. 123–29.
117. Bachaumont et al., *Mémoires secrets*, 34: 189–94. On this *parlementaire*, and the other principal officers of the court, see Le Moy, *Le Parlement de Bretagne*, pp. 576–78.
118. Bachaumont et al., *Mémoires secrets*, 34: 189–94.
119. Calonne had been the *procureur-général* of the commission established in Brittany in 1765 by Louis XV's government to judge de La Chalotais as the alleged ringleader of parlementary oposition to royal policies in the province.
120. On Euzénou de Kersalaün, see Egret, *The French Prerevolution*, pp. 120, 259 (n. 11). On Du Couëdic de Kergoualer, see his *Précis historique* and its two sequels of the same year.
121. Bachaumont et al., *Mémoires secrets*, 34: 189–94.
122. Ibid. Robinne, "Les magistrats du parlement de Normandie," pp. 328–45, discusses Godart de Belbeuf and other *parlementaires* as rural seigneurs. Some of Godart de Belbeuf's observations on the May Edicts of 1788 are given in Egret, *The French Prerevolution*, p. 157.
123. Egret, *The French Prerevolution*, p. 120. On this judge refer also to d'Estaintot, *Notes manuscrites d'un conseiller au parlement de Normandie*, p. 26.
124. *Gazette de Leyde*, 28 December 1787.

125. As quoted in Egret, *The French Prerevolution*, p. 135. As far back as the early 1760s, Joly de Bévy had been shut up in the Bastille because of his vociferous opposition to government policies and to the activities of the local Estates. See La Cuisine, *Le Parlement de Bourgogne*, 3: 214–42.

126. Egret, *The French Prerevolution*, p. 135.

127. Egret, "L'Aristocratie parlementaire française," pp. 12–13; Ferrand, *Mémoires*, pp. 8–9; Sallier, *Annales françaises*, p. 80; and Pasquier, *Histoire de mon temps*, 1: 27–28.

128. See Egret, "L'Aristocratie parlementaire française," pp. 12–13, for some pertinent statistics. Further information on the ages of the provincial judges can, of course, be culled from the local studies cited in the preceding notes.

129. See Doyle, *The Parlement of Bordeaux*, pp. 24–25, and Robinne, "Les magistrats du parlement de Normandie," pp. 116–23. On the other hand, Robinne does admit that the situation at Rouen regarding the judges' ages was not as extreme as was the situation at Paris.

CHAPTER 2

1. Sallier, *Annales françaises*, pp. 78–79.

2. Barentin, *Mémoire autographe*, pp. 95–96.

3. *Almanach royal* for 1790.

4. Egret, *The French Prerevolution*, p. 97.

5. So asserted Moreau, *Mes Souvenirs*, 2: 356, and Hardy, *Mes Loisirs*, 8: 102–3 (MS Fonds fr. 6687). As late as the *séance royale* of 19 November 1787, though, Tandeau was still discharging the functions of king's *rapporteur* in the Parlement.

6. Refer again to Moreau, *Mes Souvenirs*, 2: 381–83 for particulars on this alleged maneuver by the two magistrates.

7. See, for example, Lescure, *Correspondance secrète*, 2: 364 for rumors concerning Lefebvre d'Amécourt, and Hardy, *Mes Loisirs*, 8: 215 (MS Fonds fr. 6687), for rumors about President Joly de Fleury.

8. For the following comments by the *procureur-général* on this subject, consult Bibl. nat., MS Joly de Fleury 1038, fols. 26–27, and 1041, fols. 109–10. The Notables rejected this proposal for reasons substantially the same as those adduced by Joly de Fleury.

9. For a discussion of this issue and, more specifically, of the judges' memorandum to the government, see Stone, *The Parlement of Paris*, pp. 67–70. In their memorandum the magistrates had spoken of "royal authority, which the Parlements have always defended and indeed have so much interest to defend."

10. *Edit portant création d'assemblées provinciales et municipales* (Versailles, June 1787); see Isambert et al., *Recueil*, 28: 364–66 for the text of this legislation.

11. Bibl. nat., MS Joly de Fleury 1038, fol. 25; see also fol. 20 for more extensive remarks on this question.

12. For the correspondence between President Joly de Fleury and the acquaintance, named Varenne, see ibid., 1042, fols. 76, 77–78.

13. *Administration des pays de Bresse, Bugey, et Gex*. The memoir, dated April 1787, is found in ibid., 1037, fols. 104–8.

14. Ibid., fol. 107.

15. Ferrand, *Mémoires*, p. 10. Also, refer again to the text of the edict in Isambert et al., *Recueil*, 28: 364–66.

16. Hardy, *Mes Loisirs*, 7: 117 (MS Fonds fr. 6686).

17. *Gazette de Leyde* for 3 July 1787. Thus, there was a mixed reaction to the provincial intendants' activities in 1787. The judges could view them as part of the structure of royal (and magisterial) authority in provincial France menaced potentially by the new network of assemblies. At the same time, at least some of the jurists feared that the intendants could acquire altogether too much authority over the assemblies in administrative matters. The *Gazette* in its supplement of 6 July discusses this ambivalence in the Parlement at length.

18. Arch. nat., X^{1B} 8988, plenary session of 5 May 1788.

19. Flammermont, *Remontrances*, 3: 693.

20. *Réflexions d'un magistrat sur la question du nombre et celle de l'opinion par ordre ou par tête.* The pamphlet was dated 7 December. For the full text, see either Bibl. nat., 8° Lb^{39}, 821, or Hardy, *Mes Loisirs*, 8: 165–66 (MS Fonds fr. 6687).

21. Arch. nat., 158 AP 3, dossier 24, letter 19.

22. Ibid., letter 20. Eventually the magistrate's wife did write to the ministers, indignantly protesting her husband's and her own loyalty to the crown. *Lettre de Mme d'Eprémesnil au principal ministre*, Bibl. nat. Duval d'Eprémesnil did not, however, regain his freedom until the autumn.

23. Ferrand, *Mémoires*, p. 30.

24. Duval d'Eprémesnil was elected to the Estates General as a delegate of the nobility and continued to serve as an outspoken apologist for the old regime in that body after its transformation into the National Assembly. On his defense of the king in that assembly, see *Proposition inutilement faite par M. d'Eprémesnil à l'Assemblée (sur l'inviolabilité de la personne royale)*, Bibl. nat. On his subsequent career and execution, see Carré, "Un Précurseur inconscient de la Révolution."

25. *De la nécessité d'assembler les Etats-Généraux dans les circonstances actuelles*, Bibl. nat.

26. *Réflexions sur les pouvoirs et instructions à donner par les provinces à leurs députés aux Etats-Généraux.* Citations are from p. 6.

27. Refer to Arch. nat., X^{1B} 8986, plenary session of 9 February 1787, and Flammermont, *Remontrances*, 3: 694–95, for this address.

28. Bibl. nat., MS Joly de Fleury 1040, fols. 253–54.

29. Refer to the provisions of this legislation in Isambert et al., *Recueil*, 28: 394–400.

30. Turgot had attempted to abolish this abusive practice by legislative means in 1775. The success of his reform remains doubtful, however: the royal tax collectors, heavily pressured in subsequent years to meet their quotas of taxation, must have been as tempted as always to take from the most affluent members of the parish communities what they could not extract from the poorest or most unscrupulous peasants.

31. Flammermont, *Remontrances*, 3: 692.

32. Ibid., 3: 690.

33. On this controversy as it had raged during Necker's first ministry, consult Lardé, *Une Enquête sur les vingtièmes*; and Stone, *The Parlement of Paris*, pp. 77–85, 96–100. Parlementary remonstrances on the issue may be consulted in Flammermont, *Remontrances*, vols. 2 and 3.

34. See, on this episode, *Discours de M. Goislard de Montsabert, conseiller au Parlement de Paris*, Bibl. nat.; and Arch. nat., X^{1B} 8988, plenary session of 29 April 1788.

35. These "supplications" are given in Flammermont, *Remontrances*, 3: 664.

36. Ibid., 3: 665–66, for these reiterated "supplications." The provisions of the stamp tax legislation may be consulted in Isambert et al., *Recueil*, 28: 400–415.

37. On this point, refer to Ferrand, *Mémoires*, p. 12. The remonstrances of 24–26 July 1787 may be consulted in Flammermont, *Remontrances*, 3: 667–75.

38. Flammermont, *Remontrances*, 3: 672.

39. Ibid., 3: 667–68.

40. Ibid., 3: 671. See also Sallier, *Annales françaises*, p. 94, for some interesting comments on Ferrand's authorship of these protests to Louis XVI. The remonstrances offered some illuminating remarks on the difficulties encountered by any reformers endeavoring to slow the growth of government bureaucracy and thus reduce crippling administrative expenses.

41. For the complete text of this provocative *arrêté*, consult Arch. nat., X^{1B} 8988, plenary session of 29 April 1788; or Flammermont, *Remontrances*, 3: 736.

42. These occurred most notably in connection with controversies over royal taxation policies. Indeed, in its remonstrances of January 1778 directed against Necker's attempt to increase the effective yield of the *vingtièmes*, the court had gone so far as to assert that the "sole means of legitimizing taxation" was "to consult the Nation," and that, failing this, the "only means of rendering taxes supportable" was "to consult each individual." Stone, *The Parlement of Paris*, p. 82. But in 1778 convocation of the Estates General was probably the last thing in the world desired by the majority of judges.

43. Flammermont, *Remontrances*, 3: 674, for this fateful advice to the monarch.

44. Ibid., 3: 682.

45. Indeed, it is probably no coincidence that, from 1778 on, parlementary pronouncements upon the taxation issue bore a striking resemblance at times to language of the 1760s and 1770s used upon the same question on the other side of the Atlantic. The judges were as cognizant as any other Frenchmen of events in the British North American colonies, and willing to turn events as well as the writings of philosophes to their purposes.

46. Refer again to Flammermont, *Remontrances*, 3: 693, for this decree.

47. Ibid., 3: 714–15.

48. Ibid., 3: 727, 732.

49. Ibid., 3: 745–46, for this notorious decree, which was also transcribed by Hardy and by other contemporary memorialists.

50. For the original letters, consult Arch. nat., KK 1327, fols. 118–19. See also Hardy, *Mes Loisirs*, 7: 443 (MS Fonds fr. 6686) for details on the session of 9 May 1788.

51. Flammermont, *Remontrances*, 3: 671. Consult the later chapters of Gagliardo's *Enlightened Despotism* for some trenchant observations on the development of the bureaucratic nation-state in late eighteenth-century Europe.

52. Flammermont, *Remontrances*, 3: 736–38. The magistrates had not actually called for the Estates General as early as 6 July 1787, although admittedly their "supplications" of that date, protesting the government's extended stamp tax, were heading in that direction.

53. Ibid., 3: 740.

54. Ibid., 3: 782–84, for Séguier's speech. The anonymous tract was entitled *Délibération à prendre par le tiers état dans toutes les municipalités du Royaume de France.*

55. Flammermont, *Remontrances*, 3: 784–85.

56. Ibid., 3: 786–94. Guillotin had written a *Pétition des citoyens domiciliés à*

Paris for mercantile interests in the capital desiring to contribute to the national debate on the "formation of the Estates General." Ironically, the doctor defended himself against the judges' charges of incitement to "sedition" by referring the magistrates to their own provocative decree of 5 December. Thus came the *parlementaires* to be haunted by their own rhetoric.

57. Flammermont, *Remontrances*, 3: 795, for these agonized plaints by the court's newly created first president.

58. For these comments by Guillaume François Louis Joly de Fleury, see Bibl. nat., MS Joly de Fleury 1040, fol. 321.

59. Of course, they did so necessarily as this was an integral part of the drastic reform of May 1788 aimed against the high robe and its justice. But personal and "philosophical" considerations would have motivated them to oppose such a proposal in any season.

60. Flammermont, *Remontrances*, 3: 690.

61. Ibid., 3: 683–84.

62. Indeed, serfdom to all intents and purposes no longer existed save in Franche-Comté and several smaller regions, notably in eastern France; and even in those circumscribed areas it lacked the rigor of medieval serfdom. On the subordination of the seigneurial courts in the Parlement's jurisdiction to the eighteenth-century *procureurs-généraux*, see Barthélémy, *L'Activité d'un procureur général*, p. 227, n. 1.

63. For these two incidents, occurring in the late 1770s, see Stone, *The Parlement of Paris*, pp. 65–66, 114–15, 117. Furthermore, the jurists had seized the opportunity of a judicial *appel comme d'abus* in 1783 to reassert the supremacy of crown (and, thus, of lay-dominated robe) over miter in French justice. Ibid., p. 66.

64. Bibl. nat., MS Joly de Fleury 2114, fols. 308–9.

65. Flammermont, *Remontrances*, 3: 694–95.

66. Ibid., 3: 782–84. Lefevre d'Ormesson said essentially the same things at about this time in addressing the second Assembly of Notables and (on 21 December) the king himself. On the matter of judicial resentment over clerical immunity from taxation, consult again Stone, *The Parlement of Paris*, pp. 114–15.

67. For these observations, see Bibl. nat., MS Joly de Fleury 1040, fols. 275–76.

68. The magistrates' reflections upon the provincial noblesse, and their memorandum to the king, are discussed in Stone, *The Parlement of Paris*, pp. 115–19. Actually, the memorandum indicated here was the second of two submitted to Louis in 1781 explaining the court's opposition to Necker's provincial assemblies.

69. Bibl. nat., MS Joly de Fleury 1040, fols. 231, 233.

70. Ibid., 1038, fol. 20, for the *procureur-général's* remarks.

71. Ibid., 1037, fols. 104–8.

72. Ibid., fol. 108, for the president's remarks. Even more striking indications of the president's social conservatism in 1787 are to be found in the series of dissertations on French constitutional history that he left among his papers. See in particular the *Résultat de plusieurs vérités qui se trouvent établies par les Monuments de la Première et Deuxième Race des Rois de France*, in ibid., 2116, fols. 42–89; and the president's own favorable reaction to this consistently royalist interpretation of French history, entitled *Réflections sur le mémoire intitulé résultat* (fols. 90–98). A primary theme throughout is the emergence and utility of the Third Estate as a counterweight to the clergy and nobility.

73. Flammermont does not give this decree, but its most crucial provisions appear in Egret, *The French Prerevolution*, p. 197.

74. For these observations, consult Bibl. nat., MS Joly de Fleury 1040, fols. 295–98.

75. Pasquier, *Histoire de mon temps*, 1: 27.

76. Refer again to Ferrand, *Mémoires*, pp. 11–12. An additional indication of persisting misgivings in the court over this issue is the speech given by Huguet de Sémonville in the plenary session of 16 July to overcome just such reservations. For this discourse see *De la nécessité d'assembler les Etats-Généraux*, Bibl. nat.

77. *Rapport de M. l'abbé Tandeau*, Bibl. nat. There is another copy of this discourse in Arch. nat., X^{1B} 8987, plenary session of 19 November 1787.

78. *Procès-verbal de l'assemblée de notables, tenue à Versailles, en l'année 1788*, pp. 68–69 (session of 6 November 1788).

79. Sallier, *Annales françaises*, p. 209. He also remarked that the decree had passed by "a nearly unanimous vote." If true, this is significant, and somewhat ironic, in view of the decree's devastating effect upon the tribunal's popularity.

80. This controversy, and Duval d'Eprémesnil's role in it, are discussed in Stone, *The Parlement of Paris*, pp. 105–8.

81. Flammermont, *Remontrances*, 3: 690.

82. On the opposition within the court to this decree, see esp. Bouillé, *Mémoires*, pp. 63–64; Sallier, *Annales françaises*, p. 228; and Ferrand, *Mémoires*, p. 29.

83. The full text of the decree is given in Flammermont, *Remontrances*, 3: 780–82.

84. Egret, *The French Prerevolution*, p. 203.

85. Refer again to Duval d'Eprémesnil's *Réflexions d'un magistrat*, esp. pp. 4–6. He may have been encouraged in his course of action in early December by other individuals. At least, Sallier claimed that encouragement came from the newly reinstated minister Necker in a letter to the magistrate reproduced in full in *Annales françaises*, pp. 227–28; Ferrand alluded in his *Mémoires*, pp. 29–30, to the influence of Mme d'Eprémesnil, who was allegedly in touch with various "factions" in Paris. Certainly Mme d'Eprémesnil's earlier letter to the ministers (*Lettre de Mme d'Eprémesnil*, Bibl. nat.) hints at numerous political connections in the capital, and Necker may indeed have sought from the Parlement some clarification of its immensely controversial decree of 25 September. Yet Duval d'Eprémesnil would have insisted even without such encouragement that his company play a leading role in defining constitutional issues at this critical juncture.

86. Refer again to Flammermont, *Remontrances*, 3: 782–84, for his speech of 17 December 1788; and consult *La Constitution renversée*, Bibl. nat.

87. See *De la nécessité d'assembler les Etats-Généraux*, Bibl. nat., esp. pp. 2–6.

88. Sallier, *Annales françaises*, pp. 205–8. See also Flammermont, *Remontrances*, 3: 777, for additional details.

89. Sallier, *Annales françaises*, p. 208. On the other hand, it is well to note that even in less tumultuous times the magistrates' obsession about law and order did not preclude their showing solicitude for the rights of suspects and imprisoned criminals. For some examples under Louis XVI, see Stone, *The Parlement of Paris*, pp. 52–56, 73–74.

90. Bibl. nat., MS Joly de Fleury 1037, fols. 104–8.

91. Refer to Flammermont, *Remontrances*, 3: 782–84, for Séguier's antiegali-

tarian oratory of 17 December, and to ibid., 3: 796–97 for Lefevre d'Ormesson's similar sentiments expressed to the king on 21 December. The same parlementary concern helped Duval d'Eprémesnil secure passage of his decree of 5 December, as attested by fears of anarchy voiced at the plenary session of that day. Ibid., 3: 779–80.

92. For the complaints of the booksellers and printers, see Bibl. nat., MS Joly de Fleury 2114, fols. 24–28. In general, they asserted that the extended impost would make newspapers, almanacs, promissory notes, licenses of all kinds, and other printed matter too expensive to print or buy. On the pressure exerted by the consular courts, see Egret, *The French Prerevolution*, p. 94.

93. Flammermont, *Remontrances*, 3: 690.

94. See Arch. nat., X^{1B} 8986, plenary session of 28 July 1787, for these comments. Bourré de Corberon was a president of his chamber.

95. Ibid., X^{1B} 8987, plenary session of 4 August 1787.

96. The tribunal's minutes do not yield the decree of 24 October 1787, but its sense can be deduced from the comments upon it of Mathieu Louis de Mauperché, dean of the substitutes in the *parquet*, in ibid., X^{1B} 8987, plenary session of 24 October 1787. According to Bachaumont et al., *Mémoires secrets*, 36: 143, the *parlementaires* in the days immediately following took depositions from a large number of individuals on this subject.

97. On parlementary interest in this issue during the earliest years of Louis XVI's reign, consult Stone, *The Parlement of Paris*, pp. 130–36. Steven Kaplan discusses the "grain question" (and the judges' stance upon it) under Louis XV in his massive work *Bread, Politics and Political Economy in the Reign of Louis XV*. See also his more recent study *Provisioning Paris*.

98. See, for example, the jeremiad of Séguier against physiocratic advocates of economic freedom at the plenary session of 28 November 1768 (Flammermont, *Remontrances*, 3: 13). When one judge had attempted to refute Séguier's arguments, his address had been "vehemently attacked by the *présidents à mortier* of the Parlement." Ibid., 3: 18–19.

99. Bibl. nat., MS Joly de Fleury 1040, fol. 291.

100. Hardy, *Mes Loisirs*, 7: 123 (MS Fonds fr. 6686). He reported a vote of 95 to 81 in favor of the legislation. For its provisions, consult Isambert et al., *Recueil*, 28: 361–64.

101. Flammermont, *Remontrances*, 3: 798.

102. Ibid., 3: 798–99, for this decree.

103. Ibid., 3: 797.

104. Ibid., 3: 799.

105. See Stone, *The Parlement of Paris*, pp. 136–41, for a discussion of this subject. Monin, *L'Etat de Paris en 1789*, provides much interesting information on the wood trade in Paris and its environs in the eighteenth century.

106. See Arch. nat., X^{1B} 8988, plenary session of 1 February 1788, for the details pertinent to this incident.

107. For instance, royal edicts "freeing" the commerce in grain within the kingdom often left local authorities the option of reimposing export controls in times of scarcity, and this responded to parlementary complaints about doctrinaire physiocratic ideas as well as to the promptings of common sense. Similarly, royal legislation in the mid-1780s on the provisioning, storage, and marketing of firewood seems to have responded, at least in part, to concerns voiced at the Palais de Justice.

108. Flammermont, *Remontrances*, 3: 670–71. Interestingly, these same re-

monstrances assailed the pensions of parasitical aristocratic courtiers at Versailles. This, too, was an old motif in parlementary protests to the king. Ibid., 3: 668–70.

109. *Gazette de Leyde* for 10 July 1787 (Supplement). For the legislation itself, consult Isambert et al., *Recueil*, 28: 374–76.

110. Including Hardy, *Mes Loisirs*, 7: 126–27 (MS Fonds fr. 6686); *Gazette Manuscrite*, 1: 26 and 30 June 1787; and Arch. nat., X^{1B} 8986, plenary session of 28 June 1787. Both the *Gazette de Leyde* and the *Gazette Manuscrite* referred specifically to the debate within the court over the *corvée* obligations of *privilégiés*.

111. On this parlementary campaign against abuse of *corvéables*, see Stone, *The Parlement of Paris*, pp. 93–96, 141–53.

112. Indeed, the government acknowledged this attitude during Necker's first ministry when it promulgated legislation pledging that the *taille* could not henceforth be increased without the consent of the sovereign courts—consent that, it was tacitly understood, would likely not be forthcoming.

113. They had made this point on earlier occasions as well: for instance, in remonstrances of March 1776 against Turgot's effort to make all proprietors of the Second and Third Estates fiscally responsible for the upkeep of the kingdom's roads. Stone, *The Parlement of Paris*, pp. 94–95.

114. On this obscure but interesting incident, consult Arch. nat., X^{1B} 8987, plenary session of 20 November 1787.

115. These earlier affairs are treated at length in Stone, *The Parlement of Paris*, pp. 52–56.

116. Flammermont, *Remontrances*, 3: 784. See n. 54, above.

117. *Procès-verbal de l'assemblée de notables, tenue à Versailles, en l'année 1788*, p. 485 (session of 12 December 1788).

118. Flammermont, *Remontrances*, 3: 796.

119. Ibid., 3: 745–46.

120. Ibid., 3: 781.

121. Ferrand, *Mémoires*, p. 29; and Bouillé, *Mémoires*, p. 64.

122. *Gazette de Leyde* for 17 March 1789 (Supplement). See also Hardy, *Mes Loisirs*, 8: 246 (MS Fonds fr. 6687).

123. See Henri Carré, *La Fin des Parlements*, pp. 212–16, for some observations on the *parlementaires'* high hopes of dominating the Estates General in 1789—and for statistics documenting their meager success in the elections.

124. Sallier, *Annales françaises*, p. 80.

125. Pasquier, *Histoire de mon temps*, 1: 27–28. Ferrand in his *Mémoires*, pp. 8–9, sketched a similar picture of the youthful jurists of the Enquêtes and Requêtes.

126. In his *Mémoires*, pp. 63–64, the marquis de Bouillé claimed that the decree of 5 December 1788 was prepared in the sessions of a so-called *club des enragés*, formed by the duc d'Orléans and including Duval d'Eprémesnil, Adrien Duport, Huguet de Sémonville, and Le Peletier de Saint-Fargeau. Another memorialist, the minister Barentin, saw the decree as "the product of seditious gatherings at the residence of M. Duport" and listed the "revolutionary" *parlementaires* who supposedly frequented these assemblages. Barentin, *Mémoire autographe*, pp. 86–88. Yet, Duval d'Eprémesnil would soon be coming to a parting of the ways with his erstwhile allies Duport and Le Peletier de Saint-Fargeau.

CHAPTER 3

1. This was in the remonstrances of 11 April directed against the *séance royale* of the preceding November. The judges reserved some of their most vituperative language for Lamoignon's authoritarian discourse at that assemblage. Flammermont, *Remontrances*, 3: 733.

2. Ibid., 3: 733–34. Cited from the same remonstrances.

3. In the "reiterated remonstrances" against the *séance royale*. Ibid., 3: 743.

4. Refer again to ibid., 3: 745–46, for d'Eprémesnil's *arrêté* of 3 May 1788.

5. Droz des Villars, *Mémoires pour servir à l'histoire du droit public*, pp. 124–25.

6. Ibid., pp. 129–30, for Droz des Villars's continuing discussion of this question.

7. These protests (which seem to have drawn no royal response before the *lit de justice* of the following May) may be consulted at Besançon, Archives départementales du Doubs, B 2846, 30 August 1787.

8. This affair is treated briefly in Delmas, *Du Parlement de Navarre*, pp. 407–8. It is discussed later in chapter 5 herein.

9. Original documents relating to this controversy still exist in the departmental archives at Pau, but may be more easily consulted at Paris. For the government's memorandum and the *parlementaires'* remonstrances of 14 December 1787, consult, respectively, Arch. nat., K 711 (33) and K 711 (36).

10. On this incident see Arch. dép. d'Ille-et-Vilaine, Rennes, 1Bb 737, 17 and 18 September 1787; and Arch. nat., KK 1326, fols. 107–10.

11. On this affair, see Arch. nat., K 711 (60), esp. fols. 1–9; see also chapters 4 and 5 herein.

12. Arch. nat., K 711 (60), fol. 2.

13. Bachaumont et al., *Mémoires secrets*, 36: 314–16. See also pp. 249–50, for earlier commentary from this source upon the affair at Rouen.

14. See the published protests emanating from this tribunal on 19 January (*Très-humbles . . . Remontrances*), 1 March (*Arrêté du parlement de Metz*), and 20 June 1788 (*Déclarations et itératives protestations*), Bibl. nat.

15. *Déclarations et itératives protestations*, Bibl. nat., p. 16.

16. On the *parlements*, the crown, and the Gallican controversy during the years following Louis XIV's death, consult Egret, *Louis XV et l'opposition parlementaire*, esp. pp. 17–33 and 50–92.

17. Droz des Villars, *Mémoires pour servir à l'histoire du droit public*, p. 41.

18. Du Couëdic de Kergoualer, *Suite du Précis historique*, pp. xii–xiii.

19. Droz des Villars, *Mémoires pour servir à l'histoire du droit public*, p. 43.

20. For this missive, dated 6 December 1787, see Arch. dép. d'Ille-et-Vilaine, Rennes, 1Bc 10; or Arch. nat., KK 1326, fols. 494–95. The Bretons wrote to the king again on this issue, in an equally futile gesture, on 17 March 1788. Consult Arch. dép. d'Ille-et-Vilaine, 1Bc10.

21. *Déclaration et itératives protestations* (11 June 1788). Bibl. Mazarine, MS 2408, pp. 531–55.

22. The Normans had in recent years achieved notoriety for their intractable opposition to government policies, particularly in the realm of taxation. On their frenzied resistance to the *vingtièmes* during Necker's first ministry, see Floquet, *Histoire du parlement de Normandie*, vol. 7; and Egret, *Necker: Ministre de Louis XVI*, pp. 76–83.

23. For this decree, see Arch. dép. de la Seine-Maritime, Rouen, 1BP 1727, pp. 359–73; or Arch. nat., KK 1327, fols. 261–68.

24. The text of the royal decree of 9 July is in Arch. nat., KK 1327, fol. 269.

25. *Lettre du parlement de Pau au roi, du 31 août 1787*, Bibl. nat.

26. The story of the uprising at Pau has been most recently retold by Egret, *The French Prerevolution*, pp. 151–53.

27. This letter to the king may be most readily consulted in Arch. nat., KK 1327, fols. 372–75. The *parlement's* depiction of its especially critical role in local justice was corroborated by its *avocats* in their own appeals to Louis XVI. See ibid., K 711 (37).

28. The observer in question was one Barbet, spokesman (syndic) for the local *avocats*. Quoted in Egret, *The French Prerevolution*, p. 152.

29. See, for example, the discourse by Maurel de Callisanne, senior *avocat-général* at Aix, on 8 May 1788, in Arch. dép. des Bouches-du-Rhône, Aix-en-Provence, B 3680, 8 May 1788; or Arch. nat., KK 1327, fols. 270–72; and the declaration by the comte de la Tresne, *avocat-général* at Toulouse, on 27 May 1788, in Arch. nat., KK 1327, fol. 168.

30. Refer to Arch. dép. de l'Isère, Grenoble, B 2319, fols. 23–25; or Arch. nat., H¹ 1596 (262).

31. Arch. nat., KK 1326, fol. 531.

32. The position of the king's representatives in Languedoc was rendered even more difficult by the suspicion of many in the province, and not merely the *parlementaires*, that the local Estates were unrepresentative of the Languedocien population and too amenable to the ministers' fiscal demands. Egret, *The French Prerevolution*, pp. 136–38.

33. Arch. nat., KK 1327, fols. 219–20.

34. The Intermediary Committee of the Burgundian Estates administered the Estates' affairs between their triennial sessions and had long been considered by the Dijonnais *parlementaires* overly receptive to the government's wishes, particularly in matters relating to taxation. La Cuisine, *Le Parlement de Bourgogne*, vol. 3. The judges' stormy relationship with Amelot de Chaillou in this period is reflected in the latter's correspondence with the authorities at Versailles, preserved throughout Arch. nat., H¹ 147.

35. Arch. nat., KK 1326, fol. 237.

36. For Lamoignon's address, consult ibid., X¹ᴮ 8987—plenary session of 19 November 1787.

37. For these protests, consult Arch. dép. d'Ille-et-Vilaine, Rennes, 1Bc 10 (unnumbered document).

38. Ibid., for these six contested points.

39. Ibid.

40. Ibid. The judges here were protesting the government's use of "simple ministerial letters," rather than orders signed personally by the king, to summon three of their company's presidents to Versailles in connection with an earlier controversy. Thus, the ministers were again being portrayed as intriguing to isolate the sovereign from his sovereign courts.

41. Arch. nat., KK 1327, fol. 262.

42. Ibid., fols. 265–66.

43. This was Robert Lindet, as quoted in Egret, *The French Prerevolution*, p. 151.

44. On this latter point, see the testimony of President Fauris de Saint-Vincent in his *Journal du Parlement*, Bibl. Méjanes, MS 1037, p. 499; and the court's

deliberations of 22 December 1787, in Arch. dép. des Bouches-du-Rhône, Aix-en-Provence, B 3680.

45. On the politics of these four *parlements* in the 1774–87 period, refer to the relevant sections of the studies by Doyle, Gresset, Egret, and Floquet, respectively. For that matter, the magistrates at Dijon, Rennes, and Toulouse were hardly less restive under Louis XVI. We still lack a comprehensive study of the parlementary opposition under this monarch.

46. Refer again to Delmas, *Du Parlement de Navarre.* Also, see chapter 5 herein for further discussion of their actions in the prerevolutionary crisis.

47. Calonne had served as *procureur-général* in the Douai Parlement from 1759 to 1766; Lamoignon, of course, had served for thirty-two years in the Paris Parlement, sitting since 1758 on the Grand Banc.

48. Calonne, it will be recalled, had been instrumental in the government's prosecution of the rebellious Breton *parlementaire* de La Chalotais in 1765; Lamoignon had incensed most of the other grand' chambriers at Paris in 1783–84 by seconding the younger judges' call for the reform of justice.

49. For this *arrêté*, refer to Arch. dép. de l'Isère, Grenoble, B 2319, fols. 1–5; or Arch. nat., KK 1326, fols. 111–19.

50. Arch. dép. du Doubs, Besançon, B 2846, 1 September 1787; or Arch. nat., H¹ 1596 (150).

51. Arch. nat., KK 1326, fol. 231.

52. Arch. dép. d'Ille-et-Vilaine, Rennes, 1Bc 10; or Arch. nat., KK 1326, fol. 492. These *Objets des Remontrances* are dated 6 December at Rennes.

53. Arch. nat., KK 1326, fols. 236–37. The former controller general had fled the country in the wake of the Paris Parlement's calls for his prosecution in late July and early August.

54. The denunciations of Calonne at Paris, culminating in the court's announcement that it would undertake his prosecution, may be followed in the official minutes in Arch. nat., X¹ᴮ 8987. The crown intervened almost immediately, however, with its *lit de justice* and subsequent banishment of the jurists to Troyes.

55. The prodigious popularity of Necker's *Compte rendu* and his quarrel with Calonne and others over state finances in the 1780s have been treated anew in Egret, *Necker: Ministre de Louis XVI,* pp. 169–79 and 199–205. Whether either protagonist ever "won" the argument remains unclear even today.

56. Arch. nat., KK 1326, fol. 231.

57. Refer to Stone, *The Parlement of Paris,* pp. 85–90.

58. See, for example, Egret, *Necker: Ministre de Louis XVI;* Bosher, *French Finances;* and Harris, *Necker: Reform Statesman of the Ancien Régime.*

59. Egret (*The French Prerevolution,* pp. 154–62) analyzes the arguments on both sides in the great debate over the May Edicts in 1788. For additional commentary on the judges' arguments, see my discussions in chapters 4 and 5.

60. Refer again to Arch. nat., KK 1327, fol. 267.

61. Ibid., fol. 262.

62. Arch. dép. d'Ille-et-Vilaine, Rennes, 1Bb 738, 31 May 1788; or Arch. nat., KK 1327, fol. 322. The reference here, of course, was to the government's use of troops to enforce its will at the *lits de justice* at Rennes and elsewhere.

63. Arch. dép. de l'Isère, Grenoble, B 2319, fol. 41; or Arch. nat., KK 1327, fol. 172.

64. Arch. dép. de l'Isère, Grenoble, B 2319, fols. 44–51, for the original text of this major *arrêté;* Arch. nat., KK 1327, fols. 173–74, for the excerpt quoted here.

65. See the discourse of senior Avocat-Général Maurel de Callisanne on 8 May 1788 in Arch. dép. des Bouches-du-Rhône, Aix-en-Provence, B 3680, 8 May 1788; or Arch. nat., KK 1327, fols. 270–72. See also the court's *Protestations* of 7 June, in Arch. dép. des Bouches-du-Rhône, B 3680, 7 June 1788; or Arch. nat., KK 1327, fols. 290–96. The Aixois were by now every bit as audacious in their language as were the men of the other sovereign courts.

66. Faulcon, *Correspondance*, 1: 289–90. Letter dated 3 October 1787.

67. Ibid., 1: 332–33.

68. Egret, *The French Prerevolution*, pp. 161–62. This was the case even though many of these illuminati "refused to make common cause" with the stricken law courts.

69. On the provincial intendants, see Gruder, *The Royal Provincial Intendants*. But as Egret (*The French Prerevolution*) shows, parlementary suspicions about these powerful royal agents were shared by many other Frenchmen in 1787–88.

70. This includes the famous royal declaration of August 1780 abrogating the *question préparatoire*, the torture that up to then had still been occasionally employed to extract confessions from individuals suspected of having committed capital crimes. The Parisian judges had grudgingly registered this legislation in September 1780; the magistrates at Besançon had never gone along with it.

71. The original documents relative to this affair are found in Arch. dép. du Doubs, Besançon, B 2846 (unnumbered documents).

72. For these protests, consult ibid., B 2846 (unnumbered document); or Arch. nat., K 708 (23).

73. Arch. dép. du Doubs, Besançon, B 2846 (unnumbered document); or Arch. nat., K 708 (22). Lamoignon's letter is discussed in greater detail in chapter 5.

74. For this missive of 9 July 1787, consult Arch. dép. du Doubs, Besançon, B 2846 (unnumbered document). See also Droz des Villars's comments upon the *corvée* controversy of 1786–87 in Franche-Comté in his *Mémoires pour servir à l'histoire du droit public*, pp. 115–16.

75. For material pertinent to this affair, see Arch. dép. du Doubs, Besançon, B 2846 and 2850 (unnumbered documents); and Arch. nat., H¹ 1596 (150, 153, 161, 164). The Estates in Franche-Comté had not met since the French conquest of the province in the seventeenth century.

76. The remonstrances discussed in this paragraph may be most readily consulted in Arch. nat., H¹ 1596 (150).

77. Ibid., H¹ 1596 (153).

78. Though of course those *parlements* whose jurisdictions coincided with provinces boasting active Estates did not have to confront such legislation in 1787.

79. Refer to Doyle, *The Parlement of Bordeaux*, pp. 264–75, for a thorough discussion of this controversy at Bordeaux.

80. Arch. nat., KK 1326, fols. 199–201.

81. For the remonstrances, consult Arch. nat., K 708 (83¹), or H¹ 1596 (183). On their wide circulation, see Bachaumont et al., *Mémoires secrets*, 36: 177, 201–2, 207.

82. Correspondence dated 26 July 1787. Arch. nat., H¹ 1596 (217).

83. Ibid., H¹ 1596 (280).

84. For the interdictory decree of 6 October 1787, and the subsequent protests of 15 December, consult Arch. dép. de l'Isère, Grenoble, B 2319, fols. 6–10 and 11–13, respectively; or Arch. nat., H¹ 1596 (287) and (275), respectively.

85. For the correspondence of Caze de la Bove, dated 30 December, see Arch. nat., H¹ 1596 (264). See also Egret, *Le Parlement de Dauphiné*, 2: 169–201, for a more detailed treatment of the magistrates' opposition on this issue.

86. Arch. dép. de la Haute-Garonne, Toulouse, 51 B 29 (27); or Arch. nat., KK 1326, fol. 520.

87. *Lettre du parlement de Normandie au roi, pour demander les anciens états de la province*. Bibl. nat., pp. 9–10. For another copy of this missive, see Arch. nat., K 711 (62).

88. Arch. nat., H¹ 1596 (232). The intendant defended himself vigorously in a letter to the ministry dated 18 August. Ibid. (229).

89. Refer again to Arch. dép. de l'Isère, Grenoble, B 2319, fols. 6–10; or Arch. nat., H¹ 1596 (287).

90. At least, he mentioned as a subsidiary factor in the jurists' opposition to the new assemblies their concern over "the inconveniences that can result from organizational changes in the local communities," and over various other practical problems. Arch. nat., H¹ 1596 (280).

91. See the Grenoble Parlement's remonstrances of 10 March 1787 in Arch. dép. de l'Isère, Grenoble, B 2318, fols. 273–83; and the Besançon Parlement's remonstrances of 5 February 1787 and letter of 9 July 1787 to Lamoignon in Arch. dép. du Doubs, Besançon, B 2846.

92. From the remonstrances of 1 September 1787, Arch. nat., H¹ 1596 (150), or Arch. dép. du Doubs, Besançon, B 2846.

93. Arch. dép. de l'Isère, Grenoble, B 2319, fols. 1–5; or Arch. nat., KK 1326, fols. 111–19.

94. From the Besançon Parlement's *arrêté* of 30 August 1787, Arch. nat., KK 1326, fol. 218.

95. See, for example, the Rennes Parlement's *Objets des Remontrances* of 6 December 1787, in which the Bretons criticized the Parisian judges for having too readily ratified the major loan presented by the government at the *séance royale* of the preceding month. Arch. dép. d'Ille-et-Vilaine, Rennes, 1Bc 10; or Arch. nat., KK 1326, fols. 491–92. Yet the charge was somewhat unfair, given the compulsory nature of that "ratification" on 19 November.

96. The edict extending the second *vingtième* through 1791 and 1792, registered at Paris in September, was only submitted to the provincial *parlements* in the course of October.

97. For the complete text of this revealing *arrêté*, see Arch. dép. de la Seine-Maritime, Rouen, 1BP 1727, pp. 14–19; or Arch. nat., KK 1326, fols. 498–504.

98. For the *arrêté* of 27 August 1787, consult Arch. nat., KK 1326, fols. 44–50; for the remonstrances of 12 January 1788, see Arch. dép. de la Haute-Garonne, Toulouse, 51 B 29 (27); or Arch. nat., KK 1326, fols. 520–34.

99. Arch. nat., K 709 (36).

100. From the remonstrances of 31 October 1787, Arch. nat., H¹ 1596 (183); or K 708 (83¹).

101. From the Rennes Parlement's *arrêté* of 22 August 1787. Arch. dép. d'Ille-et-Vilaine, Rennes, 1Bb 737; or Arch. nat., KK 1326, fols. 39–40.

102. Fauris de Saint-Vincent, *Journal du Parlement*, Bibl. Méjanes, MS 1037, pp. 498–501.

103. *Réponse du Garde des Sceaux, Au nom du Roi, aux Remontrances du Parlement de Lorraine du 24 November 1787*, Arch. nat., K 710 (71).

104. As reported in Hardy, *Mes Loisirs*, 7: 21 (MS Fonds fr. 6686).

105. Bachaumont et al., *Mémoires secrets*, 34: 253–54. The rendition of the Provençal magistrate's address in this source agrees almost verbatim with that in Hardy's journal.

106. Refer to Fauris de Saint-Vincent's *Journal du Parlement*, Bibl. Méjanes, MS 1037, pp. 498–501; and to the court's deliberations of 22 December 1787, in Arch. dép. des Bouches-du-Rhône, Aix-en-Provence, B 3680.

107. Arch. nat., KK 1327, fols. 270–71; or Arch. dép. des Bouches-du-Rhône, Aix-en-Provence, B 3680, 8 May 1788.

108. Arch. nat., KK 1327, fols. 292–93; or Arch. dép. des Bouches-du-Rhône, Aix-en-Provence, B 3680, 7 June 1788.

109. Arch. dép. des Bouches-du-Rhône, 21 October 1788.

110. Arch. dép. du Doubs, Besançon, B 2846 (unnumbered document); or Arch. nat., H¹ 1596 (150).

111. From the court's *Protestations* of 4 June 1788, signed by all the presidents, counselors, and *gens du roi*. Arch. nat., KK 1327, fols. 218–19.

112. The *parlementaires* were all the more insistent upon this in that they had for so long accused the Burgundian Estates of falling too readily in step with ministerial fiscal policies. The Dijon Parlement and Chambre des Comptes must defend Burgundy where (they alleged) the Estates had failed to do so.

113. Arch. nat., KK 1326, fol. 234.

114. For this bold *arrêté* of 6 May 1788, consult Bibl. Mazarine, MS 2409, pp. 1353ff.

115. Refer to the Nancy Parlement's *Déclaration et itératives protestations* of 11 June 1788, Bibl. Mazarine, MS 2408, pp. 531–55.

116. This significant development is discussed extensively, if in general terms, in Bickart, *Les Parlements et la notion de souveraineté nationale*.

117. From the remonstrances of 31 October 1787, Arch. nat., H¹ 1596 (183), or K 708 (83¹).

118. Arch. dép. de l'Isère, B 2319, fols. 1–5; or Arch. nat., KK 1326, fols. 114–15.

119. From the *arrêté* of 20 December, Arch. dép. de la Seine-Maritime, Rouen, 1BP 1727, pp. 16–17; or Arch. nat., KK 1326, fol. 501.

120. Arch. dép. de la Haute-Garonne, Toulouse, 51 B 29 (27); or Arch. nat., KK· 1326, fol. 532.

121. From the court's *arrêté* of 21 August 1787, Arch. dép. de l'Isère, Grenoble, B 2319, fols. 2–3; or Arch. nat., KK 1326, fols. 114–15.

122. From the court's remonstrances of 15 April 1788, Arch. nat., K 708 (65), fols. 6–7.

123. From the court's remonstrances of 12 January 1788, Arch. dép. de la Haute-Garonne, Toulouse, 51 B 29 (27); or Arch. nat., KK 1326, fol. 534.

124. From the major *arrêté* of 20 December 1787, Arch. dép. de la Seine-Maritime, Rouen, 1BP 1727, pp. 17–18; or Arch. nat., KK 1326, fol. 502.

125. Cited from the court's remonstrances of 12 January 1788, Arch. dép. de la Haute-Garonne, Toulouse, 51 B 29 (27); or Arch. nat., KK 1326, fol. 534.

126. The magistrates at Besançon spoke of Louis XVI as king "of the French" in their *arrêté* of 30 August 1787. Arch. nat., KK 1326, fols. 216–17. The judges at Perpignan referred to Louis in this fashion, and to the Estates General as the "national asssembly," in an *arrêté* four days later. Ibid., fols. 237–38. A number of the other tribunals would soon be employing the same phraseology.

127. Arch. dép. de l'Isère, Grenoble, B 2319, fols. 17–19; or Arch. nat., KK 1326, fols. 508–11.

128. See, for example, their self-justificatory letter to the Paris Parlement of 21 December. Arch. nat., KK 1326, fols. 486–87.

129. From the Nancy Parlement's *Déclaration et itératives protestations* of 11 June 1788, Bibl. Mazarine, MS 2408, pp. 549–51.

130. Consult Egret, *Louis XV et l'opposition parlementaire*, pp. 50–92, for a discussion of this controversy.

131. Egret, *The French Prerevolution*, pp. 138–43.

132. As evidenced by remarks in their lengthy remonstrances of 31 October 1787. Interestingly, this was pointed out in Bachaumont et al., *Mémoires secrets*, 36: 206–7. As we have already noted, the Parisians were to commend their Bordelais cousins' opposition to the government somewhat belatedly the following spring.

133. For the Bretons' comments, in remonstrances of 16 February 1788, see Arch. dép. d'Ille-et-Vilaine, Rennes, 1Bc 10 (unnumbered document). For the comments of the Comtois in their strong "protestations" of 26 May 1788, consult Arch. dép. du Doubs, Besançon, B 2850 (unnumbered document), or Arch. nat., KK 1327, fol. 383. Several other *parlements* also invoked judicial solidarity in the face of ministerial policies, but in somewhat more general terms.

134. Arch. nat., H¹ 1599 (29), for this intriguing letter.

135. These examples are cited in Egret, *The French Prerevolution*, pp. 125–26.

136. Consult Fauris de Saint-Vincent's *Journal du Parlement*, Bibl. Méjanes, MS 1037, pp. 591–95.

137. Arch. nat., H¹ 147 (94). Correspondence with the government dated 30 November 1787.

138. For the Toulousains' *arrêté* of 24 October 1788 and "supplications" of 21 January 1789 on this subject, see Arch. dép. de la Haute-Garonne, Toulouse, 51 B 29 (29) or 51 B 30 (13). The Estates of Languedoc (as noted earlier) had long been notoriously unrepresentative of the local population, even by old regime standards. The *parlementaires* may have wished to acquire influence in reorganized Estates in 1789.

139. See Egret's discussion of magisterial motives in Dauphiné and Franche-Comté in this connection in *The French Prerevolution*, pp. 126–27.

140. Refer to this court's "reiterated remonstrances" of 4 March 1788, in Arch. dép. de la Seine-Maritime, Rouen, 1BP 1727, pp. 109–20.

141. See Carré, *La Fin des Parlements*, pp. 212–16, for statistics documenting the judges' overall lack of success in the elections for the Estates General. Only a handful of *parlementaires* ever actually sat in that body—and those few who did were from the beginning split along ideological lines.

CHAPTER 4

1. See Lefebvre, *The French Revolution*, 1: 88.

2. See Soboul, *The French Revolution*, pp. 28, 37, 91, 111.

3. See Egret, *The French Prerevolution*, p. 217.

4. Egret, "La Révolution aristocratique en Franche-Comté et son échec, 1788–89," p. 262.

5. Droz des Villars, *Mémoires pour servir à l'histoire du droit public*, pp. 156–57.

6. Arch. dép. du Doubs, Besançon, B 2846 (unnumbered document); or Arch. nat., H¹ 1596 (150).

7. Arrêté du parlement de Franche-Comté, in Bibl. nat. Jean Egret discusses this decree in the context of the politics of 1788–89 in Franche-Comté in "La Révolution aristocratique en Franche-Comté et son échec, 1788–89," pp. 261–63.

8. Arrêté du parlement de Franche-Comté, in Bibl. nat., p. 17. Significantly, the arrêté also challenged the popular wrath by invoking the precedent of 1614 for the upcoming Estates General. The justices at Besançon were reacting specifically to Necker's controversial Résultat du Conseil of 27 December 1788, which had declared for the "doubling" of the Third Estate contingent in the impending national convocation. But they were also quite deliberately endorsing the Paris Parlement's fateful commendation of the precedent of 1614 in its decree of 25 September 1788. Here, then, is one example of a provincial parlement willing to do that which had already cost the tribunal in the national capital its national popularity.

9. The Grenoblois, for instance, would have accepted (and indeed proposed) the notion of provincial Estates in Dauphiné according "double representation" and voting by head to commoners—although admittedly those Estates would have been subject in all substantive deliberations to a parlementary veto. Chapter 5 discusses more fully this innovation mooted in 1787.

10. Arch. dép. de l'Isère, Grenoble, B 2318, fol. 281. The extent of and limitations upon the Grenoble Parlement's humanitarianism where the corvée royale was concerned in 1787–88 receive fuller treatment in chapter 5.

11. Arch. nat., KK 1327, fols. 261–62.

12. Egret, The French Prerevolution, p. 151.

13. Egret makes this very clear in his lucid discussion of Provençal politics in 1787–88. "La Pré-Révolution en Provence, 1787–89," pp. 97–126.

14. Arch. dép. des Bouches-du-Rhône, Aix-en-Provence, B 3680—deliberations of 27 February 1788.

15. Ibid., deliberations of 12 March 1788.

16. Refer again to Fauris de Saint-Vincent, Journal du Parlement, Bibl. Méjanes, MS 1037, pp. 572–73. The president registered further impatience with the commoners' dissatisfaction in Provence, p. 590.

17. This illuminating correspondence is found throughout Arch. nat., H¹ 1238.

18. For these denunciations, and a wealth of related information, see ibid., H¹ 1240.

19. Du Couëdic de Kergoualer, Suite du Précis historique, Bibl. nat., pp. xiii–xv.

20. Droz des Villars, Mémoires pour servir à l'histoire du droit public, pp. 152–53.

21. Ibid., pp. 154–55.

22. Ibid., p. 160.

23. That is, Lamoignon's legislation specified those functionaries and legal experts who were henceforth to be deemed indispensable for the continued administration of justice in seigneurial courts. Lacking such personnel—and it was plain that the government expected this to be generally the case—the local lords would no longer be entitled to hold "feudal" court upon their lands. One of the most detailed and technical critiques of the judicial reform came from the parlementaires at Nancy. Refer to their "Declaration and reiterated protestations" of 11 June 1788 in Bibl. Mazarine, MS 2408, pp. 531–55.

24. Arch. nat., KK 1327, fol. 175.

25. Ibid.

26. The Dijon Parlement argued thus in its lengthy "Protestations" of 4 June 1788, Arch. nat., KK 1327, fol. 217. The Dijonnais, it is worth noting, analyzed the judicial reform of 1788 in as minute detail as did their counterparts at Nancy.

27. Consult Bibl. Mazarine, MS 2408, pp. 536–37.

28. Arch. nat., KK 1327, fols. 264–65.

29. Arch. nat., KK 1326, fol. 230. That the "allotment and assessment" of the *subvention territoriale* was to be entrusted in Burgundy to the Elus (leaders chosen by the crown) of the Estates could only render the new impost yet more odious in magisterial eyes, given the judges' long-standing animus against the Elus.

30. La Cuisine, *Le Parlement de Bourgogne*, vol. 3.

31. Documents pertaining to this affair are found in Arch. nat., H¹ 163 (20–91). On related fiscal and administrative disputes between the Dijon Parlement and the Elus of the Burgundian Estates in 1786–87, see Arch. nat., H¹ 186 (313–44). For two anonymous contemporaries' comments upon the controversies over the *chemins finerots* and related issues in Burgundy, see the *Gazette manuscrite*, entry of 27 January 1787, in Bibl. nat.; and *Documents concernant le règne de Louis XVI*, Bibl. nat., fol. 110.

32. Arch. nat., H¹ 163 (51).

33. There are two copies of these protests. Ibid. (89) or (91).

34. Ibid.

35. For that matter, none of the wrangles between the *parlementaires* and the officers of the Burgundian Estates were resolved before the advent of the Revolution. Ibid., H¹ 186 (313–44).

36. On this incident at Rouen, see Arch. nat., K 711 (60), and Bachaumont et al., *Mémoires secrets*, 36: 249–50 and 314–16.

37. Arch. nat., K 711 (60), fol. 3.

38. Refer to Arch. dép. de l'Isère, Grenoble, B 2318, fols. 283–92.

39. On the noble origins and connections of monks and nuns in one eighteenth-century town, see McManners, *French Ecclesiastical Society*, pp. 57–102.

40. Arch. dép. de l'Isère, Grenoble, B 2318, fols. 291–92.

41. Ibid.

42. Ibid. There is something here of the magisterial "patriotism" that invariably surfaced when ultramontane ecclesiastical claims were at issue.

43. *Discours de M. de La Boissière*, Bibl. nat., pp. 8–9 and 17–18.

44. Fauris de Saint-Vincent, *Journal du Parlement*, Bibl. Méjanes, MS 1037, pp. 796–97.

45. Ibid., pp. 800–801. On the other hand, the president was to note apprehensively in March 1789 "that the government is conspicuously favoring the third estate. Projects of independence are being authorized. There is not only some talk of obliging the first two orders to accept a more equitable tax burden, which may be fair. There is [also] talk of abolishing all distinctions of social rank. This is not announced but it is being prepared." Ibid., p. 820.

46. For Leblanc de Castillon's address, consult the Aix Parlement's deliberations of 21 October 1788 in Arch. dép. des Bouches-du-Rhône, Aix-en-Provence, B 3680.

47. This illuminating ninety-six-page treatise is found at Besançon's Bibliothèque municipale. A publication date of December 1788 seems indicated by certain topical references in the text.

48. Ibid.

49. The Parisians had spoken with irritation of "each provincial gentleman"

wanting to take up an administrative (and, by implication, a political) career. On this memorandum of 1781, see Stone, *The Parlement of Paris*, p. 118.

50. Droz des Villars, *Réflexions sur les inconvéniens*, pp. 40–43.

51. Consult, in President Joly de Fleury's papers, the *Résultat de plusieurs vérités qui se trouvent établies par les Monuments de la Première et Deuxième Race des Rois de France*, Bibl. nat., MS Joly de Fleury 2116, fols. 42–89; and the *Réflections sur le mémoire intitulé résultat*, fols. 90–98.

52. Arch. nat., K 708 (65), esp. fols. 5–6.

53. Arch. nat., K 711 (40 bis), fols. 4–5.

54. *Remontrances et arrêts du parlement de Navarre*, in Bibl. nat., pp. 3–4. This denunciation of the projected Plenary Court in 1788 resembles nothing so much as the Paris Parlement's censure of an earlier ministerial reference to an envisioned Plenary Court in remonstrances of 8 January 1775. Stone, *The Parlement of Paris*, pp. 112–13. On that occasion, too, various elements of the nonrobe nobility had come in for severe criticism.

55. For this affair, refer to Arch. dép. d'Ille-et-Vilaine, Rennes, 1Bc 10. The remonstrances of 20 August 1787 and the associated documents bear no pagination.

56. For some thoughts on the relationships among the provincial courts in this period, see Dawson, *Provincial Magistrates and Revolutionary Politics in France*, pp. 63–65.

57. Consult the documents in Arch. dép. d'Ille-et-Vilaine, Rennes, 1Bc 10.

58. Ibid.

59. On this revealing episode, consult Stone, *The Parlement of Paris*, pp. 105–8.

60. Duval d'Eprémesnil especially lampooned the aspirations of certain military nobles of past centuries in his *Du Connétable, des Maréchaux de France, de leurs fonctions, et de leur pouvoir*, Arch. nat., 158 AP 3, dossier 5.

61. Even Egret, fair-minded as he was in evaluating the arguments of proparlementary and antiparlementary polemicists in 1788, seemed to share this common skepticism. *The French Prerevolution*, esp. pp. 159–60. And, of course, he may have been right to do so. But see below, n. 65.

62. Arch. nat., K 711 (40 bis), fol. 5.

63. Ibid.

64. Arch. dép. d'Ille-et-Vilaine, Rennes, 1Bc 10; or Arch. nat., K 712 (132), fols. 6–7.

65. It should also be pointed out in this connection that the sovereign courts did not necessarily wait until their professional ways were in jeopardy in 1787–88 to declaim (and even on behalf of commoners) against *lettres de cachet*. For examples of this at Paris well *before* the prerevolutionary crisis, refer again to Stone, *The Parlement of Paris*, pp. 52–55.

66. Egret, "La Révolution aristocratique en Franche-Comté et son échec, 1788–89," esp. pp. 246–47.

67. Ibid. Against this should be set descriptions of popular agitation in May 1788 and popular merrymaking in October 1788 at Besançon. See, for example, Pingaud, *Le Président de Vezet*, pp. 19–20.

68. As reported by the marquis de Saint-Simon to the comte de Brienne in a letter of 10 November 1788. Egret, "La Révolution aristocratique en Franche-Comté et son échec, 1788–89," p. 261.

69. *Arrêté du parlement de Franche-Comté*, in Bibl. nat., pp. 5, 15–16.

70. This rendition of events at Bordeaux is taken from Doyle, *The Parlement of Bordeaux*, pp. 292–97.

71. Ibid., p. 294.

72. Ibid., pp. 296–300. As Doyle shows, some active or "honorary" members of the *parlement* participated in the assemblies held in other *sénéchaussées* of the region as well.

73. The premier source for developments in Dauphiné is, of course, Egret, *Le Parlement de Dauphiné*, 2: 171ff.

74. President de Vaulx informed President de Montferrat that, prior to registration of the government's plan in plenary session, there had been "a very numerous party in favor of persisting in the request for the Estates and refusing establishment of the provincial assembly." Ibid., 2: 174. And of course other provincial *parlements* across the realm were insisting upon similar reservations, whether with respect to new provincial assemblies or with respect to revived Estates.

75. Ibid., 2: 175.

76. Ibid.

77. Ibid., 2: 111.

78. Ibid., 2: 178–79.

79. Ibid., 2: 186–89. The judges, this nobleman charged, had the effrontery to regard themselves as "the true successors to the general Assemblies of the Nation" of past times.

80. Thus, Jean-Joseph Mounier and Antoine-Pierre-Joseph-Marie Barnave, along with a host of pamphleteers of lesser reputation, voiced this fear at the time—though in no wise attempting to gloss over the magistrates' shortcomings. Ibid., 2: 190–92.

81. The court's *procureur-général* pointedly sent a copy of this decree to Keeper of the Seals Lamoignon the day after its promulgation. The magistrates threatened in their decree to strip the marquis de Belmont of all his "privileges in the Court in his capacity there as Baron de Montmar" should he at any future time "endeavor to transgress against this Decree, against the laws of the Province and against the Ordinances of the Court." Ibid., 2: 109–10.

82. Ibid., 2: 110. Nor (as Egret shows) was this the only contemporary to accuse the judges of displaying insufferable arrogance toward all ranks of Dauphinois society. As we have seen, moreover, the same charge was being leveled at that very time against the *parlementaires* in Franche-Comté.

83. This intriguing manifesto is to be found in Arch. nat., K 692B (7).

84. Ibid., pp. 171–72.

85. Ibid.

86. Egret, *The French Prerevolution*, p. 174.

87. Refer, in the specific case of Brittany, to Le Moy, *Le Parlement de Bretagne*, passim; and Saulnier, *Le Parlement de Bretagne*, passim.

88. Brienne plainly did attempt to drive a wedge between military noblesse and *parlementaires* in Dauphiné and Franche-Comté (and hoped to do likewise in Normandy) by dangling before the nobles' eyes the prospect, not of a reinstated magistracy, but rather of a revival of their cherished provincial Estates. Egret, *The French Prerevolution*, pp. 181–82. Brienne seems, however, to have entertained less hope for the success of this tactic in Brittany, whose nobility, he was to observe after his disgrace, "was so full of prejudices, so stubborn, so bullheaded in its resistance, that nothing but disorder and trouble could have been expected." Ibid., p. 182.

89. *Gazette de Leyde*, 5 December 1788 (Supplement).

CHAPTER 5

1. The most thorough analysis of the arguments on both sides in this national debate over the May Edicts is that of Egret, *The French Prerevolution*, pp. 154–62.

2. For an excellent example of magisterial expatiation upon these and related points, refer to the Nancy Parlement's *Déclaration et itératives protestations* of 11 June 1788, in Bibl. Mazarine, MS 2408, pp. 531–55.

3. As cited in Egret, *The French Prerevolution*, p. 159.

4. Arch. nat., K 709 (36), fol. 6.

5. Ibid. On the fiscal interdependence of all rural taxpayers, from seigneurs to peasants, see Behrens, "Nobles, Privileges, and Taxes in France."

6. Arch. nat., K 709 (36), fol. 6.

7. Ibid., fol. 7.

8. Ibid., fol. 6.

9. Ibid., fols. 7–8. The judges also complained that the royal act of 27 June 1787 providing definitively for commutation of the *corvée royale* had not been sent to their company. They probably would have objected to it—as several other major *parlements* were doing at that time.

10. Ibid., fol. 9. The magistrates claimed that over the preceding twenty-five years the total *increase* in revenue demanded from the province for each *vingtième* had only amounted to 67,500 livres. Thus it was the sudden *acceleration* in the rate of increase of taxation that especially exercised them.

11. Ibid., fols. 6–7. The jurists offered no hard statistics to substantiate this charge, though they *were* able to show that the Burgundian Estates had been compelled in recent years to borrow huge amounts of money to cover the cost of construction of roads, canals, and various unspecified edifices in the province. Ibid., fols. 8–9.

12. See Egret, *The French Prerevolution*, pp. 136–37, for details of this projected reform.

13. The original of these remonstrances is found in Arch. dép. de la Haute-Garonne, Toulouse, 51 B 29 (27). Excerpts here are cited from the copy in Arch. nat., K 713 (49).

14. Arch. nat., K 713 (49), fols. 1–2.

15. Ibid., fol. 3.

16. Ibid., fols. 3–4.

17. That the rural producer was so easily discouraged an entrepreneur reflected (among other things) his deeply rooted conservatism in all agricultural matters. The classic commentary upon this dilemma in the French countryside appears in Bloch, *French Rural History*.

18. *Objets de itératives remontrances* of 1 March 1788, and the *arrêté* protesting and "nullifying" the forced ratification of the October legislation on 10 March, in Bibl. nat.

19. *Arrêt de la cour du Parlement de Toulouse*, Bibl. nat.

20. The government had been assured by several of its agents in Languedoc that the province would accept a higher quota of taxation, especially if this increased levy were assessed in a more equitable fashion on the basis of the new survey of properties. But the Estates had not yet actually sanctioned *any* tax increase; this consequently remained (at least in local eyes) a matter for further negotiation between the ministers and the province. See Egret, *The French Prerevolution*, pp. 136–37.

21. Ibid., p. 137.

22. Arch. dép. de la Seine-Maritime, Rouen, 1BP 1727, pp. 14–19; or Arch. nat., KK 1326, fols. 498–504.

23. The original of these remonstrances is found in Arch. dép. de la Seine-Maritime, Rouen, 1BP 1727, pp. 45–72. They are more readily accessible in *Remontrances du Parlement de Normandie*, Bibl. nat. as *Remontrances du Parlement de Normandie au Roi.*

24. *Remontrances du Parlement de Normandie*, pp. 2–3.

25. Ibid. The Rouennais also maintained, as did so many of their counterparts elsewhere, that oppressive taxation of the land discouraged agricultural initiative and drove capital investment into other sectors of the economy—meaning above all annuities and other kinds of loans. For the most part landed proprietors themselves, the provincial judges tended naturally to condemn such *fortunes mobilières* as "sterile" forms of wealth, useless to the community at large.

26. Ibid., pp. 14–15.

27. Ibid.

28. Ibid., pp. 12, 14–15.

29. Ibid., pp. 16–17. The Normans' use of the term *impôt unique* may owe something to its widespread currency in the writings of the physiocrats, those eighteenth-century proponents of agricultural reform whose pet project was a simplified and more equitable land tax.

30. *Remontrances du parlement de Flandres*, Bibl. nat., pp. 9–10. The jurists at Douai reiterated these sentiments in protests of 1 February 1788.

31. *Mémoire présenté au roi par le parlement de Nancy*, Bibl. nat., pp. 26–28. The judges at Nancy alleged that the imposts levied upon the inhabitants of their province had more than quadrupled over the preceding fifty years.

32. From the jurists' *arrêté* of 3 September 1787 condemning Loménie de Brienne's *subvention territoriale* and stamp tax. Cited by Hardy, *Mes Loisirs*, 7: 226–27 (MS Fonds fr. 6686). Interestingly, the judges referred with candor in this pronunciamento to commoners' "property already so burdened by what is owed to ecclesiastics and seigneurs" as well as to other authorities.

33. Arch. nat., H¹ 163 (51).

34. Ibid., H¹ 163 (89) or (91).

35. Ibid.

36. Ibid., H¹ 163 (81).

37. In a letter dated 4 January 1787, ibid., H¹ 163 (82). He expressed similar opinions in another letter, addressed specifically to Calonne four or five days later. Ibid., (79).

38. Ibid., K 711 (60), fols. 5–6.

39. Bachaumont et al., *Mémoires secrets*, 36: 314–16.

40. The controversy at Bordeaux receives thorough treatment in Doyle, *The Parlement of Bordeaux*, pp. 249–63.

41. See Arch. nat., K 711 (60), fols. 2–3, for the magistrates' vague and perfunctory allusions to the provincial assemblies of Normandy. The Rouen Parlement was not among the first sovereign courts to proclaim a preference for revived provincial Estates over the government's provincial assemblies, but would be demanding them vociferously by late 1788. In the meantime, the judges' own political role took precedence (at least in their own eyes) over any role in local administration that could be accorded to the provincial assemblies.

42. Droz des Villars, *Réflexions sur les inconvéniens*, pp. 43–45, 49–50.

43. Cited from the *arrêté* of 3 September 1787. Hardy, *Mes Loisirs*, 7: 226–27 (MS Fonds fr. 6686).

44. Arch. nat., KK 1326, fols. 230–31.

45. *Règlement pour les paquebots des correspondances avec les colonies.* Versailles, 14 December 1786. Isambert et al., *Recueil*, 28: 272–75. *Arrêt du conseil concernant l'établissement des paquebots pour la correspondance avec les colonies françaises et les Etats-Unis de l'Amérique.* Versailles, 20 December 1786. Isambert et al., *Recueil*, 28: 281–83.

46. Ironically, I came across the documents pertaining to this affair (extracts from the Bordeaux Parlement's official records in a reprinted edition) not at Bordeaux but rather at Rennes. See Arch. dép. d'Ille-et-Vilaine, Rennes, 1Bc 10 (unnumbered document without pagination). It would be interesting to ascertain how the *parlementaires* at Rennes acquired these copies of the Bordelais judges' minutes, and whether they played a role in inspiring the Bretons' action on the same issue the following month.

47. Ibid.

48. Ibid.

49. Ibid., 1Bb 737 (unnumbered documents).

50. Ibid.

51. See Arch. dép. des Bouches-du-Rhône, Aix-en-Provence, B 3680 (minutes of session of 2 October 1787).

52. On this latter subject, see Egret, "La Pré-Révolution en Provence, 1787–89."

53. A copy of the protests quoted in these paragraphs is appended to the official minutes of the session of 13 February, in Arch. dép. des Bouches-du-Rhône, Aix-en-Provence, B 3680.

54. Consult Isambert et al., *Recueil*, 28: 601, for notification of this decree. Its full text, however, is not given here.

55. Droz des Villars, *Mémoires pour servir à l'histoire du droit public,* pp. 162–64. He also observed that his company's first president and *procureur-général* had apprised the ministry of the "difficulties in which the province found itself" at the time of the first Assembly of Notables in early 1787. Ibid., pp. 163–64.

56. Arch. dép. du Doubs, Besançon, B 2175, fols. 187–88.

57. Consult Arch. nat., H¹ 723 (103).

58. These fruitless decrees of March, April, and May 1789 are inscribed among the "important acts of the Court" in Arch. dép. du Doubs, Besançon, B 2175.

59. This *arrêt d'enregistrement* (voted on 6 August 1787) is given in Arch. dép. de la Côte-d'Or, Dijon, B 12145, fol. 466.

60. Bibl. mun. de Dijon, MS Fonds de Juigné 1309, fols. 328–29.

61. Ibid.

62. Ibid. For these later decrees, consult fols. 330–31, 338–39, 342–43, and 354–55, respectively.

63. On the efforts of the Parisian *parlementaires* during the mid-1780s to ensure an adequate supply of firewood for the capital, refer to Stone, *The Parlement of Paris,* pp. 136–41. The analogous activities of the judges at Rouen are discussed by Floquet, *Histoire du parlement de Normandie,* vol. 7.

64. Floquet, *Histoire du parlement de Normandie,* 7: 503–4, for this incident. On several occasions during this difficult decade, Floquet informs us, the *parlementaires* had little choice but to adopt urgent measures on behalf of the indigents of Rouen. The latter, desperate from the cold, actually invaded the Palais de Justice demanding attention to their plight. The jurists sought and received special royal subsidies for the purchase of wood several times during these years.

65. Ibid., 7: 509–10. The minutes of the Rouen Parlement's plenary sessions of

1789 apparently no longer exist, and thus it has proven impossible to consult this missive to Louis XVI. It seems, however, that Floquet was more fortunate in the mid-nineteenth century, for he cites extensively from the letter in ibid., 7: 517–18.

66. Ibid.

67. Refer to the works of Robert Forster, Philippe de Péguilhan de Larboust, and Jean Sentou cited earlier on this point. This is not necessarily to say, however, that in the subsistence crisis of 1788–89 the Toulousain *parlementaires* made no provision for the hungry in their community and their jurisdiction. Unfortunately, the sorry state of the late eighteenth-century parlementary archives at Toulouse (at least as far as public affairs are concerned) permits little investigation of this issue.

68. For the full text of this decree, see Bibl. mun. de Dijon, MS Fonds de Juigné 1309, fols. 300–301.

69. On this matter, see Stone, *The Parlement of Paris*, pp. 141–53; and Doyle, *The Parlement of Bordeaux*, pp. 231–48.

70. For the original of these protests, consult Arch. dép. du Doubs, Besançon, B 2846 (unnumbered document). For a more accessible copy, see Arch. nat., K 708 (23). Quotation here from Arch. nat., K 708 (23), fols. 2–3.

71. Arch. nat., K. 708 (23), fols. 5–7.

72. Ibid., fol. 10.

73. The original is found in Arch. dép. du Doubs, Besançon, B 2846 (unnumbered document); the copy quoted here is in Arch. nat., K 708 (22).

74. This letter in rejoinder must be consulted in Arch. dép. du Doubs, Besançon, B 2846 (unnumbered document).

75. Droz des Villars, *Mémoires pour servir à l'histoire du droit public*, pp. 115–16.

76. On the Grenoble Parlement and the problem of the *corvée royale* in the late 1780s, consult Egret, *Le Parlement de Dauphiné*, 2: 163–69.

77. The original of these protests is found in Arch. dép. de l'Isère, Grenoble, B 2318, fols. 273–83.

78. This counterproposal was found by Egret in the provincial archives of Drôme and is discussed in *Le Parlement de Dauphiné*, 2: 163–69.

79. See Arch. nat., KK 1327, fol. 176. The original of this major decree is found in Arch. dép. de l'Isère, Grenoble, B 2319, fols. 44–51.

80. For this memorandum, see Arch. nat., H¹ 1599 (2).

81. On 12 July the Alsatian judges had, in protests to Louis XVI, enumerated imposts—*fourrages, épis du Rhin*, and so on—levied exclusively upon the *taillables* of the province and (so they claimed) arbitrarily increased by the ministers to help defray expenses unrelated to the administration of Alsace. See Arch. nat., H¹ 1596 (232). The jurists had also censured Intendant Chaumont de la Galaisière for his allegedly oppressive management of affairs in the province. The intendant angrily denied the magistrates' charges in a letter of 18 August to the ministers.Ibid., document 229.

82. For this missive, see Arch. nat., H¹ 1599 (31).

83. Ibid., document 33.

84. See chapter 3, and Delmas, *Du Parlement de Navarre*, pp. 407–8.

85. For this ministerial memorandum, see Arch. nat., K 711 (33). More specifically, these "Observations" insisted that those inhabitants of the region demonstrably injured in their proprietary or other rights by the Franco-Spanish border negotiations had been or would be fully indemnified for their losses. The judges'

attack upon the comte d'Ornano was termed totally unjustified and irresponsible. See ibid., document 32 or 40, for the earlier magisterial protests (of 11 December 1786).

86. Ibid., document 36, fols. 3–4.

87. Ibid., fols. 4 and 5.

88. Ibid., fol. 3. They had, of course, descanted as well upon the principle of the inalienability of royal domain; still, the plaints of aggrieved local landowners probably counted for more in moving them to remonstrate on this question.

89. Delmas, *Du Parlement de Navarre*, pp. 407–8.

90. See Bachaumont et al., *Mémoires secrets*, 35: 88–89. Although this source maintained that the jurists' "foolish" protests had been motivated in part by magisterial fears concerning a possible reduction in the size of the jurisdiction stemming from the readjustment of the Franco-Spanish border, such misgivings do not surface in the protests of December 1787.

91. On the ten-year recession immediately preceding the Revolution, the classic studies remain those of Labrousse, *Esquisse du mouvement des prix et des revenus;* and Labrousse, *La Crise de l'économie française.*

92. Arch. dép. d'Ille-et-Vilaine, Rennes, 1Bb 736 (minutes of 16 and 23 February 1786). A copy of the letter itself, an unnumbered document, is found in ibid., 1Bc 10.

93. These missives are unnumbered documents in ibid.

94. On this incident, consult ibid., 1Bb 736 (minutes of 11 and 15 May 1786). A copy of the missive is found in ibid., 1Bc 10.

95. This letter is found in Arch. dép. de la Seine-Maritime, Rouen, 1BP 1727, pp. 205–16. This excerpt is from p. 207.

96. Ibid., p. 212.

97. Ibid., pp. 213–16, for the quotations in this paragraph.

98. Ibid., pp. 215–16.

CONCLUSION

1. See Greer, *The Incidence of the Emigration*, p. 85. Greer's numbers are somewhat larger than those given in Carré, *La Fin des Parlements*, pp. 263–76.

2. Refer to Carré, *La Fin des Parlements*, pp. 277–91; Greer, *The Incidence of the Terror;* Doyle, *The Parlement of Bordeaux*, pp. 311–13; and Duboul, *La Fin du Parlement de Toulouse.*

3. On the fates of the Parisian *parlementaires*, refer again to Carré, *La Fin des Parlements*, pp. 263–309, and to the apposite biographical entries in Bluche, *L'Origine des magistrats.* Some of the veterans of the Parisian and provincial tribunals attended convocations of old regime judicial and governmental personnel held abroad in the 1790s and mapped out strategies and issued appeals for the restoration of the old institutions in France. Such efforts, of course, came to naught.

4. Consult, in addition to the sources listed in the preceding notes, Egret, *Le Parlement de Dauphiné*, 2: 358–59; and Robinne, "Les magistrats du parlement de Normandie," pp. 387–92.

5. On this point, see Lucas, "Nobles, Bourgeois, and the Origins of the French Revolution," and Egret's analysis of the political propaganda of late 1788 and early 1789 in *The French Prerevolution.*

6. Refer to Doyle, *Origins of the French Revolution*, pp. 7–40, for the most

recent overview of this orthodox interpretation and of the dissenting "revisionist" historiography of the past generation.

7. Cobban, *The Social Interpretation*, pp. 67, 79, 68–80. Furthermore (as Cobban could have added), the industrial revolution in France hardly got under way on a major scale before the middle and later decades of the nineteenth century. See also Crouzet, "Les conséquences économiques de la Révolution à propos d'un inédit de Sir Francis d'Invernois," pp. 182–217.

8. Cobban, *The Social Interpretation*, p. 82.

9. Lucas, "Nobles, Bourgeois, and the Origins of the French Revolution," p. 86.

10. Ibid., pp. 124–25.

11. Ibid., p. 103. See pp. 97–98 and 116–18, for Lucas's discussion of the crown's long-term impact upon the evolution of the social elite, and the attitude of the elite toward the government in the eighteenth century.

12. Taylor, "Noncapitalist Wealth and the Origins of the French Revolution," p. 491.

13. Doyle, *Origins of the French Revolution*, pp. 158, 41–114.

14. See, for some other straws in the wind, J. F. Bosher's introduction to Egret's *The French Prerevolution*; Keith Baker's remarks in a review article, "Enlightenment and Revolution in France: Old Problems, Renewed Approaches," pp. 281–303; and Furet's *Penser la Révolution française*, esp. pp. 145–51.

15. Furet, *Penser la Révolution française*, pp. 148–50.

16. Ibid., pp. 149–51, 148.

17. Skocpol, *States and Social Revolutions*. Skocpol has not been without her precursors in this interpretative tradition. See, for a brilliant if controversial example, Von Laue, *Why Lenin? Why Stalin?*

18. Skocpol, *States and Social Revolutions*, pp. 51–67. On the critical role of the financiers in the deepening governmental crisis under Louis XVI, see also Bosher, *French Finances*, pp. 304–5.

19. Skocpol, *States and Social Revolutions*, pp. 59–60, 64.

20. Ibid., pp. 64–67.

Bibliography

It has seemed most natural to divide the bibliography for this study into the following five sections: (1) essential reference works, including almanacs, dictionaries, bibliographical articles, published documentary collections and parlementary proceedings, and the like; (2) unpublished Parisian and provincial parlementary records and proceedings; (3) pamphlet literature in various forms authored by, or especially concerning, the Parisian or provincial *parlementaires*; (4) memoirs and journals from the pens of contemporary observers; and (5) subsequent scholarship on the *parlementaires* and their affairs in this period. Readers desiring to cast their nets more widely for the immense wealth of historical research on late eighteenth-century and revolutionary France are advised to consult the bibliographies of more general works.

ESSENTIAL REFERENCE WORKS

Almanach royal. Paris: Debure, for the years from 1774 to 1790.

Antoine, Michel. "Les Remontrances des Cours supérieures au XVIIIe siècle. Essai de problématique et d'inventaire." *Comité des travaux historiques et scientifiques. Bulletin de la section d'histoire moderne et contemporaine* 8 (1971):7–81.

Bluche, J. François. *L'Origine des magistrats du Parlement de Paris au XVIIIe siècle.* Paris: Fédération des Sociétés historiques et archéologiques de Paris et de l'Île-de-France, 1956.

Egret, Jean. "Note d'orientation de recherches sur les Cours souveraines, particulièrement au XVIIIe siècle." *Comité des travaux historiques et scientifiques. Bulletin de la section d'histoire moderne et contemporaine* 5 (1964):45–53.

Etat nominatif des pensions sur le trésor royal, imprimé par ordre de l'Assemblée nationale. 3 vols. Paris: Imprimerie nationale, 1789–90.

Flammermont, Jules. *Les Remontrances du Parlement de Paris au XVIIIe siècle.* 3 vols. Paris: Imprimerie nationale, 1888–98. Flammermont published in the third of these three volumes nearly all parlementary speeches and protests delivered to Louis XVI during the 1774–89 period, as well as certain deliberations within the court's plenary sessions. The complete minutes and registers of those plenary sessions make up parts of series X^{1A} and X^{1B} in the Archives nationales (see below, second section).

Isambert, François André, et al., eds. *Recueil général des anciennes lois françaises: Depuis l'an 420 jusqu'à la révolution de 1789.* 29 vols. Paris: Belin-LePrieur, 1822–33. The full texts of legislation discussed in this study are not always found in this compilation of French laws. In such cases the reader wherever possible is directed to copies of royal acts (and parlementary decrees) found elsewhere.

304

Bibliography

Marion, Marcel. *Dictionnaire des institutions de la France aux XVII et XVIII*
siècles. Paris: A. Picard, 1923.
Monin, Hippolyte. *L'Etat de Paris en 1789: Etudes et documents sur l'ancien ré-*
gime à Paris. Paris: Jouaust, 1889.
Mousnier, Roland. *The Institutions of France under the Absolute Monarchy.*
Trans. Brian Pearce. Chicago: University of Chicago Press, 1979.
Procès-verbal de l'assemblée de notables, tenue à Versailles, en l'année 1787.
Paris, 1788.
Procès-verbal de l'assemblée de notables, tenue à Versailles, en l'année 1788.
Paris, 1788.
Roton, A. de. *Les Arrêts du Grand Conseil portant dispense du marc d'or de no-*
blesse. Commentés et complétés par J. de la Trollière et R. de Montmort.
Paris: S. G. A. F., 1951. As Jean Egret has pointed out, the decrees in question
were almost certainly issued by the Conseil des Dépêches rather than by the
Grand Conseil during the 1770s and 1780s. The decrees excused young and
noble *parlementaires,* among other noblemen, from the obligation of paying
the *marc d'or de noblesse,* upon assuming office, and they thus provide information about the social origins of the young entrants into the court during
this period. The vast majority of these initiates were lay rather than clerical,
and it is these lay jurists whose decrees of dispensation were published by de
Roton and his collaborators.

UNPUBLISHED PARLEMENTARY RECORDS AND PROCEEDINGS

The official records of the Paris Parlement make up the several X series in the
Archives nationales. The judicial decrees, minutes, and registers found therein
constitute one of the most imposing documentary collections surviving from the
old regime in France. Other series in this national repository contain genealogical
and administrative information germane to the membership and functions of the
Paris Parlement. However, most collections of personal papers surviving from the
eighteenth-century judges repose in the Bibliothèque nationale, most notably the
copious holdings in the manuscript archive of the Joly de Fleury family. Although, for the years prior to 1774, there are abundant and valuable parlementary
papers housed in other Parisian repositories, documents essential to the historian
of the 1774–89 period are concentrated entirely in the Archives nationales and
Bibliothèque nationale. Copies of some of the documents deriving from the late
1780s may be found elsewhere in the capital, as, for example, at the Bibliothèque
de l'Arsenal, Bibliothèque historique de la Ville de Paris, Bibliothèque Mazarine,
Bibliothèque Saint-Geneviève, Bibliothèque du Sénat, Société de l'Histoire du
Protestantisme Français, Archives de Paris et de l'Ancien Département de la
Seine, and Archives du Ministère des Affaires Etrangères. Nevertheless, specialists in the Paris Parlement of Louis XVI's reign may safely spend all their scholarly hours at the Archives nationales and Bibliothèque nationale.
    The story regarding the provincial *parlements* is considerably more compli-
cated. Even if (as in the case of this study) a distinction be made for research
purposes between eight of the oldest and most extensive provincial jurisdictions
and the lesser jurisdictions of provincial France, the student of the
prerevolutionary provincial magistracy must still range all over the country in
search of the pertinent official parlementary records. Inadequacies in the archives

of even some of the most important provincial *parlements* are, fortunately, miti-gated in large measure by what is available at Paris: what cannot be found at Toulouse, for instance, usually turns up at the Archives nationales or Bibliothèque Mazarine. There are doubtless personal papers of magistrates of the late 1780s that lie yet undiscovered in series E and other documentary series of the provincial archives, in rustic châteaus and *maisons de campagne,* among holdings deriving from the Revolutionary Tribunal at the Archives nationales, and elsewhere.

Manuscript Sources at Paris (1786–89)

Archives nationales

Although pertinent documents may be found in many series at the Archives nationales, ranging from the old regime series O^1 and U to the "modern" series AD^{XVI}, AP, BB^{30}, and F^{1a}, the principal sources are the following:

158 AP, especially cartons 3 and 9. Personal papers of Jean Jacques IV Duval d'Eprémesnil.

H^1 147, 163, and 186. Parlement of Dijon, Estates of Burgundy, correspondence between Burgundian intendant and central government.

   723. Parlement of Besançon, affairs of Franche-Comté.

   731. Parlement of Douai, affairs of Flanders, Hainaut.

   1238 and 1240. Parlement of Aix, affairs of Provence.

   1596 and 1599. Parlementary remonstrances and correspondence concerning the provincial assemblies in 1787.

K 160 and 700. *Lits de justice,* protests over reform legislation of 1787–88.

   692(B). Parlement of Rouen, affairs of Normandy.

   707. Parlement of Aix; Conseil Supérieur of Alsace (Colmar).

   708. Parlements of Besançon and Bordeaux.

   709. Parlements of Dijon and Douai.

   710. Parlements of Grenoble, Metz, and Nancy.

   711. Parlements of Pau and Rouen.

   712. Parlement of Rennes.

   713. Conseil Souverain of Roussillon (Perpignan); Parlement of Toulouse.

KK 1326–27. *Troubles du Royaume de France au sujet des édits, déclarations, etc., enregistrés aux lits de justice de 1787 et 1788 par le Parlement de Paris et ensuite par les autres Cours du Royaume.* An enormous two-volume collection of anonymously transcribed protests of all kinds by the parlements and other sovereign courts during the prerevolutionary crisis.

O^1 352. Personal information about the Parisian and provincial judges during the prerevolutionary crisis.

X^{1B} 8986–89. Minutes of Parisian parlementary sessions (including the plenary sessions on judicial and public affairs held in the so-called Conseil Secret) during 1787–89. Remonstrances and other pertinent political documents are usually to be found transcribed here or even in published form. (The court's official registers for this period no longer exist.)

Bibliothèque Mazarine

MSS 2407–9. *Recueil des actes des Parlements de France, durant l'année 1788.*
A three-volume collection of transcribed parlementary protests similar to, if
not nearly as voluminous as, that indicated above in Arch. nat., KK 1326–
27.

Bibliothèque nationale

Collection Joly de Fleury. This collection of more than 2,500 volumes, a legacy
of the famous Parisian family of the eighteenth-century robe, provides crucial information on the *parlementaires* (especially the Parisians) of that era.
Volumes consulted for the 1787–89 period:

1037. Provincial assemblies (1787).
1038–44. A wide range of political, administrative, and social issues of the
prerevolutionary crisis, including the Assemblies of Notables of 1787 and
1788, taxation, and preparations for and discussion of the Estates-General in
1788–89.
1466. Material on the stamp tax and *subvention territoriale* of 1787.
2114–16. Various public controversies of the period, such as the Paris Parlement's exile to Troyes in 1787, the government's projected *cour plénière*, Loménie de Brienne's financial legislation, and so on.

Nouvelles acquisitions françaises 945. An anonymous eighteenth-century commentary upon the Paris Parlement.

Manuscript Sources in the Provinces (1786–89)

Aix-en-Provence

Archives départementales des Bouches-du-Rhône (Dépôt annexe à Aix):
B 3680. *Délibérations du Parlement de Provence, 1786–90.*

Bibliothèque Méjanes:
MS 634. *Notice du Parlement de Provence. 1788.*
MS 1037. *Journal du Parlement, du Président Fauris de Saint-Vincent.*

Besançon

Archives départementales du Doubs:
B 2175. *Actes importantes. Edits et Déclarations. (1779–90).*
2846. *Remontrances, Lettres et Réponses (1787).*
2850. *Correspondance avec les ministres (1787–88).*

Bibliothèque municipale de Besançon:
Collection Dunand.
MS 13. *Journal du Père Dunand (1752–87, 1789).*

307
Bibliography

Dijon

Archives départementales de la Côte-d'Or:
B 12145. *Enregistrement des édits, ordonnances, etc. (1781–87).*
Bibliothèque municipal de Dijon:
Fonds de Juigné.
MS 1309. *Recueil d'arrêts du Parlement de Dijon. Imprimés et manuscrits* (vol. 6, 1781–89).

Grenoble

Archives départementales de l'Isère:
B 2318–19. *Arrêtés, remontrances, etc. (1787–89).*
Bibliothèque municipale de Grenoble:
Fonds Gariel.
MS 1629 (Q 6). *Correspondance du procureur-général au Parlement de Grenoble avec les ministres, du 12 avril 1780 au 20 juillet 1790.*
MS 1630 (Q 7). *Copie des lettres écrites au procureur-général du Parlement par les ministres . . . du 17 avril 1780 au 10 octobre 1788.*
MS 1632 (Q 4 [6]). *Correspondance du procureur-général au parlement de Grenoble avec la province, du 18 avril 1786 au 16 avril 1789.*

Rennes

Archives départementales d'Ille-et-Vilaine:
1Bb. *Registres secrets de la Chambre du Conseil.*
736. Novembre 1785–Octobre 1786.
737. Novembre 1786–Octobre 1787.
738. Novembre 1787–Octobre 1788.
739. Novembre 1788–Octobre 1789.
1Bc. *Remontrances du Parlement.*
9. 1783–87.
10. 1786–89.
11. 1788.
12. 1788.

Rouen

Archives départementales de la Seine-Maritime:
1BP 1727. *Chambre de Secret (12 Novembre 1787–11 November 1788).*

Toulouse

Archives départementales de la Haute-Garonne:
51 B 29. *Remontrances (1712–89).*
51 B 30. *Remontrances (1652–1789).*
51 B 37. *Administration intérieure et événements politiques (1551–1790).*
51 B 38. *Imprimés importants relatifs à l'organisation et à la juridiction de la Cour (1671–1789).*

PAMPHLET LITERATURE

Parlementary protests, decrees, letters, and the like are listed here in alphabetical order by the seats of justice.

Arrêtés du parlement de Franche-Comté. Des 4 et 9 janvier 1788. N.d. Bibl. nat., 8° Lb³⁹, 501.

Arrêté du parlement de Franche-Comté. Du 27 janvier 1789. N.d. Bibl. nat., 8° Lb³⁹, 1026.

Arrêté du parlement de Franche-Comté, du 31 janvier 1789. N.d. Bibl. nat., 8° Lb³⁹, 6956.

Très-humbles et très-respectueuses remontrances qu'adressent au roi, notre très-honoré et souverain seigneur, les gens tenant sa cour de parlement de Bordeaux à Libourne, du 4 mars 1788, sur les lettres de cachet. N.d. Bibl. nat., 8° Lb³⁹, 528.

Lettre du parlement de Bordeaux au roi, du 23 janvier 1789. N.d. Bibl. nat., 8° Lb³⁹, 1008.

Arrêté du parlement de Dijon, séant en temps de vacations. Du lundi 10 septembre 1787. Arrêté du parlement de Dijon, séant en temps de vacations. Du mercredi 12 septembre 1787. N.d. Bibl. nat., 8° Lb³⁹, 447.

Très-humbles et très-respectueuses remontrances qu'adressent au roi . . . les gens tenant sa cour de parlement et aides à Dijon. N.d. Bibl. nat., 8° Lb³⁹, 510.

Remontrances du parlement de Flandres. (30 novembre 1787.) N.d. Bibl. nat., 8° Lb³⁹, 6356.

Remontrances du parlement de Flandres. (1ᵉʳ fevrier.) [1788] N.d. Bibl. nat., 8° Lb³⁹, 517.

Très-humbles et très-respectueuses remontrances qu'adressent au roi . . . les gens tenant sa cour de parlement, chambre des comptes et cour des aides de Metz. (19 janvier 1788.) N.d. Bibl. nat., 8° Lb³⁹, 6370.

Arrêté du parlement de Metz. Du premier mars mil sept cent quatre-vingt-huit. N.d. Bibl. nat., 8° Lb³⁹, 527.

Déclarations et itératives protestations du parlement de Metz. (20 juin 1788.) N.d. Bibl. nat., 8° Lb³⁹, 6472.

Remontrances du Parlement de Nancy, arrêtées le 12 janvier 1788 sur l'ordre d'exil et lettres de cachet. N.d. Bibl. nat., 8° Lb³⁹, 12274.

Mémoire présenté au roi par le parlement de Nancy. (Février 1788.) N.d. Bibl. nat., 8° Lb³⁹, 6376.

Arrêté du parlement de Nancy, du 22 décembre 1788. N.d. Bibl. nat., 8° Lb³⁹, 6737.

Lettre du parlement de Pau au roi, du 31 août 1787. N.d. Bibl. nat., 8° Lb³⁹, 429.

Remontrances au roi, par le Parlement de Navarre, sur la translation du parlement de Bordeaux à Libourne. (14 décembre.) [1787] N.d. Bibl. nat., 8° Lb³⁹, 478.

Arrêté du Parlement de Navarre du 12 janvier 1788. 1788. Bibl. nat., 8° F. 9930.

Très-humbles et très-respectueuses remontrances présentées au roi par le parlement de Navarre, sur une lettre qui lui a été écrite le 2 janvier 1788, par M. le garde des sceaux; avec la réponse à cette même lettre. N.d. Bibl. nat., 8° Lb³⁹, 495.

Arrêté du parlement de Navarre, à la suite d'un arrêt du conseil, du 1ᵉʳ de ce mois, signifié le 11. Du 20 février 1788. N.d. Bibl. nat., 8° Lb³⁹, 6375.

309
Bibliography

Remontrances et arrêts du parlement de Navarre. Des 21 et 26 juin 1788. N.d.
Bibl. nat., 8° Lb³⁹, 601.

Extrait des registres du parlement de Navarre, du 13 mars 1789. 1789. Bibl. nat.,
8° Lb³⁹, 7024.

Arrêté du parlement de Bretagne. Du 18 aout 1787. Arrêté du 20 aout 1787.
N.d. Bibl. nat., 8° Lb³⁹, 406.

*Lettre de MM. du parlement de Bretagne au roi, du 29 janvier 1789. Arrêt de la
cour, du jeudi 12 février 1789.* N.d. Bibl. nat., 8° Lb³⁹, 6984.

Remontrances du Parlement de Normandie au Roi, du 5 février 1788. N.d. Bibl.
nat., 8° Lb³⁹, 518.

*Lettre du parlement de Normandie au roi, pour demander les anciens états de
la province. (Novembre.)* [1788] N.d. Bibl. nat., 8° Lb³⁹, 793.

*Supplications du parlement de Toulouse au roi. Du 5 janvier 1788. Supplica-
tions du parlement de Toulouse au roi, au sujet du parlement de Bordeaux.
Du 5 janvier 1788.* N.d. Bibl. nat., 8° Lb³⁹, 499.

*Objets des très-humbles et itératives remontrances du parlement de Toulouse,
sur l'édit du mois d'octobre dernier, portant prorogation du second vingtième. (1ᵉʳ mars.) Arrêté du parlement de Toulouse, du 10 mars 1788.* N.d.
Bibl. nat., 8° Lb³⁹, 529.

*Arrêt de la cour du Parlement de Toulouse, qui fait inhibitions et défenses de
donner aucune exécution à l'ordonnance des commissaires des vingtièmes de
la province de Languedoc, du 30 janvier 1788, à peine d'enquis, etc. Extrait
des registres du parlement. Du 27 mars 1788.* N.d. Bibl. nat., 8° Lb³⁹, 533.

Pronouncements by individual *parlementaires* are listed below in alphabetical
order by the individuals.

Droz des Villars, François-Nicolas-Eugène. *Mémoires pour servir à l'histoire du
droit public de la Franche-Comté, principalement en matière d'administration et d'impôts.* 1789. Bibl. nat., 8° F. 33087.

―――――. *Réflexions sur les inconvéniens et les dangers des nouveaux systèmes
d'administration relativement à la province de Franche-Comté.* N.d. Bibliothèque municipale de Besançon.

Du Couëdic de Kergoualer, Amand. *Précis historique de ce qui s'est passé à
Rennes, depuis l'arrivée de M. le Comte de Thiard, commandant en Bretagne.*
Rennes, aux dépens de la province de Bretagne, 1788. Bibl. nat., 8° Lb³⁹, 560.

―――――. *Suite du Précis historique des événemens de Bretagne.* Rennes, aux
dépens de la province de Bretagne, 1788. Bibl. nat., 8° Lb³⁹, 561.

―――――. *Précis historique des événemens de Bretagne. 3ᵉ partie.* Rennes, aux
dépens de la province de Bretagne, 1788. Bibl. nat., 8° Lb³⁹, 561 bis.

*Avertissement de M. d'Eprémesnil, à l'occasion de trois libelles anonymes qu'il
a reçus de Beaucaire, par la poste.* 1789. Bibl. nat., 8° Lb³⁹, 6957.

*Déclaration de M. d'Eprémesnil, au sujet d'un imprimé faussement répandu
sous son nom.* 1789. Bibl. nat., 8° Lb³⁹, 6826.

*Discours de M. d'Eprémesnil à l'Assemblée nationale, au sujet de l'affaire des
magistrats de Rennes.* 1790. Bibl. nat., 8° Le²⁹, 423.

Discours et opinions de d'Eprémesnil, précédés d'une notice sur sa vie. 1823.
Bibl. nat., X 18835 bis.

*Observations sur une assertion de M. de Menou, au sujet des frais de l'ancienne
administration judiciaire comparée à la nouvelle, proposées le 30 août 1790 à
l'Assemblée nationale, par M. d'Eprémesnil.* 1790. Bibl. nat., 8° Lb³⁹, 3980.

Proposition inutilement faite par M. d'Eprémesnil à l'Assemblée (sur l'invio-

labilité de la personne royale) . . . *le 28 mars 1791, suivie d'un aperçu de l'opinion qu'il aurait prononcée, s'il avait eu la liberté de parole.* N.d. Bibl. nat., 8° Le²⁹, 2094.

Réflexions d'un magistrat sur la question du nombre et celle de l'opinion par ordre ou par tête. December 1788. By Duval d'Eprémesnil. Bibl. nat., 8° Lb³⁹, 821.

Lettre de Mme d'Eprémesnil au principal ministre. N.d. Bibl. nat., 8° Lb³⁹, 6395.

Discours de M. Goislard de Montsabert, conseiller au Parlement de Paris . . . *le* . . . *29 avril 1788, à M. le premier président, sur les vérifications ministérielles entreprises pour accroître la masse des vingtièmes.* N.d. Bibl. nat., 8° Lb³⁹, 6383 or 6385.

De la nécessité d'assembler les Etats-Généraux dans les circonstances actuelles, et de l'inadmission du timbre: Fragment du Discours de M. [Huguet] de Sémonville, conseiller au Parlement, dans la séance du 16. July 1787. Bibl. nat., 8° Lb³⁹, 377.

Réflexions sur les pouvoirs et instructions à donner par les provinces à leurs députés aux Etats-Généraux. N.d. Attributed to Huguet de Sémonville by the revolutionary and Napoleonic librarian and editor Antoine-Alexandre Barbier. Bibl. nat., 8° Lb³⁹, 11117.

Discours de M. de La Boissière, conseiller, avocat général au parlement du Dauphiné, prononcé le jour de l'ouverture de ce parlement, du 17 novembre 1788, à la séance pour la prestation du serment, et analogue aux circonstances de l'année 1788 et aux états généraux. N.d. Bibl. nat., 8° Lb³⁹, 6627.

Discours de M. le premier président (Louis-François de Paule Lefevre d'Ormesson), lors de sa réception, prononcé en parlement, toutes les chambres assemblées, le 12 novembre 1788. N.d. Bibl. nat., 8° Lb³⁹, 687.

Discours de M. Savoye de Rollin, avocat général au parlement de Dauphiné, prononcé lors de la séance de cette cour, du 21 octobre 1788, pour l'enregistrement et la publication de la Déclaration du roi, du 23 septembre 1788, qui ordonne que l'assemblée des états généraux aura lieu dans le courant du mois de janvier de l'année prochaine. N.d. Bibl. nat., 8° Lb³⁹, 6595.

Façon de voir d'une bonne vieille, qui ne radote pas encore. Attributed to Antoine Louis Séguier by Barbier. N.d. Bibl. nat., 8° Lb³⁹, 750.

La Constitution renversée: Réflexions de M. Séguier, avocat général au Parlement à Paris. N.d. Bibl. nat., 8° Lb³⁹, 5604.

Rapport de M. l'abbé Tandeau, de l'édit d'emprunt enregistré à la séance du roi au Parlement, le 19 novembre 1787. N.d. Bibl. nat., 8° Lb³⁹, 470.

GENERAL MEMOIRS AND JOURNALS

d'Allonville, Comte Armand. *Mémoires secrets, de 1770 à 1830.* 6 vols. Paris: Werdet, 1838–45.

Augeard, Jacques-Mathieu. *Mémoires secrets . . . (1760 à 1800).* Paris: H. Plon, 1866.

Bachaumont, Louis Petit de, et al. *Mémoires secrets pour servir à l'histoire de la république des lettres en France depuis 1762 jusqu'à nos jours.* 36 vols. London: J. Adamson, 1777–89.

Barentin, C.-L.-F. de Paule de. *Mémoire autographe sur les derniers conseils du roi Louis XVI.* Paris: Comptoir des imprimeurs réunis, 1844.

Bibliography

Bésenval, Bon-Pierre-Victoire, baron de. *Mémoires*. 3 vols. Paris: P. Buisson, 1805.

Beugnot, Jacques-Claude, comte de. *Mémoires, 1783–1815*. 2 vols. Paris: E. Dentu, 1867–68.

Bouillé, François-Claude-Amour, marquis de. *Mémoires*. Paris: Baudouin fils, 1821.

Choiseul, Etienne-François, duc de. *Mémoires*. Paris: Fernand Calmettes, 1904.

Croy, Emmanuel, maréchal duc de. *Mémoires . . . sur les cours de Louis XV et Louis XVI*. Paris: aux bureaux de la "Nouvelle Revue retrospective," 1897.

Documents concernant le règne de Louis XVI, 1er janvier 1783–22 décembre 1792. Bulletins d'informations rédigés à Versailles et à Paris par un témoin, familier de la Cour. 3 vols. Bibl. nat., MSS Nouv. acq. fr. 13276–78.

Dufort, J.-N., comte de Cheverny. *Mémoires sur les règnes de Louis XV et Louis XVI et sur la Révolution*. 2 vols. Paris: E. Plon, 1886.

Faulcon, Félix. *Correspondance*. 2 vols. Poitiers: G. Debien, 1939–53.

Ferrand, Antoine François Claude, comte de. *Mémoires*. Paris: A. Picard et fils, 1897.

Gazette de Leyde. Nouvelles politiques publiées à Leyde. 57 vols. Leiden, 1760–1810.

Gazette manuscrite, ou Bulletin à la main. 1787–1789. 3 vols. Bibl. nat., Réserve, 4° Lc², 2225.

Georgel, Abbé Jean-François. *Mémoires pour servir à l'histoire des événements de la fin du XVIIIe siècle, depuis 1760 jusqu'en 1806–1810, par un contemporain impartial*. 6 vols. Paris: Eymery, 1817–18.

Hardy, Siméon-Prosper. *Mes Loisirs, ou, Journal d'événements tel qu'ils parviennent à ma connaissance (1764–1789)*. 8 vols. Bibl. nat., MSS Fonds fr. 6680–87.

Lescure, A. M. de, ed. *Correspondance secrète inédite sur Louis XVI, Marie-Antoinette, la cour, et la ville, de 1777 à 1792*. 2 vols. Paris: H. Plon, 1866.

Métra, François, Imbert, G., et al. *Correspondance secrète, politique et littéraire, ou Mémoires pour servir à l'histoire des cours, des sociétés et de la littérature en France, depuis la mort de Louis XV*. 18 vols. London: J. Adamson, 1787–90.

Montbarey, Alexandre-Marie-Léonor de Saint-Mauris, prince de. *Mémoires autographes*. 3 vols. Paris: A. Eymery, 1826–27.

Montmorency-Luxembourg, Anne-Charles-Sigismond, duc de. Cited in Paul Filleul, *Le Duc de Montmorency-Luxembourg*. Paris: Labergerie, 1939.

Moreau, Jacob-Nicholas. *Mes Souvenirs*. 2 vols. Paris: E. Plon, 1898–1901.

Pasquier, Etienne-Denis, baron et duc de. *Histoire de mon temps: Mémoires du Chancelier Pasquier*. 6 vols. Paris: Plon, 1893–95.

Sallier-Chaumont de la Roche, Guy Marie. *Annales françaises: Depuis le commencement du règne de Louis XVI jusqu'aux Etats-Généraux, 1774–1789*. Paris: Leriche, 1813.

———. *Essais pour servir d'introduction à l'histoire de la Révolution française, par un ancien magistrat du Parlement de Paris*. Paris: Leriche, 1802.

Ségur, Louis-Philippe, comte de. *Mémoires ou souvenirs et anecdotes*. 2 vols. Paris: Didier, 1843.

Sémallé, Jean René Pierre, comte de. *Souvenirs*. Paris: A. Picard et fils, 1898.

Soulavie, Jean-Louis Giraud. *Mémoires historiques et politiques du règne de Louis XVI*. 6 vols. Paris: Treuttel et Würtz, 1801.

Talleyrand-Périgord, Charles-Maurice, duc de. *Mémoires*. 5 vols. Paris: C. Lévy, 1891–92.

Vitrolles, Eugène François Auguste d'Arnaud, baron de. *Mémoires*. Paris: Farel, 1950.

SUBSEQUENT SCHOLARSHIP

Alatri, Paolo. *Parlamenti e lotta politica nella Francia del Settecento*. Rome: Laterza, 1977.
Amiable, L. *La Franc-maçonnerie et la magistrature en France à la veille de la Révolution*. Aix: J. Remondet-Aubin, 1894.
Antoine, Michel, ed. *"Le Mémoire" de Gilbert de Voisins "sur les cassations": Un épisode des querelles entre Louis XV et les Parlements, 1767*. Paris: Sirey, 1958.
Baker, Keith. "Enlightenment and Revolution in France: Old Problems, Renewed Approaches." *Journal of Modern History* 53 (1981): 281–303.
Barthélémy, Paul Bisson de. *L'Activité d'un procureur général au Parlement de Paris à la fin de l'ancien régime: Les Joly de Fleury*. Paris: Société d'édition d'enseignement supérieur, 1964.
Behrens, C. B. A. "Nobles, Privileges, and Taxes in France at the End of the Ancien Régime." *Economic History Review*, 2d ser., 15, no. 3 (April 1963): 451–75.
Bickart, Roger. *Les Parlements et la notion de souveraineté nationale au XVIIIe siècle*. Paris: F. Alcan, 1932.
Bien, David D. *The Calas Affair: Persecution, toleration and heresy in eighteenth-century Toulouse*. Princeton, N.J.: Princeton University Press, 1961.
Bloch, Marc. *French Rural History: An Essay on its Basic Characteristics*. Trans. Janet Sondheimer. Berkeley: University of California Press, 1966.
Bluche, J. François. *Les Magistrats du Parlement de Paris au XVIIIe siècle (1715–1771)*. Paris: Les Belles-Lettres, 1960.
Bosher, J. F. *French Finances, 1770–1795: From Business to Bureaucracy*. Cambridge: Cambridge University Press, 1970.
Burckard, François. "Organisation, personnel et rôle du Conseil souverain d'Alsace, de 1715 à 1790." Thèse de l'Ecole des Chartes, 1951.
Carcassonne, Elie. *Montesquieu et le problème de la constitution française au XVIIIe siècle*. Paris: Presses Universitaires de France, 1926.
Carey, John A., *Judicial Reform in France before the Revolution of 1789*. Cambridge, Mass.: Harvard University Press, 1981.
Carré, Henri. *La Fin des Parlements, 1788–1790*. Paris: Hachette, 1912.
———. "Les Parlements et la convocation des Etats-Généraux (1788–1789)." *La Révolution française* 53 (1907): 5–24, 168–77, 193–217.
———. "Un Précurseur inconscient de la Révolution: Le Conseiller du Val d'Eprémesnil." *La Révolution française* 33 (July–December 1897): 349–73.
———. "La Réaction parlementaire de 1775 et le procureur général de Moydieu." *Revue d'histoire moderne et contemporaine* 11 (1908–February 1909): 349–58.
———. "La Tactique et les idées de l'opposition parlementaire." *La Révolution française* 29 (July–December 1895): 97–121.
———. "Turgot et le rappel des Parlements." *La Révolution française* 43 (July–December 1902): 193–208.
Cavanaugh, Gerald J. "Turgot: The Rejection of Enlightened Despotism." *French Historical Studies* 6 (Spring 1969): 31–58.

313
Bibliography

Clapiers-Collongues, Balthasar de, et al. *Chronologie des Officiers des Cours Souveraines de Provence*. Aix: B. Niel, 1909.

Cobban, Alfred. *A History of Modern France*. Vol. 1: *Old Regime and Revolution, 1715–1799*. Baltimore: Penguin Books, 1968.

_____. "The Parlements of France in the Eighteenth Century." *History* 35 (1950): 64–80.

_____. *The Social Interpretation of the French Revolution*. Cambridge: Cambridge University Press, 1964.

Colombet, Albert. *Les Parlementaires Bourguignons à la fin du XVIIIe siècle*. Lyons: Bosc frères, 1936.

Crouzet, François. "Les Conséquences économiques de la Révolution à propos d'un inédit de Sir Francis d'Invernois." *Annales historiques de la Révolution française* 168 (1962): 182–217.

Dakin, Douglas. *Turgot and the Ancien Régime in France*. London: Methuen, 1939.

Dard, Emile. *Un Epicurien sous la terreur: Hérault de Sechelles, 1759–1794*. Paris: Perrin, 1907.

Darnton, Robert. *Mesmerism and the End of the Enlightenment in France*. Cambridge, Mass.: Harvard University Press, 1968.

David, René, and de Vries, Henry P. *The French Legal System: An Introduction to Civil Law Systems*. New York: Oceana Publications, 1958.

Dawson, Philip. "The Bourgeoisie de Robe in 1789." *French Historical Studies* 4 (Spring 1965): 1–21.

_____. *Provincial Magistrates and Revolutionary Politics in France, 1789–1795*. Cambridge, Mass.: Harvard University Press, 1972.

Delmas, Pierre. *Du Parlement de Navarre et de ses origines*. Bordeaux: Y. Cadoret, 1898.

Doyle, William. *Origins of the French Revolution*. Oxford: Oxford University Press, 1980.

_____. *The Parlement of Bordeaux and the End of the Old Regime 1771–1790*. New York: St. Martin's Press, 1974.

_____. "The Parlements of France and the Breakdown of the Old Regime, 1771–1788." *French Historical Studies* 6 (Fall 1970): 415–58.

_____. "Was There an Aristocratic Reaction in Pre-revolutionary France?" *Past and Present* 57 (November 1972): 97–122.

Dubédat, Jean Baptiste. *Histoire du Parlement de Toulouse*. 2 vols. Paris: A. Rousseau, 1885.

Duboul, Axel. *La Fin du parlement de Toulouse*. Toulouse: F. Tardieu, 1890.

Egret, Jean. "L'Aristocratie parlementaire française à la fin de l'ancien régime." *Revue historique* 208 (1952): 1–14.

_____. *The French Prerevolution, 1787–1788*. Trans. Wesley D. Camp. Chicago: University of Chicago Press, 1977.

_____. *Louis XV et l'opposition parlementaire, 1715–1774*. Paris: Armand Colin, 1970.

_____. *Necker: Ministre de Louis XVI, 1776–1790*. Paris: Honoré Champion, 1975.

_____. "Les Origines de la Révolution en Bretagne." *Revue historique* 213 (1955): 189–215.

_____. *Le Parlement de Dauphiné et les affaires publiques dans la deuxième moitié du XVIIIe siècle*. 2 vols. Grenoble: B. Arthaud, 1942.

———. "La Pré-Révolution en Provence, 1787–89." *Annales historiques de la Révolution française* 26 (1954): 97–126.

———. "Un Récit inédit sur la Journée des Tuiles." *Annales historiques de la Révolution française* 29 (1957): 70–74.

———. "La Révolution aristocratique en Franche-Comté et son échec, 1788–89." *Revue d'histoire moderne et contemporaine* 1 (1954): 245–71.

Eisenstein, Elizabeth. "Who Intervened in 1788? A Commentary on *The Coming of the French Revolution*." *American Historical Review* 71 (October 1965): 77–103.

d'Estaintot, Robert-Charles-René-Hippolyte-Langlois, Comte. *Notes manuscrites d'un conseiller au parlement de Normandie [L.-A. de Gressent]*, 1769–1789. Rouen: E. Cagniard, 1889.

Estignard, Alexandre. *Le Parlement de Franche-Comté, de son installation à Besançon à sa suppression, 1674–1790*. 2 vols. Paris: A. Picard, 1892.

Everat, Edouard. *La Sénéchaussée d'Auvergne et siège présidial de Riom au XVIIIe siècle: Etude historique*. Paris: E. Thorin, 1885.

Faure, Edgar. *La Disgrâce de Turgot*. Paris: Gallimard, 1961.

Flammermont, Jules. *Le Chancelier Maupeou et les Parlements*. Paris: A. Picard, 1883.

Floquet, Amable-Pierre. *Histoire du parlement de Normandie*. 7 vols. Rouen: E. Frère, 1840–42.

Ford, Franklin L. *Robe and Sword: The Regrouping of the French Aristocracy after Louis XIV*. Cambridge, Mass.: Harvard University Press, 1953.

Forster, Robert. *Merchants, Landlords, Magistrates: The Depont Family in Eighteenth-Century France*. Baltimore: The Johns Hopkins University Press, 1980.

———. *The Nobility of Toulouse in the Eighteenth Century: A Social and Economic Study*. Baltimore: The Johns Hopkins University Press, 1960.

Frondeville, Henri de. *Les Présidents du parlement de Normandie, 1499–1790*. Rouen: A. Lestringant, 1953.

Furet, François. *Penser la Révolution française*. Paris: Gallimard, 1978.

Gagliardo, John. *Enlightened Despotism*. New York: Thomas Y. Crowell, 1967.

Galibert, Paul. *Le Conseil souverain de Roussillon*. Perpignan: L'Indépendant, 1904.

Galy, Germain. *Le Cadastre de la France, son intérêt juridique*. Paris: Sirey, 1942.

Gaxotte, Pierre. *La Révolution française*. Paris: Arthème Fayard et Cie, 1928.

Glasson, Ernst. *Le Parlement de Paris: Son rôle politique depuis le règne de Charles VII jusqu'à la Révolution*. 2 vols. Paris: Hachette, 1901.

———. "Le Parlement de Paris sous Louis XVI." *Revue parlementaire* 24–26 (1900).

Gomel, Charles. *Les Causes financières de la Révolution française*. 2 vols. Paris: Guillaumin, 1892–93.

Goubert, Pierre. *L'Ancien régime*. 2 vols. Paris: Armand Colin, 1969–73.

Greer, Donald. *The Incidence of the Emigration During the French Revolution*. Cambridge, Mass.: Harvard University Press, 1951.

———. *The Incidence of the Terror During the French Revolution*. Cambridge, Mass.: Harvard University Press, 1935.

Gresset, Maurice. *Le Monde judiciaire à Besançon, de la conquête par Louis XIV à la Révolution française, 1674–1789*. 2 vols. Lille: Service de reproduction des thèses de l'Université, 1975.

Gruder, Vivian R. *The Royal Provincial Intendants: A Governing Elite in Eighteenth-Century France.* Ithaca, N.Y.: Cornell University Press, 1968.

Hanley, Sarah. *The Lit de Justice of the Kings of France: Constitutional Ideology in Legend, Ritual, and Discourse.* Princeton, N.J.: Princeton University Press, 1983.

Harris, Robert D. *Necker: Reform Statesman of the Ancien Régime.* Berkeley and Los Angeles: University of California Press, 1979.

Hudson, David Carl. *Maupeou and the Parlements: A Study in Propaganda and Politics.* Dissertation, Columbia University, 1967.

Jacomet, Pierre. *Vicissitudes et chutes du Parlement de Paris.* Paris: Hachette, 1954.

Kaplan, Steven. *Bread, Politics and Political Economy in the Reign of Louis XV.* 2 vols. The Hague: Martinus Nijhoff, 1976.

_____. *Provisioning Paris: Merchants and Millers in the Grain and Flour Trade during the Eighteenth Century.* Ithaca, N.Y.: Cornell University Press, 1985.

Krug-Basse, Jules. *Histoire du parlement de Lorraine et Barrois.* Paris: Berger-Levrault, 1899.

Labrousse, C. E. *La Crise de l'économie française à la fin de l'Ancien Régime et au début de la Révolution.* Paris: Presses Universitaires de France, 1944.

_____. *Esquisse du mouvement des prix et des revenus en France au XVIIIe siècle.* 2 vols. Paris: Dalloz, 1933.

Lacour-Gayet, Robert. *Calonne: Financier, réformateur, contre-révolutionnaire, 1734–1802.* Paris: Hachette, 1963.

La Cuisine, Elisabeth-Françoise de. *Le Parlement de Bourgogne depuis son origine jusqu'à sa chute.* 3 vols. Dijon: J.-E. Rabutot, 1864.

Lardé, Georges. *Une Enquête sur les vingtièmes au temps de Necker: Histoire des remontrances du Parlement de Paris (1777–78).* Paris: Letouzey et Ané, 1920.

Laurain, E. *Essai sur les Présidiaux.* Paris: L. Larose, 1896.

Lavergne, Léonce de. *Les Assemblées provinciales sous Louis XVI.* Paris: Michel Lévy Frères, 1864.

Lefebvre, Georges. *The French Revolution.* Trans. Elizabeth M. Evanson. 2 vols. London: Routledge and Kegan Paul, 1969.

Le Moy, Arthur. *Le Parlement de Bretagne et le pouvoir royal au XVIIIe siècle.* Angers: A. Burdin, 1909.

_____. *Remontrances du Parlement de Bretagne au XVIIIe siècle.* Angers: A. Burdin, 1909.

_____. *Le XVIIIe siècle breton: Autour des Etats et du Parlement. Correspondances inédites de Mm. de Robien et de la Bellangerais, 1765–1791.* Rennes: J. Plihon, 1931.

Lesort, André. "La Question de la corvée des grands chemins sous Louis XVI après la chute de Turgot (1776–1778)." *Comité des travaux historiques et scientifiques: Section d'histoire moderne et contemporaine* 8 (1927): 49–95.

Lucas, Colin. "Nobles, Bourgeois, and the Origins of the French Revolution." *Past and Present* 60 (August 1973): 84–126.

McManners, John. *French Ecclesiastical Society under the Ancien Régime: A Study of Angers in the Eighteenth Century.* Manchester: Manchester University Press, 1960.

Mahuet, Antoine, Comte de. *Biographie de la Cour souveraine de Lorraine et Barrois et du Parlement de Nancy, 1641–1790.* Nancy: Sidot frères, 1911.

Bibliography

Mahuet, Hubert, Comte de. *La Cour souveraine de Lorraine et Barrois, 1641–1790.* Nancy: Société d'impressions typographiques, 1959.

Mandrou, Robert. *La France aux XVIIe et XVIIIe siècles.* Paris: Presses Universitaires de France, 1970.

Marion, Marcel. *Le Garde des Sceaux Lamoignon et la réforme judiciaire de 1788.* Paris: Hachette, 1905.

———. *Histoire financière de la France depuis 1715.* Vol. 1: *1715–1789.* Paris: A. Rousseau, 1914.

Mathiez, Albert. *The French Revolution.* Trans. Catherine Alison Phillips. New York: Russell and Russell, 1962.

Merval, Stéphane de. *Catalogue et Armorial des Présidents, Conseillers, Gens du Roi et greffiers du Parlement de Rouen.* Evreux: A. Hérissey, 1867.

Meyer, Jean. *La Noblesse bretonne au XVIIIe siècle.* 2 vols. Paris: S. E. V. P. E. N., 1966.

Michel, Emmanuel. *Biographie du Parlement de Metz.* Metz: Nouvian, 1853.

———. *Histoire du Parlement de Metz.* Paris: J. Techener, 1845.

Michelet, Jules. *Histoire de la Révolution française.* 10 vols. Paris: Calmann-Lévy, 1909–10.

Michon, Georges. *Essai sur l'histoire du parti feuillant: Adrien Duport.* Paris: Payot, 1924.

Palmer, Robert R. *The Age of the Democratic Revolution: A Political History of Europe and America, 1760–1800.* 2 vols. Princeton, N.J.: Princeton University Press, 1959–64.

Péguilhan de Larboust, Philippe de. "Les Magistrats du parlement de Toulouse à la fin de l'ancien régime (1775–1790)." Diplôme of the Faculty of Letters of Toulouse, 1965.

Petot, Jean. *Histoire de l'administration des Ponts et Chaussées, 1599–1815.* Paris: M. Rivière, 1958.

Pillot, G.-M.-L. *Histoire du Parlement de Flandres.* 2 vols. Douai: Adam d'Aubers, 1849.

Pillot, G.-M.-L., and Neyremand, Ernest de. *Histoire du Conseil souverain d'Alsace.* Paris: Durand, 1860.

Pingaud, Léonce. *Le Président de Vezet.* Paris: Nogent-le-Rotrou, 1882.

Prost, François. *Les Remontrances du Parlement de Franche-Comté au XVIIIe siècle.* Lyons: Bosc frères, 1936.

Renaudet, A. *Les Parlements: Etudes sur l'histoire de la France, 1715–1789.* Paris: Centre de documentation universitaire, 1946.

Renouvin, Pierre. *Les Assemblées provinciales de 1787: Origines, développements, résultats.* Paris: A. Picard, 1921.

Richet, Denis. "Autour des origines idéologiques lointaines de la Révolution française: Elites et despotisme." *Annales, E. S. C.* (January–February 1969): 1–23.

Robert, Paul-Albert. *Les Remontrances et Arrêtés du Parlement de Provence au XVIIIe siècle, 1715–1790.* Paris: A. Rousseau, 1912.

Robinne, Paul. "Les Magistrats du parlement de Normandie à la fin du XVIIIe siècle (1774–1790)." Thèse de l'Ecole des Chartes, 1967.

Saulnier, Frédéric. *Le Parlement de Bretagne, 1554–1790.* 2 vols. Rennes: J. Plihon et L. Hommais, 1909.

Saulnier de la Pinelais, Gustave. *Les Gens du Roi au Parlement de Bretagne, 1553–1790.* Rennes: J. Plihon et L. Hommais, 1902.

Sentou, Jean. *Fortunes et groupes sociaux à Toulouse sous la Révolution, 1789–1799.* Toulouse: E. Privat, 1969.

_____. *La Fortune immobilière des Toulousains et la Révolution française.* Paris: Bibliothèque nationale, 1970.

Shennan, J. H. *The Parlement of Paris.* London: Eyre and Spottiswoode, 1968.

Skocpol, Theda. *States and Social Revolutions: A Comparative Analysis of France, Russia, and China.* Cambridge: Cambridge University Press, 1979.

Soboul, Albert. *The French Revolution, 1787–1799.* Trans. Alan Forrest and Colin Jones. New York: Vintage Books, 1975.

Somerset, H. V. F. "Le Correspondant français à qui Burke adressa ses Réflexions sur la Révolution française." *Annales historiques de la Révolution française* 23 (1951): 360–73.

Stone, Bailey. "The Old Regime in Decay: Judicial Reform and the Senior *Parlementaires* at Paris, 1783–84." *Studies in Burke and His Time* 16 (Spring 1975): 245–59.

_____. *The Parlement of Paris, 1774–1789.* (Chapel Hill, N.C.: The University of North Carolina Press, 1981).

_____. "Robe Against Sword: The Parlement of Paris and the French Aristocracy, 1774–1789." *French Historical Studies* 9 (Fall 1975): 278–303.

Taylor, George V. "Noncapitalist Wealth and the Origins of the French Revolution." *American Historical Review* 72 (January 1967): 469–96.

Tocqueville, Alexis de. *The Old Regime and the French Revolution.* Trans. Stuart Gilbert. New York: Doubleday, 1955.

Truchis de Varennes, A.-J.-S., Vicomte de. *Le Rétablissement du Parlement de Franche-Comté en 1674, suivi de la liste des membres de ce Parlement de 1674 à 1789.* Besançon: Jacques et Demontrond, 1922.

Villers, Robert. *L'Organisation du Parlement de Paris et des Conseils Supérieurs d'après la réforme de Maupeou, 1771–74.* Paris: Jouve et Cie, 1937.

Von Laue, Theodore H. *Why Lenin? Why Stalin? A Reappraisal of the Russian Revolution, 1900–1930.* Philadelphia: J. B. Lippincott, 1971.

Wattinne, Adolphe. *Un Magistrat révolutionnaire: Michel Lepeletier de Saint Fargeau, 1760–1793.* Paris: Marchal et Godde, 1913.

Wolff, Louis. *Le Parlement de Provence au XVIIIᵉ siècle: Organisation, Procédure.* Aix: B. Niel, F.-N. Nicollet, 1920.

Index

discussed by *parlementaires* at Rouen, 128–29, 184–86, 222–23

Territorial subvention. See *Subvention territoriale*

Tobacco, sale of: supervised by *parlementaires* at Dijon, 236

Tournelle. *See* Grand' Chambre: origins and functions of

Trébons, Charles Blanquet de Rouville, vicomte de, 48

Turgot, Anne-Robert-Jacques, baron de l'Aulne: deregulates grain commerce in 1775–76, 111; reforms *corvée royale* in 1776, 116, 177, 237, 284 (n. 113); attempts to abrogate *contrainte solidaire* as applied to peasant taxpayers in 1775, 210, 279 (n. 30)

Union des classes, 166–67

Union of *parlements. See Union des classes*

Vaulx, François de, 50

Vaulx, Pierre-Marie de, 37, 50, 69, 295 (n. 74)

Verthamon, Jean-Baptiste-Maurice, 49

Verthamon, Martial-François de, 69

Vezet, Joseph-Luc-Jean-Baptiste-Hip-

polyte de, 65, 72, 146

Vingtièmes: abolished briefly by government in 1787, 4; reimposed by government in late 1787, 8–10, 76; levied upon parlementary *gages*, 55; criticized by Paris Parlement in 1788, 85, 87, 96; criticized by provincial *parlementaires* in 1788, 129, 135, 140, 142, 151, 154–56, 158, 163, 167, 177, 180, 209–19, 224, 242, 246, 296 (n. 10); accepted temporarily by *parlementaires* at Aix in 1787, 174; criticized by Paris Parlement in 1778, 280 (n. 42); condemned by *parlementaires* at Rouen during late 1770s, 285 (n. 22)

Virieu, François-Henri, comte de, 202–3

Vitrolles, Eugène François Auguste d'Arnaud, baron de, 68

Voltaire, François Marie Arouet de, 63–65

Wood trade: investigated by Paris Parlement in 1788, 113–15; supervised by *parlementaires* at Rouen during 1780s, 235, 298 (n. 64); supervised by Paris Parlement during 1780s, 283 (n. 107)